Library of Congress Cataloging in Publication Data
Main entry under title:

Sport in higher education.

   Bibliography: p.
   1. College sports--United States--Addresses,
essays, lectures.   I. Chu, Donald.   II. Segrave,
Jeffrey.   III. Becker, Beverly J., 1930-
GV351.S66   1985   796'.07'1173   85-143
ISBN 0-87322-000-5

Developmental Editor: Sue Wilmoth, PhD
Production Director: Sara Chilton
Copy Editor: Olga Murphy
Typesetting: Yvonne Sergent and Aurora Garcia
Text Layout: Gail Irwin
Cover Design and Layout: Chu Usadel
Printed by: Edwards Brothers

ISBN: 0-87322-000-5

Printed in the United States of America

10 9 8 7 6 5 4 3 2 1

Human Kinetics Publishers, Inc.
Box 5076, Champaign, IL 61820

Acknowledgments

As in any undertaking of this kind, thanks must be extended to those who have made possible this manuscript and to the "Conference on Sport and Higher Education," on which the book is largely based. To the administration of Skidmore College, gratitude must be expressed for their continued support of the academic study of sport and their recognition of the importance of many types of research within the liberal arts environment. The ability to pursue sport studies within the liberal arts college indeed demonstrates the breath and quality of the institution. To the faculty and staff of Skidmore's Department of Physical Education and Dance, a hearty thank you is appropriate. This is especially true for our fine secretaries Nancy Homiak and Dorothy Broring whose selfless determination to make things "right" manifest itself in "lists," in "plans," in problems attended to before they become problems, and in taking care of countless details.

Finally, I wish to thank my two colleagues who helped in this endeavor. Perhaps because neither was reared within the intercollegiate athletic tradition, each has brought a fresh perspective to this work. Beverly Becker has been an inspiration and firm guiding hand during my years at Skidmore. Though too wise to believe she knows all, all who have had the honor to know her have benefited from that association. To my other compatriot, Jeffrey Segrave, I must express my warmest appreciation for his moral support and technical expertise. Our long friendship has indeed been productive as well as enjoyable.

Donald Chu

Contents

Preface

"The college of character has the power to lift our spirits and focus our abilities, to exemplify true character so strongly that students will always have their experiences in the college as a point of reference, to unify a community and make it a model for society." (Martin, 1982:79)

"Simply, I had grown tired of losing. I didn't cheat because the Joneses did or because it made me a big man. I did it because I didn't want to get beat anymore. That's all." (Coach Tates Locke, 1982:61)

These quotes describe conflicting images of the college and its sport. One views the institution of higher learning and its programs as the exemplars of human character, while the other demonstrates the dark side of the institution. Both sides of the ivy-covered tower of American higher learning are visible in intercollegiate sport.

From its student controlled recreational origins in the 19th century, American college sport has become an institutional program of major significance and an integral part of the public image of higher education itself. Concomitant with the growth of intercollegiate athletics, however, has been controversy concerning sport's process and propriety. From the football brutalities which so appalled Teddy Roosevelt in 1905, from the Carnegie Foundation Report of 1929 which documented the radical changes in funding and governance structures in college sport, and from the American Council on Education Reports of 1952 and 1974, sport in higher education has aroused the gamut of emotions from exuberant support to indignant condemnation or unmitigated apathy.

As will be repeated many times and in many ways, the theme of this book focuses on the idea that intercollegiate sport is experiencing a crisis. The crisis has historical roots. Public awareness of the unequal treatment of blacks and women and unethical improprieties of big-time recruiting and eligibility maintenance now loom as dark clouds over the uncertain horizon of American higher education. With the defense of academic governance from external groups and economic survival such pressing concerns in the 1980s, big-time athletic's justification within higher education has become extrémely problematic. With empirical refutation of the myths of "character development" (that sport participation promotes positive personality, attitude, and behavior changes) and the "doctrine of good works" (that big-time sport makes money for the institution), many questions are being raised concerning big-time sport's appropriateness to the higher learning in America. This book will examine these concerns more factually than would be possible solely through journalism and in greater depth than would be possible solely through empiricism.

REFERENCES

LOCKE, T., & Ibach, B. (1982). *Caught in the net*. West Point, NY: Leisure Press.

MARTIN, W.B. (1982). *A college of character*. San Francisco: Jossey-Bass.

Introduction

The Intercollegiate Sport Scene

> The American university has become unique in the world. One aspect of that uniqueness is the existence to say nothing of the character and effect of our Big Game. These are facts: they are among the 'givens' of our situation and can neither be wished away nor ignored with impunity. They demand to be understood more explicitly and broadly than we have managed hitherto.
>
> Edwin Cady, from *The Big Game*

Intercollegiate sport programs today are as different as the American higher educational institutions of which they are a part. Among the more than 3000 2- and 4-year colleges and universities in the United States, sport programs range from the smallest level to the big-time athletic program. The smallest level programs play against strictly local competition and are usually staffed by part-time coaches and faculty. In contrast, the big level programs field over 20 teams, and are supported by an athletic corporation which is not even under the formal control of the university president.

Governing the competitive programs of these schools are a number of organizations including the National Collegiate Athletic Association (approximately 800 member schools), the National Association for Intercollegiate Athletics (approximately 520 member schools) and the National Junior College Athletic Association (approximately 580 member schools).

The most influential of all these organizations is the National Collegiate Athletic Association (NCAA) which divides its membership into three categories, based upon the type and level of sport supported by the college or university. Average budgets for NCAA institutions are presented below.

Table 1

**Total Revenues and Expenses for Men's and Women's
Athletics Fiscal Year 1981
(Thousands of Dollars)**

Average Financial Results by Responding Category	Men's Athletics	Women's Athletics	Total	Average Deficit
Division I Institutions with Football				
Average revenues	$3,391	$124	$3,515	$120
Average expenses	3,243	392	3,635	
Division II Institutions with Football				
Average revenues	248	19	267	226
Average expenses	392	101	493	
Division III Institutions with Football				
Average revenues	56	7	63	234
Average expenses	249	48	297	
Division I Institutions without Football				
Average revenues	476	44	520	299
Average expenses	631	188	819	
Division II Institutions without Football				
Average revenues	102	27	129	175
Average expenses	232	72	304	
Division III Institutions without Football				
Average revenues	30	15	45	136
Average expenses	144	37	181	

Note: Adapted from Mitchell H. Raiborn. (1982). *"Revenues and Expenses of Intercollegiate Athletic Programs."* Mission, Kansas: National Collegiate Athletic Association.

College sport is costly. Division I football-playing schools on the average spend over $3.5 million on their athletic programs and incur an athletic deficit of $120,000. This annual deficit rises to $234,000 for the Division III institution that fields football teams. Division I schools not playing football average an athletic budget of over $819,000. For these schools that usually emphasize basketball, the average deficit produced is almost $300,000.

Although the college athlete accounts for less than 5% of the total student population (170,304 men and 64,375 women) (Atwell, 1979), the popularity of the athlete's sporting efforts brings tremendous visibility to those institutions blessed with media attention. The public relations benefits of intercollegiate sport attracted Notre Dame's administration which consciously developed football in the 1890s as a student recruitment instrument; nor did the publicity value of the successful Cornell crew team of the 1870s escape the attention of Cornell's president who charged the teams indebtedness to the advertising expenses of the university (Smith, 1976). In fact, the vigor with which sport was promoted as representative of institutions of higher education was decried in Bulletin #26 of the Carnegie Foundation for the Advancement of Teaching (1931):

> The avidity of the colleges themselves for publicity has in the past been partly to blame for the unsatisfactory relation between newspapers and college sports. Comparatively few institutions have attempted to give newspaper writers the opportunity to learn that athletics are only one of the activities of a college or university.

Sport's salience remains an important avenue for gaining public visibility today. The sports page which earlier heralded the efforts of collegians in the 1920s continues to laud the triumphs of today's heroes. While Red Grange brought glory to the Illini in the 1920s, John Elway has brought attention to the Stanford Cardinals. Sport captures public attention and displays and promotes the banner of that institution over the thousands of American colleges and universities.

What then has the casual spectator seen in college sport? Certainly the observer has witnessed greatness—the courage of seemingly defeated teams that triumph through the force of their determination. The public has witnessed transcendent moments of glory—the superhuman effort which reminds us of the possibility of greatness. At the same time, however, the public has been witness to abuses and improprieties in college sport, scandals in athletics which become visible with such regularity that they lead the observer to ask whether this is deviancy or the norm? Consider the following situations in college athletics listed below:

- Physical abuse of athletes by coaches (Shaw, 1972)
- Alteration of high school transcripts to gain entry to college
- The addition of "phantom" courses on the transcripts of college athletes to promote continued eligibility (Underwood, 1980)
- The enticement of high school athletes to colleges with under-the-table payments, running as high as $20,000 per year (Alfano, 1984)

While one must hope that such abuse in college sport is the exception, accounts such as these in the popular press do little to bolster the image of higher education. This is particularly troublesome considering the degree to which American institutions of higher learning are dependent upon the public for support.

Unlike the Oxbridge English models of early American higher education, the colonial college was continually beset by financial concerns. Without consistent support from religious, royal, or the landed elements of society, and without the accumulation of endowments sufficient to fund the development of interest bearing accounts, the American college historically has had to make resource acquisition a prime concern (Kneller, 1955; Curtis, 1959; Nearing, 1917).

The American college president had to be continually concerned with finances. In order to survive, institutional colleges have raised money by changing their names to match wealthy benefactors (i.e., Col. Henry Rutgers, James Bowdoin,

William Carleton) (Rudolph, 1968). Colleges have charged ferry tolls and have even taken poultry in barter. More recently, one college offered trusteeships for donations of $1 million (Jacobson, 1982). That intercollegiate sport might be used as a means to attract potential students and money is, then, of no surprise.

In a land where the American dream posited success for anyone willing to work hard enough, the more than 2,000 4-year colleges and universities find themselves competing for students as well as for money. Except for the handful of the most prestigious Ivy and "seven-sister" colleges, within the financial means of most students, there are numerous choices from which potential collegians may select. In the competition to attract the human lifeblood of higher learning, the American school might use the great respect afforded its academic curriculum, or it might use the visibility and tradition of its spirited athletic programs.

Whatever the reason for intercollegiate sport in the 1980s, however, it is clear that athletics and higher education in America are closely related. It is difficult indeed to think of Notre Dame or even Slippery Rock, for that matter, without football. Images of Lew Alcindor and Elvin Hayes, Big Red, and the Orangemen come quickly to mind when we think of UCLA, Houston, Illinois, and Syracuse. Despite decades of financial and ethical problems and of loud criticisms, college sport has endured, holding America's imagination. The excitement of the New Year's Day bowl games and the race for basketball's "final four" indicates the strength of intercollegiate sport today. Because campus athletics dominate the public image of higher education and because sport may so elevate the spirit or degrade the integrity of the educational institution, intercollegiate sport demands inspection.

Another reason exists, however, for looking at college sport. As the programs of an organization reveal something about the nature of the organization, the sports of a school tells us something about the character of the social institution of higher education in America. Our colleges and universities have developed into a form unique among the world's places of higher learning. The presence of sport as a formal part of the school attests to this fact. How those sport programs are run, the behaviors that are tolerated or demanded, and the problems which remain unsolved tell us something of the nature of higher education and the American society on which it is dependent.

The financial and demographic realities of the '80s have made apparent the need for rigorous study and for open discussion of such concerns as intercollegiate sport's economic realities, its intra- and interinstitutional governance, and the matter of campus sport's consistency with the mission of higher education.

This book provides perspective on the intercollegiate athletic situation in America. Based upon presentations at the "Conference on Sport and Higher Education" (Skidmore College, March 18-19, 1983), other invited manuscripts, and papers previously published elsewhere, the authors look at intercollegiate athletics' current situation, at seemingly endemic problems and at prospects for future change. Observing intercollegiate sport from the eyes of the scholar, the athletic director, the higher education administrator, and the foundation leader, these papers provide various viewpoints. While some of these authors maintain rigid scientific orientation in their reporting, other writers present an admittedly emotional view. Discussion of the propriety of intercollegiate sport's practices and objectives may benefit from both approaches.

The book is divided into six parts: "The Intercollegiate Sport Scene" introduces the diverse scope of campus athletics; Part I, "The Development of Intercollegiate Sport" provides a historical account of the evolution of sport programs and the student/athlete role, and suggests reasons for the somewhat "improbable" inclusion of athletics on the historically intellectual campus; Part II, "Abuses and Concerns," presents journalistic, empirical, and philosophical discussion of some controversies in college sport; Part III, "Governance," presents an account of the administrative structures both within and external to the college and university which control campus athletics; Part IV, "The Rationalization of Intercollegiate Athletics," considers the justification for intercollegiate athletics: The different sections within Part IV examine purported socialization, educational and career benefits, the campus sport's economic situation, and the issues of race and women in intercollegiate athletics. The book concludes with proposals for change in Part V and a final consideration in the "Epilogue," Part VI.

REFERENCES

ALFANO, P. (1984). "NCAA head asks assault on rampant abuse of rules." *New York Times*, CXXIV, #46, Oct. 13, 1984:p. 1, 48.

ATWELL, R. (1979). *The money game*, Washington, D.C.: American Council on Education.

CADY, E.H. (1978). *The big game*. Knoxville: University of Tennessee Press.

CARNEGIE Foundation for the Advancement of Teaching Bulletin #23. (1931). New York.

CURTIS, M.H. (1959). *Oxford and Cambridge in transition 1558-1642*. Oxford: Clarendon Press.

JACOBSON, R.L. (1982). Position available: University trustee; price: $1-million. *Chronicle of Higher Education*, **24**, 3.

KNELLER, G.F. (1955). *Higher learning in Britain*. Berkeley: University of California Press.

NEARING, S. (1917). Who's who among college trustees. *School and Society*, **6.**

RAIBORN, M.H. (1982). *Revenues and expenses of intercollegiate athletic programs*. Mission, Kansas: National Collegiate Athletic Association.

RUDOLPH, F. (1968). Financing the college. *The American college and university*. New York: Alfred A. Knopf.

SHAW, G. (1972). *Meat on the hoof: The hidden world of Texas football*. New York: St. Martin's.

SMITH, R.A. (1976, January). Reaction to "Historical Roots of the Collegiate Dilemma." *Proceedings of the 79th Annual Meeting of the National Collegiate Physical Education Association for Men* (pp. 154-162).

UNDERWOOD, J. (1980, May). The shame of American education: The student-athlete hoax. *Sports Illustrated*.

Part I

THE DEVELOPMENT OF INTERCOLLEGIATE SPORT

Perspective...knowing how some situation stands relative to significant conditions or circumstances is important to the understanding of any social phenomenon. If the world is viewed strictly from the present, one gains a very different picture than the reality of the world when considered against other worlds and other times.

The purpose of this part of the book is to provide the perspective of time, culture, and space which frees us from the blindness of temporal and spatial provincialism. A broader perspective will be gained by looking at campus sport's historical development and the peculiarity of the American relationship between the college and athletics relative to its European models.

Far from having a unitary view of the college's purposes and appropriate processes, the American school has seen many changes since its colonial origins. Diversity of immigrants, varying beliefs, large expanses of land, and the distance that promotes insulation of peoples, the lack of a strong central government with a ministry of education, and the absence of a national religion were all factors contributing to a curriculum and college life marked by continuous change. In fact, the distinguishing characteristic of American higher education is its pluralism, a pluralism which parallels the multifaceted society on which the college and university is dependent. Historically, the American campus has been marked by alteration of programs, models of education, student, faculty, and societal expectations. The incorporation of seemingly inconsistent or even contradictory organizational goals and programs is somewhat commonplace for the American college and university.

In this part's first paper Joanna Davenport traces the historical chain of events leading to the "paradoxical" relationship between winning and money on the

1

one hand, and "scholarship, leadership, honesty, financial integrity (and) ethics" on the other. From the first student-controlled intercollegiate contest between the crew teams of Harvard and Yale in 1852 to the big time sports of today, the increasingly formalized relationship between sport programs and college governance and financial structures is described. From accounts of abuses, from reports on these abuses, from recommendations for change and the development of regulatory bodies such as the Big-10 and the NCAA, it is apparent from Davenport's paper that reform has been long called for and just as long ignored. As Davenport's paper points out, there is a constancy to the repeated calls for reform and the unheeded criticisms of campus sports excesses and abuses. To this day, the relationship between intercollegiate sport and the purposes of higher education in America remain ill-defined, and the translation of educational philosophy into sporting reality remains unrealized at the big-time levels of play.

In his paper, Gregory Sojka historically considers the changing image of the student-athlete. Far from there being one conception of the "All-American" athlete, closer inspection shows many views of the ideal sporting student. From the ascetic puritan "moral athlete" to the Ivy League hero, from the Anglo-Saxon male to blacks and women, from the "paid gladiator" to the "criminal-entrepreneur," the public image of student-athlete in America has varied diversely. During different historical periods the publically perceived raison d'etre for the student-athlete on campus has changed from primary concern with religion and academic study, to promotion of All-American values, to winning and money. College athletics has mirrored shifts in American values. These shifts, have in the author's view, come full-circle from the student-athlete as "moral athlete" to athlete as representative of the "moral majority."

Donald Chu offers a very different perspective in his paper. Rather than presenting a historical view of the development of intercollegiate sport, Chu offers a sociological interpretation of the symbolic reasons for the inclusion of intercollegiate sport within the formal programs and responsibilities of the American college. Why did these schools of higher learning come to view athletics as an integral part of their educational programming when the English and German models on which the American college was based had no such athletic structures? Chu argues that the answer lies in the assumed understandings of the people in a society about the progams and purposes of social institutions. Because there was no well-accepted understanding of what the American college should and should not do, presidents of schools concerned with the survival of their institutions were able to employ athletics as a means of attracting money, students, and visibility.

In summary, the papers in this part of the book serve to dispel any notions of a singular view of American higher education and sport. Both the school organization and its programs have changed many times over the relatively brief 300 or so years of higher education in America. There is little reason to believe that change in institutional programs such as intercollegiate sport will end in this era. In fact, if there is any lesson to be learned from this brief review of history, it is that more change is inevitable and central to the maintenance of compatibility between societal needs and higher education's legitimate programs.

Yet amidst all this change there is constancy. The "survival question"—the constant need for money, for students, and for the publicity that attracts both have been constant problems for American higher education. As we will see from this part of the book, the problems and abuses of today are historically rooted and have defied change. The "survival question" for schools so dependent on consistent annual support has helped reshape the view of programs and students appropriate for the American college and university.

Chapter I

From Crew to Commercialism— The Paradox of Sport in Higher Education

Joanna Davenport
Auburn University

A few years ago, a well-known coed university mailed out an attractive white flyer on which the title "Grants/In/Aid" appeared in blue letters (Grants-In-Aid). Cleverly inserted in the background of the title were the drawings of men engaging in football, basketball, baseball, and track. The important part about this anecdote is the following message contained in the flyer! "What's it take to make [X University] a winner?" The answer: "Guts...and Grants/In/Aid." Some of the message was as follows:

> It's just that simple. Or complex. Take the guts part. Guts has a lot to do with winning....[X University] players have the right kind of coaches. The right kind of spirit. The right kind of teamwork. You've seen it. You've seen them win....These kids don't just wander in off the streets. The good athletes. They don't just 'happen to suit up' and then play a heck of a ball game....They're recruited. And a part of the recruiting package is an athletic scholarship to the University. It takes lots of money to provide room, board, books, and tuition for a top-notch athlete. (Grants-In-Aid)

The flyer than mentions the cost of the scholarship differentiating the in-stater from the out-of-stater. For dramatic emphasis about the expenses, that particular section ends with the sentence, "And that's every year for four years" (Grants-In-Aid). The last part of the flyer is the "kicker"—the benefits a person accrues with a donation to this fund. For $1,000 the donor belongs to the President's Club, which entitles him or her to Number 1 ticket preference, President's Club parking, Varsity Room privileges, and Special Grants/In/Aid Events: These events usually mean free programs, free food and drinks, and all the niceties to ensure that the donor is so well treated that the gift will be repeated the next year. The person contributing $500, naturally receives less benefits: Number 2 ticket preference, special (though less special) parking, Varsity Room privileges, and the Special Events "perks." For $100, the donor receives the Number 3 ticket preference, the special parking (though a little less convenient), and the Special Events, but no Varsity Room privileges. Furthermore, short messages from both the president and the chancellor of the University are included in the brochure. The brochure concludes with "...help [X University] to win" (Grants-In-Aid). Notice that the word "academics" is never mentioned, and the only reference to such is the phrase from the chancellor in which he states that "we wish to achieve excellence in all our programs including athletics" (Grants-In-Aid).

Was the omission of material about academics an oversight or just not germane to the purpose of the Grants-In-Aid program? The answer may not be important, but the main ideas were that winning and money are the underlying facets of the huge question—What is the role of intercollegiate athletics in higher education? This topic is so multifaceted that covering all the aspects of the question would be impossible in this paper. However, the topic to be examined is the affect of sport on higher education.

This paper's title reflects the point of sport's origins—with crew—to where we are today with the lurid reports of illegal inducements, transcript falsifications, and the use of athletes merely as physical performers with no thought of their obtaining degrees. A further explanation of my title is the use of the phrase, "The paradox of sport in higher education." Paradox is defined as "something...with seemingly contradictory qualities or phrases" (*Webster's New Ideal Dictionary*, 1978). The paradox of college sport comes from the public's expectation that institutions of higher education should espouse the epitome of scholarship, leadership, honesty, financial integrity, ethics, and all other such positive qualities. Unfortunately, however, when winning and money interface with sport, the positive qualities are sometimes forgotten. This paper will look at the growth of intercollegiate athletics and their oftentimes unethical commercialization. What was the chain of events that created this paradoxical situation?

IN THE BEGINNING

The faculties and administrators in early colleges and universities never planned anything as frivolous as sports and games as part of the curriculum. The concentration was solely on academics. Yet, as we all know, times changed and students were soon engaging in recreational activities which college authorities viewed as a method for students to release pent-up energies.

As the recreational pursuits became more organized, it was natural that a group from one college wished to test its ability against a corresponding team from another institution. Keep in mind that all this activity was done outside the jurisdiction of the university and was completely organized and managed by the students. The historic year for the beginning of intercollegiate sport was 1852 when a crew race was organized between Harvard and Yale (Scott, 1951, p. 16). It soon became apparent to many college authorities that the news about the crew races was helping to publicize the college and, thus, aiding admissions.

The next intercollegiate sport was baseball, and the first contest was in 1859 between Amherst and Williams. But it was 10 years later in 1869 that the real watershed occurred in the saga of intercollegiate athletics. On November 6, 1869, the first game of intercollegiate football was held between Rutgers and Princeton. No other sport, especially in the big universities, was received with such enthusiasm, created more controversy, or caused more meetings. This has brought us to the original question—the place of athletics in higher education.

As football was played by more and more colleges, it soon became an important part of campus life but still was without the official sanction of the colleges and universities. Students raised the necessary monies from loyal alumni and faithful followers. Eventually, the sport that raised the most money (football) was categorized as major, and the sports with less money were labeled minor.

Colleges and universities discovered that football increased the prestige of the institution. This publicity, especially if the teams were winning, increased alumni donations, attracted prospective students, and "in the case of state-supported colleges, increased appropriations from the state legislature." (Eitzen & Sage, 1978, p. 52). Nevertheless, the administrators viewed the intercollegiate situation as outside the main purview of higher education.

By the 1890s sports were becoming small business enterprises on college campuses, the situation aptly described by these remarks:

> The 1890s were a critical time for American collegiate sports. Big name universities were determined to win at any cost and were committing bigger and bigger excesses to do so. Professional baseball pitchers were becoming campus stars. Coaches were inserting non-students for football games and putting themselves in their own line ups. Jampacked college grandstands went wild rooting for 'heroes' who attended school only during baseball and football seasons. Street brawls between players and townspeople often followed hotly-contested games.

> Collegiate sports were at a critical crossroads and might have been set back many years—or even abolished—had it not been for the urgent and historic meeting in Chicago on January 11, 1895. (Wilson & Brondfield, 1967)

This meeting was the beginning of "The Intercollegiate Conference of Faculty Representatives," better known as The Big Ten. This conference became one of the first to have regulations regarding students' eligibility and participation; many of The Big Ten rules were copied by other parts of the country. An important concept in the formation of The Big Ten was that the control of intercollegiate athletics would be in the hands of faculty, not athletic personnel.

Thus, rules and regulations were formulated, but the situation in football by 1905 was climactic when it was reported that during that year, 18 had been killed and 143 seriously injured while playing the game. President Roosevelt met with representatives from Harvard, Yale, and Princeton and urged them to do something about the appalling reports he was receiving about football. Consequently, a meeting was held in New York in December 1905 with about 30 institutional representatives present. Even though the reason for the meeting was football, the Intercollegiate Athletic Association of the United States was formed (its name changed to the NCAA in 1910), and its purpose was to oversee all sports, as thus defined in the original constitution:

> Its object shall be the regulation and supervision of college athletics throughout the United States, in order that the athletic activities in the colleges and universities of the United States may be maintained on an ethical plane in keeping with the dignity and high purpose of education. (Applin, 1979)

A few paradoxes emerge here as well. The institutions were to have their own autonomy with this new NCAA, and yet, they relied on an outside agency for regulations. Furthermore, the early NCAA did not have regulatory control or an enforcement mechanism. In essence, it was a sports rule-making advisory body and a good forum for discussion of concerns at the National NCAA meeting each year. The NCAA did promote the growth of conferences, and these conferences helped bring member institutions "into line." Is it not amazing that these original student-organized sports were still not formally in the educational mainstream at any individual college or university but were publically prominent enough to cause the formation of a national body? However, an attempt had been made for control and though problems existed, sports continued to grow.

BY THE 1920s

The 1920s saw "The Golden Age of College Sports." As one author stated, "There came new freedoms, new drives, new searchings for emotional and physical outlets; and sports seemed to provide the one big national denominator." (Wilson, 1967, p. 109)

Finally, in the 1920s institutions of higher education formally recognized intercollegiate athletics as part of education and, for the most part, placed them in the physical education departments. It was also recommended that coaches be faculty members and that they be given appointments in the physical education department. This change was viewed with some alarm by many physical educators who had strived and secured academic respectability for the profession of physical education. Furthermore, the importance of physical education was recognized by the faculty and administration; in addition, almost all institutions of higher education in the 1920s had a requirement in physical education which did much to enhance its importance to the academic community. There was justifiable concern from the physical education viewpoint that the hired coach who was also to teach physical education would neglect his teaching duties in favor of his first love, coaching. Many people did both jobs very conscientiously, but the reverse was also true.

Now that athletics was part of the educational program, intercollegiates received institutional funds which allowed sports to grow even further. Thus, the commercialization of collegiate sports increased, especially in football. The game was making big money and, hence, critics attacked it as being big business. It is important not to forget some of the outgrowths of these financial gains on our college campuses. In his book, *Football, Today and Tomorrow*, published in 1928, Roper comments on this situation:

> The man who pays for a football ticket in the fall always pays for half a dozen other sports which he may not care to see but which are just as important to the all-around development of the student body as football itself. (p. 131)

The tennis courts, the golf courses, the ice rinks, and so forth, that grace many campuses were a concomitant outgrowth of the big revenue producing game of football, especially in the 1920s. Even though it is perpetual fiction at some institutions, it is truth at others that the majority of the other sports in which colleges participate are financed by the monies made from football and basketball.

During the Golden Age of Sports, there were also an increase of alumni associations, identifying with the college through sport. This situation was reinforced by the discovery of how important a publicity office and, more currently, sports information office could be to the school. The alumni were kept informed about their school through news about the teams. The importance of sport to the alumni is described in the book, *The Development and Scope of Higher Education in the United States* (Hofstadler & Hardy, 1952):

> Athletics, because they are a symbolic link between the alumnus and his youth, are also the strongest link between the alumnus and his school. In some, yet undefined because no social psychologist has yet made a study of the alumnus—renewed contact with intercollegiate athletics revives his youth as no other experience could. He returns to the stadium with a sense of expectation that he could not think of getting from a visit with a former teacher or a visit to the library....The alumnus is important to the university: He is a major source of direct support...he joins the undergraduate in underwriting commercialized athletics. (p. 114)

Intramurals, too, became popular programs on college campuses in the twenties as more students wished to engage in sporting activities. One important aspect about the intramural movement in the 1920s, rarely present today, was its close relationship to the intercollegiate program, undoubtedly due to the fact that freshmen were ineligible for the varsity teams. Mitchell (1939) in his book *Intramural Sports* indicated that one of the objectives of intramurals was to have students learn skills so they would be proficient enough for the intercollegiate teams (p. 20). The famous Carnegie Report of 1929 (Savage, 1929) extensively comments on the dichotomy of the intramural programs at some institutions and states that "another negative tendency is the intimate connection of intramural athletics with intercollegiate athletics under personnel that is interested primarily or exclusively in intercollegiate contests (p. 84)."

Even though the twenties was a boom time, the old problems had not gone away and in some respects had increased due to the commercialism and popularity of winning teams. In 1925, the following was written about sport and higher education:

> In the eyes of the general public, a college...stands high or low in the public estimation largely on the basis of the performance of its athletic teams; specifically its football...teams....The fame and value of a university have come to be measured by the space it occupies in the sporting pages of newspapers, and the size of the crowds that gather in its million-dollar stadium. As things now stand, the only thing that college athletics advertises is—athletics. The whole business has got out of proportion and out of hand. What is needed is not a general housecleaning but a revolution. (Gavit, 1925, pp. 143-144)

The twenties ended with the Crash of '29 and the release of the famous Carnegie Report entitled *American College Athletics* (Savage, 1929). The publication was the compilation of the findings of a 3-year investigation including visitations to campuses on the whole issue of athletics in the colleges and universities. It described all the abuses in college sport and urged the college administrators to take charge and to clean up the situation. As can be expected, most of the allegations or wrongdoings were involved with football. Obviously, the report was not well received, and most people involved in athletics claimed that the bad practices mentioned were not going on at their institution but somewhere else. Consequently, nothing much changed, but the report itself is a treasure trove of facts and figures about intercollegiate athletics. It is important to mention some of the report's opening statements as they illustrate the somewhat paradoxical connection of sport and higher education.

> In the United States the composite institution called a university is doubtless still an intellectual agency. But it is also a social, a commercial and an athletic agency, and these activities have in recent years appreciably overshadowed the intellectual life for which the university is assumed to exist.
>
> ...the football contest...is not a students' game, as it once was. It is a highly organized commercial enterprise. The athletes who take part in it have come up through years of training; they are commended by professional coaches; little if any personal initiative of ordinary play is left to the player. The great matches are highly profitable enterprises. (Savage, 1929, p. VIII)

The solution to correct the abuses in intercollegiate sports is stated as thus:

> But there can be no doubt as to where lies the responsibility to correct this situation. The defense of the intellectual integrity of the college and of the university lies with the president and faculty....The responsibility to bring athletics into a sincere relation to the intellectual life of the college rests squarely on the shoulders of the president and faculty. (Savage, 1929, p. XXI)

THE GREAT DEPRESSION

The great Depression, which affected all facets of our society, certainly had an impact on higher education and concomitantly, intercollegiate athletics. Budgets were drastically slashed; gate receipts went down; teachers and coaches were released; and athletic contests were scheduled with opponents in closer proximity to reduce travel costs. Yet, even though sports programs were faced with financial changes, there seemed to be no changes in the problems regarding illegal inducements and recruiting. The NCAA attempted to address the situation in 1933 by appointing a special committee to study recruitment and subsidization. In 1934 the traditional Round Table meetings at the annual convention discussed the findings of the committee who presented a code of legal and illegal acts. The chairman of the committee, Z.G. Clevenger of Indiana University, opened the Round Table with these remarks:

> There isn't a man in this room who believes that this recruiting and subsidizing
> problem can be solved completely here today, or next year, or the year after...all
> I think we can do is to approach as nearly as we can to a set of ideals that the most
> of us at least can agree upon, and then try to see if we cannot approximate those
> ideals in the way we carry out the programs...and of course, that will depend to
> a great extent upon the integrity of those handling the athletic programs...and the
> integrity of those having charge of the various colleges and universities. (NCAA,
> 1934, pp. 101-102)

The delegate from Georgia commented that the real problem was that there was no clear-cut definition of subsidization. The NCAA president stated in closing the Round Table that the NCAA "has never assumed the responsibility of trying to be a governing body....These are local problems. Perhaps, all that the NCAA can do is in an educational way to try to state standards or ideals" (NCAA, 1934, p. 115).

In 1937 the Round Table discussions centered on the conduct and control of intercollegiate sports. The two dominant themes in that Round Table were presented in the form of questions that continue today: Is it high time that colleges and universities take charge? And is the athletic program a part of the educational program? (NCAA, 1937, pp. 19, 21).

WORLD WAR II

The advent of World War II caused a hiatus in the growth of intercollegiate sports as the nation's energies were channeled into the war effort. There were some suggestions to eliminate athletic schedules, but athletic programs were maintained at reduced levels. Due to decreasing enrollments eligibility restrictions were relaxed, allowing freshmen and first-year transfers to play on the varsity teams.

When the war ended in 1945, intercollegiate sports started anew on over-emphasis, and at some institutions the game of basketball was becoming as big time as football.

THE 1950s AND 1960s

An indication that sports were becoming more commercial was the move in the late 50s and early 60s to separate athletics from physical education departments. In many colleges and universities athletics not only split administratively but were housed in different facilities. Furthermore, there was a return to the status of years ago where coaches were full-time coaches and were not given faculty rank. The move certainly raised the question once again—the role of athletics in higher education.

Intercollegiate athletics were moving rapidly to even a bigger business operation where money and winning were the overriding factors. To win meant good recruiting, and stories were abundant of abuses and irregularities, both financial and academic. Presidents and faculties were unable at this juncture to exert control, and the fortunes of the athletic program often determined the fate of the chief executive officer. This unfortunate state of affairs is illustrated by the following example from 1949, but happened far too often at many institutions of higher education.

> President Homer L. Dodge of Norwich University said today that the poor showing of Norwich football team this season was among the reasons for his decision to resign. He added that he was influenced to some extent by the pressure applied by sports-minded alumni....I have been aware of some criticisms of the administration, partly because of our lack of success athletically....I would like to remark for the record that Norwich has spent more money on athletics since I've been president than during any other equal period in its history. (Scott, 1951, pp. 118-119)

With the popularity of television, a new commercial dimension and a new challenge faced college sports in the early 50s. At first, the NCAA and conferences did not wish to have football games televised, believing it would hurt ticket sales for the games. Then, as the monetary aspect became apparent, being on TV assumed another big business aspect to collegiate sport. Its importance is certainly illustrated by the litigation now going on between the NCAA and the College Football Association as to who controls the rights to negotiate TV contracts for institutions' contests.

Abuses in intercollegiate sports reached a peak in the early fifties with the basketball scandals; thus it was time for the NCAA to change from an advisory body to a governing body with full power to police and penalize. An initial attempt at control had been a Sanity Code of Ethical Practices with expulsion of violators from the NCAA, but it proved ineffective and was dropped within a few years. Thus, Walter Byers was made executive director of the NCAA and the constitution was revised, whereby the Committee on Infractions had the power to censure institutions in violations of NCAA rules. Now there was no doubt that control for the most part was in an outside agency, not at a respective institution.

However, the new regulatory body did not stop the illegalities, and irregularities in collegiate sports and reports of violators poured in to the NCAA office. To try and combat some of the unethical conduct, more and more rules were adopted as evidenced by the present day NCAA Rule Book.

The 1950s at the time may have appeared traumatic with the growing commercialism, scandals, and illegal operations but historically was the calm before the storm of the 1960s and 1970s. The student protests on campus in the 1960s and early 70s had a major impact on all higher education and intercollegiate athletics. On some campuses students voted to divert those funds usually specified for athletics to ghetto projects or social action causes. The demands of athletes to determine their own dress and to wear long hair and beards was a constant challenge to the coaches. Racial discrimination was brought out into the open and there was a demand for parity and more black coaches. The emergence of the drug culture was another component that challenged all of higher education and athletics.

TITLE IX AND THE 1970s

Higher education was faced with a new dimension with the passage of Title IX in 1972. Colleges and universities were mandated by a federal law to provide equal opportunities for women in athletics as had been provided for decades for the men. Here again, a thrust was made by NCAA to further compound the issue of the place of sports in higher education. Even though Title IX simply states that there shall be no sex discrimination in any educational institution that receives federal funds, the NCAA sued to have athletics exempt from this law. When the lawsuit was denied, they sued again to have the revenue-producing sports exempt under Title IX. When, again, that lawsuit was rejected, the guidelines were finally released 3 years later in 1975. Who would have believed then that in January 1981 the NCAA would not only vote to sponsor women's championships, but within 1 month's time after the vote would have a new logo with both a man and a woman in the centerpiece. A paradox? Undoubtedly, quite a change of heart, as indicated by this 1977 statement in *Women's Sports* (Hogan, 1977): "NCAA had spent more money lobbying against equal opportunity than it costs AIAW to run 17 National Championships" (p. 46).

The outlook for women's sport is somewhat frightening. Apparently women are going down the same path as the men. Back in 1977 with AIAW still in existence these pointed remarks were in *Life Special Report:*

The women...seem...imperiled by the same system of vassalage that has claimed, controlled, financed, and often demeaned male participants in intercollegiate athletics.

Title IX has not only prompted American colleges into offerings increasing athletic opportunity, but has also made it possible for them to repeat all the old mistakes they made with the men. In a sense, the institutions have little choice; the government insists on athletic scholarships for women as long as there are athletic scholarships for men. But U.S. colleges want winning teams at every level, and women's coaches (who think no differently than men's coaches) are already doing their level best to get blue-chip value for their investments. (p. 83)

In the 70s another study was done on intercollegiate athletics by the Commission on Collegiate Athletics of the American Council on Education. The findings were similar to all previous investigations and the problems seemed to have escalated in relation to the "size, popularity and scope of intercollegiate sports" (Coakley, 1982, p. 157). The Director of the Commission, Harry Marmion (1979), offered these remarks about intercollegiate athletics:

The role of sports on some college campuses is more important than many realize. Strong collegiate athletic programs can have significant economic, social, and even political effects on the institution, a state, and even an entire region....We must be aware, concerned, and involved with this unique aspect of our educational system. If key administrators do not get involved, then the inevitable will happen. There will be scandals, governmental involvement, and even worse, public condemnation. (pp. 343-344)

ATHLETIC'S PLACE IN HIGHER EDUCATION

It has been 131 years since the first collegiate crew races held on Lake Winnipesaukee and 114 years since the first football game. The former student-run, student-organized activities have become at some campuses the most dominant aspect of collegiate life. During the Christmas of 1983, one Big Ten institution changed its final examination schedule so the student body would be free to attend the bowl game where their football team would be competing.

The former student sports that solicited funds from students and followers for uniforms and equipment have become multimillion dollar enterprises with equipment and facilities that no one would have dreamed of years ago. It certainly is paradoxical that in these tight financial times with reduced budgets and no faculty raises, money is still somehow found to build an addition to the football stadium. Can there be any doubt of the commercialized aspect of big-time football when a college coach is paid $287,000 a year and when a junior in college is offered $5 million to sign a professional football contract? Is not the complexity and almost the absurdity of this situation exemplified by the fact that the members of the Georgia State Legislature wore black and red armbands (Georgia's colors) the day after Herschel Walker made his announcement that he was leaving the University of Georgia?

Thus, we are back to the original question: Are athletics a part of higher education?—Whose responsibility is it to answer this question? In retrospect, there can be little doubt that if the basic question of the relationship of athletics to higher education had been addressed by the presidents and faculties years ago, we would not even have to ask this question. Unfortunately, the issue remains unanswered. All these many years the administrators and faculties have relied on the answer from outside agencies, such as the NCAA, the American Council on Education, and so forth. George Hanford (1979) reaffirms this predicament when he states that "the problems of intercollegiate athletics will be solved only when its relationship to the education process is finally defined..." (p. 366).

Therefore, the paradox of intercollegiate athletics remains with us today and is as follows:

> Athletics are the most severely criticized activity of college life and they are the most loved. They are the most rational channel into which to direct the energies of youth, and they are, when improperly administered, the most dangerous and diseased. They are the most vulnerable activity of the American college life, and they are one of the most vital....Football commands a devotion unequaled in any other sport....The situation rightly controlled will satisfy one of the most basic demands of the educational program. (Kent, 1930, pp. 587-588)

These are not my words. The last five sentences were taken from the book, *Higher Education in America*, and were written 53 years ago. Let us hope that the paradox can be resolved before the passage of another 50 years.

REFERENCES

APPLIN, A.C. (1979, May). *The recent historical development of the NCAA*. Paper presented at the annual meeting of the North American Society for Sport History, Austin.

BRONDFIELD, J. (1974). *Woody Hayes and the 100-yard war*. New York: Berkley Publishing Corporation.

COAKLEY, J. (1982). *Sport in society*. St. Louis: The C.V. Mosby Company.

EDWARDS, R.H., Artman, I.M., & Fisher, G.M. (1928). *Undergraduates*. Garden City, New York: Doubleday, Doran.

EITZEN, D.S., & Sage, G. (1978). *Sociology of American sport*. Dubuque, Iowa: William C. Brown Co.

FREEMAN, W. (1977, April). *College athletics in the twenties: The golden age or fool's gold*. Paper presented at History Symposium of the National Association for Sport and Physical Education, Seattle.

GAVIT, J. (1925). *College*. Rahway, NJ: Harcourt, Brace and Company, Inc.

GRANTS-IN-AID. Unpublished brochure. University of Illinois, Champaign, IL.

HANFORD, G.H. (1979). Controversies in college sports. *Educational Record, 60*, 366.

HOFSTADLER, R., & Hardy, C.D. (1952). *The development and scope of higher education in the United States*. New York: Columbia University Press.

HOGAN, D. (1977). NCAA and AIAW: Will the men score on women's athletics? *Women Sports, 4*, 46.

KENT, R.A. (1930). *Higher education in America*. Boston: Ginn and Company.

MARMION, H.A. (1979). Collegiate athletics: An overview. *Educational Record, 60*, 343-344.

MITCHELL, E.D. (1939). *Intramural sports*. New York: A.S. Barnes and Company.

NCAA Proceedings of 29th Annual Convention. (1934, December). New York.

NCAA Proceedings of 32nd Annual Convention. (1937, December). New Orleans.

ROPER, W. (1928). *Football, today and tomorrow*. New York: Duffield and Company.

SACK, A. (1977). Big time college football: Whose free ride? *Quest, 26*, 36.

SAVAGE, H.J. (1929). *American college athletics*. New York: The Carnegie Foundation.

SCOTT, H.A. (1951). *Competitive sports in schools and colleges*. New York: Harper and Brothers.

SEPPY, T. (1975, April 17). Pressure to win pushes colleges to recruiting war. *The Kansas City Star* (1975, May 11), p. 23.

THE new youth. (1977). *Life special report*, p. 83.

WEBSTER'S new ideal dictionary. (1978). New York: G. & C. Merriam Company.

WILSON, K.L., & Brondfield, J. (1967). *The big ten*. Englewood Cliffs, NJ: Prentice-Hall.

Chapter 2

The Evolution of the Student-Athlete in America: From the Divinity to the Divine

Gregory S. Sojka
Wichita State University

Four years ago, Rindge & Latin High School basketball coach Mike Jarvis raised the collective blood pressures of the media, the academic community, and the basketball coaches of America by sending a letter to 150 colleges outlining the academic weaknesses of his star center, Patrick Ewing, and setting forth a program to compensate for these weaknesses. The fortunate university which would enroll the 7-foot center, perhaps the best high school player in the country, must provide careful guidance in course selection, daily tutoring, help with writing and proofreading papers, review of reading material, untimed testing and the permission to use a tape recorder for lectures (*The Washington Post*, reprinted in the *Wichita Eagle-Beacon*, 19 April, 1981, p. 32). Jarvis created the guidelines to avoid exploitation of his star player by success-hungry recruiters. Georgetown University coach John Thompson, who signed Ewing to a national letter of intent, had to counter many loud charges of "special deals" and "special treatment" from critics who complained that student-athletes like Ewing become more athletic and much less academic.

The Jarvis-Ewing controversy illustrates the "business of intercollegiate athletics" whereby the athletes provide public entertainment, gain attention and money for their academic institution, and prepare for professional careers during their college years. How has such a system evolved in our country? What role has the student-athlete played on college campuses over the centuries? This historical survey reveals that student-athletes have played many different roles and their image has changed as rapidly as they run back and forth across stadium fields and basketball courts. The metamorphosis of the student-athlete provides a reliable index of changing American values and attitudes toward such subjects as work, play, and higher education.

PRAYER AND PLAY

In colonial America, the few select students at Harvard and later at Yale and Princeton prepared for the ministry with a rigid curriculum which included Latin, Greek, Hebrew, logic, and rhetoric. Harvard's goal, according to Samuel Eliot Morison, was to educate clergy "who would spell the difference between civilization and barbarism" (Morison, 1936, p. 6). Their divinity studies tested their wills but not their bodies. Puritan society emphasized useful industry for survival as much as for salvation; games and play were carnal pleasures and frivolous diversions from devotion, survival, and salvation. King James I's *Book of Sport*, issued in 1618, justified exercise as necessary to a person's well-being, but the Puritans preferred prayer and tilling the soil to dancing and other "fruitless diversions." They opposed bear-baiting, for example, not because of the torture of animals, but because of the pleasure gained by spectators of these events (Dulles, 1965, chapter 1). Leaders such as William Bradford held the entire community together in labor with no distraction from amusements. Within this constrictive and somber environment, Puritans trained and tested their wills as so many "moral athletes," as Ralph Barton Perry calls them (Perry, 1944, p. 245).

The Age of Enlightenment: Balance of Mind and Body

The return of Charles II to the throne marked the end of Puritanism and the restoration of the more secular Anglican Church in 1660. John Locke's belief that "a sound mind in a sound body is a short but full description of a happy state in this world" typifies the Age of Enlightenment in the 18th century which combated attitudes toward sports such as expressed by the President of Princeton in 1787, who banned sports from campus as "low and unbecoming gentlemen and scholars and as attended with great harm to the health" (Locke, 1946, p. 138). New England colonies survived the Great Awakening led by Jonathan Edwards to give birth to such beliefs by Reverend Joseph Seccomb that "when the Body has been long wearied with Labour, or the Mind weakened with Devotion....Our Diversion, if rightly used, not only fits us for, but leads us to Devotion (Seccomb, 1743, pp. 17-19).

A Boston physician, Dr. John Jeffries, published a paper titled "Physical Culture: The Result of Moral Obligation" in 1833 which harkened back to the Greek ideal of balance; mental and physical skill could fulfill man's potential (Jeffries, 1833, p. 252). Jacksonian Democracy accompanied the rapid growth of the academy in America: More than 250 institutions existed prior to the Civil War, a large increase over the 9, small denominational colleges that operated during the Revolutionary War (Rudolph, 1962, p. 201). A new found faith in the inevitable perfectedness of man and an average life expectancy of 35 years provided inspiration for reformers who touched college campuses.

Dull, Spartan, well-regulated, and academically rigorous, the post-Revolutionary War students were oppressed by a faculty not much more tolerant of nonacademic pursuits than their Puritan predecessors. In return, rebellious energetic students harassed faculty and destroyed buildings in protest over food, curfews and classes (Lewis, 1970, p. 222-9).

Emergence of the Field of Physical Education

Thus, university administrators welcomed the physical education classes established around gymnasium exercises imported by Frederick Ludwig Jahn and his "turnverein." One president simply stated that "thorough fatiguing of the body" could promote "pure living and pure thinking" (Geiger, 1958, pp. 238-9). The formalized physical training did not provide an outlet for undergraduate energies; students preferred their own "ball" games informally organized and irregularly played on "Bloody Monday" by Harvard sophomores against the Frosh (Lucas and Smith, 1978, pp. 193-195). "Bloodball," a part of the class rush system at Cambridge, was a mass assault conducted in Harvard Yard described by one New York *Evening Post* reporter who witnessed "eyes...bunged, faces blackened and bloodied and shirts and coats torn to rags" (Durant and Bettmann, 1965, p. 28).

However, it was the intercollegiate and not the intramural contests that gained students' attention; campus sport clubs took shape and regular competition resulted. August 3, 1852, was the date for the first intercollegiate athletic contest: a crew match between the Harvard and the Yale clubs on New Hampshire's Lake Winnepesaukee (Whiton, 1967, p. 639). The first intercollegiate baseball game (Amherst defeated Williams 73-32 on July 1, 1859) and the first intercollegiate football game (Rutgers defeated Princeton 6-4 on November 6, 1869) followed.

Such contests of muscle, not mind, would go a long way in negating the observation by a British visitor that a Boston boy is "a picture of prematurity" with "no breadth either of shoulders, information or ambition" (Grattan, 1928, pp. 250-1). Americans themselves recognized their boys as "an apathetic-brained, a pale pasty-faced, narrow chested, spindle-shanked, dwarfed race—mere walking manikins to advertise the last cut of the fashionable tailor (Anonymous, 1856, p. 646). Oliver Wendell Holmes realized that "such a set of black-coated, stiff-jointed, soft muscled, paste complexioned youth as we can boast in our Atlantic cities never before sprang from the loins of Anglo-saxon lineage" (Holmes, 1858, p. 881). Thomas Hughes' popular story of boys' sports at Rugby, *Tom Brown's Schooldays* (1857), inspired Harvard, Brown, Trinity, and Yale to form the College Rowing Association which staged an annual regatta. American schools developed a pride in their athletic exploits. When Yale outstroked Harvard, the Cambridge school paper reported that "Yale was still a little in the rear of Harvard in its *machinery* for education" but the Elies declared the victory to be "sacredly connected with the glory of Alma Mater herself" (The Regatta, 1864, and The College Regatta, 1864, p. 13).

Superiority in athletics could provide a new institution with instant prestige. When Massachusetts Agricultural College celebrated a victory over Harvard in 1870, observers believed that the win "gave the agricultural college standing as a real college" (True, 1929, p. 107). An alumnus of Williams College dramatized another truth about intercollegiate athletics when he stated "you do not remember whether Thornwright was valedictorian or not, but you can never forget that glorious run of his in the football game" (Tenney, 1890, p. 142).

Newspaper coverage of intercollegiate athletics increased and alumni as well as people who could not attend an institution identified with their *alma mater* or geographical school as intersectional rivalries grew. Despite President Andrew D. White's protest, "I will not send thirty men to travel four hundred miles only to agitate a bag of wind," his Cornell University eventually played a football game against Michigan in 1874 (Sagendorph, 1948, p. 150). In fact, an upstart institution such as Michigan could establish itself as an academic peer and spread its reputation by playing Harvard, Princeton, and Yale—which it did, all in one week in 1881 (Rudolph, 1962, p. 376).

However, college sports was not without growing pains, and critics of intercollegiate athletics verbalized doubts about the financial side, the sportsmanship, the values, and relationship between athletes and the student body. Albert Bushnell Hart speaking in 1890 spoke of "athletic recruits as the few young men who became members of the college in order to develop and to exhibit their skill as athletes" not scholars (Hart, 1890, p. 65). Another critic at the rapidly growing University of California believed that athletics "as conducted now in our large arenas is but for the few picked teams while the many students who need physical development the most become stoop-shouldered from rooting from backless bleachers" (Ferrier, 1930, p. 457).

Stanford University's President called for an end to the abuses and hypocrisy with an open honesty. "Let the football team become frankly professional," he suggested. "Cast off all deception," he continued. "Get the best professional coach. Pay him well and let him have the best men the town and alumni will pay for" (Denlinger & Shapiro, 1975, p. 23).

Establishing a Balance: Beginning of the NCAA

However, the man who personified the "strenuous life" and preached "muscular Christianity," and who discouraged President Eliot from abandoning football at Harvard for fear of producing "mollycoddles" instead of "vigorous men," intervened only after a particularly bloody 1905 season which produced 18 fatalities and over 150 serious injuries. Teddy Roosevelt called a White House Conference with representatives of several Ivy League Schools and encouraged Chancellor Henry B. McCracken of New York University to call a National Conference. The 62 attending members formed the Intercollegiate Athletic Association of the

United States, which effectively confronted Walter Camp and his Intercollegiate Football Rules Committee and eventually developed into the National Collegiate Athletic Association (Lewis, 1969, pp. 717-24).

The forward pass, the neutral zone between the lines, 10 yards to make a first down, and the outlawing of "hurdling" were introduced to improve the game's safety. In addition, the organization would hopefully eliminate "tramp" athletes like Fielding H. Yost, who drifted from West Virginia College to Lafayette College in order to help defeat unbeaten Pennsylvania, and James Hogan, who was lured by Yale to play amateur football with a suite in Vanderbilt Hall, free tuition and meals, a trip to Cuba, all profits from scorecards sales, and a job as a cigarette agent for the American Tobacco Company (Boyle, 1963, p. 22).

DEVELOPMENT OF INTERCOLLEGIATE ATHLETICS

Nowhere is the movement from student-supported, recreational club sports to full-scale intercollegiate athletics better illustrated than in the beliefs and career of William Rainey Harper, president of the University of Chicago from 1892 until 1906. His conception of a "societal service station" which deals with practical affairs, social problems and students' needs, rather than an "island of leisurely urbanity and free intellectual inquiry" prompted him to raise student enrollment from 1,815 to 5,500, to hire Amos Alonzo Stagg as Director of Physical Education and Athletics, and to devise a physical education requirement within a rapidly expanding, flexible curriculum. His influence upon the University of Chicago lasted until Robert Maynard Hutchins became president in 1929. Under his direction, the University of Chicago dropped college football in 1939, after repealing the physical education requirement and upgrading intramural athletics. Hutchins once stated that "just as much courage, and courage of a higher sort, is required to tackle a 200-pound idea as to tackle a 200-pound fullback" (Lawson & Ingham, 1980, pp. 37-67).

Cultural Diffusion

David Riesman and Reuel Denney notice the great "culture diffusion"—evidence of ethnicity and social class diversity—in college football players. On the 1889 All-American Football Team only Howard "Pudge" Heffelfinger suggested non-Anglo-Saxon participation. Irish names appeared frequently after 1895, and Jews, Poles, and Germans populated many of the later All-American teams, suggesting American heterogeneity (Riesman & Denney, 1951, 309-25). The student-athlete was as likely to be named Herschberger, McCracken, Schoellkopf, Piekarski, Levine, and Pazzetti as early gridders named Eaton, Channing, Beecher, Poe, Cranston, and Adams. The student-athlete's image reflects America's increasing ethnic populations.

Promoting College Athletics

Small denominational colleges followed the lead of the large state universities in promoting college athletics. The citizens of Lancaster, Pennsylvania, for example, conducted a successful gymnasium building campaign at Franklin and Marshall College in 1890 following a successful football season (Leslie, 1976, p. 215). The coaching career and salary history of Glenn "Pop" Warner demonstrates the shift in power from the student manager and team captain to a paid professional coach who could parlay success at one institution into a higher salary at another school. Beginning at Georgia on $34 per week, Warner moved on to Cornell in 1898 for $800, to Carlisle College the next year at $1,200, onward to Pittsburgh for $4,500 in 1915, to a final annual salary of $20,000 at Stanford (Lucas & Smith, 1978, pp. 193-195).

Emergence of the Sports Heroes

Throughout this entire controversy which discouraged many university administrators about the value of intercollegiate sports programs within the realm of higher education, the image of the student-athlete as "Ivy League hero" survived particularly within the fictional realm of Gilbert Patton's fictional Frank Merriwell, the "unreal ideal" (term coined by Boyle, p. 241). From 1896 to 1914 Frank Merriwell performed incredible feats in football, boxing, baseball, hockey, lacrosse, crew, track, shooting, bicycle racing, billiards, and golf at Ferndale Academy, Yale College, and wherever he might engage in an athletic contest. Gilbert Patten's Merriwell, like Lester Chadwick's "Baseball Joe Matson," Allen Chapman's "Fred Fenton," and other fictional sports heroes provided moral patterns of behavior, societal ethos, and entire value systems which perpetuated the college athlete as moral leader and American hero (Lowe & Payne, 1974, pp. 383-91; Erisman, 1970, pp. 29-37; Evans, 1972, pp. 104-21; Sojka, 1979, pp. 113-21). Furthermore, the occasional appearance of a real hero like Yale's Albie Booth, who won eight varsity letters and captained nearly all of the Eli teams for which he played, kept his image alive even though college football powers began to move westward with the evolution of such schools as Notre Dame, Michigan, Minnesota, Army, Chicago, and Illinois as college gridiron powerhouses. When Harvard broke off athletic relations with Princeton from 1926 until 1934 in order to schedule emerging Midwest power Michigan, the Ivy supremacy over college football was ended (Synnot, 1976, p. 189).

The college football hero was far from dead: Harold "Red" Grange of Illinois generated as much publicity and media attention as his professional contemporaries—Jack Dempsey, Babe Ruth, and Bobby Jones—during the Golden Age of Sports in America's 1920s, along with bigger stadiums and larger attendance. On October 18, 1924, during the dedication game of Illinois' new 70,000 seat Memorial Stadium, Grange achieved instant immortality when he ran for four touchdowns against Michigan, the only four times he touched the ball in the first quarter of play. He returned later in the contest to run for one additional touchdown and pass for a sixth for a total of 402 yards gained on the ground alone.

Nicknamed the "Galloping Ghost," the "Wheaton Iceman," and the "Football Phantom," Grange ushered in the new era of the student-athlete as American mass-media hero: Millions of words were written about him (the *New York Times* called him "the most famous, most talked of and written about athlete of the time"); hundreds of thousands saw him play (370,000 during his junior and last year); hundreds of thousands heard him play professional football on the newly invented radio; and businessmen (like his manager C.C. Pyle) contracted Grange to make movies ($300,000 in contracts) and to sell other types of endorsements ($120,000 annually to sell Florida real estate). A valuable "property," Grange alone is credited with legitimizing professional football—he generated over 70,000 fans while playing for the Chicago Bulls in 1925—even though his pro career was continually hampered by injuries and other distractions.

Grange, along with innovative if not rhapsodic sports writers like Grantland Rice (he wrote about the "Four Horsemen" of Notre Dame galloping against Army the same year Grange sauntered against Michigan), encouraged interest in and support of college athletics by the alumni and by athletic directors who dominated programs plagued by weak presidents, disorganized faculties, and powerless students. Alarmed with this state of affairs, the Carnegie Foundation launched a 3-year study of American College Athletics which concluded with the publication of a volume written by Walter Savage in 1929. After condemning the

> Paid coach, the gate receipts, the special training tables, and costly sweaters and extensive journeys in special Pullman cars, the recruiting from high school, the demoralizing publicity showered on players, the devotion of an undue proportion of time to training, the devices for putting a desirable athlete but a weak scholar, across the hurdle of examinations.

Savage and his predictably naive colleagues called for a return to student-controlled programs conducted for recreation and enjoyment (Savage, 1929, p. xxii). Not surprisingly, Savage's attack "codified" rather than eliminated treatment of students as athletes. George Hanford rightly points to the hiring of Dick Harlow as Harvard's first nongraduate football coach as the end of the alumni-coach era, and as the end of the era in college sports when loyalty to one's alma mater was valued more than producing a winning team for a salary (Hanford, 1975, p. 33).

BLACK STUDENT ATHLETES

With expanding recruiting programs fulfilling the pressure to win, the image of the black student-athlete grew to be more commonplace. Early pioneers like William H. Lewis at Amherst (1890-93, and on Walter Camp's All-Time All-American Team), Fritz Pollard at Brown (1915-19), Paul Robeson at Rutgers

(1917-21), and Fred "Duke" Slater at Iowa (1918-21) were such talented men that their universities overlooked their color in deference to their intelligence as students, as well as to their talent as athletes. Kenny Washington, Jackie Robinson, and Woodie Strode started a parade of UCLA black athletes which continues from UCLA and Southern California today. But not until the Supreme Court's desegregation rulings in 1954 were black athletes a common sight in universities across the country. The Southwest and Southeast conferences went from having no blacks at all participating in sports to a substantial number in a 10 year period; from 1963-1973 Texas added 6 black football players, Mississippi 5, and Alabama 13. In addition, Pittsburgh went from 2 to 31 black varsity football players and 21 at Oklahoma (Denlinger & Shapiro, 1975, p. 33). The decrease in professional prospects originating from traditionally black football powerhouses like Grambling and Florida A & M demonstrated that large state universities were recruiting local talent regardless of skin color.

Jesse Owens, the "Buckeye Bullet" from the Ohio State University, became perhaps America's first black sports hero when he won four gold medals at the 1936 Olympic Games in Berlin. In a Big Ten meet one year earlier, Owens set four world records to demonstrate athletic equality. However, the fact that fewer black student athletes actually earn degrees outside of racial motivation raises the charges by critics such as Jack Olsen and Harry Edwards that they are "paid gladiators" expected to win games and to bring notoriety and money to an institution which excludes them from social life and serious academic pursuits.

PROBLEMS OF THE 1950s

College point-shaving scandals of the early 1950s prompted the American Council of Education (a group of university presidents) to analyze once again the problems of intercollegiate athletics. They concluded that, among other items, spring football practice and postseason bowl games (which disrupted the academic calendar) should be abolished (*Educational Record*, 1952, pp. 246-55). Predictably, spring football practices continued and football bowl games multiplied rather than dwindled.

The most obvious oversight by this well-intentioned group led by John A. Hannah, president of Michigan State University, was the growing value of televised broadcasts of intercollegiate contests. From rather meager days in the 1950s when the NCAA contested televised broadcasts of football games, events proceeded to a $12 million contract for the 1972-73 season to a $29 million contract for the 1980-81 season (Odenkirk, 1981, p. 63). A media celebrity like O.J. Simpson could not only gain conference victories for South California, but increase alumni contributions to his institution while utilizing his college career to advance his economic livelihood and to gain a professional career in show business.

Alumni contributions dropped by one-half million dollars when the Ohio State University's record dropped to 4-5 during the 1966 season, proving that a losing season could contribute to a failing fund-drive (Denlinger and Shapiro, p. 30). For those schools that did not entice the talented athlete, television showed no interest. For example, during the 1974-75 season, Penn State University gained over $1 million in television and bowl game contracts, while nearby Villanova University received nothing; Penn State's continual top-ten status, and Villanova's recent dropping of intercollegiate football were logical results (Michener, 1976, p. 204).

Recruiting expenses increase, but the return on attracting talented athletes who can perhaps guide their school to a bowl game is equally growing. When Bud Wilkinson began coaching at the University of Oklahoma, his entire recruiting budget totaled $3,000, increasing to $7,588 over his long illustrious career. Current Sooner coach Barry Switzer admits that $10,000 alone was spent in recruiting one athlete, Elvis Peacock from Miami, Florida, in 1974, only 11 years after Wilkinson's last coaching season (Denlinger & Shapiro, p. 32). No wonder former Oklahoma University President George Cross stated at his inauguration that he hoped to be a president of whom the football team could be proud (Cross, 1977).

Student-athletes become media celebrities and valuable pieces of property since college sports have become so dependent upon television revenues for profit and for survival. Teams constantly reschedule contests to suit television priorities; in fact, teams schedule around media needs. "I'll play at midnight if that's what TV wants," stated Alabama coach, the late Bear Bryant. Michigan's resourceful athletic director-entrepreneur Don Canham agrees that television is "everything" (Michener, 1976, pp. 238, 371).

WOMEN MAKE THEIR PLACE IN ATHLETICS

A very persuasive argument can be made on behalf of the female as truly both student and athlete from her origins during the second half of the 19th century to present in comparison to her male counterpart. Women attending colleges in the last half of the 19th century did so to prove that they were the intellectual equals of men. In addition, the reformers who championed the women's rights movement were the same people who introduced exercise, physical education, and eventually team sports into higher education institutions. Therefore, it should come as no surprise that the few fortunate early female college students participated fully in recreation and in physical activity programs: the ultimate means to erase, perhaps forever, the Victorian stereotype of women as frail, delicate, and passive. Women at Vassar, Smith, Radcliffe, and other such schools swam, played tennis and golf, rode horses, and otherwise supplemented their intellectual endeavors with physical exercise.

Unlike men's athletics, women's collegiate sports were governed by women physical educators with little outside interference from students and alumni. Sports such as croquet, walking, ice skating, and tennis became part of the curriculum, while team sports of basketball, volleyball, field hockey, and occasionally lacrosse existed mostly on the intramural level. The first intercollegiate women's competitions were basketball games in 1896 between Cal Berkeley and Stanford and between the University of Washington and Ellensburg Normal School. Because participation was the most important reason for athletics, intramurals remained more popular than intercollegiate competitions. Lucille Eaton, director of Physical Training at Wellesley College, expressed a typical view toward competitive athletics for women. She believed that "fiercely competitive athletics have their danger for men but they develop manly strength." For women, however, "dangers are greater and the qualities they tend to develop are not womenly" (Gerber et al., 1974, p. 69). While Eaton's ideas do not seem liberated from the antiquated views which the women's colleges were refuting, other physical educators like Elizabeth Burchenal in 1919 encouraged "sports for sports sake" and not highly competitive intercollegiate schedules and teams coached by hired male coaches (Burchenal, 1919, p. 274). Another physical educator, Agnes R. Wayman, hoped that women's sports could avoid the mistakes and abuses frequently cited in men's programs. She once told a crowd: "We are setting forth under our own sail, with women at the helm and women manning the whole craft" (Wayman, 1924, p. 517).

In 1923, the Women's Division of the National Amateur Athletic Federation drew up a platform which stressed promotion of programs encouraging participation but not intercollegiate athletics. Their "play for play's sake" was summarized in their motto, "A game for every girl and every girl in a game" (Lucas & Smith, p. 352). In fact, until 1951, only 27% of the country's coeducational institutions fielded varsity teams of any type. Although varsity teams were never formally eliminated, the Division of Girls' and Women's Sports as late as 1957 discouraged intercollegiate competition unless it formed an equal triumvirate with intramural and curricular programs. Only in 1966 did a Commission of Intercollegiate Sports for Women actually encourage intercollegiate competition and create national championships. When the AIAW (Association for Intercollegiate Athletics for Women) convened in 1971 under the auspices of the American Alliance for Health, Physical Education, and Recreation to establish educational athletic programs, its 278 charter members agreed participants were to be students first and athletes second (Grant, 1979, p. 414).

Title IX, part of the Educational Amendment Act of 1972, denied discrimination against women, providing funds necessary to increase the number of female student-athletes. Despite claims from athletic directors such as Darrell Royal of Texas—"The end result very well could be that we have to give up all our athletic programs"—and coaches such as Woody Hayes, formerly of Ohio State—"To play football you need a bullneck, and I don't like girls with bullnecks"—women's athletics will remain closer to the historical origins of college athletics as long as college football remains an exclusively male sport (Parkhouse & Lapin, 1980, p. 116). In a period when 69% of all men's athletic programs lose money and 81% of football programs are not self-supporting, the outlook for women' athletics, especially with many program mergers taking place, is not all rosy (Lopiano, 1979, p. 394). The recent NCAA takeover of championship events for women's athletics from the AIAW indicated potential revenue growth but also the possibility that women student-athletes, too, may become valuable assets to their institutions as well as money-making attractions. The inevitable cheating, distortion of values, and recruiting problems will follow if the women follow the money and leave the academics behind.

THE ATHLETE AS A POLITICAL ACTIVIST

The close relationship between the changing image of the student-athlete and the emerging values and attitudes of America and its institutions of higher education is best illustrated by the appearance of the student-athlete as political activist and radical during the late 1960s. Until this time, the student-athlete might well be accused of reflecting the party-line of America's universities: They build respected, well-rounded citizens, business leaders, moral warriors, well-conditioned fighting men, and prepare student-athletes to enter into the boardroom via their experiences in the locker room. However, this period of social protest, antiestablishment values, and revolutionary rhetoric engaged student-athletes to question their competitory instincts as well as the institutions they represented.

While American black tracksters and student-athletes, (many from San Jose State University) protested, under the guidance of Dr. Harry Edwards, their paid gladiator status in the 1968 Mexico City Olympics, thousands of American youth, under the exhortation of Bobby Seale and Jerry Rubin, protested that same summer in the streets of Chicago during the Democratic National Convention. Although their means and locations differed, the student-athletes like their nonathlete comrades protested against oppression, against excessive imperialism of the United States in Viet Nam, and for individual civil rights.

Publications of this period by such athletes-become-scholars as Jack Scott (*The Athletic Revolution*, 1971) and Harry Edwards (*The Revolt of the Black Athlete*, 1969); more recently, defected student-athletes such as Dave Meggysey (*Out of their League*, 1970), Gary Shaw (*Meat On The Hoof*, 1972), and Chip Oliver (*High For The Game*, 1971), all voice a dislike for the contradictory values found in intercollegiate competition.

President Homer D. Babbidge of the University of Connecticut summarized the rhetoric of rebelling student-athletes when he told a not very receptive group of athletic directors that the need to gratify spectators, raise revenues, and to gain institutional recognition has replaced recognition of individual participating players and values of amateurism. "We have lent credence to the notion that we pay lip service to the values of sport, as we so often pay lip service to peace, to improved race relations and to academic values" (Scott, 1971, pp. 30-31). Jack Scott summarized the arguments of the student activist athletes by concluding that humanized athletic programs cannot result without changes in our educational institutions. "There cannot be athletics for athletes without a concomitant emphasis on education for students," he states, dramatizing just how substantially America's institutions evolved since the years of Yale College, the Ivy League hero, and sports programs for students controlled by students (Scott, p. vi).

One of the famous cries from this period, especially from critics such as Harry Edwards who deplored the use and subsequent disposal of black athletes, was that student-athletes were merely paid gladiators; once their eligibility expired, along with their scholarships, they had nothing to show for 4 years of athletic competition except a modest accumulation of miscellaneous college credits, usually not including degree requirements and memories of glorious days which would bring no immediate job offers.

ATHLETES AS FOREIGN LEGIONNAIRES

A recent NCAA track and field championship highlighted the evolution of another breed of student-athlete, very much the paid gladiator in his own right: the student-athletes as "immigrant-import." Coach Ted Banks' Texas-El Paso squad, as expected, captured their third straight outdoor championship. His runners have earned no worse than a second place finish in the last 21 track events conducted by the NCAA. The Miners' victory came as no surprise, but unlike previous years, the team's entire point-production was generated by non-American participants, nicknamed the "Foreign Legion" by rival coaches. Leading the imports was eight-time NCAA champion Suleiman Nyambui: As an Olympic silver medalist from Tanzania, he took firsts in the 5,000 and 10,000 meter runs, while teammate Mike Mysyoke finished third in both distance events. Sophomore Bert Cameron from Jamaica captured the 400 meter race, edging 1979 World Champion Kasheff Hassan of the Sudan and Oregon State. Milt Ottey, a freshman high jumper from Toronto, gained third place in his event. Another import, Steve Hanna, gained victory in the triple jump. However, Texas-El Paso was not the only squad to rely upon imported student-athletes to represent their university. Included among top finishers were Reidar Lorentzen of Oregon; Juba Hentunen, Brigham Young; Hans Koeleman, Clemson; Sidney Maree, Villanova; Sammy Koshei, SMU; Goran Swensson, and other non-Americans.

The only comparable example of foreign legionnaires in intercollegiate athletics would be the increasing number of Samoan football players appearing on West Coast Pac-10 Conference teams. When academic institutions labor under the pressure of credit-hour production quotas, and the emphasis on victory remains strong in college athletics, imported student-athletes will inevitably increase.

THE ATHLETE AS AN ENTREPRENEUR

The evolution of the student-athlete would not be complete without the image in the last 30 years of the student-athlete as "criminal" and/or "entrepreneur." In the early 1950s, college basketball was rocked by a series of "point-shaving" scandals investigated by New York City District Attorney Frank Hogan of Manhattan. College basketball matured with sell-out crowds which filled Madison Square Garden for double-headers involving such local teams as CCNY (NIT and NCAA champions in 1949), LIU, NYU, and St. John's. College basketball followed the lead of football as it emerged into a large-scale money-making venture and gained valuable media coverage: Fans paid $5 to $50 to see games; Garden promoter Ned Irish staged the contests; athletic directors gained revenues from the games; players gained recognition but nothing else according to NCAA rules which kept their amateur, student status intact. However, gamblers approached players and offered them money to "shave" points off the predicted margin of victory.

Not asked to "throw" or lose games and seeing the opportunity to profit from the contests, players from all major New York City teams except for St. John's cooperated and eventually were arrested. Coach Forrest "Phog" Allen of Kansas blamed the incident on the "unsavory atmosphere" of the urban east. Adolph "The Baron" Rupp of Kentucky said gamblers "couldn't touch our boys with a ten-foot pole" (Isaacs, 1975, p. 105). But both men proved too idealistic or naive as the "unsavory atmosphere" spread to the heart of the Midwest to Peoria, Illinois, and the Bradley Braves. Two of Rupp's own players were convicted of similar charges (Cohen, 1977; Rosen, 1978).

Ten years later, Oregon, Iowa, North Carolina, and countless other schools became implicated in another point-shaving scandal engineered by Jack Molinas, former All-American basketball player at Columbia and a law school graduate. Molinas, who learned the point-shaving system in college and during a brief professional career, sought to entice poor black student-athletes like Connie Hawkins into "playing for pay." Men like Hawkins had their college careers cut short and professional opportunities destroyed by association with the scandals (Wolf, 1972, pp. 78-126).

Most recently, three Boston College players have been accused of taking part in another point-shaving scandal by taking bribes to influence the outcome of nine games during the 1978-79 season. Unlike Connie Hawkins who was relatively innocent in the 1960s scandals, Rich Kuhn, Jim Sweetney, and Ernie Cobb allegedly received $2,000 for each game. Henry Hill, who master-minded the plot, claims "They were selling me. They were the salesmen, not me" (Hill & Looney, 1981, p. 18). In addition, Hill believes that the three players knew that their professional possibilities were slim, so they determined to make some money while they could. This image of the student-athlete as criminal and entrepreneur should come as no surprise: They are illegally recruited with financial inducement, and they, like the rest of the American public, read printed "point-spreads" in the newspapers as well as reports of white-collar crime and government fraud. This moral morass and ethical vacuum in society will, of course, influence our sports.

ATHLETICS AND THE MORAL MAJORITY

College athletics, mirroring shifts in American values and changes on university campuses, appears to be coming full circle with the influence of the moral majority; many student-athletes evoke times when the moral athlete represented a heroic ideal and personified the educational, intellectual, and cultural mission of such institutions of higher education like Yale. In particular, one student-athlete at the New Haven school recalls the "moral warriors" and the Frank Merriwells of the past.

Ronnie Darling, whose name alone could easily qualify him as a character in a Gilbert Patton novel, played many positions as an All-American baseball player at Yale. He personifies the values which school president A. Bartlett Giamatti describes: "a strong spirit compounded of respect for the glories of mind and body striving in harmony." Likewise, Giamatti deplores "that vile phrase 'student-athlete'," and "the very fraudulence of the college athletic enterprise and its acceptance as mere ornament in the academic process" (Deford, 1981, pp. 32, 33, 34). Darling's penchant for the dramatic game-ending hits and clutch relief-pitching, tempered by a Merriwellian modesty, combine to make his feats at Yale seem like an episode out of the glorious past of intercollegiate athletics. Darling once lost a NCAA playoff game to St. John's 1-0; after a record 11 hitless innings, a teammate's error allowed the winning run. Darling's reply was typical All-American Ivy League hero in tone: "What's the big deal, we lost the game," he stated.

President Giamatti describes competition as "something as necessary to the strong spirit as striving is necessary to the healthy character." Ronnie Darling, who reasoned "If I was going to get a college education, why not go for the best?" keeps the college hero alive and well in a time when America looks for past heroes to provide incentive for an optimistic future (Deford, 1981, p. 33).

Recently, Robert Thompson, master of Yale University's Timothy Dwight College, cancelled a noncredit course in thoroughbred horseriding on moral grounds. Thompson believed that instructor Bill Drew would emphasize the skilled reading of past-performance charts, thus encouraging students to test their skills at New Haven's closed-circuit off-track betting facility. Thompson acted in the tradition of former Yale President Dwight who punished students in 1822 for playing football and handball on college grounds and buildings, assessing a "50 cent fine, suspension or dismissal." Thompson protected Yale students from such "idle recreations" as horse-betting. Yale, which does not provide athletic scholarships, keeps an eternal vigil against the materialism and immorality which sports may breed among undergraduates.

CHRISTIAN ATHLETES

Moral athlete, paid gladiator, media celebrity, female, All-American Ivy League hero, black, criminal-entrepreneur, radical-activist, and foreign legionnaires: All joined by the Christian student-athletes currently being produced by men such as Oral Roberts, who perceive sports as having "a mission to bring people to God." After Oral Roberts University defeated Hofstra University in Madison

Square Garden, Roberts told a group of his followers "that this was a victory for God, not for basketball" (Michener, 1976, p. 236). The rise of the "moral majority" as a powerful political force parallels a rebirth of interest in the Fellowship of Christian Athletes movement, which strives to "apply muscle and action to the Christian faith...to strengthen the moral, mental and spiritual fiber of the athletes and coaches of America."

Former college players such as Roger Staubach, Craig Morton, Donnie Shell, and Archie Griffin, and current college coaches such as Grant Teaff (Baylor), Dean Smith (North Carolina), Tom Osborne (Nebraska), Bill Yung (West Texas State University), and others see their work as bearing "witness" to Christ's presence on earth; they believe Christian values and intercollegiate athletics can live side by side in a profession racked with cheating, violation, and corruption.

Occasionally, ambition and greed will cause the downfall of coaches such as Texas track coach Cleburne Price, who had recently offered scholarships to Francis Garbrah and Samuel Quaicoe from Accra, Ghana. Perhaps Price hoped to stay competitive with fellow-Texan Ted Banks of Texas-El-Paso, who built a power-house of such foreign legionnaires. Garbrah claimed 25½" in the long jump, 50'8" in the triple jump, and 13.9 in the 110 meter hurdles, while Quaicoe claimed 25'5½" in the long jump, 51'4" in the triple jump, and 46.9 in the 400 meters. Upon arriving in the United States, Garbrah could only manage 17'5½", 38'8" (he barely reached the sandpit in the jumps) and 57.2 in the 400 meters (well below the UT women's times for the event); Quaicoe managed performances well under his best claimed times. The two Ghanaians perpetrated the hoax through a counterfeit newspaper story in which names were substituted and stripped in over original headlines. These two con-men illustrated that ambitious college coaches had better reevaluate the student-athlete who in the past was exploited, but who in the future may become the exploiter.

REFERENCES

ANONYMOUS (1856, October). Why we get sick. *Harper's,* 13.

BOYLE, R.H. (1963). *Sport—Mirror of American life.* Boston, Massachusetts: Little, Brown.

BURCHENAL, E. (1919). A constructive program for school girls. *American Physical Education Review,* 24.

COHEN, S. (1977). *The game they played.* New York: Farrar, Straus, and Giroux. See also Rosen, C. (1978). *Scandals of '51,* New York: Holt, Rinehart, and Winston, for detailed analysis of the point-shaving incidents.

CROSS, G. (1977). *Presidents can't punt.* Norman, Oklahoma: University of Oklahoma Press.

DEFORD, F. (1981, March). A desire to excel. *Sports Illustrated,* 30.

DENLINGER, K. & L. Shapiro. (1975). *Athletes for sale.* New York: Crowell.

DULLES, F.R. (1965). *A history of recreation: America learns to play,* 2nd ed. New York: Appleton-Century-Crofts.

DURANT, J. & Bettmann, O. (1965). *Pictorial history of American sports.* New York: A.S. Barnes.

FELLOWSHIP of Christian Athletes brochure.

FERRIER, W.W. (1930). *Origin and development of the University of California.* Berkeley: The Sather Gate Bookshop.

GEIGER, L.G. (1958). *University of the Northern Plains: A history of the University of North Dakota, 1883-1958.* Grand Forks.

GERBER, et al., (Eds.). (1974). *The American Woman in Sport.* Reading, Massachusetts. Addison-Wesley Publishing Company.

GRANT, C.H.B. (1979, Fall). Institutional autonomy and intercollegiate athletics. *Educational Record,* **60**.

GRATTAN, T.C. (1928). *Observations of a British consul, 1839-46.* London: 1859. In A. Nevins (Ed.), *American social history as recorded by British travelers.* New York.

HANFORD, G.H. (1979). Controversies in college sports. *Educational Record,* **60**, 353.

HART, A.B. (1980, July). The status of athletics in American colleges. *Atlantic Monthly,* **66**.

HILL, H. & Looney, D.S. (1981, February 16). How I put the fix in. *Sports Illustrated.*

HOLMES, O.W. (1859, May). The autocrat of the breakfast table. *Atlantic Monthly,* **1**.

ISAACS, N.D. (1975). *All the moves.* Philadelphia: J.B. Lippincott.

JEFFRIES, J. (1883, October). Physical culture, the result of moral obligation. *The American Quarterly Observer,* **1**.

LAWSON, H.A. & Ingham, A.G. (1980, Winter). Conflicting ideologies concerning the university and intercollegiate athletics: Harper and Hutchins at Chicago, 1892-1940. *Journal of Sport History,* **7**.

LESLIE, B. (1976, Winter). The response of four colleges to the rise of intercollegiate athletics, 1865-1915. *Journal of Sport History,* **3**

LEWIS, G. (1970, Summer). The beginning of organized sport. *American Quarterly,* **22**.

LEWIS, G. (1969, December). Theodore Roosevelt's role in the 1905 football controversy. *Research Quarterly,* **40**.

LOCKE, J. (1946). *Some thoughts concerning education.* Boston, Massachusetts: Gray & Bowen, 1830; T.J. Wertenbaker. *Princeton, 1746-1896.* Princeton: Princeton University Press.

LOPIANO, D.A. (1979, Fall). Solving the financial crisis in intercollegiate athletics. *Educational Record,* **60**.

LOWE, B. & Payne, M.H. (1974, Fall). To be a red-blooded American boy. *Journal of Popular Culture,* **8**. See also Erisman, F. (1970, April). The strenuous life in practice: the school sports stories of Ralph Henry Barbour. *Rocky Mountain Social Science Journal,* **7**; Evans, W. (1972, Summer). The all-American boys. *Journal of Popular Culture,* **6**; and Sojka, G.S. (1979). Going 'From rags to riches' with Baseball Joe: Or a pitcher's progress. In T.D. Clark (Ed.), *Onward and upward: Essays of the self-made American.* Bowling Green, Ohio: Popular Press.

LUCAS, J.A. & Smith, R.A. (1978). *Saga of American sport.* Philadelphia: Lea & Febiger.

MICHENER, J. (1976). *Sports in America.* New York: Random House.

MORISON, S.E. (1936). *Harvard College in the seventeenth century.* Cambridge: Harvard University Press.

ODENKIRK, J.E. (1981, April). Intercollegiate athletics: Big business or sport? *Academe.*

PARKERHOUSE, B.L. & Lapin, J. (1980). *Women who win.* Englewood Cliffs, New Jersey: Prentice-Hall.

PERRY, R.B. (1944). *Puritanism and democracy.* New York: Vanguard.

REGATTA, The. (1859, August 3). *Worcester Palladium.* Also, The college regatta. (1864, October). *Yale Literary Magazine,* **30**.

REPORT of the Special Committee on Athletic Policy. (1952, Spring). *Educational Record,* **43**.

RIESMAN, D. & Denny, R. (1951, Winter). Football in America: A study in culture diffusion. *American Quarterly, 3*.

RUDOLPH, F. (1962). *The American college and university: A history*. New York: Knopf.

SAGENDORPH, K. (1948). *Michigan, The story of a university*. New York: E.P. Dutton.

SAVAGE, W.H. (1929). *American college athletics*. New York: Carnegie Foundation for the Advancement of Teaching.

SCOTT, J. (1971). *The athletic revolution*. New York: Free Press.

SECCOMB, J. (1743). *Business and diversion inoffensive to God, and necessary for the comfort and support of human society*. Boston: S. Kneeland and T. Green. See also Struna, N. (1977, Spring). Puritans and sport: The irretrievable tide of change. *Journal of Sport History, 4*.

SYNNOT, M.G. (1976, Summer). The "Big Three" and the Harvard-Princeton football break, 1926-1934. *Journal of Sport History, 3*.

TENNEY, S.G. (1890). Athletics at Williams. *Outing, 17*.

TRUE, A.C. (1929). *A history of agricultural education in the United States, 1785-1929*. Washington, D.C.: U.S. Government Printing Office.

THE Washington Post. Reprinted in the Wichita *Eagle-Beacon* (1981, April 19).

WAYMAN, A.R. (1924). Women's athletics—All uses—No abuses. *American Physical Education Review, 29*.

WHITON, J.M. (1901, June). The first Harvard-Yale Regatta. *Outlook, 58*. Also Lewis, G.M. (1967, December). America's first intercollegiate sport: The regattas from 1852 to 1875. *Research Quarterly, 38*.

WOLF, D. (1972). *Foul! The Connie Hawkins story*. New York: Holt, Rinehart, and Winston.

Chapter 3

The American Conception of Higher Education and the Formal Incorporation of Intercollegiate Sport

Donald Chu
Skidmore College

When placed in cross-cultural perspective, the rise of sport at American institutions of higher education is utterly peculiar. In no other country is there a similar proximity between athletics and the formal structure of educational institutions. This connection has been chronicled in a number of major historical treatments of the rise of sport in the United States. Betts (1974) noted the importance of advances in transportation and communications in the development of America's sport. Barney similarly noted the significance of the industrial revolution in the burgeoning of sport in the late 19th and early 20th centuries (Zeigler, 1979, p. 187). Lucas and Smith (1978), in their well-documented *Saga of American Sport*, noted the importance of the British origins of sport on the campus and the differences in the character of sport due to the lack of a gentlemanly amateur ideal in this country.

The focus of the aforementioned works and of most other accounts of intercollegiate sport has been, however, on sport itself. The usual center of attention has been on the documentation and description of the major events in the history of sport on campus. Early student efforts to develop alternatives to the boring, outmoded, classically oriented curriculum are usually described, as is the eventual triumph of big-time athletics during the Golden Age of Sport.

Few studies have focused on the institutions of higher education into which athletics would eventually be incorporated. While such descriptive works are a necessary stage in the determination of historical truth, they must lead to more analytical works whose purpose is more an explanation of why these chronicled events have taken such a peculiar pattern. Why did athletics become so much a part of the formal college/university structure? What was it about the universities and colleges in this country that suited them, unlike their European counterparts, for such a relationship with sport?

This paper suggests that an ill-defined "charter" (i.e., a societally legitimized understanding of what the college/university should strive to do and the means to be employed to reach those goals) created a particularly fertile atmosphere for the incorporation of radically different programs into the academic structure.[1] Without a strong American consensus and an assumption and understanding of the goals and technologies appropriate for institutions of higher education, the very structure of the college/university was open to redefinition to suit the particular needs and desires of America's higher educational institutions and their constituencies.

Willing academicians, government leaders, and the American general public entertained the notion of new programs and objectives for higher education, and the colleges' business-minded presidents and trustees used athletics as a means of remedying financial and enrollment difficulties. Without a well-accepted understanding of the importance and responsibilities of the American college and university, leadership in higher education had to search creatively for funds and students, altering programs and educational philosophies in the process.

THE "CHARTER" OF HIGHER EDUCATION

According to the sociologist John Meyer (1970), all viable institutions, whether they be the church, family, or education, have socially defined "charters."[2] The charter tells the members of an institution and society what that institution should be and what programs and goals should be incorporated as a legitimate part of that institution. Because of the charter, definitions of purposes and responsibilities of an institution are understood without these definitions being formally expressed. The family, for example, is understood to have certain functions involving rearing of the young. These understandings precede any formal-legal definition of the purposes of the family. Without a societal acceptance of the legitimacy of this definition of what a family should and should not be entitled to do, any formal-legal definition which goes beyond that societally accepted definition is open to serious doubt.

The charter is not a written document; instead, it is an informal understanding. Though it is informal, it is in no way less important than a school's written and usually state-registered declaration of purposes. In fact, it is precisely the charter's unwritten nature which renders it significant. Operating on the unconscious level in the minds of the population, the charter tells the people what they should reasonably expect in the way of programs from the entity called "the college." Although each school is affected by this societal perception of what is "right" for that culture's higher education, no one school has the power to change the charter so defined for that society's higher educational institutions.

The charter is the result of historical and contemporary values, attitudes, goals, and dreams of the society.

The relatively strong charters possessed by Oxford and Cambridge, for example, were forged over the centuries with the help of highly influential elements of society. Since Oxford's 12th century and Cambridge's 13th century origins as protective guilds for English scholars, the institutions have gained the strong respect of the supporting society. Such respect may have come partly from the universities' ancient affiliation with ecclesiastical institutions, all of which shared the attitude that knowledge was sacred and above the selfish yearnings of individuals or special interest groups. The perpetuation of knowledge was a responsibility shared by all in society and was owed to all mankind over all ages.

The colleges of Oxford and Cambridge were seen by the church, and the society was strongly influenced by the church as legitimately fulfilling the needs of mankind. The necessity of these services was further recognized by English aristocracy, nobility, and business leadership who were to endow the universities so well over the centuries. Today, the English government carries on this tradition of respect for the charter of these institutions. Although the control of these universities is beyond the legitimate right of the government, the financial support of these two universities is still a government responsibility.

The charter is granted by society to its institutions because it is the society which is the source of an agreed upon understanding of the institutions' goals and programs. Although an individual president or administration of a particular college may have a well-defined blueprint for that school (as has been demonstrated by case studies of specific schools), this does not mean that a society knows clearly what programs are acceptable for higher education in general (Veysey, 1965, pp. vii-viii). The governing body of a particular school may determine its own goals and programs, but such a determination must be consistent with the programs and goals deemed appropriate for higher education by the society in which that particular school is enmeshed.

Important for the purposes of this paper is the recognition that the societal grant of the "charter" varies in its clarity and strength. A "clear" charter explicitly recognizes specific objectives and technologies appropriate for an institution. A "strong" charter gives an institution great power in society. Institutions so well endowed with strong charters have little problem attracting recruits and maintaining institutional economic health. It is the contention of this paper, however, that American higher education had neither a well-defined nor a strong charter. Lack of clarity indicated by the entertainment of various models of higher education and the need to modify such models to suit America, led to an "open charter" and, therefore, a willingness to formally try new programs in the structure of higher education. The weak charter of higher education in the United States contributed to continual concerns for the flow of resources necessary for survival.

Higher education in the United States did not develop firmly entrenched in the soil of a well-defined culture (Brubacher & Rudy, 1958, p. 373). There were, in the 19th and early 20th centuries, few objectives and means of reaching those objectives accepted by all in the dynamic American society. Although there was a general agreement among the founding fathers that education in general needed to strike a fine balance between the "uniform" American and the free-thinking individual American, there was considerable diversity of opinion concerning specific objectives and the proper means of reaching those goals (i.e., the technology of higher education, classes, curriculum, etc.) (Cremin, 1980, pp. 103-128, 251; Tyack, 1966). Without the established understanding of the "charter" of higher education in the United States, the objectives and technology to be incorporated in American higher education were thrown open to question. Thus, higher education in America was open to new interpretations and programs.

Diversity of opinion concerning the legitimate purposes and technology of higher education led to a willingness to entertain numerous European and American conceptions of higher education's purposes. The distinctly American incorporation of interscholastic sport within the formal structure of the college/university was made possible by the diversity of opinions about proper curricula, programs, and resource acquisition techniques appropriate for that institution. Without a clear-cut European assumption and unquestioned understanding about what belonged and what did not belong, and about the methodology of higher education, those concerned with higher education could not easily say that "of course, large-scaled intercollegiate sport doesn't belong as an official institutionally financed part of the school." Without such a clear-cut, generally accepted definition of purposes and programs appropriate for American colleges and universities, decisions about the appropriateness of such formal incorporation could be made on pragmatic grounds.[3]

COMPETING CONCEPTIONS OF THE CHARTER OF HIGHER EDUCATION

The earliest patterns of higher education in the United States were modeled after the prestigious forms available at Oxford and Cambridge. The transplanted Englishmen, especially, sought to transfer the structure and curriculum of higher education as completely as possible from the homeland (Gilman, 1902; Warfield, 1901). To them, the goal of the college seemed clear; it would provide continuity between the New World and the Old. As Williams (1954) has argued:

> The early Puritans in New England conceived of themselves as helping to bring about a "translatio studii," that is, a transfer of the higher learning from its ancient seats in the Old World to the wilderness of America. The founders of Harvard took for granted the essential continuity of Western learning—the direct link between the American college and earlier institutions, such as the schools of Hebrew prophets, the Academy of Athens, the Palace School of Charlemagne, the medieval universities and the Reformation academies. The precious "veritas," for which the world was indebted to the Hebrews and the Hellenes, had been handed down from genera-

tion to generation, and now the settlers of the "Holy Commonwealth" must take up this torch of learning and carry it along. (pp. 298-299)

Successive generations continued to employ the technology evident at Oxford and Cambridge, primarily the required work in abstract, impractical areas of study. The Yale Report of 1828, which served as the model for many other efforts of higher education in the period from 1830 to 1850, emphasized the need for "intellectual culture" and the development of mental skills and the acquisition of a core of knowledge. To the early precepts, there was no notion of "electives," for there was one body of learning whose validity and value had been demonstrated through time immemorial (Brubacher & Rudy, 1958, p. 16; Ross, 1976). The object of higher education, according to Brown University President Francis Wayland, was "to communicate knowledge and to confer discipline" (1842, p. 81). These sentiments were echoed as late as 1868 by James McCosh in his inaugural address as president of Princeton: "the highest end of a university is to educate; that is to draw out and improve the faculties which God has given" (Veysey, 1965, p. 23). It was understood and assumed that there were certain attitudes and thought, values to be cultivated, and factual information that every cultured and educated person must acquire.[4,5]

By 1840, however, the British-inspired "cultural school" of higher education that was dominant in the minds of America's educators was challenged by a German view of the university as the seat of scholarship—a scholarship less entrenched in history than directed to the acquisition of new learning (Warfield, 1901). By 1865 a new generation of leaders was about to take power in America's colleges and universities, and soon-to-be presidents Henry Tappan of the University of Michigan and James Morgan Hart of the University of Cincinnati believed that the German university should serve as the literal model for American higher education (Hofstadter & Smith, 1961, p. 488; Veysey, 1965, p. 10).

The German system was based on the notion that institutions of higher education should be workshops of free scientific research. Empirical methods of research were to provide safeguards against personal subjectivity. By the late 19th century, the German scientific influence had spread throughout America's universities and colleges. Even humanistic fields like literature, history, and philosophy felt honorbound to demonstrate their scientific side (Brubacher & Rudy, 1958, p. 113).

Unlike the "cultural school," which declared the universal validity and value of one "veritas," the "German scientific school" did not suppose any such value. The significance of a truth or fact had to be demonstrated through rational empirical techniques. Whereas the cultural thought valued by the upper class served as the grist of the subject matter in the cultural school, the scientific model declared that although there might be one truth, such truth had to stand on its own under scientific scrutiny without ties to any social class.[6,7]

Pure research became the dominant thread in the traditional German curriculum. The ideology of that education maintained that only mature and highly competent students should work with outstanding academics in a specialized research environment as long and as deeply as their interests and abilities allowed. The goal of the traditional system was to produce scholars equipped with the methodology, background, and philosophy required for the discovery of knowledge (Burns et al., 1971).

However, while the British and German models of higher education vied for dominance, they were both affected by the emergence of an American view that higher education could not be separated from the needs of the people. "Application" was the key word. How could education serve the practical needs of the people?

The European enlightenment and the American and French Revolutions had had a major impact on the American view of the appropriate functions of its social institutions. Government as well as education should concern itself with the improvement of the human condition. The diminution of pain and suffering through the application of knowledge and resources was to be a primary goal of all in the society (Foerster, 1937). The idea that higher education should serve practical public service found specific expression in Francis Bacon's utilitarianism and the homespun philosophy of Benjamin Franklin. Regardless of the demands of culture and science, the first responsibility of all social institutions was the betterment of the human condition.

When the European curricula were transplanted to American soil, critics considered them inappropriate for the American population. The broader utilitarian training suggested by Benjamin Franklin was incorporated in 1754 by Samuel Johnson, President of King's College, and later by William Smith at the College of Philadelphia. Criticism of European models of higher education grew as the urban merchant class in the seaport towns of the colonies became more significant (Brubacher & Rudy, 1958, p. 19). Later the call of a practical curriculum to fill the needs of the emerging business class was made by the faculty of Amherst College (Cremin, 1980, pp. 270-272) and eventually by Andrew Carnege (Nevins, 1962, p. 35). Higher education should not only develop mental and moral faculties, but should answer the needs of the learned as well as the more worldly professions (Wayland, 1850).

Approval of the Morrill Act of 1862, which gave 150,000 acres of land to states for the maintenance of agricultural and mechanical arts colleges, provided tremendous impetus for the practically oriented colleges and universities. With this federal aid, there arose the land-grant institutions, schools largely devoted to the agricultural, mechanical and business needs of their constituencies (Brubacher & Rudy, 1958, p. 63). The philosophical position of the leadership of these institutions was expressed by President Welch of Iowa State Agricultural College in 1871 when he declared "that knowledge should be taught for its own uses; that culture is an incidental result" (Welch, 1871).[8]

This type of state institution thus stood for two purposes: First, through its plethora of programs, any subject that a student wanted to pursue should be available; second, the university must answer the needs of the community. As

Warfield (1901) noted, the extension of higher education to meet a variety of needs felt by the public was not limited to the public school. When Leland Stanford Junior University opened, its prospectus announced the "provision would be made for the instruction of anyone in any subject demanded."

Of course, the "service station" concept of the American university, where the institution would serve the changing needs of the community and the students was not universally accepted. In 1936, while redirecting the Rockefeller-endowed University of Chicago toward a classically oriented curriculum, President Robert Hutchins commented on the "service station" university that would serve the needs of its constituency in order to gain support:

> According to this conception a university must make itself felt in the community; it must be constantly, currently felt. A state university must help the farmers look after the cows. An endowed university must help adults get better jobs by giving them courses in the afternoons and evening. Yet it is apparent that the kinds of professors that are interested in those objects may not be the kind of professors interested in developing education or in advancing knowledge. It is sad but true that when an institution determines to do something in order to get money it must lose its soul and frequently does not get the money. (Hofstadter & Smith, 1961, pp. 26-27)

To Hutchins, the higher educational institution which altered its programs and goals in the search for money was unwise indeed. Others concurred (Hofstadter & Smith, 1961, p. 915).[10]

By the early 20th century, then, the American college and university had been exposed to a variety of educational models. There was no one definition of what American higher education should or, for that matter, should not do. There clearly was an openness in the defining process by which educational leaders attempted to determine the programs and objectives most appropriate for American higher education. The openness of this process allowed a business-minded college and university leadership to incorporate within the American school programs vastly different from those found in European schools.

A variety of factors facilitated the incorporation of radically new programs into American institutions of higher education, including intercollegiate sport. On the one hand, these included the peculiarly native conditions of newness, the isolation from developed military adversaries, the provincialism caused by the expanse of the wilderness, and the lack of both a centralized power structure or large patrician class to control and unify the purposes and methods of higher education. On the other hand were a combination of European conceptions of the charter of the college and university and what some would say an American (albeit borrowed from Bacon's utilitarianism and French Enlightenment thought) fetish with "application."

Both sets of factors contributed to an American willingness not only to consider the many potential purposes and methods appropriate to higher education, but also to actually incorporate new programs into the university or college. The willingness to incorporate such radical programs as athletics into the country's colleges and universities was also facilitated by the peculiar methods of financing and of student recruitment that were necessary for American institutions of higher education.

THE CONTROL AND FINANCE OF HIGHER EDUCATION IN THE UNITED STATES

Those unfamiliar with the control structure of the universities and colleges of the world might be misled into thinking that the contemporary pattern of educational control evidenced in the United States is the dominant form. "Education" was conspicuously absent from the Constitution as a specific responsibility of the federal government; in fact, such matters were delegated by the 10th amendment to the control of the states. As Knoles (1930, pp. 55-56) noted, this delegation of control contributed largely to the lack of a uniform "theory of education" in the United States. The states could separately determine their own standards for higher education. The lack of a unified theory of higher education was furthered by the Dartmouth College Case of 1819. The autonomy of private institutions was reinforced with the Supreme Court's decision for the college. The right of self-government for the nation's institutions was enhanced (Hofstadter & Smith, 1961, pp. 202-213).

Accompanying this autonomy, however, was instability in resources available to American higher education. In sociological terms, it was largely the lack of a guaranteed pattern of federal and state funding separate from the ephemeral appropriations priorities of resource-bearing constituencies that provided fertile ground for the incorporation of athletics into the formal structure of the university/ college as a resource-drawing vehicle.

As literally as portions of the European models of higher education were copied by early American imitators, the control and financial structure of the university/ college was not transferred as literally. At the dawning of the university during the Middle Ages, property was held in the name of the academic body. By the 16th century, Oxford and Cambridge were endowed with sufficient properties and monies to maintain the stable economies of their heads and fellows (Curtis, 1959, p. 39). The Fellows of Oxford and Cambridge were invested with the responsibility to oversee the disbursement of these resources, the land and edifices of the institution, and the day-to-day business of the college. On the other hand, the professional faculty and their representatives on the Continent bore less responsibility than did the state for the property of the institution and the curriculum, programs, and business matters of higher education. The state also maintained regular support for those institutions (Lowell, 1934).[11]

In the American colonies, however, not only the control but also the funding of the early institutions was invested in a largely nonfaculty board, distinct both from the faculty and from the centralized state. Although the colonial American institutions accepted some public subsidies, these private schools never surrendered control of policy-formation. Despite the precarious balancing act made necessary by limited resources, and by the lack of a state-provided endowment, this largely nonfaculty-governing board maintained ultimate control of programs. In large part the freedom from control by one centralized body was made possible by the diversity of sources from which funds were garnered. Resources accepted from the state were limited, perhaps to an initial endowment or a yearly increment. The irregularities of support from the public also limited the control of any one person or group over the affairs of the institution (Brubacher & Rudy, 1958, pp. 142-143).

In sum, although the irregularities of such ad hoc financing had drawbacks in the anxieties of "making ends meet," there were also advantages in that no external group exercised excessive control over the affairs of the college. The college's own controlling board exercised primary authority over the institution's programs. John Burgess echoed the necessity for such freedom from extrainstitutional control in a later period. Burgess, himself instrumental in the transformation of Columbia College into a university in 1884, believed that the university could not thrive as an institution of the state. Whatever advantages to the institution the regularities of yearly state appropriations yielded, in Burgess' mind, these were more than offset by the inconsistencies of programs and philosophies caused by the rapidly shifting policies and personnel of transient state legislatures (Hofstadter & Smith, 1961, p. 659).

Just as the English schools were earmarked by consistent support, eventually the funding of American colleges and emerging universities was characterized by diversity. Individual benefactors like Ezra Cornell ($0.5 million), Cornelius Vanderbilt ($1 million), Johns Hopkins ($3.5 million), Leland Stanford ($20 million), and John D. Rockefeller ($30 million) lent their fortunes to the development of universities. The Morrill Act of 1862 precipitated the rise of the multipurpose, state-supported universities, such as those in Columbus, Ohio; Ames, Iowa; and Madison, Wisconsin. Alumni and special-interest denominational groups (like those so important to Notre Dame in South Bend, Indiana) provided further support.

Ultimately, however, the diversity of funding sources for higher education in the United States also had the effect of making the financial solvency of the college an ever-pressing problem. Unlike their counterparts at Oxford and Cambridge, who could rely upon aristocratic, ecclesiastical, royal, business, and, eventually, reliable government support, American college and university presidents could ill afford such financial assumptions.[12] Early American colleges were not supported well by the few American gentry, who more often than not sent their capable sons to England for advanced education (Handlin & Handlin, 1970, p. 8).

An appeal by Edward Everett in 1849 to the Massachusetts legislature for desperately needed funds indicated at least one source of this problem. Everett unsuccessfully asked for a one-half million dollar higher education appropriation that would parallel the one million dollar appropriation earmarked by the legislature for Massachusetts public school education (Hofstadter & Smith, 1961, p. 385). The competition for scarce monies often pitted various forms of education against each other. Furthermore, doubts about the inherent worth of a college education in the minds of American legislators and the public did not help to guarantee a more consistent flow of resources to American higher education.

Thus, the 19th century American college/university president, himself more individually powerful and responsible than the English "vice-chancellor" or the German "rector," had to be aware constantly of any program or policy which might increase the flow of resources to the institution (Pritchett, 1905).[13] According to Jencks, the 19th century was

> a time when financial solvency was so precarious that colleges responded to even the smallest external pressures and had only the most limited ability to reshape the priorities established by their supporters. (Jencks & Reisman, 1968, p. 6)

The new business-minded leaders taking control of American higher education in the late 19th century often ran their institutions in a manner more similar to the corporation than the religiously oriented institutions of a prior era (Pritchett, 1905; Veysey, 1965, p. 10-11).[14] The business-minded administrators were often preoccupied with the financial and enrollment instabilities of their institutions. Such concerns often led to ingenious methods of school financing. Lotteries, ferry tolls, and agricultural produce all provided fuel for the early American academic machine. As Rudolph notes (1968), funds also were secured by naming certain schools after the wealthy benefactors who expressed their generosity toward particular institutions. In 1825 Colonel Henry Rutgers donated $5,000 to the institution which presently bears his name. In like manner, (James) Bowdoin, (William) Denison, and (William) Carleton immortalized themselves in academe.

Even a president as educationally respected as Charles Eliot of Harvard could not escape the push toward business-minded dispositions. In his inaugural address (1869), Eliot demonstrated both this attitude and its rationale:

> The Corporation should always be filled with the spirit of enterprise. An institution like this College is getting decrepit when it sits down contentedly on its mortgage. On its invested funds the Corporation should be always seeking how safely to make a quarter of a per cent more. A quarter of one per cent means a new professorship. (Eliot, 1869)

It was the duty of Eliot's office to seek more money. The businessman's thoughts and techniques should be borrowed when they might be of service to education. The significance of presidential advocacy of the business method and mentality was increased by the lack of counterbalancing forces which might have restrained presidential behavior. Without a strong tradition of faculty governance of higher education in America, college presidents could direct the fortunes of their institutions relatively unimpeded by this professional group.

While the European universities were founded by and governed by groups of mature scholars, American colleges, originally staffed by transient tutors, did not develop as strong a tradition of faculty control over all matters of the institution.[15] In part, because the power of policy formation in American colleges was vested in one powerful individual, one who was separate from the faculty, not entirely answerable to one centralized state regulatory unit, and only theoretically answerable to a nonresident-governing board on all matters of college policy, the American institution of higher education was not entirely concerned with strictly scholarly issues. Unlike their European counterparts, the American colleges and universities sought resources from many places. They were both required to and had the capability of responding to the desires of the many groups who had those resources. In many cases the powerful university/college presidents directed their institutions toward rapid incorporation of programs which might garner the resources necessary for survival.

Another factor which contributed to the strength of American college presidents was the openness of opinion regarding what colleges and universities should do and how they should actually behave. Without an established "charter," college leaders were relatively unhampered in making decisions concerning programs which might draw resources to their schools. Without clear understandings in the minds of the public, students, administrators, money bearing groups, and faculty at their own and other schools, the business-minded leaders were not constrained from bringing intercollegiate athletics formally into the education institution, nor from using sport for its resource-drawing capabilities. One could only imagine the reaction of the fellows and faculties of Oxford if such a proposal had been brought before them for consideration. The established understanding of the traditional programs and goals of an Oxford education in their minds apparently precluded formal incorporation of "big time" revenue-raising rugby, soccer, or cricket.

The third factor which contributed to the relative (i.e., in comparison to continental counterparts) autonomy of American college presidents concerned their theoretical responsibility to a business-dominated governing board. Nearing (1917) reported that four-fifths of the 1,936 persons who comprised the total number of trustees in 1917 were members of the merchant, manufacturing, capitalist, corporate official, banking, doctor, lawyer, educator, and religious classes. Leighton (1920) similarly found that bankers, manufacturers, commercial magnates, lawyers, physicians, and clergymen dominated the governing boards of American higher education. Beck (1947) provided a more specific breakdown for the period 1934-35: businessmen, 41.5%; lawyers, 25%; independent professionals, 11.8%; clergy, 6.6%; politicians, 4.9%; educators, 4.6%; and others, 5.6%.

Given the preponderance of business and capitalistically oriented board members and the lack of professional educators among them, it comes as no surprise that they apparently did not redirect the primary interests of college presidents toward strictly educational matters and away from business concerns. The business orientation and its measurement of organizational "success" in terms of hard outcomes contributed to determining the health of an institution according to dollar balances and student enrollments, as opposed to softer measures that are difficult to evaluate—criteria such as how much learning took place. College programs could be reshaped in order to balance the ledger sheets and attract students because such measures were acceptable indications of college success to the business-minded leadership.

Considering other means through which higher education was supported, one cannot regard the use of sport for the maintenance of economic solvency as unusual. Given the flexible definition of what was acceptable in American higher education, the open charter, and the financial instabilities of colleges and universities, Notre Dame consciously used football as a public relations device in the 1890s; the University of California similarly exploited the efforts of its track team in 1895; and Andrew D. White cancelled the expenses of the "Cornell Navy" in 1882 as advertising costs (Rudolph, 1968, pp. 384-385). The openness of the environment and the competition for clients made American higher education particularly responsive to what the populace wanted (Cremin, 1970 p. 559). The traditional definition of education was less important than were modifications to that definition made necessary by accommodations to public desires.[16] A sport-hungry populace would be given sport in a college guise.

THE INCORPORATION OF SPORT INTO THE FORMAL STRUCTURE OF HIGHER EDUCATION

In the late 19th and early 20th centuries, intercollegiate sport fulfilled a variety of needs for both the institution and the various constituencies served by each school. Of utmost importance to the administration of colleges and universities of the nation was the attraction of funds and students. Regardless of the proven or unproven validity of their beliefs, college leadership often felt that the exploits of their athletic teams attracted monies from the state, alumni, and other benefactors. The enthusiasm with which college administration embraced athletes was so pronounced that the Carnegie Foundation (1931) reported

> The avidity of the colleges themselves for publicity has in the past been partly to blame for the unsatisfactory relation between newspapers and college sports. Comparatively few institutions have attempted to give newspaper writers the opportunity to learn that athletics are only one of the activities of a college or university. (p. 32)

Certainly, the publicity provided by the "Four Horsemen" helped make Notre Dame into a major institution in the eyes of the public (Chu, 1979).

Athletics were also thought to be an important instrument in the egotistic rivalries between communities. Brubacher and Rudy (1958, p. 60) contended that there often existed a fierce competition between states to attract settlers. Quality college programs were seen as a bargaining chip in this competition.[17]

Because of the diversity of the American population, intercollegiate sport was deemed necessary as a unifying vehicle (Rader, 1978). Sport was a very important voluntary association. The intercollegiate sport that was a part of the state-funded educational institution served as a focal point of regional interest, especially in the sparsely populated vastness of the Plains states. In a similar fashion, the sport that helped unify a state was deemed necessary to unify a diverse student population. Through sport, it was hoped, a culturally diverse population could be enculturated and socialized to accept the same norms of behavior and thought. With the apparent success of sport as part of the formal programs at Harvard, Chicago, and other leading institutions in America, it was not long before other institutions followed suit.

> Trustees of existing institutions. . .sometimes preferred to risk experimentation rather than continue in the unpromising ways of the past. . . . Once one respectable institution moved in a new direction, others found themselves under a powerful compulsion to follow suit. The changes, if they meant anything, were bound to attract students. Colleges which lagged behind for any reason. . .had to face the threat of eventual starvation. (Veysey, 1965, pp. 10-11)

The economic deprivation to which Veysey (1965) alluded was a very real factor in the program consideration of late 19th and early 20th century college presidents. Despite overall growth rates in enrollments, yearly fluctuations were so great that the demise of institutions was a very real possibility (Chu, 1979, pp. 25-26; Savage, 1933). The response in many cases was an increase in efforts to reduce resource uncertainties (Henry, 1975, p. 8). The enlargement of intercollegiate sport programs was one vehicle for resource acquisition.

The acquisition of money and students through the development of intercollegiate sport may be seen as a "diversification" of the business of higher education into a new market. With the difficulties of gaining significantly more funds and enrollments through traditional means, college leaders particularly valued the publicity, contributions, and allotments that institutions gained through the exploits of their sport teams.

Emergence of the field of physical education presented an opportunity to rationalize intercollegiate sport philosophically as within the societally defined and accepted charter of American higher education. College sport could be "taught" by coaches who were faculty. Sport was rationalized as an extension of the classroom. The recruiting of scholarship athletes, so essential for winning, was rationalized as similar to the enrollment of scholarship musicians or mathematicians. The use of business-oriented methods in sport (e.g., specialization, emphasis on productivity, technical advancement) was rationalized by college leadership as the pursuit of excellence and necessary to a good public image of the college. Through sport, the "all-around" student could be developed physically as well as mentally. To help justify the inclusion of athletics within the programs of higher education, the "cultural school" of education's objectives was presented. Colleges and universities with open "charters" could now claim not only to develop students in the humanities, the sciences and professionally, but in personal character and physical health as well (Ross, 1976).

Lacking both financial security and a clear understanding of what higher education should not do, the development of winning intercollegiate sport teams became increasingly important as a formal concern of the institution.[18]

By the turn of the 20th century, big-time intercollegiate sport became incorporated within the formal structure of American higher education. No longer was such sport run or financed primarily through student associations. Full-time coaches, scholarship athletes, and contractually obligatory schedules became *pro forma* at the major institutions (Savage, 1933). By 1932 the American variant of school-related sport varied significantly from the type of sport evident at the European institutions of higher education (Kotschnigh, 1932, pp. 98-99). Despite the many similarities between American and its European heritage, the athletics incorporated into the college and university are of a scale and intensity peculiar to this side of the Atlantic. The peculiarity of institutionally sponsored sport did not escape the notice of Freiedrich Schonemann (1930), a German observer of American society.

> The big financial returns derived from the ticket sale have caused the authorities to close their eyes to the evils of the whole situation, even corruptive practices. The buying and selling of college athletes may be a sport necessary for the semi-youthful enjoyment of certain aged alumni with ample means, but it tends to cheapen both the college and its sports.

> The responsiblity for the evil results of the existing system of college athletics rests with all those college presidents and deans who do not wish to face the facts. They are the powers which really control campus activities and personalities. . . . they should be made to understand that the spirit of the whole educational system is endangered by their very indulgence. (Schonemann, pp. 126-127)

It is perhaps unfair to attribute to the college president sole responsibility for the formal incorporation of sport within American higher education. Acting within the milieu of a weak charter and lack of guaranteed funding and other resources, and subject to the beguiling temptations of business attitudes and philosophies, the college president may have been merely the agent through which otherwise inevitable incidents were enacted.

FOOTNOTES

1. This study seeks to avoid what Veysey (1965) terms "the fragmentation of the total picture into local chronicles of individual campuses that has tended to obscure the broader issues which divided academic men from one another"

(pp. vii-viii). Though the case histories of individual colleges will, of course, be referred to, an overemphasis on any one or few campuses would present a distorted view of the diversity of opinion concerning American higher education which dominated in the era under discussion. Once again quoting Veysey (1965):

> The most striking thing about the American university in its formative period is the diversity of mind shown by the men who spurred its development. Here lies the excitement of their story. Those who participated in the academic life of the late nineteenth century displayed sharply dissonant attitudes. Their outlook offered no smooth consensus, despite the eventual efforts of an official leadership to create one. Instead, theirs was an arena of continual dispute, of spirited conflicts over deeply held ideas, of partisan alignments and sharp individual thrusts, which gentlemanly loyalties might soften but could never wholly subdue. Although by the end of the century one can properly speak of "the" university, characterized by a particular structure, not even a powerful trend toward uniformity of procedure could obliterate the profound differences of opinion which subdivided the academic population. (p. vii)

Also see Cremin (1980, pp. 400-402) concerning the "provinciality" of higher education and the regional differences in perspective that it engendered.

2. "Institution" means an interrelated system of social roles and norms organized about the satisfaction of an important societal need or function. "Educational institutions" is used in its collective sense to refer to all higher educational organizations and not one particular college or university.

For another version of the notion of the "charter" in its specific application to education, see Nesbit (1971) on "dogma."

3. The America which emerged from the Revolution was one both concerned with the cultivation of its particular national identity and with its remaining European relationship. America sought new definitions for the political, economic, and educational institutions necessary for social existence. One reason for the multiplicity of competing definitions of societal institutions was the very newness of the nation. According to David Tyack (1966), "America had no feudal tradition, no encrustation of illiberal institutions, no corrupt and gothic history to live down." Without the weight of well-established institutions, missing was the inertia which in an older culture must be overcome prior to the development of radical conceptions of those institutions. For example, over time, people consciously and unconsciously develop an understanding of what the government should do and how it should carry out is functions. In addition, various layers of legal structure are developed which both legitimize and concretize the important structures of government. The very newness of America stripped away the conservatism of that inertia. The nation was ready for new definitions. There were fewer assumptions as to how things should be.

Distance also played a part in the differences of American thought. Separated by the Atlantic Ocean from the developed military might of the European states, Americans had no need to band together constantly under one centralized government. Unrestrained individualization was a luxury afforded by the Atlantic moat. The huge expanses of American land, not easily joined by a well-developed communications and transportation system, also contributed to diversity of thought and power. Localism was more the rule than the exception, due to an ever-expanding frontier and poorly developed roads.

The diversity of the many colonial groups was further reinforced by the lack of the development of a state church. The clergy, which played such an important part in the centralization of European institutions of higher education, was not to perform the same function in this country. There was not one body to disseminate *a* truth and *a* way of disseminating that truth (Jencks & Riesman, 1968, p. 2).

There was no state church to provide centralized guidance to the development of American higher education, nor was there an all-powerful ministry of education or similar body to fund and hence to control educational policy. An emerging private sector was to grow increasingly important in the maintenance of individual institutions.

On this issue of a pluralistic society leading to a parallel plurality of opinions concerning higher education, see the Carnegie Commission Report (1973). In this report they note a number of competing and sometimes conflicting purposes for higher education: (a) The provision of opportunities for the intellectual, aesthetic, ethereal, and skill development of the individuals and the provision of campus environments which can constructively assist students in their more general development and growth; (b) The advancement of human capability in society at large; (c) The enlargement of educational justice for the post-secondary age group; (d) The transmission and advancement of learning and wisdom; and (e) The critical evaluation of society, through individual thought and persuasion, for the sake of society's self-renewal (p. 93).

4. The diffuseness of the American charter, for higher education is also demonstrated by differences of opinion held by proponents of the same general model for college education. While some college leaders spoke for the importance of *a* set curriculum for the education of character, others like Charles William Eliot of Harvard (1869) maintained that character could be better developed by student selection of courses.

5. Traditional English higher education has had a relatively low regard for mechanical and scientific technical training. Only recently has university level training been made possible in these areas. Positions of this sort in the labor force could be secured without the need for a university degree (Burns et al., 1971).

6. While the reforms inspired by the German conception of the charter of higher education facilitated great change, however, it would be wrong to suggest that such changes in the heretofore dominant English charter were universally embraced. As Stephens (1909) noted, for a long time, particularly in the East, "science" was regarded as an intruder. To critics of overeager "Germanizers," apparently radical alterations in the American college were being affected without

recourse to discussions of the "true nature of the American university" (Warfield, 1901).

7. Although there are traditionally accepted definitions of higher education's charter in Britain and Germany, this is not to say that there has been no diversity of opinion within those systems. See R. Steven Turner, "University Reformers and Professional Scholarship in Germany 1760-1806" in volume 2, pp. 495-532 and Arthur Engel, "The Emerging Concept of the Academic Profession at Oxford 1800-1854" in volume 1, pp. 304-351, both in Lawrence Stone (Ed.), *The University in Society*, Princeton University Press, 1974.

8. Diversity of opinion concerning the charter of higher education may be symbolized by differences of opinion concerning the purposes of the large land grant schools. Although largely practical in orientation, Preston Sutton (1884), state senator for Iowa, argued for a liberal curriculum at Iowa State Agricultural College.

9. American higher education traditionally has been more accessible to the public than either the British or German systems. While in the mid-1960s, 2,132 American colleges and universities served 41.2% of the population ages 20-24, the total of 104 German and 217 British institutions of higher education served 8.6% and 7.6% of their country's age group, respectively. The far easier access to higher education in America has contributed to a consumer, business supply and demand orientation, whereas limited availability of student space in Germany and Britain has been a conscious choice on the part of educational leaders in Europe. American colleges and universities compete for funds and students, whereas German and British schools may choose from a highly eager pool of applicants (Burns et al., 1971, pp. 165-196, 45-90; Harris, 1972, p. 435).

10. Some would contend the existence of another conception of American higher education. Although partly subsumed under the "service station" model, the liberal arts conception of their education was supported by many educational leaders, among them Ernest Hatch Wilkins (1932), President of Oberlin College; William H.P. Faunce (1915), President of Brown University; and Edwin G. Conklin (1915), Professor at Princeton University.

Instruction in the liberal arts in the words of Ernest Hatch Wilkins (1932, p. 11) leads to development of the five fields of "social living": homelife, the field of earning, citizenship, leisure, and philosophy/religion. The liberal arts education seeks to survey the many different facets of human knowledge. In a way, it derives its character from an admixture of the English, German, and practical models of higher education.

11. The English conceive of Oxford and Cambridge as scholarly institutions which fulfill the human need for knowledge. No one power group, not even the central government has the right to dictate the sort of work carried on in these institutions. Yet the strength of the charter of these institutions is so great that they are consistently supported by Parliament. In 1948-49, for example, Oxford received fully 56% and Cambridge 50% of all their income from Parliamentary

grants. During the American 1949-50 academic year, on the other hand, higher education received only 17% of its current fund income from Washington (Harris, 1972, pp. 590-91). Lord Simon of Wythenshawe comments on the English situation:

> Foreign visitors find it hard to believe that this system in which the Government provides the greater part of the income of the universities and gives the universities ''gentle guidance'' and yet leaves them completely free in all academic matters, can really exist. It seems to good to be true. (Kneller, 1955, p. 59)

According to the understood charter for these English universities, knowledge belongs to all of men and all ages and must not be tampered with by nonmembers of the scholarly classes, *yet* it is the responsibility of government to provide for continuity of material resources.

Funds are appropriated by the University of Grants Committee (UGC) of Parliament. Composed primarily of academics, it has traditionally formed a buffer between the directions which might be imposed by the central government and the autonomy-seeking universities. Although in the past higher educational institutions have been relatively unfettered by strings attached to government-supplied monies, there has been some concern that the UGC might direct monies into areas of study where the government detects societal need (Burns et al., 1971).

In Germany all institutions of higher education (except theological and pedagogical schools) are corporate public bodies, and by 1964 statistics were 82% funded by local and federal governments (Burns et al., 1971). Also see Paulson (1906) on governance and funding differences between German and American schools.

12. Although there was an approximately 300% increase in the properties and endowments held by American higher education during the period 1892-1914, there was such an uneven distribution of this wealth that it contributed to the seemingly eternal financial instabilities of the vast bulk of colleges and universities. By 1914, Claxton (1915, pp. 188-89) reported that 60% of all institutions possessed a total of 6% of the annual working incomes, 10% of school property and endowments and 12% of all college students. By 1940, this pattern of a concentration of resources among a minority of schools continued. Twenty universities received 75% of all foundation grants, 25% was allotted to a remaining 310 institutions and 700 institutions received no foundation subsidies at all (Brubacher & Rudy, 1958, p. 361).

13. Governance systems in Great Britain, Germany, and the United States vary greatly. In both Britain and Germany there is a strong tradition of faculty control. German administrative heads, the rector and pro-rectors, are usually elected to short 1 year terms which may be renewed 1 more year. Election is by the professors of the institution. The Senate, composed of professors and representatives of other teaching staffs, has authority over all other non-teaching and research areas of the university. Some recent movement has been made,

however, in Berlin's two universities to centralize power in the form of a president elected to a 7-year term.

British institutions of higher education are also dominated by faculty control. This control takes various forms ranging from the courts and councils of civic and new universities, to the Hebdomadal Council of Oxford and the Council of the Senate at Cambridge (Burns et al., 1971).

14. For a brief discussion of the significance of the new business-minded leadership of the colleges and universities in America to the rise of sport, see Lucas and Smith, 1978, p. 217.

15. The failed attempt by Nicholas Sever and William Welsted in 1721-23 to establish the dominance of resident faculty in the control structure at Harvard had broad repercussions since it established the judicial precedent of presidential and trustee dominance of college control (Hofstadter & Smith, 1961, pp. 3-4).

16. Certainly the fortunes of the Massachusetts Agricultural College in 1870 did not escape note by the nation's college presidents. Following an athletic victory over Harvard, the agricultural institution was given increased appropriations from the state and lauded as a "real" college (Rudolph, 1968, p. 154).

17. See Arthur J. Klein and Franklin V. Thomas, "Cooperation and Coordination in Higher Education," *American Council of Education Series* (Series I), 1938, 2(5).

18. For detail on the justification of athletics into college programs, see Chu, 1979.

REFERENCES

BARNEY, R.K. (1979). Physical education and sport in North America. In E. Zeigler (Ed.), *History of physical education and sport*. Englewood Cliffs, NJ: Prentice Hall.

BECK, H.P. (1947). *Men who control our universities*. New York: King's Crown Press.

BERNS, B.B., Altbach, P., Kerr, C., & Perkin, J. (1971). *Higher education in nine countries*. New York: McGraw Hill.

BETTS, J.R. (1974). *America's sporting heritage: 1850-1890*. Reading, MA: Addison-Wesley.

BRUBACHER, J.S., & Rudy, W. (1958). *Higher education in transition*. New York: Harper and Row.

CARNEGIE Commission on Higher Education. (1973). *The purposes and the performance of higher education in the United States*. New York: McGraw Hill.

CARNEGIE Foundation for the Advancement of Teaching. (1931). *Current development in American college sport*. New York: McGraw Hill.

CHU, D. (1979). Origins of the connection of physical education and athletics at the American university: An organization interpretation. *Journal of Sport and Social Issues, 3*(1), 22-32.

CLAXTON, P.P. (1915). The American college in the life of the American people. In W.H. Crawford (Ed.), *The American college*. New York: Henry Holt.

CONKLIN, E.G. (1915). The place of the physical and natural sciences in the college curriculum. In W. H. Crawford (Ed.), *The American college*. New York: Henry Holt.

CREMIN, L.A. (1970). *American education: The colonial experience 1607-1783*. New York: Harper & Row.

CREMIN, L.A. (1980). *American education: The national experience 1783-1876*. New York: Harper & Row.

CURTIS, M.H. (1959). *Oxford and Cambridge in transition 1558-1642*. Oxford: Clarendon Press.

DOMHOFF, G.W. (1970). *The higher circles: The governing class in America*. New York: Random House.

ELIOT, C.W. (1980). Inaugural address as president of Harvard, 1869. In C.W. Eliot (Ed.), *Educational reform: Essays and addresses*. New York.

ENGEL, A. (1974). The emerging concept of the academic profession at Oxford 1800-1854. In L. Stone (Ed.), *The university in society*, (Vol. 1). Princeton: Princeton University Press.

FAUNCE, W.H.P. (1915). The aim of the New England college. In W.H. Crawford (Ed.), *The American college*. New York: Henry Holt.

FOERSTER, N. (1937). *The American state university*. Chapel Hill; University of North Carolina Press.

GIDEONSE, H.D. (1937). *The higher learning in democracy*. New York: Holt, Rinehart and Winston. Also in R. Hofstadter & W. Smith, (Eds.) (1961). *American higher education*. Chicago: University of Chicago Press.

GILMAN, D.C. (1902). The launching of a university. *Scribners Magazine, 31*, 327-332. Also in J.C. Stone and D.P. Denevi. (1971). *Portraits of the American university 1890-1910*. San Francisco: Jossey-Bass.

HANDLIN, O. & Handlin, M.F. (1970). *The American college and American culture*. New York: McGraw Hill.

HARRIS, S.E. (1972). *A statistical portrait of higher education*. New York: McGraw Hill.

HEDGE, F.H. (1866). University reform, an address to the alumni of Harvard at their triennial festival. *Atlantic Monthly, 18*, 299-307.

HENRY, D. (1975). *Challenges past, challenges present*. San Francisco: Josey Bass.

HOFSTADTER, R., & Smith, W. (Eds.). (1961). *American higher education*. Chicago: University of Chicago Press.

HUTCHINS, R.M. (1936). *The higher learning in America*. New Haven: Yale University Press. Also in R. Hofstadter & W. Smith (Eds.). (1961). *American higher education*. Chicago: University of Chicago Press.

JENCKS, C., & Riesman, D. (1968). *The academic revolution*. Garden City, NY: Doubleday.

KLEIN, J., & Franklin, V. (1938). Cooperation and coordination in higher education. *American Council of Education Series* (Series I), **2**(5).

KNELLER, G.F. (1955). *Higher learning in Britain*. Berkeley: University of California Press.

KNOLES, T.C. (1930). American education—Whence and whither. In P.A. Schilpp (Ed.), *Higher education faces the future*. New York: Horace Liveright.

KOTSCHNIGH, W.M. (1932). *The university in a changing world*. London: Oxford University Press.

LEIGHTON, J.A. (1920). Report of committee T on place and function of faculties in university government and administration. *Bulletin of the American Association of University Professors*, **6**.

LOWELL, A.L. (1934). At war with academic traditions in America. Cambridge: Harvard University Press. Also in R. Hofstadter & W. Smith (Eds.) (1961). *American higher education*. Chicago: University of Chicago Press.

LUCAS, J.A., & Smith, R.A. (1978). *Saga of American sport*. Philadelphia: Lea and Febiger.

MEYER, J.W. (1970). The charter: Conditions of diffuse socialization in schools. In W.R. Scott (Ed.), *Social processes and social structure*. New York: Holt, Rinehart, and Winston.

NEARING, S. (1917). Who's who among college trustees. *School and Society,* **6**.

NESBIT, R. (1971). *The degradation of the academic dogma.* New York: Basic books.

NEVINS, A. (1962). *The state university and democracy.* Urbana, IL: University of Illinois Press.

PAULSEN, F. (1906). *The German universities and university study.* New York: Charles Scribner's Sons.

PRITCHETT, H.S. (1905). Shall the universities become a corporation? *Atlantic Montly,* **96**, 295-299.

RADER, B. (1978). The quest for subcommunities and the rise of American Sport. *American Quarterly,* **30**, 355-369.

ROSS, M.G. (1976). *The university: The anatomy of academe.* New York: McGraw Hill.

RUDOLPH, F. (1968). Financing the college. *The American college and university.* New York: Alfred A. Knopf.

SAVAGE, H.A. (1933). *Economy in higher education.* New York: Carnegie Foundation for the Advancement of Teaching.

SCHONEMANN, F. (1930). A German looks at American higher education. In P.A. Schilpp (Ed.), *Higher education faces the future.* New York: Horace Liveright.

TURNER, R.S. (1974). University reformers and professional scholarship in Germany 1760-1806. In L. Stone (Ed.), *The university in society* (Vol. 2). Princeton, NJ: Princeton University Press.

TYACK, D. (1966). Forming the national character. *Harvard Education Review,* 29-41.

VEBLEN, T. (1918). *The higher learning in America: A memorandum on the conduct of universities by businessmen.* New York: Viking.

VEYSEY, L.R. (1965). *The emergence of the American university.* Chicago: University of Chicago Press.

WARFIELD, E.D. (August, 1901). The expansion of our great universities. *Munsey's Magazine.*

WAYLAND, F. (1842). *Thoughts on the present collegiate system in the United States.* Boston: Gould, Kendall & Lincoln.

WAYLAND, F. (1850). *Report to the corporation of Brown University on changes in the system of collegiate education.* Providence, RI: George H. Whitney.

WELCH, A.S. (1872). *Iowa State agricultural college, fourth biennial report of the board of trustees, 1871.* Des Moines, IA: G.W. Edwards. Also in J. Brubacher & W. Rudy. (1958). *Higher education in transition.* New York: Harper & Row.

WILKINS, E.H. (1932). *The college and society.* New York: Century.

WILLIAMS, G.H. (Ed.). (1954). *The Harvard divinity school.* Cambridge, MA: Harvard University Press.

YALE report of 1828 (1961). In R. Hofstadter & W. Smith (Eds.), *American higher education: A documentary history.* Chicago: University of Chicago Press.

ZIEGLER, E.F. (1979). *History of physical education and sport.* Englewood Cliffs, NJ: Prentice Hall.

Part II

ABUSES AND CONCERNS

Like I said, I think all the schools cheat. Really. Once you reach the pros you sort of joke about it amongst yourselves. You say, "who got the best deal while they were in school?" It wasn't bad for only being an amateur.

Wayne "Tree" Rollins, in
Caught in the Net. (Locke
& Ibach, 1982)

Abuses in college athletics have a long and inglorious past. Though constructed within the hallowed walls of academe, intercollegiate athletics' scandals have demonstrated that cheating, bribery, threats, and unfulfilled promises are not the province of the world outside the ivy of higher learning.

The problems of intercollegiate athletics are of many types: the unethical and illegal recruiting of secondary school athletes; abuses associated with gaining or maintaining eligibility; illegal payments; lack of graduation of college athletes or lack of adequate preparation even with paper graduation; criminal behavior in the form of point-shaving or game-fixing by athletes given illegal bribes; and the abuse of athletes by coaches.

As we have seen from the preceding chapters, however, the question of abuses in college sport must not be limited to simply listing the sort of problems outlined above. The listing of abuses removes us from the individual impact of college sport and somehow absolves us from the human effect of emotional commitment to sport and to school. In addition, new problems involving the legal rights of athletes and coaches and the societal, organizational nature of intercollegiate sport deviance must also be considered.

In the first paper in this section, Philip Boshoff questions the necessity of breaking the tamper-proof seal of the sports world to help athletes more effectively face real life problems. He looks at the ethics and values athletes gain from sport and their carry-over value to life outside of sport. He uses scenarios to depict how the accepted mores of intercollegiate athletics filter down to exert a heavy influence on youth sports. Finally he proposes the need to strike a balance between the values gained from an athlete's educational and athletic experiences.

Tates Locke, former Clemson basketball coach, presents a coach's view of the effects that pressure to win may have on those who run the ball game. Initially naive as to the degree of "rule stretching" he felt necessary to win at the big-time level, Locke soon finds himself so tired of losing that he "looks the other way" and rationalizes the unethical and illegal behavior of his assistants and avid boosters. In this emotional personal excerpt from the book *Caught in the Net*, Locke gets an enormous load off his chest and tells us something about the machinations within the big-time athletic machine.

Next, William Beezley takes a historical look at the rise and fall of the "Dixie Classic." This basketball tournament, held annually from 1949-1961, showcased some of the outstanding big-time powers of the era. The national attention and avid spectator interest of this event, however, made the classic a prime target of gamblers and those who sought to weight the dice in their favor. Although sport gambling might have been at one time more a mark of wealth and confidence, a form of conspicious consumption, the press for quick returns corrupted the ideals of English gentlemanly sport. Basketball with its published point spreads was particularly susceptible to "fixing." After all "shaving" a few points to reduce the margin of victory could beat the "point spread" and gain cash for youthful student-athletes while not usually affecting the team's won-lost record. In this historical review, Beezley carefully chronicles the ambitious individuals and vicious competition which characterized basketball in the Atlantic Coach Conference. He points out that while point-shaving was obviously illegal, such cheating merely followed a pattern of institutional cheating, under the table promises, and payments to which highly touted recruits were exposed during their courtship by rival schools.

In the paper by Ewald Nyquist, the abuses of intercollegiate athletics are vigorously condemned, as are inequities in funding for women's sports programs. The author, himself long concerned with the integrity and "goodness" of higher education in America, scathingly attacks the intercollegiate athletic and "academic" programs that do not primarily educate, but whose programmatic reason for existence is the generation of money. Nyquist decries the degradation of academic ideals and the subordination of acadmic integrity in response to perceived material needs. In his view, the underlying cause for the abuses in big-time college sport is a moral crisis in the academic institution. Too many schools at the big-time level have sold their souls for the visibility and potential profit of spectator sports.

In the next paper James Frey anticipates the future of American intercollegiate athletics. Despite current major television exposure, the growth of women's sport and the public's warm embrace, problems of rising costs, in the supply of skillful labor, and the political repercussions of well-publicized scandals have created a crisis situation for campus sport. It is predicted that schools will evolve into two types: the majority of all schools able to afford only a limited scope of operations, and a smaller elite group able to compete at the national level. This smaller group will be able to operate at this most extraordinarily expensive level primarily because of resources available from "an organizational coalition of athletic administrators and alumni/boosters who represent the political and economic power in the community. . . ." The role of the faculty, students, and even the college president will be, in comparison, less significant. Inevitably arising are questions of control of the programs which represent the institution. According to Frey, tremendous potential exists for abuses due to the professionalization of what may have been amateur sport. The affiliation of sport teams to an institution and to an educational idea will remain only "as a matter of convenience."

Linda Carpenter's paper considers a particularly pressing legal concern involving campus administration and scholarship athletes. At the core of the author's paper is the question—Can "amateur-athletes" (as defined by NCAA regulations) receive worker's compensation benefits?" Are the scholarship student-athlete workers for the university or college, and are they entitled to compensation if they are injured in the service of the school? According to Carpenter, it is necessary to establish (a) the presence of an employer-employee relationship at the time of the injury; (b) that the injury resulted from work performed for the employer and for the advancement of the employer's affairs. Ms. Carpenter, PhD, JD then reviews legal evidence speaking for and against the view of the student-athlete as a potential beneficiary of worker's compensation benefits. The repercussions of this question are far-reaching. Judicial definition of the student-athlete as a "worker" might legitimize what many critics of big-time sport already assume: that is, that the Division IA athlete is already a paid professional in the employ of the institution. If the decision were to go in this way, any myths concerning the amateur student character of college athletes might then be dispelled.

In the last chapter David Rose broadly considers the debate surrounding intercollegiate sport. Rose identifies two fundamental questions organizing the debate: (a) Are college athletes amateur or professional? and (b) Are college athletic programs education or entertainment? In response to these questions, the author identifies four positions.

The Establishment position, most closely identified with staunch supporters of the NCAA, views college sport as amateur, athletics as educational, and sport revenues as necessary to support the athletic program. Advocates of this view further contend that the major problems in athletics are caused by a few deviant individuals.

Reformers agree with the Establishment position that athletics should be amateur and that programs should be educational. Disagreement erupts over the Reformers' contention that the NCAA and other Establishment governance structures have built in an emphasis on winning and commercialism. The Reformer position was that of the now defunct Association for Intercollegiate Athletics for Women and is the current position of the National Association for Intercollegiate Athletics.

Sport Scholars and Radicals, the final two positions identified by Rose, agree that college sport is professional and profit-oriented entertainment. Sport Scholars see the NCAA not as a voluntary organization but as a cartel, while Radicals view student-athletes as exploited by the profit-oriented sport entertainment system.

Rose concludes that any one of these positions is inadequate to provide answers to the basic questions surrounding college athletics. He then proposes a way out of the present quandry by recognizing teams as "semi-professional" representatives of the colleges that sponsor them, and for American higher education in general to be "moved away from its present marketplace orientation."

The papers in this section suggest that the problems of intercollegiate sport involve more than the particular coach and the particular athlete who may be involved in under-the-table payments. While money offered as an inducement for attendance at a particular school is certainly cause for concern, this problem is but an indicator of much larger concerns. Clearly the push for revenues, for institutional visibility, and prestige, drives the athletic programs, as well as other college and university programs, to demonstrate its effectiveness. The American zeal for producitivty, for the "end" result may not be balanced by a corresponding emphasis upon the "means" used to gain those ends. Clearly the society which molds its social institutions in its image is reflected in the society's educational institutions as well as in its sport.

Chapter 4

Keep the World of Sport Hermetically Sealed

Philip P. Boshoff
Skidmore College

When we encourage the kind of simplistic, win-at-all-costs thinking that has come to be associated with sport in America, we relegate athletes to a role where decisions are made for them by trainers, teammates, officials, and coaches, who give them a highly functional, often successful set of values for the limited duration of practice or competition. Millions of fans enjoy the marvelous spectacle, the glory and competition of that hermetically-sealed world of sport. I always turn to the sports section of *The Times* first and am drawn away from a stack of freshman themes to watch Gastineau's sacks. The glorious, self-contained world of the gridiron, the arena, the diamond grabs the spectator's and viewer's attention. When Roy Hobbs' homer smashed the clock in *The Natural,* we caught a glimpse of what sport does best: It transports us to a world where Wall Street's fluctuations seem irrelevant, overdue credit card bills cease, and nameless pains go away.

Perhaps sport is an escape, a simplified world where athletes wear absurd costumes festooned with rams' heads and birds' claws. Perhaps that outdoor or indoor arena symbolizes the worst of our collective psyches of hero worship, competitiveness, and mob reaction; yet that arena still enthralls millions of us, including me. Millions of us who go through the turnstiles or schedule our weekends around the game of the week support the ideal of the arena. But we must keep these ideals within the confines of sport, within its regulated codes and rules. For when administrators, coaches, and athletes carry these ideals out-of-bounds, they pry open this self-contained world of penalty flags, called strikes, and fouls. Sadly, such oversimplified regulations do not extend beyond the end zone markers and locker rooms. When we act as though they do, we harm athletics and athletes. Educators, particularly, must recognize the potential dangers when they allow their athletic programs and their ethics of all-out victory to cross the boundaries between athletics and academics. Such reasoning encourages the rationalizations that foster excess and scandal in athletic departments; and perhaps even worse, such thinking can lead athletes to believe that the security and simplicity of the arena continue in their lives.

Former Stanford University football coach and current coach of the twice-superbowl champion San Francisco 49'rs, Bill Walsh, presents a typical scenario for many athletes:

It starts from the day a Little League coach takes a youngster under his wing and tells the boy he can be a great baseball player. 'But to do it, he tells the boy, you've got to forgo all other sports—no tennis, no swimming. Never mind the piano, practice your baseball!' The Little League coach *cares*. He enjoys his work, and, naturally, he'd like to develop a baseball player.

The boy enrolls in high school, and the coach there sees his potential. He wants the youngster to have the 'opportunity to excel.' Whether the coach realizes it or not, he starts directing the boy's life—telling him what classes to take, giving him a course of study that doesn't challenge him in the classroom or develop the disciplines of the mind that will best serve him in society.

The parents fall into the trap. They're happy their son is being 'taken care of.' If he is really exceptional in athletics, the townspeople get involved, from the mayor on down. They treat him specially, to the point where he doesn't have a real perspective on life. 'Things' are done for him. No one wants to spoil his chances to make it big.

The college recruiter visits. He tells the parents that he will 'take care' of their boy, make sure this or that doesn't happen, that he'll have the best of this and that. Still the young man doesn't have to deal with the day-to-day frustrations other youngsters face. He's quite willing to accept this attention—his name in the paper, a suit of clothes, being steered away from classes he 'won't need.' After all, he's going to be a pro.

The boy goes through his college career 'protected.' Special dormitories, special food, carefully chosen courses. He lives with youngsters of the same interests. There are no distractions, no problems, no frustrations. We coaches we feel we have to try harder and harder, because that's what our competition does, and so we do more and more to segregate the athlete. And he goes willingly.

We do everything *but* educate him. We're afraid he'll fail, so we look for ways of making it easier instead of ways to educate him. Soon his entire outlook is distorted.

It can be devastating. (*Sports Illustrated*, May 19, 1980, pp. 42-43)

BREAKING THE RULES

And devastating it has been in the numerous cases of colleges and universities whose intercollegiate sports programs have found themselves continually having to up the ante to attract and keep those blue-chip athletes, who potentially mean millions of dollars to athletic programs. NCAA Commissioner, Walter Byers, estimated that 30% of all Division I institutions are involved in some kind of dishonesty (Farrell, September 5, 1984). In a later interview he admitted that cheating had established an unsettling presence in collegiate sports: "I was surprised at first, and finally I became astonished at what I considered to be the deliberateness of strategies of getting around the rules. And I was also astonished at the level of it, the level of the dollar transactions" (Farrell, November 7, 1984, p. 31).

Byers and all who follow college athletics must worry when some of the wealthiest and most prestigious universities in the nation have their athletic departments implicated in violations of NCAA rules. Most recently the University of Florida, one of the leading research universities in the south, suffered the ignominy of having the NCAA sustain 59 charges against its football program, including recruiting violations, sales of players' complimentary tickets, maintaining a slush fund, and holding out-of-season practices (*Chronicle*, "Conference Bars U Florida," November 28, 1984).

A widely publicized case earlier in 1984 involved Oregon State University's successful basketball program, which the NCAA placed on probation for a year. The NCAA required Oregon State to return $342,634 that the team had earned for playing in the 1982 NCAA tournament. All references to the team's performances in 1980-82 tournaments were struck from NCAA records, and the basketball program received NCAA sanctions for some 40 rules violations that occurred between 1979-83 ("NCAA Tells Oregon State," 1984).

The 1984-85 academic year began with 13 Division I universities on NCAA probation; the grounds varied from improper recruiting tactics and providing illegal benefits to athletes, to admissions and academic eligibility violations ("13 Universities," 1984).

Not only institutions whose athletic programs earn them revenue and recognition on the sports page have come under scrutiny, but colleges whose academics overshadow their athletics have also been questioned. As incredible as it may seem, Johns Hopkins and the NCAA sparred over the eligibility of lacrosse players (Monaghan, September 19, 1984). The pity is not even that Hopkins succumbed to challenging NCAA rules to win more lacrosse games, but that one of America's finest universities even deigned to cross the sidelines to remove lacrosse from simply being a sport.

Even small colleges who belong to the National Association of Intercollegiate Athletics are not immune to breaking the rules. Typical infractions include using players who have not satisfied academic requirements or who have not sat out the required 16 weeks after transferring (Monaghan, October 31, 1984). The violations at NAIA schools are minor when compared with those at Division I institutions. But when NAIA schools, which have traditionally maintained a healthy balance between academics and athletics, fall victim to cheating, we see how pervasive cheating has become.

There have even been allegations that athletes' civil rights have been violated, which suggests an even more pernicious form of breaking the rules. The American

Civil Liberties Union accused members of the Memphis State University football program of imposing born-again Christian beliefs on their players ("Memphis State Coach," 1984).

The attitude that athletics should be involved with more than just the athlete's physical endurance and competitive edge within the sport begins early.

> I don't really give a whip what he does as long as he keeps good grades up and hits 'em hard. Give it all he's got both in the classroom and out here cause that's how he's gonna make it. And no way else. I'd give my eye teeth to see 'em go to SU (Syracuse University), and we'd be at every game—you could be sure.

The lines could have been part of the dialogue from *All the Right Moves*, but it was, instead, from a father and an assistant coach of Yearling football in Saratoga Springs, New York.

The spectacle before me was being played out as a miniature version of Sunday afternoons across the nation: 12-year-olds running out of the pro set, linebackers in zone coverages, coaches wearing headsets, and a barely postpubescent group of "Yearlingettes" in short skirts, tight boots, and too much make-up strutting to the tinny loudspeaker's generic rendition of "Get It On."

A freckle-faced kid who must have weighed 75 pounds held his sides and fought back tears. "You've got to suck it up damnit. That's the only way you'll get respect. The next time, hit that Decker kid so that you bust his ribs. Show him what you're made of," growled an overweight, middle-aged guy with a flat-top and "Coach Brandt" stenciled across his windbreaker.

VALUE SYSTEM IN AMERICAN SPORT

I walked away, wondering again about excesses in intercollegiate sport programs, about athletes and their coaches as role models, and about the value system of sports in America. Certainly, it begins at this level: The excitement, the simplicity of channeling aggressions and a week's frustrations into a cross-body block and the systems of rewards maintain the prominence of sport throughout the high school, collegiate, and professional levels. Doesn't it make sense to train kids early, to teach fundamentals, and, perhaps even more importantly, to coach them in forming values? The coaching of values, however, bothered me, for what I observed that October afternoon was the reinforcement of a system of values that would teach those kids to cut through ambiguity by beating the brains out of an opponent and to avoid depression by either winning or supporting a winner. The Yearling squads and Yearlingettes were seeing role models and learning values that underline American entertainment, economics, and even politics.

Newspapers hyped Joe Montana's engagement to the Schick blonde, whom he dated following a razor blade commercial—love at first lather. A grinning Vice President Bush apologized for a campaign metaphor when he said that he and the president were going to "kick some ass." No one threw a penalty flag; in fact, many members of the media applauded the metaphor as Bush and the "Gipper" went for a 50-state "sweep" on election night. Sponsors recently shelled out for the "million-dollar minute" to advertise their products on Superbowl XIX. And Tom Landry stumped for the President's reelection in Texas while marketing "Power for Living."

The rhetoric and ethics of the gridiron and arena no longer tacitly influence behavior in the classroom, on the job, in the political arena, or even in the living room—they downright shape it. When the values within the sidelines become applied to the complexities of daily life, their appropriateness is questionable. Few people can deny Joe Montana's brilliance as a passer, or Tom Landry's excellence as a coach, but when their lives become a symbol of the glamor of athletics, their values a primer for behavior, then we need to look at the influence that athletes and coaches have upon the ethics of young athletes.

Most of us value the priorities of mental alertness and physical fitness that athletes personify. Peter Antonio Gaido, a football player at Beloit College, articulates this ideal:

> College football, like any other competitive team sport, is much more than a game. It produces growth of all sorts in an individual that cannot be learned in a book or classroom. I'm talking about growth in character, maturity, self-respect and pride, the respect of others, responsibility, honesty; and the list continues with those traits that are the building blocks of any 'good' individual. An athletic experience, such as college football, is of unpriceable value. (Gaido, 1984, p. 2)

Of "unpriceable value" is a college education combined with sport that remains within its boundaries. Unfortunately, too many college athletes believe that athletics alone will sustain them in later life. Only one third of National Football League players, 20% of the National Basketball players, 16% of major league baseball players, and 8% of National Hockey League players have college degrees (Weir, 1984). Patriots' lineman Brian Holloway, Stanford graduate, refers to life after football as "similar to death,"; Holloway's teammate, Steve Moore, a 3-year starter at Tennessee State, who is still three semesters shy of his degree, adds that too many coaches approached schoolwork with the attitude that "if you don't do it, we'll still work something out" (Weir, 1984).

Gaido's statement summarizes the ideals that we ascribe to competitive sports and to being a member of a team. That guy screaming from the sidelines at the Yearlings game believes it, college and university athletic personnel believe it, Peter Antonio Gaido believes it, and I believe it—in part. But we must also see the sadder reality that Holloway and Moore mention.

I believe in the dedication. An athlete has to be dedicated to put in painful hours in the weight room. He or she has to be dedicated to put up with the long hours of practice. I also believe in all those other ideals that roll off the tongue like caramel cliches. However, I do not believe in the insidious allure sports too often perpetuates—that daily life imitates the gridiron or arena, that life *should* imitate sport. The danger underlying this belief leads university officials to cheat to make win-at-all-costs teams; it makes Coach Brandt believe that once his son wins a scholarship, his problems will be solved; and it leads athletes like Brian Holloway to wonder if there is "life after football."

Nearly anyone who has participated in or coached a sport, who has cheered heartily from the sidelines, or who is a merely a fan has been coached to regard athletics as somehow better than life and to believe that athletes shine as embodiments of young Mr. Gaido's ideals. Because these athletes appear as beacons of dedication and character in a world largely bereft of such qualities, we further believe they *must* be above the common herd, that their success at sweeping around a pulling guard and breaking into daylight is an elevated analogy for climbing over a competitor at the office and winning the raise.

But the analogy does not cease. Indeed, with the help of thousands of pages of print and hundreds of hours of sport journalism, we turn the existence of the athlete into a sacred American essence, a vision of right. We welcome the athlete into our homes for more hours than most of us welcome our relatives or friends; we read about their exploits; we crave the chance to learn about their personal lives; we welcome them into the pulpits; our presidents send them plays; we vote them into office; we make their lives beyond the confines of the playing area a paradigm for what we wish our own lives could be; and we dedicate our Sunday afternoons into making our youth believers in the vision that the best of life imitates sport.

The values of sport do transfer to our lives; at least that is the message that millions of Americans hear each Sunday afternoon. On Thanksgiving the Detroit Lions were playing the Green Bay Packers again. The folks at NFL control would have to do a feature on Lombardi's men, I thought. They did not disappoint: playboy Paul Horning, now a successful commentator; bad boy Max McGee, now a real estate magnate; all-American boy Bart Starr, former coach, now business success. Lombardi's guys—what American parent would not want a kid to grow up with those values—about as American as the turkey roasting in the oven. These guys live the way Hollywood and the NFL lead us to think they should: rough around the edges, soft around the heart. Dirty Harry's tough exterior, Mean Joe Greene's football jersey and a Coke are the constitutive symbols of American *macho*.

An all-too common interpretation of this ethic becomes play by the rules, but playing by the rules does not mean that the chain cannot be stretched. This ethical clarity seduces us into believing that the rules of the arena hold true in that world "out there." Winners, losers, legal moves, penalty flags—wouldn't it be nice if there were "zebras" in our daily life who threw the flag at us? Life outside sport, unfortunately, presents ambiguities; it lacks the clarity of life within sport. Herein lies the dilemma for the academic who loves the special world of athletics, but who also recognizes the danger of extending the values of athletics beyond its unique boundaries.

One of the goals of education is to provide students with the lenses through which to look at the complexities of life. As idealistic as it may sound, an education should provide a student with the ability to tolerate ambiguity, to accept autonomy, and even to accept loss. There is a vitality within the life of sport for educators to appreciate, but there are limitations within that world that athletes, coaches, fans, and especially educators must realize. That is the message I would like to give Coach Brandt—or better yet—I would like Bill Walsh to give it to him.

REFERENCES

The CHRONICLE of Higher Education. (1984). Conference bars U. of Florida from Sugar Bowl after NCAA sustains charges of 59 violations, **29**, p. 33.

FARRELL, C.S. (1984, September 5). NCAA admits difficulty in catching violators of recruiting and financial-aid regulations. *The Chronicle of Higher Education,* **29**, p. 29.

FARRELL, C.S. (1984, November 7). NCAA Byers: Now a vocal proponent of reform. *The Chronicle of Higher Education,* **29**, p. 31.

GAIDO, P.A. (1984, October 8) *Beloit College 1984 press kit*, report, comment, *The NCAA News*, p. 2.

MEMPHIS State coach is accused of imposing religious beliefs on players. (1984, October 3). *The Chronicle of Higher Education,* **29**, 26.

MONAGHAN, P. (1984, September 19). Hopkins—NCAA battle continues over enforcement. *The Chronicle of Higher Education,* **29**, pp. 29, 32.

MONAGHAN, P. (1984, October 31). Small-college sports: The unglamorous rulebreakers. *The Chronicle of Higher Education,* **29**, pp. 35, 36.

NCAA tells Oregon State It Must Give Back $342,000. (1984, May 23). *The Chronical of Higher Education*, p. 27.

STUDENT Athletes. (1980, May 19). *Sports Illustrated*, pp. 42-43.

UNIVERSITIES on NCAA probation. (1984, September 5). *The Chronicle of Higher Education,* **29**, p. 33.

WEIR, T. (1984, December 13). Colleges, pros must prepare athletes for life after sports. *USA Today*, p. 3C.

Chapter 5

Caught in the Net

Tates Locke
University of Nevada, Las Vegas

Bob Ibach
Freelancer

When you fly over Clemson, South Carolina—in fact, anywhere over the upper region of that state—you have to fall in love with the place. There's the beauty of the Blue Ridge Mountains and calmness of the crystal blue lakes which surround the campus. It's a place which is so much in order that it seems God meant for Clemson to be located exactly where it is on this earth.

The school, to its credit, knew the atmosphere was a selling point and had me flown over the campus in a private plane. I guess it was while viewing the loveliness from that height that I decided I would take the coaching position if Howard made me an offer. From that plane I could see the entire athletic complex—Littlejohn Coliseum and the beautiful, spacious football stadium. Then there was the tradition of the ACC, one of the most difficult conferences in the country. Well, I saw all that before me and I thought to myself, 'Tates, obviously they care about having a winning basketball program here.' That clinched it. Later, when Frank Howard said "Would you?" I responded "When do I start?"

Looking back, I realize I made a terrible mistake by letting my emotions get the best of me. I had not really asked the administration many questions about the direction of the program, and I guess, because of my passive approach, I had painted them a picture of a fellow who could be easily swayed. Ultimately, that would lead to my undoing at Clemson.

Like I said, I was partially blindfolded. I had not closely enough examined the reasons why the Tigers' basketball program had dug itself into a deep hole all those years. To begin with, Clemson had no tradition of winning, but I assumed I could overcome that with hard work. Unfortunately, the other pitfalls which

I would encounter would almost be impossible to overcome...especially if a coach had to follow the NCAA rulebook.

Probably the largest handicap was the general lack of support at Clemson for recruiting black athletes. There were virtually no blacks at Clemson University when I came in 1970. Realistically, I should not have been that surprised. After all, high schools in the South had only been integrated since 1968, and that section of the country was hardly prepared to welcome blacks into its colleges 2 years later.

It was the same feeling at Clemson, thanks to the attitude of the alumni and other heavy contributors to the athletic program. They preferred a lily-white team, which didn't leave a basketball coach much room to wander in the ghetto playgrounds of the East, where many of the best high school talent was to be found. Again, had I looked into the situation more closely before accepting the job, I would have seen such prejudice at Clemson.

The fact that I was 33 years old when I came to Clemson was no excuse. I was far from being naive about racial unrest in the South. But it's one thing to hear about racial prejudice and another to actually experience it.

I had never heard the term "nigger" used until I got to Clemson. When I first heard it used, it shocked me to death, probably because it dawned on me that an actual person was being referred to, not a people. It really shocked me. I had heard "nigra" before but never "nigger." So here I was, falling in love with God's country in a little southern college town but not really knowing the standards or attitudes of the natives with whom I was dealing. Compounding the problem of the social acceptance of the black athlete was an even larger dilemma— the academic acceptance of the black athlete.

I had been told the ACC had an 800 minimum college board score requirement for all of its athletes. Clemson, itself, didn't have such a policy but the ACC did, and as long as Clemson was in the conference, it had to abide by that rule. About the only thing Clemson and University of South Carolina, the two ACC schools most affected by the rule, did to protest the 800 minimum was threaten to withdraw from the conference. I saw that as a chicken way out. One of the schools should have tested the rule in the courts. How that rule ever stayed out of the courts I'll never know. It was so wrong. But again, it was a classic example of the hypocrisy of the South and the ACC.

What all of this did in terms of the Clemson basketball program was make it practically impossible to recruit a kid from the South. Face the facts—most of the youngsters in that section of the country were not prepared academically to go into the ACC. So it became one big nightmare for us at Clemson those first couple of seasons.

For us to attract the quality black athlete, even one who passed the 800 board score, was a tall order. By the time a youngster from New York or Ohio or somewhere else in the East had been dragged all the way through the ACC, by the time he had a chance to see life at the other campuses, Clemson had two chances of getting him—slim and none. By being the southernmost school in the league, we were geographically the last stop along the trail. Toss in our far inferior social standards, for blacks that is, and you had one big mess.

In 1970 there were still two sides of the street in Clemson, one for whites and the other for "niggers." It appalled me. I had only seen something like it once before in my life during the summer I worked at Delta State University. The administration assured me the situation would change, that within a year the 800 board requirement would be dropped, thus enabling Clemson to attract more blacks to our campus—both students and athletes. In the meantime, I was told to hang in there for another season, then go out and start recruiting the best black athletes I could find east of the Mississippi.

But there was a catch. How are we going to recruit a quality black athlete when we can't even show him a decent time socially when he visits our campus? It was a realistic question. I knew that under the present circumstances a black kid visiting Clemson would laugh at our campus atmosphere. We'd only be kidding ourselves and wasting money. Then I hit upon an idea: Why not create a *phony* social atmosphere for the blacks?

Enter the era of the Phony Black Fraternity. Boy, did we do a great job of acting on this one. The bunch of us should have won Academy Awards. Hell, we took these old, quonset-hut houses in which some of the married students used to live and fixed them up, turning them into "fraternity houses" where we could entertain our black recruits.

The charade didn't stop there—it only began. We would go into surrounding communities, places like Seneca, Anderson, and Greenville, and bring back to campus as many black high school students, seniors mostly, as we could find. Then it would appear as if Clemson was integrated on the weekends. We went out and hired bands, held dances, and even provided transportation to and from the social activities.

In 1970, the student enrollment at Clemson was 8,900. Maybe one half of one percent—and that's a high estimate—was black. However, you would never be able to tell by looking at one of our weekend fraternity functions. You'd have thought we were a branch school of Grambling. Yes sir. Reality didn't hit until Monday morning when you could look all around campus and see mostly white faces. During the weekends, life was back to normal at Clemson University.

I'll never forget a particular fall weekend. We had invited a slew of hot-shot high school basketball players to visit our campus. On Saturday they attended a football game. There must have been 50,000 fans watching when these kids walked to the 50-yard line at halftime to get introduced, one by one. A few days later I had to speak at an IPTAY boosters' club meeting in nearby Greenwood. Many of those people had been at the football game and seen only two white faces among the halftime guests. I knew it had bothered some and I was waiting for someone to mention the subject. Sure enough, a loud voice from the back of the room raised the question.

"How many of dem niggers you plan on signing?" the one fellow drawled. The room fell silent, waiting for my response.

"As many of them that want to come to Clemson," I shot back.

Now it *really* got quiet.

I couldn't ignore the facts, however. And the facts were our Phony Black Fraternity looked about as legitimate as a three-dollar bill. You could see right through the damn thing. I knew we weren't fooling any of our black guests for one minute, either. Hell, you'd walk into the dances and there would be all these blacks sitting around the room. Nobody was talking! Where I grew up in Batesville, Indiana, you could smell stuff when it wasn't right—and this black fraternity set-up smelled. I mean, those people were as uncomfortable attending those parties as I was watching them in attendance. Enough was enough.

I can laugh at the situation now. I mean, here we had spent all this effort and money to create this so-called "beautiful experience" for these people and there was nothing. Absolutely nothing.

The abolishment of the Phony Black Fraternity only led to bigger troubles. We still had the same problem before us—how to present a social atmosphere which was meaningful to our black prospects, one that would entice them enough to attend Clemson. It came down to one simple fact: If we couldn't create a social atmosphere on campus for our black students, then we had to do something to lead them into a social involvement off campus, in places like Greenville. Trouble was, how was a poor black youngster going to get to Greenville?

By car, of course. Which explains why we had to start providing some of our better black athletes with a set of wheels.

During my 5 years at Clemson, I helped many of my players out with their personal transportation, but only once did I actually purchase an automobile for a player. I use the word "automobile" rather loosely since the car I bought for Jo Jo Bethea was ready for a junkyard. Jo Jo was a talented black guard, a kid who had transferred to Clemson from Anderson Junior College in time for the 1973-74 season. He was one of two outstanding blacks we recruited that previous spring, the other being Tree Rollins. The 1967 Plymouth I bought Bethea cost $1,023 and was part of the "package" we put on him. We never said we were buying a kid, we used the phrase "put a 'package' on him."

I still cry from laughing so hard when I think about Jo Jo's ol' junker car and how the NCAA sent a bunch of investigators to our campus during the 1974-75 season to find out about the cars we had allegedly given our players. They must have been shocked when Jo Jo led them to a local trade school where he had been overhauling the engine. That junker was a mess. The NCAA investigators saw this old car up on cinder blocks and one of them looked at Jo Jo and said, "You mean *that* is the car they gave you?" I can imagine the shocked look on their faces, questioning some kid about a piece of junk.

Not all the cars were junk. A couple players had newer models. Wayne Rollins, the 7-1 center who we called Tree, had a Monte Carlo, compliments of an alumnus. Skip Wise, our star freshman guard from Baltimore, also had a car given to him. I stayed completely out of who was given what merchandise, but I knew these kids weren't buying it with their own money.

That's one of the cute ways a college coach learns to stay clean. The smart ones stay away from those kind of illegal transactions. They let someone in the boosters' club or a prominent alumnus take care of it. That way they can look you straight in the eye and say "I'm clean." Technically, they are.

The only thing I know for fact is that Jo Jo and Tree, my two black recruits in 1973, were taken care of by someone from Clemson. Mostly it was Rollins who got the royal treatment, or should I say it was his mother, Wilma Robinson. I know Tree got a car and received a monthly allowance, of which he saw very little. Most of the money was mailed to his mom's home.

As I have previously mentioned, I spent much of my personal money to provide players with personal transportation. In 5 years, I must have spent between $40,000 to $50,000, buying them plane tickets to go home for the holidays, giving them money for car rentals and for gasoline. Things like that. Spending money. It was $20 here and $30 there. It didn't seem like a week went by when some player didn't need an extra buck.

You might wonder where I was getting the money. Good question, because at $20,000 a year, I was the lowest paid coach in the ACC. I started at $20,000 in 1970 and was making $23,000 when I left in 1975. Some improvement, huh? Actually the money for my players came directly out of profits from my summer basketball camp. Without that money we wouldn't have survived—none of us— me, my assistants or my players. I made about $20,000 off the camp—but I always split it four ways with my assistants. In that way, each assistant made enough to bring his annual salary to $20,000 or more. The remainder after paying my assistants I reserved for my players.

Sometimes there were good reasons to spend money on the kids such as the time during the 1973-74 season. It was in December and we were going to Pittsburgh to play in the Steel Bowl Tournament. Tree Rollins arrived at the airport in a light windbreaker—he didn't own a winter coat. So on that trip I bought Tree a coat with my own money. I think it cost $100. It wasn't anything super, but the kid needed a coat! What was I going to do, let my star center get pneumonia?

I took a similar, personal view about the holidays. Most of my players had no money or transportation to get them home for Thanksgiving or Christmas. I believe this is a time of the year a college kid should be with family if at all possible, so I'd slip them $50 or $100, whatever it took to get him home for a day or two. But that was a criminal offense according to the NCAA rulebook. According to *my* rulebook, it would be more criminal not to help out a youngster in that kind of situation.

There was another source of money for players—a secret slush fund.

The fund was originated by three or four die-hard alums and set up in a bank in Columbia. Any check written needed two signatures. The monies for the fund were raised by a conglomerate of people soliciting to other Clemson supporters secretively. There were some real heavyweights involved in this scheme, mostly football people.

Their original intent was to supplement this secret account by the sale of Tiger Paw rags, a gimmick similar to the Pittsburgh Steelers' Terrible Towel. Because several of the boosters had connections with local textile plants, the rags could be produced quite economically, about 15 cents a piece. Then the rags were sold for 2 dollars each, with a dollar going back into the slush fund to repay monies being loaned to athletes. In this way, the money was untraceable. It was cash. That money was to be deposited in a Columbia bank, but whether it ever was I don't know.

I never got into the logistics of it. All I know is that each athlete's family, or the ones which were receiving help, were given enough money each month to meet the car payments. The players never saw the money. It was sent to their parents.

While I never got involved in the mechanics of the fund, I do know it existed because several of my friends had been approached and asked to make a contribution. They did not want to get involved either and called me to find out what was going on. I would tell them what I knew and assure them any contribution would be greatly appreciated. That was the extent of my role, but I think some of my friends lost respect for me, figuring I was endorsing the scheme. I know that is how it must have appeared to them.

Actually, I never used the slush fund as an inducement to attract a ballplayer to Clemson. I would never tell a kid that "if you come to Clemson you'll get so much money." On the other hand, let's be realistic. I was never that good of a recruiter to lure a kid like Tree Rollins away from a University of Kentucky. No, to get Rollins to come to Clemson over about six other top schools, we had to be doing *something* under the table. I knew some of the things and I had a good idea about some others, but Tree and I never spent much time discussing the subject. Again, I just didn't want to know.

Our players had a monthly spending allowance and received a number of gifts from various sources. Items like radios, stereos and items of that nature. I don't know who got what. In some cases the appliances were put in their parents' homes. Sometimes I'm not so sure it wasn't the mothers of the players who were doing the asking for these gifts.

I kept out of the details, but I knew what was coming down. I knew my players were being taken care of and that's all that counted. The kids never came to me for the heavy stuff, just some spare cash. And I gave it to them out of my pocket.

As for the slush fund, as far as I know it never really amounted to anything. It was lacking in funds and some of the heavy contributors got hurt financially. A couple of them were decent folks. I remember this one guy had to mortgage his house and sell his business because he got in debt over the slush fund.

A lot of their troubles might have been avoided—and perhaps the NCAA investigation, too—if they had worked the arrangement differently. It was ridiculous for them to put all their money into one fund. It would have made more sense for each "heavyweight alumnus" to fund an individual player. One guy would have gotten Rollins, another Wise, another Rome, and so on. That way if anybody shot a gun, the entire group wouldn't have to answer for all the problems.

That's exactly how some schools hide from the NCAA—they spread out and make 'em look in 25 different directions for clues. Clemson didn't do this...it was stupid.

And Clemson got caught.

LOOKING FOR ANSWERS

It hasn't been an easy decision to pour out my innermost thoughts and feelings on the subject of the illegal recruitment of college athletes, specifically using my own experiences at Clemson University as a point of focus. I realize many of my critics won't believe me when I say I have done a great deal of soul-searching, going back to probably that last season at Clemson in '75, before deciding to undertake this project.

I'd be lying if I didn't admit to wavering just a little myself over the winter months of 1981, wondering if my intentions would be misunderstood by the media and by the public. I wanted people to understand that I wasn't writing a book to "get back a certain people" as some thought, but actually in the hope some other young college coach might read about my self-inflicted downfall and avoid a similar embarrassment.

I guess what solidified my belief in this project occurred 2 months before my dismissal at Jacksonville. We were playing an afternoon game in Mobile, Alabama, against South Alabama. Jim Thacker, a popular television sports commentator who broadcasts Sun Belt Conference games, approached me about accompanying him to Clemson after our contest. Thacker was scheduled to do the play-by-play of the South Carolina-Clemson game and thought I might be interested in coming along on their private airplane. I agreed to make the trip.

Arriving at Littlejohn Coliseum that evening brought back many memories. For me, the nostalgia was heavy. I mean, you don't spend 5 years of your life in a small town like Clemson and walk away entirely. A piece of me always remained there.

Sitting at one of the press tables at courtside, my eyes wandered through the crowd. The faces were familiar, sometimes *too* familiar. I guess that is what aroused my emotions. I couldn't get over how certain members of the Clemson alumni and athletic department were sitting in exactly the same seats they had occupied when I had been head coach. They were all carrying on the same way. It was like one big party all over again, giving me the feeling I had slipped into some kind of a time machine. It was 1975 all over again, even though I knew the calendar read 1981.

It happened these same people were doing the same illegal things as before. Obviously, no one had learned a lesson. No one had walked away from the dirt of the early 1970s. They just *never* walked away. I saw that and I got this sick feeling in my stomach.

From that moment on, I knew *Caught in the Net* had to be completed.

I guess it was about the time of my fourth season when I began to feel badly about myself. I had gotten caught in a vicious circle. Small, innocent deceptions had led to bigger projects. I remember Harrison coming to me in October of 1973, not long after he had replaced George Hill on our staff. Charlie had seen Tree's car and wondered how the kid could afford one when he couldn't even afford a coat.

"Charlie, we got several members of the alumni to help him," I told Harrison.

"Tates, I don't know if that's right," returned Harrison. "Jesus, I just don't know if that's right.

"Charlie," I answered, "I did it because I just got tired of getting my ass beat in the ACC."

That is the truth. Simply, I had grown tired of losing. I didn't cheat because the Joneses did or because it made me a big man. I did it because I didn't want to get beat anymore. That's all.

My conscience bothered me. Here I was, the former coach of the United States Military Academy, bending the rulebook in every direction possible. I felt as if I had cheapened the game of basketball. I was also feeling badly about some of the kids who we had recruited into Clemson. Some of them weren't good kids and couldn't stand the pressures. They were succumbing to all sorts of social temptations.

But then so was I. I wasn't living a very exemplary life myself. I was taking all kinds of pills, drinking heavily, and running the streets with women. I had never run the streets before. I wasn't happy with Tates Locke. I was ashamed of what I was doing. I was cheating my profession, cheating my family, and cheating myself. I was in knots. My stomach felt like someone was hitting fungoes inside.

I kept on cheating. Common sense told me to get out, to start over, even if it meant leaving Clemson for another school. Foolishly, I didn't listen to my conscience.

I think it is difficult to say which schools and coaches are *not* cheating. I am sure there are some who are not, but you start discussing the illegal recruitment of a college athlete and you are talking about the *degree* of cheating, not the actual act of cheating itself.

What induces a certain ballplayer to attend a particular college? Let's start there. Every high school player in this country, when he begins talking about playing Division I basketball, has to have a reason for attending the school he selected. Some will tell you it is because of the academic environment but actually what has transpired is that the institution, more than likely the coach, has told this youngster "We can get you through school if you are a poor student."

That, friends, is an inducement.

You are promising this kid something you have no right to promise him— guaranteed passing grades.

If this appears to be innocent, perhaps it is, but such an inducement is only the beginning. Once a school skirts the academic part, the next step is to assist the youngster with his campus lifestyle. They may offer him transportation to and from his home, or maybe an alumnus will offer a special deal on clothing, or it could be a discount on an automobile. It just mushrooms. For those universities which are doing it big-time, the favors go beyond this stage. There are offers and promises made to a recruit's parents. Sometimes the school may build them a new home or buy them furniture, or simply pay them off in cash.

I'm always amused when I attend NCAA conventions and tournaments and see the parents of these youngsters. You look at them and their economic background and know there is no way possible they paid their own way. I know their community didn't hold a local street dance to raise the money. Yet time after time I see these parents after ballgames, coming to campus from 200 to 1,000 miles away.

How the hell do you think they're getting to campus?

I know Charlie Harrison used to tell me one of the first things he looked for when he was recruiting was whether or not the recruit automatically expected you to offer him something. Charlie told me—and he was right—a kid doesn't jump to that conclusion unless another school had been into his home before and offered him something illegal. That is a tipoff right there.

The inducements are made smoothly. Colon Abraham once told me he never saw the money B.C. Inabinet was sending him for his new car, but he knew his parents received the money on a regular basis at the end of each month through the mail. Colon never felt guilty about taking the money because he had given Clemson much of his time and ability and helped the school earn even more money from ticket receipts.

I believe there is a message for other college basketball coaches somewhere in my final season at Jacksonville University, in our miserable 8-19 record. As Al McGuire used to say, "With one aircraft carrier you could have flipped-flopped that record around."

Al was right. During the 1980-81 season, our team averaged 57.5 points a game. Our opponents average 59 points. So we lost, on the average, by 1.5 points, which shows you what one "aircraft carrier" would have meant to us. The guy could have been 6-5 or 7-0 or 5-10, but one outstanding athlete could have turned our season around without question.

The problem begins when you consider the importance of getting this "aircraft carrier." You look at the prospect and say to yourself, 'Boy, we *need* that guy.' Then it starts. After you get the one kid, you want two. Then you get the second prospect and you want another...and another. It snowballs. By then you've lost control.

I never lost control at Jacksonville as I had at Clemson. Eventually my honesty caught up with me. By going 8-19 in 1980-81, by having two horrendous recruiting seasons back-to-back at Jacksonville, proved to me everything I have felt about recruiting since I was dismissed from Clemson. Beliefs which I felt and the hatred I had for the system since 1975 were proven true: If you recruit honestly, most likely you'll end up with a losing team.

Recruiting done strictly according to the NCAA rulebook is almost an impossibility, but schools and coaches *can* skim the top of legalities and cut down on the flagrant violations. That is a very realistic goal.

For instance, if I were coaching at Indiana or Ohio State, I don't think I'd have to flagrantly cheat because you live off your own state kid. You have loyalties in those states and if a coach is smart enough to wrap his tentacles around the football people, he can survive and do quite well in his basketball program. Why anybody at schools like those would have to cheat I'll never know.

What about the private institutions? I don't know enough about the workings at a Notre Dame to comment, but I can tell you about the set-up at a military school like Army. When I was at West Point, we were not allowed to pay for a young man's visit to the Academy. So are you going to tell me we got Mike Silliman, a two-time first team high school All-American, without paying his way to West Point for a visit? Come on.

We did pay his way but that wasn't in violation of any NCAA rule, only a rule set forth by the Academy.

When Mike Silliman decided to attend the Point, here was a perfect example of harrassment on the part of other schools. He was being recruited by Kentucky, which threatened to get his father dismissed from his job if Mike didn't play for Adolph Rupp. Mike, you see, was from the Louisville area and Kentucky felt it would be disloyal of him to go elsewhere. I believe the only reason we got Mike to come to West Point was that no one could critiize him for attending a military school. That would have been disloyal to the United States!

The governing body of collegiate basketball, the NCAA, is good in *theory*. The NCAA projects itself as a nonprofit organization put together by volunteer members and member institutions for the betterment of interscholastic athletics. That looks very good on paper, but when winning becomes more important, when money comes next—or maybe it's the other way around—the NCAA rules won't suffice. College basketball has become a monster. It's big business. Look at the television monies, tournament monies and other dollars generated from gate receipts. All those things dictate winning—at all costs.

It's really absurd that only a handful of schools are put on probation by the NCAA. The really big boys are always overlooked. Remember all the garbage which went on at some of the West Coast schools like UCLA and USC recently? What trash. That whole operation should have been sent into the ocean. It was as if those schools were giving the NCAA the finger, sitting on an island and flipping them the bird.

John Wooden was a great basketball coach; I don't think anyone will argue with that. But John was also one of the best in the business at playing the ''shell game''—which one is the peanut under? John was clever.

I don't know if Wooden really knew about all the violations or if he even wanted to know. I really doubt if he set them up himself. Regardless, that operation at UCLA was strongly rumored to be the most ruthless cheating game ever established in college basketball which has *never* been caught. The monies, the contracts, and financial agreements the players at that school were said to have were totally incredible.

There have been worse leagues than the Pac-10. The greatest bandit league of all-time might have been the Missouri Valley when Cincinnati, Bradley, and Wichita were nationally ranked almost every season in the late 50s and 60s.

The Atlantic Coast Conference? I believe a lot of schools in the ACC cheated to get respectable. Clemson was a perfect example. I think years ago there was cheating at North Carolina, heavy cheating, but that subsided when the school got to be respectable and nationally ranked. I think there has been cheating at North Carolina State in the past, but again, it was done to enable the school to catch up with the rest of the pack. Once you get into the pack, and have some money to stay there, the cheating decreases if you're smart. All most alumni want is a chance, every now and then, to make a run at the top. They can live with that at most schools.

I think as long as there are young coaches who want to be head coaches and schools which want to get a piece of the pie, you will always see *some* amount of cheating. The NCAA can't hire enough investigators or make enough rules to stop them. Plus, there is always going to be a double standard of who gets caught and who doesn't. If you are one of the established Top 20 schools and you get caught, more than likely your reprimand will be less severe than say an Idaho State or a Jacksonville or a Clemson. Those are the facts of life in college basketball.

If I can offer one bit of advice to a young coach today, be he a high school head coach or a college assistant, it is that the individual must be willing to accept the unwritten code which already exists. Don't try to change it and don't act surprised and gossip about it. Just go out and get the job done. If it's recruiting, then go out and recruit. Play the game by the rules of the street.

It's like in sales or anything else—somewhere down the line you are going to have to give out green stamps. You are going to have to cheat *somewhere* along the line, but do it and don't talk about it.

There is nothing which disturbs me more than to hear a coach say his program is lily white and turn around and gossip about another coach's program. When I hear that kind of talk, I call him a liar and walk away. People who know me know I shoot right from where it hurts. I will never talk about them behind their back. I will never tell anyone, "I didn't get the guy because so and so bought him." I won't do that. But if a coach starts talking that Mickey Mouse, slobby stuff, I say, "Hey, wait a minute. You're such an actor. You cheat and you're just disappointed because you didn't get the kid."

Then I walk away. That's the way I am. Nobody will talk that kind of trash around me. I won't let them. Besides, they should know better. I've *been* there before.

Young coaches had better know what they are getting into before they plunge into the college ranks. I always tell a high school coach, 'I'll help you get a job as a college assistant, but don't go walking in there with your eyes closed. Don't think it's going to be all X's and O's and all that strategic stuff. It isn't."

They all tell me they know they have to recruit players. They'll say, "I think I can recruit." I laugh, then I tell them, "Yeah, you go recruit but remember to bring a pocketful of money along with you."

You see, every coach out there can coach; every coach out there can teach. They all can talk. But you have to have something to sell. At Jacksonville, I was fortunate that I had the sun, a small campus, and individual academic attention to promote a recruit. That is more than many coaches have to sell. But I probably didn't have enough. Jacksonville didn't have a beautiful campus arena—we used the city's. And we didn't give away clothing, cars, women, and other material items. In that sense, we were operating a disadvantage.

The end result showed what usually happens: 8 and 19.

Chapter 6

The 1961 Scandal at North Carolina State and the End of the Dixie Classic

William H. Beezley
North Carolina State University

The Dixie Classic, held on the campus of North Carolina State University, reigned as the outstanding invitational basketball tournament in the United States for 12 years from 1949 to 1961. Everett Case, the basketball coach who brought North Carolina State to national prominence in the sport and who forced rivals to upgrade their basketball programs, used the Classic to gain publicity for his program and to aid in his recruiting. The tournament instantly became a social and financial event in Raleigh. Because it was played during the Christmas holidays, fans from the community could obtain tickets that would ordinarily be used by the students. Because Case regularly invited teams ranked in the Top Ten, national attention focused on the tournament. This interest brought sportswriters from around the country to Raleigh and quickly caught the eye of gamblers as well. Commercialism, publicity, and gambling climaxed in the 1961 scandal at N.C. State and ended the Classic.

SPORT AND GAMBLING

From its beginning in the English colonies, American sport has appealed to those with the time and money for games—what today would be called the "country club" crowd first took up athletics, followed by petty crooks and big time criminals, who also had leisure and cash. Colonial Virginia horsemen always placed large wagers to demonstrate their confidence in their horses and to display their wealth before the lower classes in the colony.

Fixing athletic contests, called *hippodroming*, caused national concern in the 19th century. Gamblers fixed boat, bicycle, and foot races, but public ire turned particularly against hippodroming baseball players. Three New York Mutuals threw a game to the underdog Brooklyn Eckfords in 1865 and were banned for a time from the league. More notorious were the "Louisville Four," who played for the Grays, a member of the National League, and who fixed several games late in the 1877 season. All four were banned for life from the league. Not until 1919 did a scandal of such proportions again rock the world of sport. The nation was shocked to discover that gamblers had fixed eight Chicago White Sox players so that the Cincinnati Reds would win the 1919 World Series. Without trial or court-acceptable evidence, the commissioner banned the eight "Black" Sox players for life to preserve the purity of the game.[1]

College sports, primarily football until after 1900, remained relatively free of gamblers until the 1930s. Then gamblers expanded their activities to include college basketball. Two developments assisted them. Sports editors, intent on selling newspapers, began predicting winners of important games and, to show off their skill, also determined the margin of victory (called the *point spread*—if a game ends 79-76, the spread is three points). The daily newspapers thus began publishing a betting sheet.[2]

Basketball's popularity also encouraged gamblers. Crowds became so large that they forced games out of small college gyms into larger municipal arenas. Madison Square Garden became America's basketball capital as the management frequently sponsored double-headers and postseason tournaments. This trend spread across the country. College games were no longer played only before fellow students and alumni, but before the general public. Spectators appeared who had no interest in school spirit and healthy competition, but only a game's outcome—often for their personal profit.

Gossip about "fixed" games was soon whispered around. Some $50,000 changed hands on the 1935 Temple-New York University game according to rumors.[3] A few years later, in 1944, Phog Allan, Kansas University's coach, warned that a coming scandal "could stink to high heaven." The National Association of Intercollegiate Basketball criticized Allan for his "deplorable lack of faith in American youth and meager confidence in the integrity of coaches."[4] Within weeks it was learned that ball players at Brooklyn College had been accepting bribes for shaving points to manipulate the point spread. The National Association said it was an isolated incident and ignored reports of gambling and bribes at five other schools.

Coaches and fans could not dismiss gambling rumors in 1950-1951. The season was tremendous—for teams, spectators, and gamblers, with as much as $10,000,000 changing hands every game day.[5] With that much money at stake, gamblers soon attempted to control the margin of victory in big games. Proof of this activity came when Junius Kellogg of Manhattan College reported an attempted bribe to the New York City police. District Attorney Frank Hogan laid a trap for the gamblers, caught them, and then began an investigation that ended with shocking results.

Hogan collected evidence that 32 players from seven colleges had taken bribes to shave points in at least 86 games. The scandal scarred the reputation of the nation's greatest teams. Players caught in cheating schemes came from the City College of New York, whose team had won two straight NCAA championships and in 1950 won the National Invitational Tournament, Long Island University, and Manhattan University. Most of the players and teams hailed from New York, so it was doubly shocking when three Kentucky players confessed to shaving points. Alex Groza, Ralph Beard, and Dale Barnstable had been All-Americans and Olympic champions. They had led the Kentucky Wildcats to a National Athletic Association title and 111 victories from 1946 to 1949. All three said they has shaved points during their college careers.

These revelations gave college basketball a bad name. Attendance declined across the country (although not in Raleigh). Long Island University dropped its sports program. Players were tried on criminal charges and the NCAA handed out probation to the schools involved. The NCAA recommended schools not play in public arenas and many coaches refused to play in Madison Square Garden.[6]

Basketball gradually bounced back and by the mid-1950s attendance regained its prescandal numbers. The recaptured popularity also reached New York City. Players tried to forget the scandals, and coaches wanted to protect their teams.

At North Carolina State University, Coach Everett Case adopted the practice of periodic meetings to warn players of gamblers' techniques and to outline the penalties for accepting bribes.[7] Other coaches quickly followed Case's example.

Team meetings with a law enforcement officer who cautioned about the dangers of gambling, however, totally ignored the circumstances that made cheating scandals possible, even probable. Americans have a willingness to gamble that cannot be ignored nor denied. One of every ten adult Americans gambles in some form.[8] Universities cannot control gambling on their athletic events, but they must not contribute to circumstances that invite gamblers to tamper with college athletes. Recruiting after World War II often involved free trips, gifts, money, and promises of even more. Once the athlete reached campus, he found that he was regarded as little more than a hired hand by the faculty, the other students, and the alumni. Only the stars received much in the way of rewards. The athlete's general feeling was that he had been hired to play basketball. The prevailing feeling on the part of gamblers was that if the athlete could be hired to play the game, then he could be hired to play if not quite so well.[9]

The intense rivalry of alumni boosters, students from neighboring campuses, and townspeople results in intensive recruiting by college coaches. In the 1950s, coaches sometimes "cheated" on the rules to obtain an important recruit. Of course, the players knew this—they knew who was paid under the table, who was not qualified for admission to the college, and who was aided in easy classes by tutors. These were, and they remain today, the circumstances in which gamblers can make their pitch to players. As the competition and rivalry intensifies, so does the possibility of scandal as the one in Raleigh in 1961.

THE BEGINNING OF THE 1961 SCANDAL

New York District Attorney Hogan continued to track down rumors and protect the college game from organized crime. His persistent efforts deterred some gamblers and eventually led to the discovery of some who could not be intimidated. In March 1961 Hogan broke the second major basketball cheating scandal.

The D.A. announced the arrest of Aaron Wagman and Joseph Hacken, members of a national crime syndicate, informing the press that both men were charged with bribing college basketball players. His evidence involved players from Seton Hall. In a classic understatement, one New York Investigator remarked, "Just wait until it all comes out; it'll make 1951 look like peanuts." Arrests and revelation followed, implicating teams as far west as Colorado, throughout the middle west and east, and into the south as far as Raleigh.[10]

In the end, 50 players from 27 different schools were charged with fixing 44 games between 1956 and 1961. They had received close to $45,000 in bribe money; the gamblers had made millions.[11]

Hacken confessed to arranging dates for players, providing them with spending money, and paying $500 to $1,000 a game for shaving points. He found summer jobs for cooperative players, usually at resorts in the Catskills, playing for hotel basketball teams.[12]

Investigation identified go-betweens who hoped for big money but profited little from their association with Wagman and Hacken. One such hanger-on was Jack Molinas. Thirty years old when the scandals broke, Molinas had played basketball for Columbia University and the Fort Wayne Pistons of the National Basketball Association. In the pros he was widely suspected of gambling on games. In 1954 Molinas became an attorney and began acting as Wagman's middleman.

Molinas profited from his gambling activities, but it was not always an easy life. A Chicago gambler in 1960, for example, threatened Molinas' life because a "fix" had not occurred. Another time, syndicate "hit" men used baseball bats to beat Molinas unconscious in a Miami parking lot. New York investigators followed Molinas for 23 months before arresting him in 1960. They had evidence that he had made deals with at least 50 players from 23 schools and tried to bribe Connie Hawkins of the University of Iowa. He was found guilty in 1963 on five counts of gambling, conspiracy, and perjury with a sentence of 36 years in prison. Later released on probation, he moved to California where he was shot to death on August 4, 1975, at his Hollywood Hills home. The gunman was never identified.[13]

Scandal soon reached Chapel Hill. New York detectives investigating Wagman identified one of his contacts as University of North Carolina's player Lou Brown. Shown photographs of himself with several gamblers, Brown confessed that since

1959 he had arranged for players to shave points, but had refused to bribe his teammates. Instead, he approached friends on other teams, such as Frank Majewski of St. Joseph's and Eddie Browler of LaSalle. He also introduced fellow Tar Heel Doug Moe to Wagman. Moe took a $75 gift from the gambler, but rejected an offer to shave points. Besides receiving money for bribery activities, Brown also began betting on games.

He explained that Wagman and Hacken had learned that he was from a poor family. His only spending money was his monthly $15 laundry fee. It wasn't enough, he said, because the other kids on the Carolina campus "drove Thunderbirds," so he had accepted the gamblers' offer.

Chancellor Williams B. Aycock of the University of North Carolina suspended Brown from school. He also dismissed Moe because he had accepted $75 from Wagman and had failed to report the attempted bribe.[14]

THE SCANDAL REACHES N.C. STATE

Chancellor John T. Caldwell, worried that the scandal might reach the N.C. State campus, directed athletic officials to have each player sign a statement that he had not been involved with gamblers and had no knowledge of players who had. The players, except Anton Muehlbauer and Stan Niewierowski, who had left school in April, and Terry Litchfield, returned the statement.[15] These forms temporarily calmed officials, but gossip crisscrossed the campus.

Wolfpack players were kidded on the brickyard (the plaza in front of the library) and heard whispers in their classes. The gossip was too much for one team member, Ken Rohloff. He told Frank Weedon, sports information director, that his classmates talked about him before classes and that several refused to speak to him. Rohloff said he had done nothing wrong, but suspected teammates might be involved. He wanted to know what to do. Weedon told him to see Case immediately.[16] Rohloff left the office, Weedon assumed, to see the coach.

Case already had suspicions that a player or two might be shaving points. He had been troubled by Muehlbauer's play in the December 17, 1960, Georgia Tech game. Sometime later, he said, "I knew things did not look good. I was morally sure that something was wrong, and I got Roy (Clogston) to call Mr. Anderson (Director of the State Bureau of Investigation)." The SBI sent an agent to give the annual lecture to the team, and Anderson began some preliminary investigating. After the February 16 game in which UNC whopped State, 97-66, Case told Anderson that he was certain of cheating.[17] The coach and the SBI began working closely on the investigation.

State's involvement became public when Anderson ordered the arrest of Stan Niewierowski, team captain from Brooklyn, Anton Muehlbauer, Jr., also from Brooklyn, and Terry Litchfield of Louisville, Kentucky. Litchfield was placed under house arrest in the college infirmary; Muehlbauer was arrested in Greensboro, brought to Raleigh, and released on bond; Niewierowski was taken into custody by New York police. Anderson had another North Carolina warrant for the arrest of Lou Barshak of Brooklyn, a student at Los Angeles State College, named as the contact man. The trial of the three Wolfpack players and Barshak was set for June 5 in Wake County Superior Court.[18]

Litchfield confessed to reporters the day after his arrest that he had been involved with gamblers. But he had never received a pay-off and had never shaved points, he claimed. "I made a mistake, a bad mistake; I'm sorry for what I did, but I guess that won't make any difference now."[19]

The arrests shocked other State players. Bob DiStefano said, "I really didn't believe anyone on our team was involved." But he conceded that Niewierowski gambled on anything; "Throw a feather in the air and he'd bet whether it would hit the floor or not. I think he knew what he was doing but the others must have been talked into it."[20]

Vic Bubas, Duke basketball coach since 1959 and former State player and assistant coach, expressed sadness at the disclosures. He said no one did more than Case to warn players about gamblers. Bubas added, "I will not condemn anyone until he is proven guilty."[21]

Caldwell declared that "the evidence and facts in this type of case are obviously beyond availability to a student honor code board. It is not fair to ask the students to sit in judgment on a case in which it is not possible for them to have access to relevant witnesses, testimony, and evidence."[22] Therefore Caldwell took charge, ruling that Niewierowski and Muehlbauer, who had withdrawn from college, ostensibly because of academic difficulty, would not be permitted to return. He suspended Litchfield and said he would not be allowed to reenter school. He reminded fans that they should hold no grudge against the players who had been "confronted with temptation and succumbed." Rather, he said, "opprobrium.... (should) be directed against those who bribed them."[23]

Caldwell also prepared to meet with the UNC campus Chancellor Aycock and William Friday, president of the 16 campus North Carolina University system (called the Consolidated University) to take steps to prevent a repetition of cheating scandal. Caldwell planned to suggest that the schools offer "no scholarships for athletes except graduates of N.C. high schools or sons of bonafide graduates of NCSU." He was prepared, however, to concede scholarships for boys from Virginia.

Chancellor Caldwell wanted to restrict the schedule of games. He proposed no contests be played outside the ACC or ACC states, except for the NCAA tournament. He also wanted to convert the Dixie Classic into a "North Carolina Classic" with the Big Four hosting four other North Carolina teams.[24]

Taken together, his suggestions called for deemphasis of basketball. Caldwell, Aycock, and Friday discussed the plan at a series of three meetings. Although their final policy varied somewhat from Caldwell's proposals, the officials announced on May 22, 1961, a deemphasis of basketball. The three university executives restricted recruiting, prohibited participation in summer basketball leagues, and reduced nonconference schedules.

Players who held scholarships were assured that both UNC and N.C. State would meet their commitments to them. But the administrators advised coaches that they could offer only two scholarships to freshmen from outside the ACC area. Football coaches were also restricted; they could recruit only 12 boys from outside the ACC region.

The NCAA had banned all summer basketball play beginning in 1962. But Friday, Caldwell, and Aycock ordered an immediate restriction against participation in organized summer competition such as the resort leagues operating in the Catskills.

The most stringent action involved basketball schedules. The officials reduced the maximum number of games from 25 to 16, plus ACC and NCAA tournament contests. This ruling permitted only two nonconference games. With this decision, North Carolina State abandoned the 12-year-old Dixie Classic.[25]

Caldwell explained the deemphasis was "designed to bring basketball in the Consolidated University back into educational perspective."[26] Friday echoed this sentiment, saying, "Our aim is to save athletics by deemphasizing certain practices and removing certain influences which have been detrimental to college sports and taking away from them the very qualities which make them valuable as a part of education. Our position is a positive one. We aim to restore sportsmanship. We aim to conserve to our students their rightful privilege of taking part in wholesome athletic competition and protect them, as the University must, from exploitation."[27]

These decisions revealed, at least implicitly, what Caldwell, Friday, and Aycock considered the "certain practices" and "certain influences" that resulted in the scandals. The president and both chancellors agreed that the principal cause for the gambling episode was high-pressure college recruiting. They believed that a young man's values were badly shaken, if not completely altered, when he was courted by 10, 25, even 100 colleges. Recruiters at best pandered to a boy's ego and at worst made under-the-table promises to lure him to one college or another. They concluded that if you could hire a boy to shoot baskets, someone else could hire him to miss them.[28]

North Carolina officials did not limit the number of scholarships; instead, they restricted the area where coaches could recruit. This decision reflected a long-standing bias that periodically came to the surface, a suspicion, often downright resentment, of outsiders, especially those from the north. Everett Case pointed his finger at New York and told reporters, "Have we created a Frankenstein monster! The recruiting is too vicious, the rivalry is too vicious...I am now convinced that the trend must be to play our basketball with North Carolina boys...Maybe the ethical sense of New York boys is all screwed up, I don't know, but North Carolina boys would certainly be loyal."[29]

Many N.C. State faithfuls easily accepted this view because the gamblers came from New York and one from Louisville. Caldwell refused to say that players from any region of the country were more susceptible to gamblers than boys from North Carolina. But Friday argued, "Our basketball teams of recent years have been formed on a disproportionate number of students from regions of the country distant from our State and conference. While this, per se, may have nothing to do with the predicament in which we find ourselves at this time, it is nevertheless confirming evidence that we have recruited these players with a view primarily to their skill as performers without regard for the desirability of fielding teams which are more or less representative of the normal composition of the student bodies."[30]

New Yorkers resented implications that their boys had lower ethical standards than Carolinians. One journalist reported, "The familiar strains of an old refrain are wafting northwards from Raleigh, N.C..... It's the fault of those bad New Yorkers on the squad, says North Carolina State basketball coach Everett Case, speaking of the point-fixing scandal that has just riddled his team." The reporter suggested it was not the players' morals at fault, but rather those of coaches and university officials. "The sense of values that needs looking to is that of a university which recruits young men not because they are good students, but because they are good basketball players. Secretary of Commerce Luther Hodges, a former governor of North Carolina, who obviously knows a good deal about the athletic situation at N.C. State, had a three-word message of advice for colleges hit by the basketball scandal: 'Quit buying teams.' It strikes us a tune worth repeating and we suggest Mr. Case try it on his phonograph."[31]

State and Carolina fans accepted restrictions on recruiting with little public comment. Nor was there much reaction to the prohibition against participation in summer basketball programs. Investigations in New York City and in Raleigh made it clear that the summer basketball leagues in the Catskills provided gamblers an opportunity to contact players they wanted to bribe. Litchfield had been approached by Barshak while playing on a Catskill resort team. Muehlbauer and Niewierowski and others had also been contacted while holding jobs at summer resorts. Other state players performed in summer leagues without encountering gamblers. Nick Pond and Bob DiStefano, for example, had played in the Catskills without becoming involved with underworld point-fixers.[32]

END OF THE CLASSIC
AND PUNISHMENT OF THE PLAYERS

What shocked fans, students, and athletic officials about the deemphasis was the cancellation of the holiday tournament. No Dixie Classic—the disbelief rivaled the news that State and Carolina players had been involved with gamblers. Consolidated University President Friday anticipated the outcry and said: "Holiday tournaments, of which the Dixie Classic is a prominent example, conducted at a time when college is not in session, exemplify the exploitation for public entertainment or for budgetary and commercial purposes of a sports program which properly exists as an adjunct to collegiate education. These tournaments subject students, the coaches, and the colleges to unnecessary demands and unwise distractions."[33]

Caldwell had anticipated some change in the holiday tournament. His suggestion, a North Carolina Classic matching eight state teams, would have reduced the national attention on the tournament. The schools would still have profited from games that had reduced, but still substantial, fan interest.[34] But in the atmosphere of gamblers and fixed games, the decision was simply to end the tournament.

Some state fans thought the death of the Dixie Classic involved more than the possibility that it might attract gamblers. They suspected a conspiracy and charged that the fix scandal had been a convenient excuse for UNC's Coach, Frank Maguire, who believed State derived a recruiting advantage by hosting the Dixie Classic, to urge its termination. For 2 or 3 years there had been rumors that Maguire wanted Carolina out of the tournament; certainly there was grumbling about the advantage the Wolfpack gained by having the Classic on its campus.[35] But this advantage would have disappeared in any event with the recruiting restrictions imposed by deemphasis.

A storm of protest was gathering against the Classic's cancellation. Friday, moving swiftly, reported to the Board of Trustees about the decisions. Friday did not need the trustees' approval—the actions were within the powers of the President and the Chancellors—but he asked for their endorsement. The trustees voted overwhelmingly to support Friday. Caldwell and Aycock also moved to implement the deemphasis of athletics. Caldwell ordered Clogston, N.C. State's Athletic Director, to begin at once notifying athletic directors of State's deemphasis and revising the team's basketball schedule.[36] He also informed the athletics staff that he would accept nothing less than complete cooperation with the new program.

Friday and the Chancellors agreed that the restrictions would be reviewed in the future, but for the time being would modify no aspect of the deemphasis. These decisions completed the University System's response to the scandal.

Caldwell had to deal with the Ken Rohloff case before closing the issue in Raleigh. Caldwell had determined to investigate Rohloff's guilt or innocence. When the SBI completed its investigation on June 7, Walter Anderson gave the Chancellor a summary of Rohloff's testimony. Under questioning, Rohloff admitted that Muehlbauer had approached him about shaving points. Muehlbauer told Rohloff that he and Litchfield had received $1,000 each for shaving points in the Georgia Tech game. Rohloff had refused to become involved. Anderson concluded that Rohloff was not implicated in point-fixing. The New York District Attorney also reported that Rohloff did not figure in his investigation.

Chancellor Caldwell listened to the tape recording of the Rohloff questioning. He determined that Rohloff had cooperated fully with the SBI and that he had not been involved in point-fixing. Rohloff had, however, failed to report the attempted bribe. Rohloff explained this by saying if a gambler had approached him, he would have reported it to Case but because it was a teammate, he "just couldn't do it."[37]

Because Rohloff failed to report the bribe, Caldwell placed him on disciplinary probation from July 20, 1961, to January 27, 1962. The Chancellor said that during the fall semester he could not receive student aid nor participate in varsity athletics. Even though he did not accept a bribe or fix any games, Caldwell said that Rohloff had been willing to play on a team with players who were doing those things.

The Chancellor declared that Rohloff's unwillingness to report the bribery attempt "reflected lack of respect for the game and the College."[38]

A *Raleigh Times* editorial praised Caldwell's handling of the case. Putting Rohloff on probation demonstrated to future athletes that State intended to live by the rules. His reluctance to report a teammate, the editor said, was "typical of students everywhere (who refused) to turn in fellow students for any violation of the honor system, including cheating on examinations."[39]

But a week later, another *Times* editorial questioned Caldwell's decision. Rohloff had cooperated with authorities when asked, and besides he had some obligation to a friend. The article suggested that friendship was more immediate than the vague "moral obligations" that guided Caldwell's ruling.[40]

The decisions on Litchfield, Muehlbauer, Niewierowski, and Rohloff stood. The University had moved decisively to deal with the fixing scandal. Caldwell still had to devote a great deal of time to encouraging boosters to continue their support of N.C. State athletics. However, with the probation of Rohloff, the issue was settled as a campus question. The cheating scandal moved to the courts where it was treated as a criminal case.

PUBLIC DISCUSSION OF THE SCANDAL
AND THE END OF THE CLASSIC

Newspapers, sportswriters, sports fans, and students discussed the point-fixing scandal. Their shock prompted serious consideration of what had been responsible for making the players susceptible to the gamblers. The *Raleigh Times* identified two factors: the commercial nature of big-time athletics in which financial decisions overrode everything else and the role of the newspapers; "Honest hindsight," the editor wrote, "must tell us that the newspapers have played a major role in the development of big-time athletics. They have ballyhooed and publicized all the favorable aspects of big-time athletics. They have developed the public appetite for such big-time sports and have made possible the big gate receipts...There is nothing wrong with such ballyhoo and such publicity. The wrong comes in publicizing only the favorable aspects of such things. The newspapers have not dug into big-time athletics as they have dug into politics and government."[41]

The *Greensboro Daily News* placed the blame squarely on the university. The editor charged that the administration, the trustees, and even the General Assembly (North Carolina's State Legislature) had tolerated a "climate of professionalism in athletics" and they concluded that the Consolidated University must "put first things first."[42]

College basketball reflected contemporary society in the opinion of sportswriter Bill Lee of the *Hartford* (Connecticut) *Courant*. "Cheating seems almost to have become the fashion of the day, criminally phoney television quizzes, rigged contests, dishonest disc jockeys, bribery in the highest places, widespread tax dodging, and downright cheating." He argued that colleges offered the athletes the worst example of all. "If a university lowers the rigid bars of academic qualification to allow the matriculation of star basketball players, no one is better aware of the cheating than the player himself. If there is a further winking at standards in order to keep a faltering student of athletic excellence in school, the athlete's moral fiber is additionally weakened by the very college he represents." Lee admonished the colleges, "Stop aspiring to big tournaments, guarantees and network television shows; in short, keep basketball from becoming too big for its britches."[43]

Newly elected editor of N.C. State's student newspaper, *The Technician*, Mike Lea, expressed sympathy for the guilty. However, in his "Open Letter to Arrested Trio," he fairly distributed the blame for the gambling incident.

We students cheered you when you were on the basketball floor, and then thought of you as "poor relatives" the minute that you stepped into academic circles. We were so excited over seeing State College numbered among the top teams in the nation that we overlooked the fact that you players were human beings. We thought of you almost as hired entertainers, and when we gave you the impression that you were only important as a paid diversion for us, we know that it was hard to view yourselves in any other light. We made you mercenaries and now we condemn you for being mercenary.

The administration and the Athletics Department are guilty of the same errors. Of course, the Athletics Department wants to put forth a good showing. Primarily they want winning teams....There could be little feeling of "patriotism" to an institution which wanted you for one thing—to produce a winning basketball team.

The administration is also partly responsible. They let their academic ideals and goals be submerged to a stronger athletic program...

The general public has their share of blame, also. They made basketball so important, and demanded colleges to place too great an emphasis on winning athletic teams that the college almost had no other alternative than to forsake some of its ideals in the pursuit of trophies.

There is no need reiterating the fixers' part in this sad occurrence. No one knows better than you what a group of money-grubbing men can do to make a fast dollar without regard for the consequences that might be inflicted on someone else....

Finally, we newspapers have to assume part of the responsibility...We, also, have been one of the pressure groups which have forced athletic teams to place winning as the all-important goal. We have placed the emphasis on the wrong aspect of the game, and have indirectly forced colleges to do the same.

And, of course, you have to take the blame. What you did was very wrong, and no matter what the circumstances are, you showed a weakness of character that may nearly ruin your life.

All of State is shocked and hurt at what you three students did. We remember your last-second shot in the Duke game, Terry; and we remember your running up and tackling him, Stan. You seemed so full of spirit, and seemed so happy to see a win that it is hard to believe that you could have sold yourself to lose a game.[44]

In the midst of this public discussion of the scandal, Caldwell wrote to members of the Wolfpack Club, the athletic booster club, May 22, 1961, explaining the decisions he, Aycock, and Friday had been forced to make. "Some will be disappointed in some of the actions." Caldwell said. But he consoled boosters, "May I assure you now that our desire is to continue to maintain a strong position in the Atlantic Coast Conference in all sports, prominently basketball and football. We need your help as never before. Many of you have tied your previous contributions to tickets for the Dixie classic. Now you must tie your support to the bigger idea: This is for State College."[45]

Responses to the Chancellor's plea for support poured into his office. "Amen. Yes sir, you can count on my approval," said Eric Bell. "Swallowing our disappointment (selfishness)—We must admit you are right," reported Gray & Creech, Inc. Charles Brady remarked, "In an age and time when so many of us are guilty of cheating on income taxes, cheating on expense accounts, etc., I am not greatly surprised that some of our athletes have been tempted and some of them succumbed." Despite the "sad mistake" of eliminating the Dixie Classic, he said he would continue his donations to both UNC and N.C. State. Howell Stroup, former State athlete, declared, "You have my wholehearted support." R.J. Barnes, speaking for many who backed Caldwell, boasted, "I am proud to know we have a Chancellor who accepts athletics as part of the College and is willing to promote it rather than treat it as a wart or parasite that should be done away with."

But others doubted Caldwell's commitment to the red-and-white varsity. Critical comments ranged from disappointment with deemphasis to anger at cancellation of the Dixie Classic. "You ask...Am I right? I say no. It's the Dixie Classic that seems to me is being unfairly punished. For shame," chided one Wolfpacker. Another scoffed, "In my opinion, the actions taken were extremely shortsighted but I wish to take exception particularly to the restricting of recruiting from outside the Atlantic Coast Conference area." Asheville's WLOS-TV editorialized, "We are frankly dubious about the effectiveness of the University's new plan." Another Wolfpacker scolded Caldwell, "It occurs to a lot of people that the coaches and the schools should be penalized." And C.W. Tilson asked if the Chancellor had considered "the real down to earth problem we have in replacing the finances for our athletic program we will be losing as a result of the basketball deemphasis."[46]

Caldwell, although aware of the financial crisis, responded to another consideration. "The decisions the three of us made," he wrote Tilson, "reflect our point of view that the aspiration for national recognition and national ratings in basketball had produced pressures that had consistently led to embarrassment to this institution over the past ten years. We don't intend to continue to be embarrassed."[47]

Not only did Consolidated University officials want to avoid embarrassment, but also they hoped to avoid losing initiative to another authority. Only days after the arrest of State's players, Governor Terry Sanford had suggested the trustees investigate varsity sports. Moreover, the NCAA lurked around, ready to impose sanctions and penalties if the University failed to act. And it was just possible the North Carolina General Assembly might take up the question of university athletics. Caldwell, Aycock, and Friday recognized the need for prompt, decisive action by the University. Their program of deemphasis preempted punitive action by the Trustees, the NCAA, and the legislature.

ECONOMIC RESULTS OF THE SCANDAL

University officials might discount the economic impact of deemphasis, but Raleigh businessmen did not. The Raleigh Merchants Bureau, Inc., requested reinstatement of the Dixie Classic because it benefitted "the State of North Carolina, the University, the community where it is located, and our people at large."[48] But Caldwell explained the decision had been made with full knowledge of "public enjoyment and incidental commercial benefits that come to the city." The merchants' protest against cancelling the Classic, the *Greensboro Daily News* charged, demonstrated the commercialism College authorities wanted to eliminate. "Biggest howl of all came from Raleigh businessmen, primarily merchants, restauranteurs, and hotel and motel owners, who cried in anguish about the half million or more dollars which they might lose in business attributed to the basketball classic and the visitors which it brought to the capital city."[49] Ironically, the *News & Observer* reported that Governor Sanford left for Ohio in an effort to attract industry to North Carolina that could stick a million-dollar finger in the state's economic dike, a leak developed as a result of the cancellation of the Classic.[50]

As Tilson predicted, N.C. State soon experienced an economic crunch because of the basketball deemphasis. H.B. James, Athletics Council Chairman, told Caldwell in June, 1961 that there were problems with the 1961-1962 budget. James contended that the probable short-fall resulted from the reduction in home basketball games, which could cost the Athletic Department an estimated $52,000. According to estimates, this would result in a deficit of $22,517 in the next year's athletic budget.

James suggested they replace the money lost through deemphasis by using North Carolina State monies for coaches' salaries, eliminating minor sports, and increasing the athletic fee an additional $5.00 a student.[51]

Unwilling to adopt these extreme measures and unable to permit deficit spending, Caldwell eventually lifted some restrictions on basketball scheduling. He informed Roy Clogston in January 1962, "Chancellor Aycock and I have...agreed that each of our institutions can schedule as many as nineteen basketball games and five nonconference games plus two practice games or 'scrimmages.' " But, he cautioned, these games could not include tournaments or games played during the Christmas holidays. And within a short time the restriction on recruiting and the ban on holiday games and tournaments were also dropped.[52]

Besides the impact on the budget, the scandals and deemphasis had an impact on recruiting, although not as harshly as many anticipated. Case signed 6'9'' Charlie Grob, an all-state player from New Jersey, and 6'0'' Gary Hale from Jeffersonville, Indiana. The Wolfpack recruited three more players from North Carolina. The biggest loss was 6'2'' Tal Brody, another New Jersey player, who decided to attend Temple because of the scandals. Not one of these five played varsity in 1962. Grob and another player left State, and the other three recruits were held out of action.[53]

THE GAMBLERS AND THE COURTS

The scandal had the most immediate impact on the players involved. New York's District Attorney had given immunity from prosecution to players in exchange for testifying in the City's cases against gamblers. But North Carolina law did not provide for "turning state's evidence" and it was widely reported that the players could not receive immunity for testifying for the State.[54]

Governor Sanford determined to probe thoroughly the gambling network operating in the state. With the governor's backing, the General Assembly approved a special appropriation of $50,000 to the Attorney General's office for the investigation of point-shaving. Evidence gathered on the North Carolina State players involved with gamblers went to the Wake County Grand Jury.[55]

The country's Grand Jury reviewed testimony throughout the summer and returned indictments on September 12, 1961, against gamblers Eugene Greene, Charles Tucker, David Budin, Michael Siegel, Louis Barshak, and Bob Kraw. No players were indicted, but the true bills shocked Wolfpack fans who learned four players had cheated. The gamblers had bribed Nierwierowski, Muehlbauer, Litchfield, and Don Gallagher. Gallagher had been voted the 1960 Alumni Trophy as the Outstanding Senior Athlete.

Jurors wanted to question Gallagher who was on active duty in Germany with the U.S. Army. Governor Sanford arranged Gallagher's return from Berlin in January, 1962. After hearing the testimony, the Grand Jury issued indictments of 10 gamblers for 65 bribery charges. Solicitor Lester V. Chalmers described these fixers as members of the "biggest gambling network" in the country. Each count listed in the Jury's bills carried up to 5 years imprisonment and fines on conviction.[56]

The indictments named Dave Goldberg, Steve Lekometros, Jake Israel, Frank Cardone, Peter Martino, Morris "Moe" Heyison, Eugene Greene, Aaron Wagman, Joseph Hacken, and Paul Walker. All these defendants were investigated by the New York District Attorney; several were questioned by the U.S. Senate's Subcommittee on Organized Crime.

The indictments named 11 North Carolina State games that gamblers had attempted to fix. The games and the players implicated were the following:

1. ACC tournament game, State—75, South Carolina—72, March 5, 1959. A South Carolina player received an offer to shave points.
2. State—59, Wake Forest—73, December 5, 1959. Gallagher charged with accepting $1,000 for point shaving.
3. State—50, South Carolina—71, December 8, 1959. Gallagher charged with shaving points for $500.
4. State—58, Kansas—80, December 12, 1959. Gallagher charged with shaving points.
5. Dixie Classic, State—32, Dayton—36, December 28, 1959. Gallagher allegedly received $1,000 for shaving points.
6. State—34, Duke—47, January 9, 1960. Gallagher charged with shaving points for $1,000.
7. State—63, Duke—53, February 9, 1960. Gallagher charged with shaving points for $1,000.
8. State—48, Maryland—46, February 13, 1960. Gallagher allegedly received $1,000 and Niewierowski $1,250 for shaving points.
9. State—62, Carolina—66, February 17, 1960. Both Gallagher and Niewierowski refused offers of $1,250 each to shave points because of rivalry with UNC.
10. State—82, Georgia Tech—76, December 17, 1960. Litchfield and Muehlbauer received $1,000 each to shave points.
11. State—67, Duke—81, January 7, 1961. Niewrowski allegedly received $2,000 and Muehlbauer $1,250 for shaving points.

The Wolfpack players escaped prosecution. The Grand Jury did not indict them because of their full confessions and their cooperation with the investigators. Solicitor Chalmers focused his attention on the gamblers. Several suspected fixers—notably Walker, Wagman, and Greene—pleaded guilty or no contest and became star witnesses for the solicitor. Cardone and Morris successfully fought extradition from Pennsylvania.[57]

When the trial began in November, 1962, only Goldberg and Lekometros faced the jury. After 10 days of testimony, the Jurors deliberated for 2 hours to find them guilty.[58] Goldberg was sentenced to an active 5-year term and fined $21,000. Lekometros received an active 5-year sentence and a $9,000 fine. Both received suspended 3-year sentences for each of 16 and 14 counts respectively. The suspensions required payment of the fines and court costs.

Other sentences ranged from 18 months for Walker to 3-year suspended terms for Barshak and Siegel. Wagman and Greene received fines and prison terms, but these were suspended if they were sentenced to prison terms—which they were—by the New York City courts.[59]

For the players, the trial meant the humiliation of testifying to their complicity in shaving points. The few thousand dollars they received—at least once mailed in a comic book—was poor payment for the scar cheating left on their careers. Niewierowski explained his actions, saying, "I simply needed the money."

Muehlbauer and Litchfield seemed ignorant of the consequences of what they were doing. And Muehlbauer's mother expressed her confusion, "He was a home boy. He'd go to the movies. He drank Pepsi Cola and milk."[57] Of the four, Gallagher perhaps had the best reason for taking the money because he had a wife and child to support.[60]

The scandal, investigation, and trial did not end commercialism in college athletics, did not reduce the glare of publicity, and did not alter high-powered recruiting at State and Carolina. These aspects of intercollegiate sport were temporarily reduced, but competition in the Atlantic Coast Conference soon restored them. A few of the gamblers received prison terms, but no one believes that gambling ended, although certain players stopped shaving points. The only enduring result of the 1961 scandal was the end of the Dixie Classic.

FOOTNOTES

1. Eliot Asinof, *Eight Men Out: The Black Sox and the 1919 World Series* (New York: Holt, Rinehart and Winston, 1963). Nineteenth century and early twentieth century sports scandals are discussed in the chapter entitled, "Fixes," in George Gipe, *The Great American Sport Book* (Garden City, New York: Doubleday & Company, Inc., 1978), pp. 16-38, see especially pp. 16-18 and 22-23.

2. Fear that the newspaper was becoming a handicapper's guide for betting on North Carolina State University's varsity teams was expressed as early as 1936. See the testimony of A.E. Bowen, Anderson-Sermon Hearings, Faculty Council Meeting, December 17, 1936, Athletic Council Records, Box 4, Volume 1, p. 111, NCSU University Archives (hereinafter cited as UA).

3. Charles Rosen, *Scandals of '51: How the Gamblers Almost Killed College Basketball* (New York: Holt Rinehart and Winston, 1978), p. 28.

4. *Ibid.*, p. 29; Stanley Cohen, *The Game They Played* (New York: Farrar, Straus and Giroux, 1977), pp. 63-67.

5. Cohen, *The Game They Played*, pp. 67-68.

6. Rosen, *Scandals*, pp. 30-32.

7. Case explained the procedures he had adopted after the 1951 scandals in a letter to Athletic Director Roy B. Clogsten, May 17, 1961, "Athletics (Special Folder), "Chancellor's Office, Box 91, UA: His efforts grew out of the NCAA suggestion that coaches take some action (see 1951 NCAA Memo to member institutions, Athletic Department, Box 5, UA). Case also discussed these procedures in an interview, *Fayetteville Observer*, May 14, 1961, "Fix Scandal File," Information Services, Box 2, UA.

8. Rosen, *Scandals of '51*, pp. 23-26.

9. Cohen, *The Game They Played*, p. 227.

10. *Ibid.*, pp. 228-229.

11. *Ibid.*, pp. 229-232.

12. Rosen. *Scandals*, pp. 190-198.

13. *Ibid.*, p. 200.

14. "Observations of James H. Weaver, Atlantic Coast Conference Commissioner," February 4, 1961, in "Fix Scandal File," Information Services Box 2 UA; *Durham Herald*, May 14, 1961; *Raleigh Times*, May 15, 1961.

15. Caldwell to Roy B. Clogston, May 5, 1961, "Fix Scandal File," Information Services, Box 2, UA: The signed statements are in "Athletics (Special Folder)," Chancellor's Office, Box 91, UA.

16. Frank Weedon Deposition, June 16, 1961, "Athletics (Special Folder)," Chancellor's Office, Box 91, UA.

17. Case testimony reported in *News and Observer* (Raleigh), November 28, 1961. Clogston to Dean Joe Romoda, Southern Louisiana University, June 6, 1961, Athletic Department Box 5, UA: Smith Barrier Column, *Greensboro Daily News*, May 15, 1961; *Raleigh Times*, May 15, 1961.

18. *Raleigh Times*, May 13-15, 1961; *Greensboro Daily News*, May 14, 1961; *Fayetteville Observer*, May 14, 1951.

19. Litchfield Interview," *Winston-Salem* (North Carolina) *Journal and Sentinel*, May 14, 1961.

20. *News and Observer*, May 14, 1961.

21. *Fayetteville Observer*, May 14, 1961.

22. "Press Release," May 13, 1961, N.C. State News Bureau, Information Services, Box 2, UA. For the withdrawal of the players from the university, see N.C. State, Official Bulletin, April 13, 1961.

23. *Ibid*.

24. "Caldwell's Handwritten Notes," "Athletics (Special Folder)," Chancellor's Office, Box 91, UA.

25. *News and Observer* May 23, 1961 and *Raleigh Times*, May 24, 1961. Caldwell to various university presidents, e.g. President Herbert E. Longenecker, Tulane University, May 31, 1961, "Athletics (Special Folder)," Chancellor's Office, Box 91, UA.

26. Caldwell to Wolfpack Club Members, May 22, 1961, "Athletics (Special Folder)," Chancellor's Office, Box 91, UA.

27. *Ibid*.

28. Caldwell to C.W. Tilson, June 1, 1961, *ibid*.

29. *Greensboro Daily News*, May 15, 1961.

30. *News and Observer*, May 23, 1961; also see *Raleigh Times*, May 15, 1961.

31. *New York Herald Tribune*, May 23, 1961, "Fix Scandal File," Information Services, Box 2, UA.

32. *News and Observer*, May 14, 1964, and Testimony of Donald Michael Gallagher, Stanley Niewierowski, Terry Litchfield, Anton F.P. Muehlbauer, and Lou Barshak in *State vs. Dave Louis Goldberg and Steve Likometros*, Supreme Court of North Carolina, 1963.

33. *News and Observer*, May 23, 1961.

34. Caldwell's Handwritten Notes," "Athletics (Special Folder)," Chancellor's Office, Box 91, UA.

35. Clogston to Chuck Erickson, Dec. 16, 1959, Athletic Dept., Box 3, UA.

36. Caldwell to Cogston, May 22, 1961, "Athletics (Special Folder)," Chancellor's Office, Box 91, UA.

37. Walter F. Anderson, Director, State Bureau of Investigation, to John H. Caldwell, June 7, 1961, report on "Basketball Irregularities, File Number M-1858," and "Handwritten Notes on SBI taped Interview with Kenneth Rohloff," "Athletics (Special Folder)," Chancellor's Office, Box 91, UA.

38. "Draft Letter to Kenneth L. Rohoff," June 16, 1961, and Caldwell to Rohloff, June 19, 1961, ibid. This letter was printed in the *News and Observer*, June 20, 1961.

39. *Raleigh Times*, June 20, 28, 1961.

40. *Ibid*.

41. May 15, 1961.

42. May 15, 1961.

43. May 16, 1961.

44. May 28, 1861, in "Fix Scandal File," Information Services, Box 2, UA.

45. *Technician*, May 15, 1961.

46. Caldwell to Wolfpack Club members, May 22, 1961, "Athletes (Special Folder)," Chancellor's Office, Box 91, UA.

47. Letters to Caldwell and transcripts of television and radio editorials are contained in Chancellor's Office, Box 91, UA.

48. Caldwell to C.W. Tilson, June 1, 1961, "Athletics (Special Folder)."

49. *Ibid*.

50. Don S. Kimrey, President, Raleigh Merchants, Inc., to John T. Caldwell, June 1, 1961 (with copy to Governor Terry Sanford), and William Friday, President, the Consolidated Univesity, to Kimrey, June 2, 1961; Caldwell to Selby B. Jones, June 6, 1961, ibid.

51. *Raleigh News*, May 25, 1961, and *News and Observer*, May 26, 1961.

52. James to Caldwell, June 14, 1961, Athletics Dept., Box 5, UA.

53. Caldwell to Clogston, Jan. 6, 1962, and Case to Wolfpack Club members, Oct. 25, 1962, ibid.

54. From newspaper clippings in "Fix Scandal File," Information Servies, Box 2, UA.

55. *Daily Independence* (Kannapolis, NC), May 14, 1961.

56. *Greensboro Daily News*, May 15, 1961.

57. *News and Observer*, Jan. 10, 1962.

58. *News and Observer*, March 22, 1962.

59. *State vs. Dave Louis Goldberg and Steve Lekometros*, 1963.

60. Niewierowski testimony, *ibid.*, p. 317; *News and Observer*, Jan. 10, 1962.

Chapter 7

The Immorality of Big-Power Intercollegiate Athletics

Ewald B. Nyquist
Pace University, New York

The central issue in big-power athletics is moral, not educational, not economic, not fiscal, not social—*moral*—what is right and what is wrong. What is morally wrong cannot be educationally right. Big-power semiprofessional athletics are incompatible with the values associated with higher learning. To be immoral means that one violates moral principles knowingly. That is not true of everyone at fault in athletics. People may violate morality without evil intent, perhaps by moral blindness or by indifference. As Professor Alasdair MacIntyre of Vanderbilt University states in his new book, *After Virtue*, we have lost our comprehension, both theoretical and practical of morality. He strikes a chord when he laments and diagnoses our lack of consensus about basic moral values and states that as a liberal democracy, we have placed great value on pluralism and tolerance of divergent views; however, things seem to have gotten out of hand (Hook, 1983:25-26).

Harold Enarson, who finally had the guts to fire Woody Hayes at Ohio State, said recently,

> We live in an era in which shoddiness surrounds and drowns us in its pretenses. The sorriest president of the sorriest university in the meanest state of this land orates about the zeal of excellence. Nonsense! The impulse for mediocrity, for safety, and for security, is the strongest and more dominant impulse in our society. (Enarson, 1983)

More than one prominent spokesman for higher education is disturbed by the seeming purposelessness and drifting nature of higher education.

As Frank Rhodes, president of Cornell University said recently, we are all for a sense of purpose but against any particular direction. So few institutions seem to claim any moral or intellectual tradition. A university's service to society could be interpreted as a response to market demand as "opposed to collective moral and intellectual judgment." Thus stated Professor Thomas Bender of New York University in criticizing effectively a book by the president of Harvard entitled, *Social Responsibilities of the Modern University*. He continues by saying that universities must have the courage to stand for something substantive or else how can they be defended; a university worth affirming must have an ethos, a sense of its own integrity (Bender, 1982).

Nothing is so important for educational institutions over the long haul as to draw out man's common humanity and thus create a better community, one that will be tolerant, compassionate, just, and humane. Put that credo in juxtaposition to the scurrilous and opprobrious behavior in the conduct of big-power intercollegiate sports, and one is struck by the moral contrast. It almost seems, for example, that being put on probation by NCAA is fashionable. After all, as Dave Anderson of the *New York Times* has remarked, it surfaces to exquisite public view the proof for alumni and boosters that the institution is trying to win (Anderson, 1982).

All moral authority is founded on justice. Surely there are some transcending values that operate or should operate more universally in our society as well as in sports. What are they? Let's try equity, justice, honesty, humaneness, and trust for starters and the belief that the individual human being is still the fundamental unit of value in our society.

SPORTS IN SOCIETY

As it is, sports are a metaphor of society. The values in the latter are reflected in the former. The only problem is that athletics in the collegiate form are associated with institutions of higher learning, secular churches, really, that ought to stand for something. Someone has said that sports are the social cement of our national life. School children in Washington, D.C., were permitted to skip school to watch the Washington Redskins' victory parade. They did not get that same permission when the President was inaugurated.

We are a nation of scofflaws. Transgressions in traffic laws are rampant. Stop means go in a traffic signal. Graffiti abound; marijuana and cocaine affect all classes. One is ashamed of the American propensity for littering our environment—the parks, the forests, the cities, the highways. No place is immune. In athletics, disregard of ethical and legal boundaries, as is the case in society, goes far beyond so-called minor transgressions. They include, besides illegal use and sale of drugs, fraud, assault, rape, robbery, larceny, sexual and racial discrimination, and dehumanization.

TV, money, entertainment—these have made a difference. Power and money are the supreme troublemakers in our society. Power is winning every Saturday and being "numero uno" in the Monday polls, and money consists of operating a self-sustaining business enterprise with an entertainment function under the guise of teaching character and educating for values. If the purpose of learning, as author Robertson Davis has said, is to save the soul and enlarge the mind, in many big-power athletics plants, few souls are being redeemed and minds expanded by the values exemplified by their institutions and coaches.

I am well aware of the putative and frequently real virtues of athletics. Paraphrasing liberally William Boyd, former president of the University of Oregon in a recent article, athletics provide personal growth and self-esteem, discipline, concentration and cooperation, self-restraint, and sacrifice for the individual. For society, athletics provide the principal celebration of life, and every society requires festivals. Moreover, athletics provide an open door access to opportunity for upward social mobility for many, which is both an individual and a social benefit. For the institution, athletics help to furnish a binding force that yields a sense of community. Externally, athletics is a window on tne university, albeit a stained glass window these days (Boyd, 1980). Athletics can help to build an image of superiority, attract money, build community support, and influence legislators, although lately, many state university presidents are finding that winning football teams do not restrain legislatures from cutting their budgets. An image is often what the public thinks about a university when it is not thinking very hard.

While bad practices and abuses have not been uncharacteristic of intercollegiate athletics in other generations, the 1960s accelerated a decline in integrity in athletics, much as that decade witnessed a decline in the quality, academic standards, and integrity of higher education generally. The standards for institutional accreditation by regional accrediting agencies have declined over the years; this slippage has coincided with the troubles and counterculture movement of the 1960s when many faculties, pandering to students, pusillanimous in confronting student demands, driven by liberal guilt for minority status and economic disadvantage, along with craven presidential leadership, clearly lowered expectations for learning. Open admissions also added to the decline, not because that policy is not a good one, but because academicians did not know how, or did not want, to cope with great numbers of youth with academic deficiencies, especially the poor and minority groups. Compassion became suspended judgment.

Steve Bailey of Harvard, now deceased, once provided some motives for or causes of slovenliness in academic marketing and standards. He mentioned reaping the results of the transition over decades from an elitist system of higher education to an egalitarian one, with the additional assumption by higher education of nonacademic social purposes, like athletics, for instance. Others were "the trivialization of learning that stems from the contemporary saliency of customer convenience and job-hunger," trying to ensure institutional survival and forestalling the threat of going out of business, and coping with the uncongenial factors of demographic declines and diminished resources. He concluded that there must be "way-stations between snobbery and slobbery and that equality and quality are not sworn enemies" (Bailey, 1979).

COMMERCIALIZED SPORTS

Recently, I gave a speech on what I call the commercialization of higher education. It becomes less easy to distinguish between so-called nonprofit higher institutions and proprietary organizations. For one thing, the ethics, tactics, and taste employed by some colleges in their self-interest leave one aghast—or at least thunder and struck, as James Thurber used to say. The techniques of the corporate world and the language of Madison Avenue ad-libbing have invaded the noble halls of learning. "College development drives lavish courtship rites upon their patrons that are worthy of flamboyant Hollywood." Newspaper and magazine advertising for students is absolutely commercial in language and tone. Odius comparisons are made to the disadvantage of other, named institutions, often with the use of superlatives. Cheaper tuition rates are cited for better quality than provided by rival institutions. One institution in New York even advertises a second semester sale: Sign up for 12 credits and pay for 9. As competition for money and students grows more intense, colleges seem to be less willing to impose standards on themselves.

There are other evidences of commercialization of higher education. Some institutions are intentionally modeling themselves after big business corporations, bottom-line and all. There is a dangerous trend that may affect the integrity of universities, namely, a kind of companionate marriage between industry and research universities. One is tempted to recall and rephrase what Gerald Ford, as a Congressman, once said about Abraham Lincoln on Lincoln's birthday: If Robert Hutchins were alive today, he would turn over in his grave. Hutchins made it perfectly clear that while universities were modeled after business corporations, they were first of all a center of independent thought.

It has taken me a while to come to the morals of big-power athletics, but I hope I have made the case that society, universities and colleges, and athletics are all of a piece, inseparable. As Professor Patrick Morgan of Washington University has said,

> Higher education has become vastly more important to the daily concerns and activities of society. A perfect example of higher education's increasing involvement in society is...athletics. It is big business, big entertainment, and a big component of Americans' leisure time. Higher education provides cheap instruction in athletics for millions, is a major customer of sports equipment suppliers, serves as a farm system for the major professional sports, employs thousands who have made sports a career, provides mass entertainment, and generates a good portion of the news in sports pages and publications. (Morgan, 1983)

What are we to think of such practices and behavior as the following?

- credit for nonattendance in snap courses at remote extension centers;
- keeping athletes eligible by inducing them to take a smorgasbord of intellectually undemanding courses, the floss and the souffles of the curriculum, totally unrelated to established degree requirements, making it possible to make normal academic progress toward a degree and, hence, graduation;
- the financial power of outside booster clubs to direct the athletic programs at some universities and to buy players and coaches;
- the total disregard of established regular admissions standards in order to make allowances for otherwise inadmissible, nearly illiterate athletes who either have shallow gene-pools to begin with, or else through no fault of their own, because of poor secondary schooling and poverty status, do not know their elbows from their end zones or their acids from their bases;
- the incestuous relationships between some community colleges and universities whereby sweetheart arrangements are made that (a) permit coaches to season athletes with poor high school records in easy courses in the community college allowing them then to transfer with acceptable grade averages, or else (b) permit coaches unethically to exceed the limit of their athletic scholarships by placing excess athletes temporarily in the junior colleges;
- false promises of financial assistance;
- the uncivilized, dehumanizing, and demeaning behavior of some coaches guilty of harassment and verbal abuse as well as excessive physical conditioning drills as punishment for errors, resulting in injuries;
- actual physical assault and abuse, including the use of an axe handle to punish lazy football players at Morris Brown College;
- fraudulent transcripts, both high school and college, and illegal transfer of credit;
- illegal cash payments, free use of cars, gifts, purchases of clothes, TV and stereo sets, alleged payments by outside supporters for abortions for girl friends of athletes; and
- the frequent recruitment of foreign athletes who are given false promises of financial assistance by institutions intensely concerned with remaining competitive. (Recruiters go abroad on safaris, not recruiting trips.)

There are several instances of athletes suing their universities for several causes, among them breach of contract and misrepresentation that promised full scholarships but furnished loans instead; not receiving anything even remotely resembling a college education; and soliciting worker's compensation for injuries received on the playing field.

The courts have been sharp-tempered, cynical, and acerb in their decisions in denouncing universities for their practices. Witness the basketball coach at the

University of New Mexico who is convicted of 21 of 22 counts of fraud and the filing of false public vouchers for expenses incurred on behalf of the basketball program. The judge deferred any sentence, put the coach on unsupervised probation for one year, and ordered the dismissal of all counts after one year of good behavior. The judge stated that his court was being asked to be hypocritical in enforcing a double standard and to sentence a man because he got caught, not because his conduct was unacceptable.

In the case of the University of Minnesota, a judge restored a scholarship to a basketball player and ordered the university to put the athlete in a degree-granting program, so he could be eligible for a fourth year of play. Moreover, the judge stated that the athlete had been deprived of due process, had a constitutionally protected private interest under the due process clause of the Constitution, and that the private interest at stake was the player's ability to obtain a no-cut contract with the National Basketball Players Association.

Listen to Coach Jim Valvano, basketball coach of North Carolina State, whose transfer from Iona College in New York raised our state's average. As an editorial in the *New York Times* reported:

> We're not even really part of the school anymore, anyway. I work for the North Carolina State Athletic Association. That has nothing to do with the university. Our funding is totally independent. You think the chancellor is going to tell me what to do? Who to take into school or not to take into school? I doubt it.

I also note the sentencing of Rick Kuhn, a basketball player at big-power Boston College, to 10 years in prison for shaving points. The moral is, if you can be hired to shoot baskets, you can also be hired to miss them. Sometimes I do not understand these Jesuit colleges. Take the well-documented and televised case of Kevin Ross who played basketball at Creighton University for 4 years, and at the end, was still almost a year and a half short of a degree. Creighton University is paying his way in a famous private ghetto prep school in Chicago. When tested there, he was at the second grade level in achievement in the basics. As of last fall he was enrolled in the seventh grade. A TV documentary shows him in the seventh grade class, answering a question correctly to the applause of his 11-year-old classmates.

I deplore the harassment, the boorish, uncivil, and unethical conduct of students and fans at games, especially at basketball games in closed arenas. The coaches, themselves, do not set the best of examples.

You remember Woody Hayes of Ohio State, who was seen on national television hitting an opposing player who intercepted a pass. (Woody's hero was General Patton.) What about the snarling basketball coach at Indiana University, Bobby Knight, a cross between Billy Martin and Woody Hayes. He was ejected for misbehavior from a game in the Pan American Games a few years ago, held in Puerto Rico, and was later arrested by Puerto Rican authorities and taken to jail in handcuffs for alleged assault of a police officer.

Then there is Frank Kush, football coach and reputed sadist, who was sued by a player for physical punishment and mental harassment. Twenty-two legal documents were filed showing that when Kush felt pain or fear was needed to get better performance, he would kick players in the legs and buttocks, hit them in the face and abdomen and strike them with steel bars, wooden dowels, ropes, boards, and sticks. After leaving Arizona State, he was hired by the Baltimore Colts.

I wonder about values when I see the University of Washington proposing to drop 24 degree programs because of fiscal austerity in the state, while its football team, Rose Bowl winner in 1982 and still a contending big-power, is separately and fully funded, undiminished in its outside support.

In the same year Bear Bryant was earning $104,000 in base salary, receiving $300,000 in radio and television income and $46,000 in various benefits, not to mention other monetary rewards, the University of Alabama lost its doctoral accreditation by the National Commission on Accreditation of Teacher Education, an accrediting agency that is quite probably the least respected in the higher education community. Add to that, pay increases for 9,800 faculty and staff have had to be deferred because of a projected shortfall in state revenues.

Concerning salaries, the $287,000 per year in money and benefits given to Jackie Sherrill at the Texas A&M University, exceeding anything any full distinguished professor receives in oil-rich Texas or the compensation of any Nobel prize winner anywhere, was thus justified in answer to criticism by the chairman of the university's board of trustees: "Higher education is a business, and I think Sherrill's contract is part of that process." It should also be noted that Bo Schembechler, football coach at the University of Michigan, was offered the Texas A&M position first but turned it down, saying at a news conference, "There are other things in the world more important than money—that's why I'm staying at Michigan." He was then given a $25,000-a-year raise in his base salary, from $60,000 to $85,000.

Of concern also is the letter of intent athletes must sign and that cannot be broken without losing a year of eligibility. If coaches can break a legal contract promise, why can't students break their simple pledges? Isn't there some not so obscure moral principle at stake here?

It seems to me that too many coaches and too many institutions are totally unfettered by a conception of good faith, good sportsmanship, or by ethical and moral precepts in athletics. The rule seems to be that of self- or institutional interest: One must, on occasion, rise above principle.

BLACK ATHLETES

Some statistics reveal other moral dilemmas and badly ordered priorities. It should be an embarrassment to predominantly white universities that have a greater proportion of blacks on their intercollegiate football and basketball teams than they have in their general student populations. It is astounding that this is especially true of southern and southwestern institutions, many of which have resisted racial integration under federal court orders with a passionate zeal worthy of affluent white suburbs undergoing public school racial desegregation. Fifty-four of Bear Bryant's last football team numbering over a hundred were black. It is an easy bet that the general student body does not number more than 5 to 10% blacks. Texas A&M probably has a similar ratio.

There is a serious question of substantial exploitation of athletes, especially black athletes. Tempting athletes by extolling the value of sports as a ladder for upward social and economic mobility has appeal and is demonstrable in many cases. However, it is less a ladder than an optical illusion precisely because the path really is a funnel turned upside down—many climb but few emerge at the top. The odds are at least 10,000 to 1 against a high school athlete ever signing a pro contract. By one estimate, only 2% of high school athletes ever sign professional contracts and only 1 or 2% of college players will play professional football or basketball. A pro career lasts about 3 to 4 years. Statistically, it is easier to become a doctor or a lawyer than a professional athlete.

Almost two-thirds of all collegiate basketball and football players fail to earn a degree during their 4 years in college. About four out of five NBA players do not have diplomas. Harry Edwards, a distinguished black professor at the University of California at Berkeley, once found that about 75% of black scholarship athletes did not graduate, even the ones who came with 2 years of junior college.

A few years ago, the University of Miami shamelessly produced a four-color recruiting poster captioned "A Pipeline to the Pros" that included pictures of its players who made it. Miami, of course, is now on probation, and I note that its president, along with one or two other presidents whose institutions are on probation, have recently made strong, but late-in-the-day, pious statements about the importance of cleaning up collegiate athletics.

Racism permeates many segments of collegiate athletics and results in discrimination and inequitable and exploitative treatment. Increasingly in our society, there is ample evidence that there is a diminishing concern for the plight of minority groups and for the maintenance of civil rights. That evidence is clear in federal policies and practices, in the fact that blacks are entering college and form a lesser proportion than before, in the alarming diminished concern for affirmative action, and even in the retrogression in providing equal opportunity, including equitable treatment of women.

The growing indifference to minority groups, especially blacks, is a part of moral failure in our society and in our higher institutions. What goes on in intercollegiate athletics is one part of it. At stake is a matter of equity and justice, and, as I have expressed earlier, all moral authority is founded on justice.

WOMEN ATHLETES

Along that same vein, another injustice is that of the continuing biases against the equitable treatment of women in higher education, particularly with respect to athletics. Higher institutions do not like the imposition of legislative controls and the mandates of court decisions, but without them, a great deal of social movements and changes would not have taken place in our colleges and universities: The courts and the threat of going out of business are the biggest educational innovators around. Although great progress has been made, there is still some distance to go.

While I have great admiration for Father Hesburgh, President of the University of Notre Dame, I also know the now coeducational Notre Dame has been one of the most vociferous opponents of Title IX which ensures equity for women. A couple of years ago, Notre Dame offered no athletic scholarships for women, while, of course, basketball, football, and hockey were fully subsidized. Now Notre Dame defends giving athletic scholarships to women in proportion to their enrollment in the university, but not counting the scholarships for football and basketball. That is, the ratio of men to women at Notre Dame is 70 to 30. All grants-in-aid, except for men's football and basketball, are apportioned approximately 70% to men and 30% to women. It takes a determined effort to achieve a desired end to accept that logic with equanimity.

While many colleges have been so evangelical in promoting the benefits of athletics for men and in devoting huge resources on their behalf, that same zeal has not been mustered in preaching the identical gospel for women. As legal and social provisions for equitable treatment of women and their access to opportunity in athletics have increased, their positions in professional decision making, such as athletic directors, and in coaching jobs have declined. Eighty percent of all athletics departments are now merged. Fifteen percent still have separate men's and women's departments. About 5% are at women's colleges, but less than 1% of Division I departments are headed by women and there is a continuing decline: Women are endangered species in athletic positions.

But infractions and abuses in athletics are now neuter in gender. There is no reason to believe that women are more virtuous than men, for money and power also lead women into temptation and often astray.

Some further statistics: 30% of the participants in college are women, but women are 51% of the student population. Female students have 16-18% of the athletics budgets and 20-21% of the athletics scholarships. There is a leveling of expenditures for women in athletics across the world. Women's programs are taking cuts for the first time since 1972. Sports are being dropped for which the former AIAW sponsored championships, but for which that macho organization, the NCAA, the dominant organization, has no championships (for example, badminton, softball, archery) despite the fact that four of the five sports involved are Olympic events. This fact strongly supports the view that sports for women are forced into a major-minor configuration with institutions tending to drop those that are minor. I have developed Nyquist's second law of predictable consequences of fiscal austerity: Whenever higher education is faced with diminished resources, women (and blacks) will suffer disproportionately in access to and equality of opportunity.

THE NCAA

I should now like to turn to one of my favorite subjects, the National Collegiate Athletic Association. Let us begin with the matter of integrity and control of the campus. Prestigiously sponsored reports in recent years, entitled *Fair Practices in Higher Education, The Integrity of Higher Education*, and, more recently, one by Ernest Boyer entitled *Control of the Campus*, do not so much as mention the lack of integrity in the institutional conduct of intercollegiate athletics, or the outside control exercised by athletic organizations over institutional internal affairs concerning athletics.

The NCAA is a prime infringer on the inner sanctum of institutional autonomy and increasingly encompasses within its purview greater portions of the administrative and academic prerogatives of higher institutions. It has become a monopolistic cartel in intercollegiate athletics. Not being satisfied with dominance in male athletics, it has now absorbed women's athletics as well. Furthermore, big-power institutions have increasingly come to dominate internal NCAA policy to the extent that greedy competition for TV money has threatened the organization, itself, in a proposal to form divisions of down-graded institutions on the basis of criteria that have absolutely nothing to do with education (e.g., attendance at games, size of stadiums). There is good evidence that the NCAA and the College Football Association exist to defend the economic interests of their members; property rights and profits are the dominant concerns, not the education of athletes.

The NCAA has become a guardian of the academic, administrative, and admissions morals of higher institutions. It now forbids recruitment of athletes by alumni even though alumni are extensively used by many institutions to recruit students in general. It requires institutions to include in coaches' contracts a provision that a coach may be suspended or fired if he or she violates NCAA rules.

What can be said about an organization which runs a deficit because of $2.3 million in legal fees in one year, up $1.5 million from the year before, and another $1.5 million projected for next year? These deficits result from antitrust suits involving Georgia and Oklahoma, who are challenging NCAA football television policy, and from the AIAW.

It has been said that money ranks with love as the greatest source of pleasure and with death as the greatest source of anxiety. Television money has induced universities to shift their football games to mornings, to Thursday evenings, and to Sunday afternoons (during the professional football strike); to playing consecutive basketball games on short notice on highly compressed schedules with no regard for the players; to continuing attempts to reorganize NCAA internally in order to narrow the big-power group that generates and receives the most TV income; to the formation of the CFA, the big-power football institutions, purely for the purpose of self-aggrandizement of power and money. Surely the huge sums of golden TV dollars have caused many institutions to become venal and exploitative. Changing the eligibility rule a few years ago to permit freshmen to play reflects, as a writer has said, a quantum jump in priorities from books to TV megabucks.

Take note also that ABC and CBS will pay $264 million to NCAA for broadcasting football games in the next 4 years, and CBS will pay $16 million a year to broadcast the basketball championships in the next 3 years.

The present egregious state of big-power athletics and the short half-life of the reforms of the past can be charged in great part to the indifference, ignorance, or cooperation of university presidents and other administrative and academic officials, and, of course, trustees. The rhetoric of reform in the past reminds one of the warrior monuments in the Washington, D.C. parks: The posture is heroic, the sword is held high, but the movement is nil. For the past half-year or so, we have witnessed an unprecedented outpouring of presidential concern which, of course, correlates perfectly with the culmination this past year of a growing series of scandalous revelations. My nomination for a hero's award from the American Council of Education or even the NCAA among university presidents goes to Father John Lo Schiavo, President of the University of San Francisco. (Here's where the Jesuits redeem themselves). He abolished big-power basketball last summer because he could not control alumni boosters who paid athletes, and for which the University had twice been put on NCAA probation in the last few years.

One can admire or commend the emergence of presidents as a force in NCAA affairs; however, one may criticize the proposals stemming from the American Council on Education—sponsored ad hoc group and adopted by the NCAA in January of this year. Recall, however, that there was not a black university president in the group. There have been many unconvincing rationalizations of why this grave mistake was made.

Other than that I have serious reservations about letting NCAA determine academic requirements for eligibility in athletics, I can applaud the efforts (a) to raise the high school gradepoint average requirement to 2.0 while also requiring an academic high school curriculum of basic subjects in order for athletes to qualify for playing in their freshman year; and (b) to insist on maintenance of satisfactory progress toward a degree. These particular requirements will have a general salutary effect on secondary schools, but they are hardly stringent requirements or cause for trumpeting.

ADMISSION STANDARDS

As an aside, higher institutions can take much of the blame for flabbiness in the secondary school curriculum and the decline of quality therein for several reasons, including in the last couple of decades, undemanding requisites for admission and incoherent or ambiguous curricular requirements. The secondary schools have not been given a message on what to expect.

I do take strong exception to requiring a minimum combined score of 700 on the Scholastic Aptitude Test or 15 on the American College Testing examination, low as those scores are. What are the likely consequences of this requirement?

1. About a third of those now playing football and basketball in Division I schools would not have been admitted, or, if admitted, been permitted to play during the freshman year, even though grades and especially test scores are not infallible predictors.
2. Minority groups, particularly blacks, are disproportionately affected. About half of the male blacks who take the SAT score below 700 (60% for female blacks); about 28% of blacks have scores above 15 on the ACT test. In the Big 8 conference, an analysis shows that 60% of the black athletes now attending would have been barred from competition in their freshman year, this affecting only about 10-27% of white athletes. At one institution, over 80% of the black athletes would have been barred. The historically black colleges in Division I would be especially affected.
3. While athletes can be admitted as freshmen and even receive scholarships, though they could not play because they do not meet the requirements, it is highly improbable that coaches are going to deplete their varsity playing squads by this kind of warehousing. The consequence, then, is that many economically disadvantaged athletes, especially blacks, are going to be deprived of a college education and a chance for upward mobility. It seems to me that the ill-considered test-score requirement is yet another indication of the new conservatism, the increasing apathy and indifference to minority groups and the economically disadvantaged.

It would have been much better if there had been a return to a former rule, namely, the one that barred freshmen from playing at all. Some now play before they take their first classes. Combine such a rule with requirements for making satisfactory normal progress toward a degree in one's own institution after satisfying an institution's own *regular* admissions requirements, serious charges could have been avoided and justice would have prevailed. The Reverend Jesse Jackson and some angry black university presidents will, I am confident, bring about wholesome changes in the test-score requirement.

However, I am uncertain whether this new group of requirements will make the great difference expected. How does one monitor normal or satisfactory progress toward a degree or the new academic admissions requirements? One way to cheat, among others, is to channel recruits to community colleges who can later transfer. I predict that community colleges will become a prime recruiting ground. Moreover, how does one prevent the doctoring of high school transcripts, an abuse that is not now infrequent?

Therefore, the emergence of college and university presidents as a force in NCAA is totally desirable. Can the involvement of presidents be sustained? Probably not. One may hope that the presidents can force a change in the governance structure of NCAA that will ensure a major role for presidents in the conduct of that organization.

I would rather see, though, all aspects of athletics—from admissions to financial aid, to academic counseling, for all expenditures and income from whatever source, for responsibility for the fulfillment of regular degree requirements, and for making normal progress through to graduation—placed under the regular offices in an institution responsible for these requirements, functions, and procedures for all students, with all of it under the firm and exclusive control of the president and faculty. It would also help to have all regional accrediting agencies include athletics in their evaluation procedures.

Does no one find it regrettable that an ad hoc group under the sponsorship of the American Council on Education, after its attempt at what I call "grope dynamics," finds it necessary to go hat-in-hand to the NCAA convention and lobby for changes that affect their own institutions? They should be brave enough to make these changes at home without help from an organization (the NCAA) that is constituted by those same institutions and in which they have membership. What those presidents have said in effect is this: We as presidents representing institutions cannot be trusted to be without wickedness in these affairs. You, the NCAA, must monitor us so that we, the presidents, can get on with other important things, like raising money and building public relations.

Can things be turned around? I am optimistic, but I have no hope. There is something endemic in the American public that, given the vicarious pleasures and psychological catharses, some of them are biologically founded in primordial urges of watching violent sports; there is something endemic that overlooks or even invites misbehavior, however immoral. I doubt that the public will want competition of a lesser quality in what has become a secular religion (or a minor branch of theology). In addition, the media, especially sportswriters (except for the *New York Times*), really act more like advocates than critics of big-power athletics, abuses and all. Finally, I wonder how long presidential concern and oversight will last. It has not in the past in similar eras of abuse and aroused concern.

There is a clear need for self-regulation and renewed institutional leadership in college and university affairs, but as Fred Hechinger has said, What are the prospects when "trustees too often are fearful of appointing strong and outspoken university presidents, and especially after the riotous 1960s, have looked for safe crisis managers, fundraisers, and compromisers"?

REFERENCES

ANDERSON, D. (1982, February 7). *New York Times*.

BAILEY. S.K. (1979). *Academic quality control: The case of college programs on military bases*, American Association for Higher Education.

BENDER, T. (1982, May 23). *New York Times Book Review*.

BOYD, W.B. (1980, Summer). A commentary on collegiate athletics, College Board Review, No. 116.

ENARSON, H. (1983, Winter). Educational Record.

HOOK, J. (1983, March 9). Selling the idea of virtue in an amoral society, Chronicle of Higher Education, pp. 25-26.

MORGAN, P.M., (1983, Winter). Higher education in a conservative era, Educational Record.

Chapter 8

Boosterism, Scarce Resources, and Institutional Control: The Future of American Intercollegiate Athletics

James H. Frey
University of Nevada, Las Vegas

American intercollegiate athletics face a resource dilemma of a magnitude unlike any confronted in their exciting, yet controversial history. Despite a trail of crises, mostly of an ethical nature, growth and expansion seemed to be the norm, especially in the 1960s and early 1970s. More sports, including those for women participants, were added to already lengthy lists on most campuses; television served as a cornucopian funnel of dollars and visibility to national regulatory bodies for dispersion to members; fans were attending at stadium-bursting rates; and intercollegiate events had captured the hearts and minds of students, faculties, and administrators. In some cases, these same events were even promoted as major folkloristic celebrations or public art forms crucial to the survival of American society (Cady, 1978; Novack, 1976). The picture, indeed, was rosy, until recently.

During the last 5 to 7 years, many college athletic programs have fallen on hard times largely because the trends of tax-cutting legislation, mandated growth in women's sports, and large inflationary bites out of the American leisure time and charitable dollar. In addition, revelations of scandal and impropriety, of discrimination and inequality, of education irresponsibility, and illegal financial wizardy have presented additional obstacles to justifying the growth and expansion of athletic programs. There is also evidence that fewer quality athletes are available to fill the labor pool required to maintain high-level programs. Thus, faced with resource supply problems in the form of labor and capital unlike any previously encountered, college and university athletic decision makers will have to make some hard choices in the 1980s.

It is not clear what the future of intercollegiate sports will bring in the face of this dilemma. Some of these programs continue to grow and prosper, some will suffer drastic change, and some will possibly experience a structural "demise." It is my prediction that American intercollegiate athletics will evolve into a formalized two-class system with a small, elite group of institutions maintaining very prosperous and visible programs; and a larger, but less fortunate group will operate programs of limited scope, if they have any at all. The major source of survival for the elite corps of programs rests with their ability to draw maximum resources from an organizational coalition of athletic administrators and alumni/boosters who represent the political and economic power in the community or region contiguous to the institution. The role of this coalition in the maintenance, and even survival, of athletic programs will be more prominent than that of the faculty, students, or even college presidents (Frey, 1982). Thus, the 1980s may be the last hurrah for a number of college athletic programs; but, it may also be a time of even greater glory for the group able to survive the current resource procurement problems.

ATHLETIC BOOSTERISM: THE POLITICAL AND ECONOMIC REALITY

Boosterism has a long history in America, particularly in association with colleges (Boorstin, 1965). As the country grew and expanded, a group of individuals, usually the economic elite of an area, took on the task of promoting their community in order to attract capital investment and political visibility. They were optimistic, growth-oriented, and willing to take risks even if it meant going outside the law (1965, p. 3). An easy way to mark a community as "up and coming" or destined for greatness was to establish hallmarks of permanence and legitimacy. According to Boorstin, these were a newspaper, a hotel, and a college. Not to boost a community showed total lack of community spirit and a lack of business sense (1965, p. 117). A college in town not only enhanced the image of a community, but it also increased land values; that is, it was profitable for the booster. It was only natural that colleges be promoted and controlled by boosters because this was the way American institutions were established by community, not royal or ecclesiastical decree. If a social unit did not have the support of the booster element, it usually could not survive politically or economically. In the case of the college and universities, boosters gravitated to athletics because these elements were able to generate instantaneous visibility and support. The attachment of boosters to athletic programs, as opposed to their academic counterparts, gave the former significant power and a high degree of operational autonomy.

For generations intercollegiate athletic programs have been able to operate from a position of political autonomy and priority because a coalition of alumni/ boosters, coaches, and athletic administrators represented a formidable structure of allies. The booster-alumnus provided the interconnection with the business and the political world; the coach provided the winning product; and, the administrator guided the athletic program through the academic maze. The promotion of athletics was enhanced by support from academic administrators, even in the face of faculty distress over the emphasis on athletics. Presidents supported athletics because they believed that a winning program attracted students, financial contributions, and favorable legislative appropriations. Athletics was apparently the only element of higher education which could unite all of its diverse constituencies.

It was good business to promote athletics, particularly a winning athletic program. Businessmen saw athletics as a stimulus to their profits, and because most athletic programs ran deficits, even in their early history, it was only natural that they "boost" the activity with a financial subsidy.[1] These boosters/alumni were viewed as necessary to the development and maintenance of a "big time" athletic program because legislative appropriations, university budgets, or gate receipts did not provide sufficient funds for a high-level program (Atwell et al., 1980). Faculties were either disinterested or had given up all hope of rekindling educational goals with athletes; or professors became the athletic department's greatest fans. Students, who once controlled intercollegiate athletics, willingly gave up decision-making authority when interschool contests became too complex for their administration, too expensive to operate, and too important to alumni (Lucas & Smith, 1978).

It was only a matter of time before college presidents, faculty, and students would lose the control battle because they do not have the resources to compete with those available to the booster coalition. Academics could not fund and supervise an athletic program with extrinsic, commercial goals; a booster coalition could, and still does today. If the latter can provide the money, then it can also command some power in athletic decision-making. Therein lies the focal point of the current controversy over "institutional control," that is, the academic institution's ability to run the athletic program consistent with its policy and goals, not necessarily with those of community interests.

The booster coalition is represented by three forms of organizational affiliation with the university athletic departments. The first usually takes on a name like "Cougar Club" or "Tiger Club" and maintains a formal connection with university control of funds disbursement. These have come to be known as "booster clubs," and they raise money for athletic departments through various promotions or by soliciting direct gifts, either in-kind or cash. These groups will also subsidize coaches' salaries, entertain prospective athletes, provide cars for coaches and administrators, and provide influence for political, economic, and media favors on behalf of athletes and athletic programs. Booster Club members have also been known to influence event scheduling to subsidize team travel, and to provide incentives in the form of monetary reward to coaches, administrators, and players.[2] It is these groups which have attracted the most attention from the National Collegiate Athletic Association (NCAA) enforcement division (Evans, 1974; Denlinger & Shapiro, 1975; Looney, 1978).

The nonprofit foundation, incorporated independently of the university, has the major purpose of securing funds for land procurement and capital expansion. Its ability to raise money is amazing. One school in the southeast was able to raise over $4 million in less than a month for a stadium renovation (Marcin, 1979, p. 26). The Sun Angel foundation at Arizona State raised $4.5 million to expand a stadium and to also provide funds for the construction of a baseball field and golf course (1979, p. 26).

A third type of athletic organization which includes booster/alumni association is that of the independently incorporated athletic department. Many "big-time"[3] schools where athletic departments do not receive legislatively appropriated monies (e.g., University of Michigan, University of Kansas) have corporate status with the state apart from the university. This poses questions of accountability to the larger institution and the extent to which credit lines can be negotiated for capital funds with or without university approval. The booster coalition may be able to establish a "hidden interest" in this corporation by virtue of the fact that the independent corporation can exist under rules and procedures that may or may not be consistent with the sponsoring organization. Thus, it is easier to influence an athletic program without the encumbrance of university rules and regulations.

Athletic administrators see a great deal of difficulty in bringing these groups under internal control. In fact, any effort to control these groups has been largely superficial because the need for the resources these groups provide is so great. As a result of the financial dependence of athletic department on booster groups, the latter are able to exercise a great deal of influence, direct or indirect, on athletic policy. Program and personnel decisions often cannot be made without consulting these groups. In fact, these groups will even withhold donations if the current athletic situation is not to their liking (Atwell et al., 1980).

While it is profitable for the athletic department to have affiliated booster organizations, these groups also become the source of tax and other economic benefits for their members.[4] For example, the booster groups can become a major vehicle by which one can attain access to the political and economic elite. Booster membership can be the source of reciprocal business arrangements (e.g., "If you purchase your trucks from me, I'll give you my electrical business"). Booster members also receive "perks" or special treatment from athletic departments in the form of complimentary tickets, free rides on charter flights, and so on.

The affiliation of booster clubs with colleges and universities is not new. What is apparent, however, is that these groups have dropped their general interest in the functioning of the university and concentrated their attention on athletics.[5] This is because academic governance has been financed by government dollars, and private philanthropy is not as significant as it once was. However, more importantly, athletics can do more for booster political and economic interests than can philosophy or sociology. The booster coalition represents a network of individuals who reap economic and political benefit from their common association with athletics. Historically, their power was measured by the ability to attract immigrants to a growing community (Boorstin, 1965); today, that power is measured by the ability to attract high-caliber athletes and coaches to a growing and successful athletic program. The college or university athletic program with a well-organized booster club of political and economic elite will survive in the 1980s; those without will not. The cost of surviving is great—the loss of institutional control of athletics.

INSTITUTIONAL CONTROL: CAN ACADEMIA GOVERN?

Institutional control of athletics by traditional academic means is virtually impossible in the face of the dominance exercise by the booster coalition. This is particularly true for the colleges and universities which belong to Division IA in the NCAA organization. These schools operate the most expansive programs demanding the greatest resources, and they depend a great deal on booster support for their financial survival. Because this group includes the political and economic decision makers of a community, university faculty and administration who are not representative of the elite, have very little influence.

The power of this booster coalition is actually beyond the comprehension of most faculty and academic administrators. The coalition is run by individuals who are used to getting what they want; they make decisions daily involving millions of dollars and thousands of people; and, these are the individuals who have the most political influence. No one faculty member or administrator can stand up to their power. Athletic directors, the modern-day "athletic managers," tend to hold ideological and behavioral similarities to boosters; that is, they are cut of the same mold. Therefore, athletic directors rarely provide a source of resistance to booster enthusiasm and involvement. Colleges and universities cannot deny these groups the opportunity to forge their allegiance to the campus, unless the institution has alternative bases of political fiscal support. This is rarely the case.

Nothing raises the cynical anger of a professor more than abuses of the educational goals of higher education by the athletic department (e.g., circumventing entrance requirements or pushing athletes into "easy," irrelevant courses). Rarely, however, does the faculty member follow his verbal assault with concerted collective action. University senates pass resolutions that are ignored; faculty leaders discuss the problem in ineffectual, informal settings; committees are created and dissolved with no result; or, the control of abuse is left to a faculty athletic committee which is often a mouthpiece of the athletic program and easily circumvented by external booster interests. Faculties will never be effective in controlling large-scale athletic programs because they do not operate at the same political and economic levels as boosters/alumni. The faculty voice might be more readily acknowledged if it came from an organized group (e.g., a labor union), but the prospects for this are not good (Blackburn & Nyikos, 1974). Faculties have simply lacked the courage and organizational apparatus to tackle the athletic program. They have, in their intellectual frustration, absolved themselves of responsibility for the academic credibility of athletics or any other extramural activity. Organizing the faculty will stimulate activism and subsequent demands for greater input and control of the athletic operations on campus, but unless faculties can move in the circles of the elite, these efforts will be in vain.

Faculties can lend an air of respectability to athletic programs by asserting themselves in such areas as admission standards, academic counseling and eligibility reviews. This has been suggested as a mechanism by which faculties can control athletic operations (Blackburn & Nyikos, 1974; Hanford, 1974; Plant, 1961; Marco, 1960). But when it comes to decisions about the level of program, key personnel, and general policy, the booster coalition has the greatest influence.

There is evidence that college presidents and faculties are asserting their authority in NCAA governance and rule-setting practices in order to win back the long-lost control. However, the NCAA devotes only one section of three brief paragraphs to the topic of institutional control (*NCAA Manual*, 1980-81, pp. 15-16). Its position is to hold the weakest component, the faculty, responsible for control. The regulatory power of the NCAA, or any other athletic regulatory body, is compromised by the fact that the interests of these bodies are the same as those of the booster coalition-athletic growth for economic and political benefit. The NCAA is a cartel-like organization designed to promote the athletic enterprise. It does so by monopolizing athletes' labor value and mobility as well as controlling the commercial aspect, for example, TV monies (Koch, 1971; Sage, 1979). Regulatory bodies need the booster coalition to maintain attractive and financially profitable, to these bodies at least, athletic programs. NCAA rules hold the institution responsible for acts of boosters; the result is that the regulatory body sanctions individuals, that is, requests that certain persons disassociate themselves from the athletic program, but it would never request the dismantling of a group representing the booster coalition.

Academic control of athletics will only exist at a moderate and even superficial level at schools with high-level ambitions. Those with lesser goals will find academic control more feasible. Big-time programs require more resources than an institution can provide by its own efforts. The booster coalition is needed for financial and political solvency for the most expansive programs. Even the NCAA will not be able to combat the forces of boosterism. In fact, the NCAA may be replaced by an association of elite schools which will develop regulations which permit more flexible procedures and a more advantageous division of the athletic financial pie, particularly the distribution of television revenue. Such an association already exists in the form of the College Football Association (CFA). The 60 or so members of this group desire an autonomous organization in order to circumvent current NCAA television restrictions which prevent these schools from getting maximum television coverage and, therefore, more dollars for their programs. In 1981, this group came very close to disaffiliating itself with the NCAA. Because the CFA includes the most powerful football programs, this disaffection would have been financially disastrous for the NCAA and other member schools which depend on the television monies generated by these elite teams.

FINANCIAL CONTINGENCIES AND BOOSTER ACTIVITY: COUNTERACTING ENTROPY

The growth dilemma presents itself at this time because the traditional financial resources of athletes are peaking and even decreasing. Even booster revenues are reaching a saturation level. Consequently, athletic programs are placing more emphasis on maintenance rather than growth. The result is what has been called the "stationary state" (Nisbet, 1979) or state of negative entropy (Frey, 1978a). Athletic programs are consuming more energy than they are able to generate. Several factors have produced this condition.

Attendance and Gate Receipts

Even though it may not appear to be true, stadium seating has reached its saturation point, both in terms of the number of new seats constructed and in the rate of attendance. Between 1960 and 1965, attendance at college events rose 21%; between 1965 and 1970, it was up 19%; it rose only 7.5% between 1970 and 1975; and since 1975, attendance is up only 2.1%. Since 1975 there is evidence that attendance is on the decline (Broyles et al., 1976). The rate of attendance is declining while the costs of athletic programs, which are predominantly dependent on gate receipts, are up 61% since 1972 (NCAA, 1978). Thus, revenue from gate receipts, as a portion of the total athletic budget for income, is on the decline (Atwell, 1980).

In addition, the exclusive right of season ticket holders, including corporate entities, who now take up a large portion of the seats in any stadium and arena, makes it physically impossible to expand the market by attracting or creating "new" fans.[6] For example, one school in the West has not added a new booster-season ticket holder for over 2 years because of the unavailability of seats in a basketball arena. These restrictions reinforce the elitist connotation of the college game plus limit the supportive "sense of community" that every institution seeks to create surrounding its athletic program. This means that college programs will have to get more money from the same number of persons. Only those schools with well-organized booster groups will be able to turn this trend.

A second factor, which will contribute to the decline of community interest in local or regional athletic programs, as well as gate receipts, is the development of cable television. Beginning January 1, 1978, all cable systems could carry non-network programs from distant television stations (Hochberg, 1979). Microwave or satellite distribution makes it possible for a viewer in Denver, Colorado, to watch a sporting event originating in New York, Chicago, or another distant city. While cable television triples the potential audience for an event, it can also be harmful to local gate receipts. Fans may stay home to watch an event originating from elsewhere, rather than attending the local event. In effect, college competition will be placed in competition with professional athletics even though a pay-for-play franchise is not located in or near a college or university. Many of the successful collegiate programs such as Ohio State, Oklahoma, and Nebraska attribute some of their notoriety to the fact that they are the "only game in town." Schools can gain revenue because they will hold the copyright to the broadcast and can sell permission at a fee. However, problems arise because a game may not be purchased by the cable TV outlet unless it has national appeal. This means intersectional scheduling which is becoming prohibitively expensive for most institutions. Financial restrictions on national scheduling can be overcome by programs which have a large contingent of booster dollars available to subsidize travel.

Legislative Appropriations

The reduction of available tax dollars will prevent the expansion or creation of new athletic facilities and programs on campuses. More frequently, legislators will give higher priority to capital improvements that are more consistent with the educational goals of the university. Presidents and alumni will also lobby less actively for athletic appropriations because they will be fighting for favorable appropriations for other university functions, thus leaving the door open for the capital expansion of athletic facilities to be financed by booster interests. This has already occurred on many campuses (Marcin, 1979). Athletic programs cannot expect to improve upon their appropriation because of the larger problem of fewer dollars available for any social or educational program. Combine this fact with the decline in gate receipts, and the result can only be either change the level of program—no growth or declining growth—or increase the booster coalition contribution.

Insurance

More practical economic factors will make it difficult for athletic programs to maintain their current practices. Rising liability and medical insurance rates, particularly for football, are forcing schools into a severe cost crunch on some programs. For example, in 1975 the University of California paid a liability insurance premium of $437,602; in 1977, it was $1,144,000. The "sue syndrome" plus the tendencies for juries to favor the plantiff have contributed to the escalation of product liability suits which cost considerable money regardless of outcome (Appenzeller, 1979).[7]

Inflation

In addition, inflation and rising energy prices can have serious effects on travel, equipment purchase, and facility utilization. If a team cannot travel, it cannot maintain the kind of schedule that gives its program the notoriety, exposure, and financial guarantee it needs. Add these problems to the exigencies of Title IX regulations, even with the football exemption, and changes in traditional operations will have to take place.[8] Economic problems are even more significant when it is noted that 81% of the NCAA football programs lost money in 1977, and only 30 athletic programs operated in the black. The athletic revenue growth rate for institutions has been just over 8%, but inflation has been rushing away at 11 to 12% (Raiborn, 1977).

Constituency Support

These economic problems are exacerbated by the fact that even the potential pool of contributors is dwindling. First, college enrollments have leveled off and, in many areas, are on the decline. This will make fewer alumni available for political and financial support in the future. Additionally, the alumni that do exist will have fewer real dollars for peripheral contributions and expenses. Also, these alumni will be less likely to contribute because they can draw on few intimate and positive experiences with the athletic programs of their schools. One study of alumni found that less than 1% of alumni felt athletics represented their most remembered experience in school (Frey, 1978b). This same group listed athletics 11 on a list of 12 priorities for university spending, and they also resented the preferential treatment athletes and other special groups of students received. Few were involved in direct participation because only a select number had the talent and skill it took to participate in a college athletic program. As a result, athletics may not carry the extensive alumni support that is so often suggested by athletic protagonists.

This same study demonstrated that the board of directors of the surveyed alumni group were strong supporters of athletics. Thus, athletics remain a priority, despite the apparent lack of support from the total alumni body, because the strong association of alumni with athletics is an artifact of the membership of elite alumni in booster groups which strongly endorse the athletic program.[9] Presidents and athletic directors tend to listen to the influential, not average alumnus (Frey, 1982).

In addition, recent studies of college students demonstrate that a large percent feel that college sports are operated on behalf of outside interests, not students. Fifty-eight percent of the students in one study felt the boosters controlled athletics, not the institution (Frey, 1980). Just under half felt that athletics were more important to the community than the school and were run on behalf of alumni rather than students. Seventy-six percent agreed with the notion that students have no voice in athletic governance. In another study (Jensen et al., 1980), 42% of the students felt that the "big business" aspect of college athletics is a perversion of educational goals. Yet, these students and those in the Frey study generally supported athletics on campuses. They believed athletics were valuable from the traditional standpoints of character development and campus social life. What is important here is to note that the percentage favoring athletics is not as high as the promoters of these programs would have us believe. I predict that future studies will reveal a lowering of the student support quotient for athletics.

Labor Supply

Successful athletic programs obviously cannot operate without a substantial pool of athletic labor from which to draw the most talented performers. Until recently, this supply seemed endless. Virtually any school could recruit athletes at any level of sophistication and intellect. It they were not admissible under normal circumstances, entrance requirements could be circumvented by the use of junior college enrollments, manipulated transcripts, bogus courses or minority admissions variances. Recent NCAA rulings have made it illegal to use certain courses or schools in attaining elegibility. Championship rules make it more difficult and problematic to play a transfer. These factors, combined with the exclusivity of college athletics, means that fewer athletes, particularly male, qualify, from the standpoints of either academic potential or physical skill, for college athletics.

There has, in fact, been a first-ever decline in the number of males who participate in college sports. While women's participation doubled from 32,000 in 1972 to 64,000 in 1978, men's participation declined from 172,000 to 170,384 during this same time period (U.S. Commission on Civil Rights, 1980). Still, schools spend twice the money per capita on male athletes as compared to female athletes. As the supply of available labor declines, the competition for the remaining qualified few will be intense. The edge may be provided by the resources of booster coalition.

Affirmative Action and Civil Rights legislation has opened the doors of opportunity, to some extent, for one of the major subgroups of athletic labor— the black. At one time, the only avenues out of the ghetto and an existence of despair were athletics and entertainment. College coaches flocked to the playgrounds and athletic fields of American urban centers to find the "diamond in the rough" who would lead their teams to glory (Telander, 1978). The black and white communities supported this association of success and athletics. However, it was not long before the injustice of this effort and attention became known.

For every athlete from these circumstances who made it to either the collegiate or professional big-time, a thousand did not. For those who made it, the career was short-lived with few long-term benefits of money or fame. Many a "star" was forced back to his origination with only stories of his experience, some reputation, but few tangible assets. It was not long before stories and reputation lost their luster. It is possible that many blacks who could have been athletes will pursue vehicles of success other than athletics because they have become aware of these injustices. In fact, leaders of the black community such as Jesse Jackson and Harry Edwards are openly challenging black youth to look at alternatives to athletics and to funnel their energies to pursue careers which have a more reliable pay-off, in addition to making some contribution to society.[10] If such admonitions are taken to heart, the labor pool available for college athletics will suffer a considerable deficit. The black portion of that labor pool will be even more decimated if faculty assert themselves on admission and degree requirements and expect higher standards of academic performance. Then, only a few academically and athletically qualified blacks will be available.

Athletes, in turn, are becoming more sophisticated about the recruiting dynamics; that is, they recognize that they have a product that is in demand. It is only natural to sell one's services to the highest bidder. The bids are ordinarily channeled through "representatives of athletic departments," for example, athletic boosters. Money payments, use of cars, travel for relatives, and other incentives are offered and often requested by the athlete. As a result, few schools will be able to stay in the bidding market for the elite athlete without the external sources of support, both legal and illegal.

The labor pool of athletics is also decimated by the high rate of disabling injuries which can keep a player from performing for a season or even a lifetime. It is estimated that nearly one million high school players, 70,000 college players, and all of the players on the National Football League suffer injuries in 1 year (Underwood, 1978). Thus, additional player resources are required. The decline of available scholarships, fewer number who are eligible or desire to play, and lowered skill of those available to replace the "star" potentially reduce the quality of the available athletic resources of a winning season, which in turn, leads to lowered alumnus and booster support. In addition, if a team has no star to attract media attention, program visibility, as well as revenues, will also be reduced. It truly is a vicious circle.

The problem of maintaining the labor pool for college athletics is further complicated by the fact that an increasing number of high school districts are dropping sports, particularly football. Between 1969 and 1979, there was a 2.3% and a 10.0% decline in the number of schools offering football and basketball, respectively (National Federation of State High School Associations, 1979). During this same time, the number of participants dropped 6.7% for football, 19.5% for basketball.

Many high schools no longer carry coaches as faculty and therefore must recruit as part-time, interested persons. In all but seven states, coaches are no longer required to have a teaching credential in order to be employed by a school system (Seefeldt & Gould, 1980). Both of these facts point to the prospect of fewer well-trained athletes being available for college programs.

Finally, there now exists a "Sport Establishment"—a network of organizations and occupations that depends on athletics as currently construed for their maintenance and survival. This network contains some 800,000 organizations with memberships in the millions and revenues/expenses exceeding one and one-half billion dollars (Frey, 1978a). College programs are part of this network, and over the years, as the administrative and organizational components have grown, greater proportions of expense has gone to organizational maintenance rather than to enhancing the participatory experience of athletes. As a result, college athletic programs are spending more money on fewer and fewer participants.

As college programs become more rationlized and organized under this athletic-industrial complex, the athlete, realizing that athletics are a business, will be less loyal to his team or nation. He or she will be less willing to sacrifice himself or herself for the sake of the team. The reason for his or her participation is extrinsic and based on self-interest, which means higher turnover of personnel. A player will not remain at "Good Ole U" for the sake of teammates and tradition. He or she will transfer to a school that will give him or her the most toward meeting his or her goals (e.g., professional career). As any foreman or manager will tell you, high turnover of key personnel is disruptive of productivity and morale.

CONCLUSION: THE FUTURE

All of these factors are intertwined. The environment of intercollegiate athletics is deteriorating. The supports are no longer there; they are missing, not because of Title IX or another singular element, but because of systematic conditions which are subtle yet pervasive. It is only a matter of time before drastic changes in the intercollegiate athletic world will come.

The most significant change will be that only a few schools will be able to grow or expand their athletic program. These schools will become an elite corps which will dominate any national attention athletics receives. Schools like Alabama, University of Southern California, and Nebraska University with programs augmented by a strong booster/alumni coalition, will form national conferences, dominate television coverage, secure the services of the best available athletes, and will essentially operate regulation-free. These programs will represent the last stage in the nationalization of college athletics and the professionalization of the college athlete. The affiliation with a college or university campus will remain only one of convenience and tradition. The elite sport clubs of America will exist in connection with a university; the booster groups will be the sponsors of these sport clubs and will provide them with the resources necessary to compete in the national marketplace for the elite athlete in a declining labor pool.

The less endowed or committee schools will see the 1980s as their last hurrah. These institutions will bear the brunt of all financial, and thus program, cutbacks. Title IX is only a temporary roadblock for the elite athletic programs, but Affirmative Action plus other financial exigencies represent the death knell for many smaller, less-endowed programs. The rich get richer and the poor fall by the wayside. The final result will be a two-class athletic system which will only be a facsimile of current organization.

FOOTNOTES

1. As early as 1852 businessmen "boosted" an intercollegiate athletic event to enhance their economic interest. The owners of the Boston, Concord, and Mon-

treal Railroads paid all of the expenses for Harvard and Yale crews to compete in the very first intercollegiate event—a Regatta on Lake Winnipesaukee. The aim of the railroads was to get people to use rail transportation to the event. It worked; the businessmen and the athletes made money (Smith, 1976).

2. A dramatic example of this influence occurred recently when Texas A&M University hired a new football coach with a 5-year contract for over $1 million. This contract was negotiated by a member of the Board of Trustees who also was a leader in the A&M booster group. The offer was tendered without the president's knowledge and before the present coach knew he was being terminated.

3. ''Big Time'' refers to those schools in the NCAA Division IA. These tend to be the largest in size, have access to a football stadium which seats at least 30,000 spectators, have an average attendance of 17,000 persons at home games, and field teams in at least 12 sports. There are 120 schools in this division out of the approximately 1,000 which compete in intercollegiate athletics. The problems of boosterism are not limited, however, to the elite schools even though the latter receive the most public attention.

4. The involvement of business and political elite in booster groups has an analogy with professional team ownership. Few professional teams make money, yet potential owners line up in order to purchase an available team. It has been suggested that through player depreciation allowance and the ability to demonstrate an ''on-paper'' loss, team owners are able to accrue considerable tax advantages (Noll, 1974). In fact, major conglomerates find it desirable to own a losing team in order to be able to demonstrate that the profit in one company was drained to service another. Thus, overall earnings are shown to be minimal and less available to taxes. Contributions to booster clubs and booster foundations provide a similar tax advantage to the contributor. It may also give him the vicarious thrill of ownership because along with his contribution comes decision-making influence as well as the opportunity to form personal associations with a revered group—athletes.

5. Booster groups can continue to influence college and university administration because of their ties to state legislatures and the governing boards of the institution. Regents and trustees are often also booster club members, or they represent groups which have dealings with other booster members.

6. An analysis of the list of booster club members of one institution revealed that 26% held corporate memberships. This figure is most likely conservative because many who were listed by name, such as medical doctors or lawyers, probably purchased memberships (i.e., made donations) through a business account.

7. At this time, there are over 100 football helmet-related injury cases pending in court with claims totaling over $300 million.

8. It is interesting to note that many athletic directors are viewing women's sports as a possible salvation from the financial requirements of maintaining a winning athletic program. From one standpoint, transferring money to women's

programs can be a justification for deemphasizing some men's sports, including the major programs. On the other hand, accelerated women's sports can mean additional revenue-producing avenues including gate receipts and women boosters-alumni. Title IX of the 1972 Education Act forbids sex discrimination in any educational institution receiving funds from the federal government. In athletics, this means a similar number of male and female participants, equivalent scholarships, equal facilities and equal availability of athletic program support services (e.g., trainers, coaches, etc.). Schools were to come into compliance by September, 1979; at this writing few have fully met the requirement.

9. Sigelman and Carter (1979) have demonstrated statistically that no relation exists between win-loss records and donation patterns by alumni. Sack (1980) reanalyzed the Sigelman and Carter data and reached the same conclusion.

10. The major problem with the arguments of individuals like Jackson is that they suggest the pursuit of professional careers (e.g., doctor, lawyer) as an alternative. Success in these careers is unlikely. Greater emphasis should be placed on the acquisition of more generalized skills such as writing or mathematical proficiency, which can be utilized in a number of job arenas.

REFERENCES

APPENZELLER, H. (1979). Product liability litigation continues to escalate, *Athletic Purchasing,* **3**, 17-20.

ATWELL, R.H., Grimes, B., & Lopiano, D. (1980). *The money game: Financing collegiate athletics.* Washington, DC: American Council on Education.

BLACKBURN, R.T., & Nyikos, M.S. (October, 1974). College football and Mr. Chips: All in the family. *Phi Delta Kappan,* **56**, 110-113.

BOORSTIN, D.J. (1965). *The Americans: The national experience,* New York: Random House.

BROYLES, F., Hay, R.D., & French, H.A. (Summer, 1976). Some facts about college football attendance. *Athletic Administration,* **10**, 13-15.

CADY, E.H. (1978). *The big game: college sports in American life.* Knoxville: The University of Tennessee Press.

DENLINGER, K., & Shapiro, L. (1975). *Athletes for sale.* New York: Thomas Y. Crowell.

EVANS, J.R. (1974). *Blowing the whistle on intercollegiate sports.* Chicago: Nelson-Hall.

FREY, J.H. (February, 1978a). The organization of American amateur sport: Efficiency to entrophy. *American Behavioral Scientist,* **21**, 361-378.

FREY, J.H. (September, 1978b). The priority of athletics to alumni: Myth or fact? *Phi Delta Kappan,* **60**, 63.

FREY, J.H. (1980). *Survey of college students' participation in athletics and intramurals.* Unpublished report, University of Nevada, Las Vegas.

FREY, J.H. (1982). *The governance of intercollegiate athletics.* West Point, NY: Leisure Press.

HANFORD, G.H. (1974). *An inquiry into the need for the feasibility of a national study of intercollegiate athletics.* Washington, DC: American Council on Education.

HOCHBERG, P.R. (Fall, 1979). Cable television's impact on college athletics. *Athletic Administration,* **14**, 6-7.

JENSEN, T.M., Leonard, W.M., & Liverman, R.D. (October, 1980). *College students' attitudes toward intercollegiate athletics: An exploratory model.* Paper presented at the meetings of the North American Society for the Sociology of Sport, Denver, Colorado.

KOCH, J.V. (1971). A troubled cartel: The NCAA. *Law and Contemporary Problems,* **38**, 129-150.

LOONEY, D.S. (July, 1978). Deep in hot water in Stillwater. *Sports Illustrated,* **49**, 18-23.

LUCAS, J.A., & Smith, R.A. (1978). *Saga of American Sport.* Philadelphia: Lea and Febiger.

MARCIN, J. (November, 1979). Booster clubs: Boon. . .or bane? *Sporting News,* pp. 26-27.

MARCO, S.M. (1960). The place of intercollegiate athletics in higher education: The responsibility of the faculty. *Journal of Higher Education,* **21**, 422-427.

NATIONAL Collegiate Athletic Association (NCAA) (1978). The sports and recreational programs of the nation's universities and colleges. *NCAA manual, 1980-81.* Shawnee Mission, Kansas.

NATIONAL Federation of State High School Associations (1979). *Sports participation survey.*

NISBET, R. (June/July, 1979) The rape of progress. *Public Opinion,* **2**, 2-6.

NOLL, R.G. (1974). The U.S. team sports industry: An introduction. In Roger G. Noll, *Government and the sports business* (pp. 1-33). Washington, DC: The Brookings Institution.

NOVACK, M. (1976). *The joy of sports.* New York: Basic Books, Inc.

PLANT, M.L. (January, 1961). The place of intercollegiate athletics in higher education. *Journal of Higher Education,* **22**, 1-8.

RAINBORN, M.H. (1978). *Revenues and expenses of intercollegiate athletic programs.* Report to the National Collegiate Athletic Association.

SACK, A.H. (1980). *Another look at winning and giving.* Paper presented at the meetings of the North American Society for the Sociology of Sport.

SAGE, G.H. (1974). Socialization of coaches: Antecedents to coaches' beliefs and behaviors. *Proceedings: National College Physical Education Association for Men,* pp. 124-132, Chicago, University of Illinois.

SEEFELDT, V., & Gould, D. (1980). *Physical and psychological effects of athletic competition on children and youth.* Washington, DC: ERIC Clearinghouse on Teacher Education.

SIGELMAN, L., & Carter, R. (September, 1979). Win one for the giver? Alumni giving and big-time college sport. *Social Science Quarterly,* **60**, 284-294.

SMITH, R.A. (January, 1976). Reaction to "Historical roots of the collegiate dilemma." *Proceedings: National College Physical Education Association for Men,* pp. 154-161, Chicago, University of Illinois.

TALENDAR, R. (1978). *Heaven is a playground.* New York: Grosset and Dunlap.

THOMPSON, J.D. (1967). *Organizations in action.* New York: McGraw-Hill.

UNDERWOOD, J. (1979). *The death of an American game.* Boston: Little and Brown.

UNITED States Commission on Civil Rights. (July, 1980). *More hurdles to clear: Women and girls in competitive athletics,* **63**. Clearinghouse Publication.

Chapter 9

The Scholarship Athlete and Workers' Compensation

Linda Jean Carpenter
Brooklyn College, New York

An injured athlete can typically seek financial compensation for the injury only through a lawsuit based on negligence principles. To win the suit, the athlete must prove each of the four elements of negligence:

1. *Duty*—a duty of reasonable care was owed by the defendant to the athlete.
2. *Breach*—the defendant breached that duty.
3. *Proximate cause*—the defendant's breach of duty was the proximate cause of the athlete's injury.
4. *Harm*—the athlete was actually harmed.

Although many sports injuries occur in the absence of negligence, it is often difficult to prove negligence in those cases where it does exist.

The difficulty encountered by the athlete in proving each of the elements of negligence is compounded by the frequently successful use, by the coach or school, of defenses such as assumption of risk, contributory negligence, and comparative negligence. For instance, the assumption of risk defense is successful when the athlete knew of the reasonably foreseeable risks of participation in a sport and participated anyway. There are very few instances when an athlete did not assume the risk of sports participation. Thus there are very few times when the athlete will be able to establish a claim of negligence without being blocked by the institution's defense of assumption of risk.

This paper explores the theory of workers' compensation as an alternative to an unsuccessful claim of negligence. Worker's compensation is a creation of state legislatures. Worker's compensation is intended to provide an informal, easily accessible form of recovery for the employee's job-related injuries. Under its provisions, the notion of fault is not involved. Therefore, the employee need not prove the four elements of negligence, and similarly, the employer does not have the defenses available as mentioned earlier.

Both the employer and employee benefit under the provisions. The employer benefits because the amount of the recovery is limited, and once the employee recovers under workers' compensation, he or she no longer can sue the employer for additional damages. The employee benefits because proof of the four elements of negligence is not required. Instead the employee must only demonstrate two elements. First, an employer-employee relationship must have been present at the time of injury. Second, the injured employee must show that the injuries sustained resulted from the work performed for the employer and that such injuries were received while engaged in the business of the employer and in the furtherance of the employer's affairs (Oleck 1969, p. 438).

When applying the concept of recovery under worker's compensation to college and university scholarship athletes, the primary hurdle to overcome is the classification of the athlete as an employee. On the surface, the terms *employee* and *amateur athlete* seem to be mutually exclusive. However, the prominent linkage of the terms *amateur* and *athletics* on college and university campuses does not put to rest all the issues concerning the employment status of the scholarship athlete with as much facility as most administrators might hope.

The recent redefinition of amateur to mean someone who meets stated eligibility requirements, rather than the old definition of someone who participates for the joy of participation adds to the dilemma.[1]

Furthermore, in many colleges and universities athletic programs present very high profiles. They often serve as standard bearers for alumni support and pride in the institution. Even though all but a handful of intercollegiate athletic programs are a drain on the budget rather than the money-raisers they are often purported to be, they still have a flavor of big business about them. In the majority of schools where athletic-generated revenue only supports a portion of the athletic expenses, there is still frequently seen the dream of a first step to fiscal independence and then the ultimate step to a fiscal contribution to the university's general operating budget. Arrival upon the ultimate plateau involves a financial benefit to the school as well as an increasing power base for those in charge of the athletic program. Certainly those schools which have athletic programs that contribute to the general operating budget would find it difficult to deny that their intercollegiate athletic programs are big business.[2]

The increasing budget constraints on institutional general funds have also provided an additional, strong motivation for an ever-larger portion of the athletic budget to be self-generated. When

> substantial portions of the expense of the program must be self-generated or secured from outside the institution there is pressure for income-producing 'spectator' sports. This may cause difficulties in maintaining institutional control sufficient to keep

the program effectively contributing to the broad educational purposes of the institution. There is a concomitant danger of considering the participant as an employee rather than as a student and even a danger of substituting the outsider's standards for those of the institution in the relationship. (Cross, 1973, p. 164)

Even the *Wall Street Journal* (1969, p. 22) has commented on the business status of intercollegiate sports by intimating that in some cases schools have come to see and to treat athletes less as students than as tools to be manipulated for profit. Thus, the question at hand is, What elements must exist for a scholarship athlete to be considered an employee (either actually or constructively) in the eyes of a workers' compensation board reviewing his or her potential eligibility for benefits and the school's obligation to pay workers' compensation insurance premiums for the athlete? If there are circumstances in which the athlete might be eligible for such benefits, it is vitally important for the institution to be aware of it. This is true because the institution which has eligible athletes but which has not paid workers' compensation premiums for those athletes is in potentially extreme financial jeopardy. When an employer should but does not pay workers' compensation premiums for eligible employees, the injured employee may elect to sue under the theory of negligence without the institution being permitted to use any of its defenses. Thus, the limitations of recovery under workers' compensation are removed.

On the other hand, an institution which elects to pay workers' compensation premiums for its athletes would certainly not wish to expend a large portion of its already tight budget unless its athletes did, in fact, fall within the eligibility requirements.

INTERNAL REVENUE SERVICE RULINGS AND THE SCHOLARSHIP ATHLETE

The Internal Revenue Service has found it necessary to tangentially address this question by determining whether an athlete's scholarship is includable in the athlete's gross income (and therefore add weight to the theory that a scholarship is salary), or excludable as a "true" scholarship[1] (IRS Code, 1979), (and therefore add weight to the theory that the scholarship athlete is truly an amateur in the old sense of the term).

To not be considered taxable income, a scholarship must meet the following two requirements: (a) The primary purpose of the studies supported by the scholarship is to further the education and training of the recipient; and (b) the amount does not represent compensation or payment for services. In a 1969 IRS tax case, the Supreme Court upheld the above two requirements as being necessary if a scholarship is to be nontaxable (*Bingler v. Johnson*, 1969).

The point of the court in this 1969 case is summarized in the following statement:

> The thrust of the provision dealing with compensation is that bargained-for payments, given only as the *quo* in return for the *quid* of services rendered, whether past, present, or future, should not be excludable from income as 'scholarship' funds. *(Bingler v. Johnson*, 1969, p. 741)

Thus, it might be inferred that the IRS might view a scholarship athlete as an employee of the institution providing his or her scholarship funds if that scholarship happened to be contingent on the athlete's playing on a team.

The IRS again addressed the question in 1977 (Internal Revenue Service, 1977) when it ruled that a scholarship granted under the following rules imposed by the athletic governing association was nontaxable (and thus probably evidence of the lack of an employment relationship).

1. The recipient had to be accepted to the university according to admission requirements applicable to all students.
2. The recipient must have been a full-time student.
3. The award had to be made by the agency of the university that is responsible for awarding scholarships in general.
4. Once awarded for a given academic year, the award could not be terminated even upon the student's unilateral decision to not participate in athletics, nor could the student be required to engage in any other activities in lieu of participation in a sport.
5. The amount of the scholarship could not exceed the expenses for tuition, fees, books, and supplies.

In this 1977 case, the university required no particular activity of any of its scholarship recipients. The revenue ruling held that

> although students who receive athletic scholarships do so because of their special abilities in a particular sport and are expected to participate in the sport, the scholarship is not cancelled in the event the student cannot participate and the student is not required to engage in any other activities in lieu of participating in the sport. The athletic scholarships are awarded primarily to aid the recipients in pursuing their studies. Therefore, the value of the scholarships is excluded from gross income. (Internal Revenue Service, 1977, p. 263)

The court's reasoning may not be based on a firm foundation of reality today. In actuality, when a student cannot participate in a sport, the scholarship can be and often is cancelled at the end of the semester. Furthermore, some scholarship agreements do require alternative service for an injured athlete.[3] Third, the idea that athletic scholarships are awarded primarily to aid the recipient pursue his or her studies is often not consistent with the reality of athlete's restrictions on course loads, freedom to have sufficient study time, participation in degree oriented programs, and so forth.[4]

As we turn our attention elsewhere, we leave the IRS cases with the feeling that they could be effectively used to argue both for and against the notion that a scholarship athlete might be considered an employee.

CASE LAW AND THE SCHOLARSHIP ATHLETE'S ELIGIBILITY FOR WORKERS' COMPENSATION BENEFITS

Now let us turn to the case law to look for less tangential statements concerning our question, "What elements must exist for a scholarship athlete to be considered an employee in the eyes of a workers' compensation board?" Unfortunately, the case law is somewhat sparse in the area of workers' compensation and scholarship athletes. However, there are a few significant cases where courts have examined the position of the athlete-claimant and have held that he or she is an employee for purposes of workers' compensation coverage.

The first of these cases was *University of Denver v. Nemeth* (1953). While engaged in spring football practice, Nemeth suffered an accidental injury to his back. At the same time, he was receiving $50 per month from the university for work related to tennis court maintenance. His work on the tennis courts was suspended during football practice. The university argued that to apply the Workers' Compensation Act to scholarship students would be against public policy (public policy being interpreted as favoring the awarding of scholarships, and the imposition of workers' compensation would dampen this).

The court in the *Nemeth* case held that the football player was an employee and therefore entitled to workers' compensation. In its opinion the court reflected that "higher education in this day (1953) is a business and a big one." Furthermore, it is important to note that Nemeth was told that "it would be decided on the football field who receives the meals and the jobs" (*University of Denver v. Nemeth*, 1953, p. 425).

The court presented the following rationale for its finding.

> The obligation to compensate Nemeth arises solely because of the nature of the contract, its incedent and responsibilities which Nemeth assumed in order to not only earn his renumeration, but to retain his job. The University hired him to perform work on the campus, and as an incident of this work to have him engage in football. (*University of Denver v. Nemeth*, 1953, p. 430)

Thus it appears that the court, at least in this case, was willing to look beyond the "fictional" records of a student employed to maintain a tennis court to the reality of the relationship between the employment and the student's athletic participation. When trying to draw a parallel between the *Nemeth* case and the revenue ruling discussed above, it appears that the tennis court job, if viewed as a scholarship, failed to meet the criterion of being irrevocable for the academic year.

A tender for a scholarship award takes on the form of a contract. The question of importance is, however, Is that contract an employment contract? In the *Nemeth* case, the contract was one of employment without doubt, but the stated job was to maintain tennis courts, not play football. The court found it necessary to look beyond.

A decade later, a California court addressed much the same issue with one major difference. In *Van Horn v. Industrial Accident Commission* (1963) there was no overt employment relationship as existed in the tennis court job held by Nemeth. Rather the deceased football-playing husband was the recipient of a scholarship and of rent money. The deceased was killed in a 1960 plane crash that occurred while the football team was returning from a game in Ohio. The widow and her minor children applied for death benefits under workers' compensation.

The deceased Van Horn had been on a scholarship and, after playing football for a year, married and decided not to continue playing football. Following a year off the team, Van Horn was approached by the coach and arranged a "pretty good deal to play football in order to support (his) family" (*Van Horn v. Industrial Accident Commission*, 1963, p. 171). He had told his wife that the coach had agreed to assure assistance from the college if he would resume playing football. Van Horn depended on the college assistance rather than working for his father as he had in the past because football practice took too much of his time. A portion of the funds received by Van Horn came from a booster club via a special account controlled solely by the coach. In addition, Van Horn received academic credit for each semester of team participation.

The District Court of Appeals overturned the lower court and held that Van Horn's widow and children were entitled to death benefits under workers' compensation because of the existence of an employment status due to Van Horn's receipt of compensation for playing football. Funds received do not need to be labeled "wages" in order for the athlete to be considered an employee (*Union Lumber Co. v. Industrial Accident Commission*, 1936). In the *Rensing* case discussed later, the defendant argued that tuition, room and board, books and fees are not "wages" because the NCAA so specifies. Neither does the receipt of academic credit destroy any possible employee/employer status. To the issue of academic credit the *Van Horn* court said, "one may have the dual capacity of student and employee in respect to an activity" (*Van Horn*, 1963, p. 172). Similarly, student teachers and nurses have been held to be employees in like circumstances (Department of Natural Resources, 1932; Edwards, 1946).

The National Collegiate Athletic Association (NCAA) and the Association for Intercollegiate Athletics for Women (AIAW) rules demand amateur status. If the college pays workers' compensation insurance premiums for its athletes, the institution itself would be acknowledging the nonamateur status of its athletes. On the other hand, if the college elects to exclude its athletes from its workers' compensation rolls, and if the courts, in liberally construing the typical workers' compensation act, hold that an employment relationship exists, the college's liability for compensation may be considerable as well as a larger obligation for increased workers' compensation premiums in the future.

Most colleges have chosen to exclude athletes from their workers' compensation rolls. Scholarship agreements are carefully written to abide by the NCAA and AIAW rules. (In 1984 AIAW lost its appeal and terminated its existence.)

WHAT ELEMENTS ARE ESSENTIAL FOR A *VAN HORN* TYPE RESULT?

The *Van Horn* court distinguished between athletes and other student performers such as actors and musicians. Athletes performing on the school's behalf may be expected to increase the financial gain to the school through endowments, gate receipts, and so on, whereas no such expectation exists for the services of other students. If there is no such gain to the recipient as in the court's example of the student musician, the student is not rendering services and thus is not an employee.

The *Van Horn* court also indicated that an athlete's services help the school prosper and sustain itself (apparently through gate receipts and increased alumni support) even though the school might be nonprofit. The athlete resembles an employee much more closely than a donee of charitable benevolence.

1. Thus it appears that one essential element is that services be rendered from which the college benefits in its fund-raising ability. This factor would almost always be present in the typical revenue sports of football and men's basketball. Women's basketball, along with a number of other sports, is, however, joining the ranks of revenue sports complete with television and radio contracts.
2. A second essential element for a *Van Horn* type result is that the dispensing of athletic scholarship funds must be somehow conditional. Scholarship agreements are generally written to comply with the NCAA and AIAW rules. Among these rules is the provision that scholarship funds cannot be withdrawn before the completion of the school term even if the athlete simply walks away from the team (NCAA, 1981-82).

This provision is included to disrupt the connection between sport participation and scholarship funds. It does not, however, satisfy the *Van Horn* requirement for unconditional dispensing or renewal. This is because there generally exists a tacit understanding between the athlete and his or her school that the *renewal* of the scholarship depends on team participation. Although such an understanding does not disturb the athlete's eligibility in the eyes of the NCAA, the purity of ''amateur'' athletics has been strained nonetheless.

The second essential element necessary for a *Van Horn* type of imposition of workers' compensation can be met by the dispensing of scholarship funds (a) on the condition that the athlete is currently on the team (a condition seldom found in scholarship agreements today), or (b) on the condition of a promise of future participation as a prerequisite for scholarship renewal (very common today in either expressed or implied form).

In review, it appears the holding in *Van Horn* is applicable to those situations where at least the following elements are present:

1. The college benefits from the services rendered by the athlete.
2. The present payment or renewal of scholarship funds is in some way conditional on the athlete's performance or participation.

IS THE HOLDING IN *VAN HORN* BROADLY APPLICABLE?

The *Van Horn* case involved a male football player. Would other types of athletes be included in the court's holding?

> There is authority for the proposition that one who participates for compensation as a member of an athletic team may be an employee within the statutory scheme of the Workers' Compensation Act...(but) it cannot be said as a matter of law that every student who receives an athletic scholarship and plays on the school team is an employee of the school. (*Van Horn*, 1963, p. 170)

The critical issue here seems to be if the school is receiving financial benefit in one way or another from the services of the athlete.

Is football the only sport that may provide financial benefit to the school? The financial resources made available to the athletic programs of the nation by its institutions of higher learning in hopes of even larger financial benefits from alumni support, television contracts, and gate receipts have certainly brought athletics into the realm of big, BIG, business. Football is no longer the sole big-time sport. The massive growth in sports participation by females chronicled in the longitudinal study by Acosta and Carpenter (1983) makes it unlikely that males will remain the only athletes with the potential for being identified as employees. So, it appears that the *Van Horn* holding could be broadly applied today to a much larger spectrum of sports.

A more recent case decided the issue in Indiana (*Rensing v. Indiana State University Board of Trustees*, 1983), but because of the wording of the decision, might encourage cases in other states. The plaintiff, Rensing, was rendered a quadriplegic as a result of an injury suffered during a spring football practice at Indiana State University. The Industrial Board of Indiana reviewed his case and denied workers' compensation benefits to the scholarship athlete, Rensing. He appealed to the Indiana Court of Appeals and there received a successful outcome and was granted workers' compensation benefits for the injuries sustained as a member of the university's football team. In February of 1983, however, the Supreme Court of Indiana (highest court in the state) overturned the Appeals Court decision and found that

Rensing enrolled at Indiana State University as a full-time student seeking advanced educational opportunities. He was not *considered* (italics added) to be a professional athlete who was being paid for his athletic ability. (*Rensing*, 1983, p. 79)

Although the Appeals Court decision seems to follow the pattern set by the *Van Horn* case, the Supreme Court's decision focuses on the intent of the parties. Seven factors are sometimes used to determine if an employer-employee relationship exists. Even though the court found some of the seven to be present, it found that one, the belief of the parties in the existence of an employer-employee relationship, was not.

As mentioned earlier, the NCAA defines "pay" as something other than tuition, books, room and board, and fees. An athlete loses amateur eligibility if his or her remuneration exceeds the items defined as "not pay." In effect, the *Rensing* court was unwilling to look behind the statements which many professionals in sport today might label as "fiction" to the reality of an individual being provided remuneration for and because of athletic participation.

The *Rensing* case involved an additional point not found in earlier cases. The tender letter received by Rensing included a statement requiring Rensing to perform other services for the university if he should be injured and unable to play football. The *Rensing* court did not directly address the question of this atypical clause, but it seems likely that post-Rensing tender letters will not contain such a clause.

A few months after the February, 1983, Rensing decision, the Michigan Court of Appeals denied workers' compensation benefits to Willie Coleman, a former scholarship player at Western Michigan University. Coleman lost his scholarship, and thus his financial ability to continue at the university following a wrist injury (*Vance*, 1983, p. 21). Contrary to the *Rensing* court, the *Coleman* court found that the scholarship was compensation/wages for playing football. The court denied benefits, however, and based its decision mainly on two findings: First, the court determined that football was not an integral part of the university's business; second, the court believed that the university supposedly lacked the typical employer's ability to control, discipline, and fire an employee.

The *Rensing* and *Coleman* courts arrived at their similar conclusions by different rationales. In one case, the scholarship was not a wage, yet the court found that a contract existed. In the other, the scholarship represented wages for football, but the university failed to meet the requirements to be considered an employer. The consistency of rationales which should mark consistent decisions is still lacking in the area of workers' compensation for the scholarship athlete. The athletic community must await further decisions such as Coleman's appeal and a pending case involving a Southern Illinois University at Carbondale athlete.

At the present time, however, one might at least safely characterize the successful claimant. In jurisdictions which are willing to acknowledge the business component of athletic programs, a male, catastrophically injured ex-football player at an institution which views football as a source of benefit to the school is the most likely successful plaintiff.

CONCLUSION

The subtleties of loyalty and a sense of team spirit have probably been as responsible as any other reason for the small numbers of cases. However, if

> institutions of higher education persist in retaining a contractual (type) constructive employment relationship with their scholarship athletes, whereby financial aid is only dispensed as long as the student is participating as a team member, it is only just that the student is protected and receives the benefits under workers' compensation for any injuries sustained while employed by his school. (Steinbach, 1970, p. 527)

The path apparently being followed by both men's and women's intercollegiate athletics seems to include a commitment to contractual relationships (within the *Van Horn* meaning) with their scholarship athletes. Three possible solutions exist: First, the granting of full, 4-year scholarships rather than scholarships for 1 year only, removes the option of appearing to withdraw an athlete's scholarship by failing to renew it; second, institutions of higher education could stop offering athletic scholarships, thus removing any chance of viewing the scholarship as pay; and third, premium payment of either workers' compensation insurance or appropriate disability insurance (not merely accident insurance) provides for the financial needs of injured athletes. Although the NCAA is currently considering the pursuit of the third solution, it seems unlikely that any of the three solutions will be pursued with sufficient vigor to remove the need for workers' compensation claims by scholarship athletes.

Thus, the 1980s may see more workers' compensation cases involving scholarship athletes. As a result, institutions of higher education will be compelled to squarely face the issue of athletes: amateurs or employees?

FOOTNOTES

1. Such mechanisms as the TACTRUST provide for amateur athletes to receive compensation for their participation in amateur competitive events by placing the funds in trust until the athlete's competitive days are completed.

2. Many schools realize the financial size of their athletic programs when they are placed on probation. For instance, the University of Southern California's inability to play in televised football games has been variously reported to be costing the school hundreds of thousands of dollars.

3. See the *Rensing* case discussed later for an example of a case involving a requirment for alternative work.

4. Although none has been successful yet, there are many educational malpractice cases filed by athletes who found it impossible to perform up to the college's

expectations on the playing field and still take degree-oriented courses successfully. Thus, although the athlete might be promised an education, his or her participation on an athletic team might preclude the opportunity of taking advantage of his or her portion of the benefits.

REFERENCES

BINGLER v. Johnson, 394 US 741 (1969). *Cumulative Bulletin, 17*, (1969-2).

CARPENTER, L., & Acosta, R.V. Status of women in intercollegiate athletics. Unpublished manuscript, 1983. (Available from Professors Carpenter and Acosta, Department of Physical Education, Brooklyn College, Brooklyn, New York 11210).

CROSS, H. (1973). The college athlete and the institution. *Law and Contemporary Problems, 38*, 151-171.

DEPARTMENT of Natural Resources v. Industrial Accident Commission. 216 Cal 434, 14 P2d 746 (1932).

EDWARDS v. Hollywood Canteen. 27 Cal 2d 802 (1946).

FOOTBALL finance. (November 25, 1969). *Wall Street Journal*, p. 22.

INTERNAL Revenue Code Regulations. (1979). Section 1.1117-4(c).

INTERNAL Revenue Service Revenue Ruling. Number 77-263 (1977). *Cumulative Bulletin* (1977, p. 2).

NATIONAL Collegiate Athletic Association Constitution. Article 3, section 4(c) (2) (iv) (1981-82); Article 3, section 4(d) (1981-82).

OLECK, H. (1969). Horseplay by employees. *Cleveland Marshall Law Review, 17*, 438-450.

RENSING v. Indiana State University Board of Trustees. 437 NE 2d 78 (reversed, Feb. 1983, 444 NE 2d 1170).

STEINBACH, S.E. (1970). Workmen's compensation and the scholarship athlete. *Cleveland State Law Review, 19*, 521-527.

UNION Lumber Co. v. Industrial Accident Commision 12 Cal App. 2d 588, 55 P2d 911 (1936).

UNIVERSITY of Denver v. Nemeth. 127 Colo. 385, 257 P2d 423 (1953).

VANCE, N.S. (May 4, 1983). Court rejects athlete's appeal for workers' compensation. *Chronicle of Higher Education, 26*, p. 21.

VAN HORN v. Industrial Accident Commision. 33 Cal. Reporter 169 (1963).

Chapter 10

The Controversy Over College Sport: Will It Ever End?

David A. Rose
Los Angeles, California

For the greater part of its history, college athletics have been both a highly popular and a highly controversial aspect of American higher education. Throughout this history, the level of controversy has waxed and waned regularly. The present period has been one of increasing controversy. Media reports in recent years have cited a lengthy list of problems and possible problems, including at least the following: a point-shaving scandal, a gambling scandal, recruiting abuses, drug abuse, various forms of antisocial behavior, including sexual abuse of women, and of course, subversion of academic integrity. Such problems have become so rampant that college presidents are now worried that the integrity of their institutions will be tarnished. For example, Charles Young, the Chancellor of UCLA, noted in an editorial to the *Los Angeles Times* (1982),

> The American Council on Education and the Association of American Universities and practically every other higher-education association have appointed special committees to deal with the athletic crisis or placed that item on the agenda of their next major meeting. The NCAA itself has appointed a blue-ribbon committee that has been given a mandate to discover, analyze, and right any wrongs. (p. 5)

Young himself identified several ways that college athletics "should, and can, be straightened out."

All this official concern looks impressive until it is realized that the effort to straighten out the game is almost as old as the game itself. While a detailed recounting of these episodes is beyond the scope of this paper (Lucas & Smith, 1978), suffice it to say that the NCAA exists because of an effort to straighten out the game. Until recently, women's college sport did not exist because women physical educators were disgusted with what they saw in men's programs and decided to stay out of intercollegiate competition (Spears & Swanson, 1978). When women finally did get involved in intercollegiate competition, women leaders tried to avoid the pitfalls they had previously decried. They even set up a separate administrative organization, the Association for Intercollegiate Athletics for Women (AIAW). That organization no longer exists, its members having left it for the NCAA. In other words, answering the question of how to straighten out college athletics is not at all obvious.

As the recent skirmishing within the NCAA demonstrated, there are three general conceptions of how to straighten out college sport. One alternative advocates "cracking down"—tightening regulations and enforcement. Another advocates "being more realistic"—modifying rules to permit certain practices now deemed unacceptable. The third alternative advocates "opening up"—completely professionalizing the game by dropping rules governing academic qualifications of and financial aid to athletes. These alternatives are aspects of the major positions in what is now an 100-year-old debate over college sport.

In an effort to examine this debate, three tasks will be undertaken: First, the four positions in the debate will be identified; second, each of these positions will be shown incapable of pointing a way out of the present crisis; and third, a way out of this crisis will be briefly developed.

THE DEBATE

Two basic questions organize the debate about American college athletics. The first question asks, Are college athletes amateur or professional? The difference in concepts is defined as a difference in the motive of the participant: An amateur plays for fun; a pro, for money. The second question asks, Are college athletic programs education or entertainment? The difference here is in the purpose of the program: education of the participants or entertainment of the spectators. There are four identifiable positions addressing these questions: The *Establishment*, the *Reformers*, the *Sport Scholars*, and the *Radicals*.

The Establishment

The Establishment position is most closely identified with the National Collegiate Athletic Association (NCAA), the body which has traditionally governed men's intercollegiate programs at the nation's larger colleges and universities. The Establishment position is that college athletes are amateur, programs are educational, and commercialism through entertainment in some sports is necessary to support the entire athletic program.[1]

College athletes are amateur because they are "students first and athletes second." An individual may receive financial support (an "athletic grant-in-aid") to be an athlete, but such support is thought to be like a scholarship (often called such) given to a student talented in sports. In other words, such support is seen as a concession to the democratic distribution of skill in the population and to the time constraints training imposes on the individual. Because support is not perceived to corrupt the athlete's attitude, according to the Establishment, he or she cannot be considered a professional.

Programs are educational because sports build character. The content of this education, which has been labeled the "Athletic Creed" (Edwards, 1973), is a moral code balancing sportsmanship and competitiveness. Given the presumed applicability of this code to adult life, intercollegiate programs are appropriate to higher education because they reinforce learning taking place in the classroom, and because they teach other lessons not easily gleaned from books.

The commercialism in college sports is seen by the Establishment as a benefit not only to the athletic department but also to the university as a whole. Certain sports, notably football and basketball, are operated as commercial enterprises in order to support the expenses of the rest of the athletic program. This policy, known as the "Doctrine of Good Works" (Jackson, 1962), is necessary because school officials are often unwilling to support college sport—either out of philosophical opposition or fiscal shrewdness. College athletics are said to benefit the university as a whole because they help build and maintain student, alumni, and legislative interest and financial support.

According to the Establishment, the major problem of college athletics is their *over*commercialization. This overemphasis is believed to be the work of a few deviant individuals swept up in the glamor and power brought by commercial success. These individuals may be athletes using the programs to get to the pro leagues, alumni or administrators interested in bringing glory to their school, or coaches wanting to protect or advance in their jobs. In this environment of temptation, the Establishment sees the NCAA as an organization trying to prevent the encroachment of professionalism. Preventing professionalism now includes regulating (with penalties) key parts of the college sport process, especially recruiting, academic eligibility, financial support, and televising of contests.

The Reformers

Reformers agree with the objectives identified by the Establishment: Athletes should be amateur; programs should be educational. Disagreement lies in the assessment of what is actually happening in NCAA-governed programs.[2] Reformers see a gradual professionalizing of college athletics because of a built-in emphasis on winning and commercial success—"winning at all costs," as it is called. Thus, the Reform position is that college athletes are at the least semi-professional, that programs are primarily entertainment, and that commercialism could be avoided if schools supported athletics as part of the curriculum.[3] While this position has been voiced within the NCAA, it is most closely associated with physical educators and with two other bodies administering college sport, AIAW and the National Association for Intercollegiate Athletics (NAIA).[4]

That college athletes are semipro means that they now display, either individually or collectively, a combination of motives when they participate. In effect, what Reformers see is a morally ambiguous situation brought about by the coming together of individuals with different goals and different motives but with the same athletic abilities. In particular, they see a blending of athletes who want to be pro, with athletes who want to be educated, with athletes who just want to keep playing. Reformers doubt, in other words, that all individuals are "students first and athletes second." Because individuals have this combination of motives, financial aid to athletes manifests a combination of meanings. For some athletes, a grant is a scholarship affording an opportunity otherwise unavailable. For others, it is a wage with certain distracting obligations known as "staying eligible." For still others, it is a base pay, accompanied by lucrative opportunities for making money and getting other perquisites.

Purposes of programs are also ambiguous. Reformers see both entertainment and education manifested in programs, but they see entertainment predominating because of the commercial importance of winning. With commercial success being so important, ambiguity moves inexorably in the direction of professionalism. This shift arises because of the pressure to pander to academically deficient but highly talented athletes in order to win. In this setting, programs look increasingly like "minor leagues" of professional sport.

To the Reformer, the regulatory efforts of the NCAA are not intended to curb this increasing professionalism. Indeed, they point to the fact that the Doctrine of Good Works applies to only a minority of NCAA schools, the ones with the most commercially successful—and morally suspicious—programs. Reformers also contend that NCAA rules are changed whenever they become unenforceable. The most recent and notable example of this process was the change in the definition of amateur itself. Where before an individual was either professional or amateur, now he can be professional or amateur on a sport-by-sport basis. To the Reformer, this sleight-of-hand implicitly acknowledges that college athletes are semipro.

Given the morally ambiguous predicament Reformers find, they see a need for "improved leadership." Improved leadership means eliminating moral ambiguity, either by getting new leaders or by forcing current leaders to strive for their purported objectives. Reformers who believe neither of these alternatives is viable contend that current NCAA programs should be completely professionalized and new amateur programs should be established. New programs would not be dependent on commercial success and would emphasize broad-based participation rather than winning.

The Sports Scholars and the Radicals

The other two positions in the debate, the Sports Scholars and the Radicals, agree that college athletes are professional and that programs are intended to be profit-making entertainment. While space does not permit a complete discussion of these latter two positions (Rose, 1982), several key points can be mentioned. One idea Sports Scholars have contributed to the debate is that the NCAA is not primarily a voluntary association opposed to professionalism, but rather that it is a cartel regulating professionalism in college sport (Koch, 1971; 1973).[5] Another idea put forth by Sports Scholars is that individual freedom of action is constrained by the environment in which action takes place. In the case of college athletics, this means that leadership cannot be expected to improve (as Reformers may wish) if the system does not allow it. Finally, the politically more sensitive Radicals have suggested the idea that the amateur label is itself part of the exploitation of the system (Sack, 1973; 1977).[6] The NCAA, it is believed, is an organization which takes advantage of the mass of laborers for the advantage of those already in power. If athletes were called professional, as Radicals believe they already are, athletes would be in a better position to combat the exploitation they experience because of their recognition of their role.

EVALUATING THE DEBATE

Although discussion of the anti-Establishment positions has suggested the NCAA and its position are susceptible to attack, none of the alternatives has mounted a very serious challenge. Part of their inability here is attributable to weaknesses in their own positions.[7] One weakness in the Reformer position has already been alluded to—a lack of sensitivity to the importance of structural constraints. The cartel idea can be attacked on the grounds that no cartel has ever had as many members as the NCAA. The Radical position is most susceptible regarding its claims of exploitation: Many people, including many athletes, do not believe athletes are being exploited.

Nevertheless, history supports the claim that the present system of college sport is hypocritical. That is, history shows that the NCAA has changed rules and practices while leaving labels in tact. This conclusion suggests a way of eliminating the hypocrisy, however, by leaving rules and practices as they are now and changing labels. In particular, concepts could be defined according to the purpose of the program rather than the motives of the participants. Three concepts—amateur, semiprofessional, and professional—would be defined according to whether a program is intended to be educational, profit-making, or a combination of both. Applying these definitions to the NCAA, programs at Division I schools would be called "professional," at Division II schools, "semi-professional," and at Division III schools, "amateur."

Are the problems of college athletics substantially reduced if programs are relabeled in this fashion? Or are other, more substantive changes necessary as well? One important question in this regard is, What ideas will replace the Athletic Creed and the Doctrine of Good Works as the guiding and unifying principles of the NCAA? If one looks at developments within the NCAA in the past 15 years, two likely candidates can be seen emerging. Replacing the Doctrine of Good Works is a modified doctrine which operates at a national rather than at an institutional level. That is, big-time football and basketball would financially support not just other sports in Division I athletic departments, but athletic programs at other schools in the NCAA. Replacing the Athletic Creed would be another value held high in the NCAA, the value of institutional self-determination. With this value taking formal precedence over the Athletic Creed, schools would be free to implement the Creed as they wished, including of course, not at all.

While certain logistical problems might make it difficult to implement such ideas within the NCAA (Rose, 1982), there are other, deeper difficulties with relabeling and with abandoning the Athletic Creed. One problem is this: If the Athletic Creed were dropped, if Division I programs were acknowledged to be professional, their separate identity would be lost. The *label* "professional" would denote that college sports are only minor leagues to the major professional leagues; and programs in football and baseball could expect to suffer the same decimation the minor leagues of baseball suffered in an era of televised major league games. This fate has not befallen big-time football and basketball because of their separate identity; their commercial success is linked intimately to their social location as contests with great status and prestige. Without the separate identity, an NCAA champion or bowl game winner would be no more than a Triple A champion; and Triple A champions are not televised, lionized, eulogized, or remembered.

In other words, in the present system of college sport, the notion of the student-athlete must be maintained, regardless of how hypocritically, not just for political, but more crucially for financial reasons. The Establishment knows this: Its awareness is manifested in the regulatory monster known as the *NCAA Rulebook*. If Radicals do not already recognize this fact, they will soon discover it when college athletes remind them that a hypocritically named ticket to the riches of privately owned pro leagues is better than no ticket at all.

There is another problem with dropping the Athletic Creed and the concept of the student-athlete: Dropping both ideas would imply that the integrity of American higher education had been systematically undermined in the past. More importantly, dropping the facade would not restore integrity to the system. Why not? Because no college could then employ its standard line of defense[8] to justify its sport or physical education program once the institutions with the highest academic reputations had admitted they had been systematically lying. Physical education programs are emphasized here because of a crucial, though underappreciated link between college sport and PE. Stated succinctly, the link is this: Schools support PE departments not because school leaders believe in promoting academic quality in this area; rather schools support PE departments because their existence assuages some of the criticism of and lends credence to the professed aims of intercollegiate sports (Lewis, 1969; Rose & Oglesby, 1982). In other words, changing labels would reveal that educational integrity is subverted most fundamentally not by celebrated cases of cheating among athletes, but by the routine operation of an academic department whose existence is accepted but whose worth is largely in doubt (Henry, 1978). Because neither Reformers nor Sports Scholars are prepared to expose this latter hypocrisy, they too are party to the former, well-known one.

WHAT CAN BE DONE?

At this juncture, several points should be made clear: (a) Corruption in college sport cannot be eliminated as long as the debate over college sport remains intractable; (b) the debate over the nature of college sport cannot be resolved within the present line of thinking; and (c) therefore, a new line of thinking must be developed. In the space remaining, this task will be undertaken. In particular, research implementing such reconceptualized thinking will be discussed briefly to illustrate how the debate can be resolved and the corruption eliminated.

Rose (1980) induced that the existing concepts were defined inadequately, and that there was also a missing concept. This missing concept was called "semiprofessional sport" and was defined as participation undertaken to represent the quality of the sponsoring organization. This definition was an important breakthrough for several reasons. First, it was oriented toward the structural context of participation, not to the motives of the participants. Second, the notion of representation identified the previously missing basis upon which to see why certain sports programs could become "increasingly professionalized." Third, this orientation opened up the possibility of identifying pro sports programs other than those operated by private owners. A new question was therefore posed, College sport: semipro or pro?

It was hypothesized that the answer to this question was that programs were now professional because they had been conducted previously as semipro sport. The hypothesized explanation for this shift was the pattern of higher education in the U.S. In this pattern, schools compete with each other for money and students. Hence, if a school's sports programs were perceived to represent the college's quality, college leaders would be structurally constrained to compete in sports (to hire athletes likely to produce victories) in order to compete in the marketplace of higher education.

All these hypotheses were supported. Particularly noteworthy in this regard is that research revealed a way to identify the intermediate phases of the often cited process of "increasing professionalization." These phases could be seen as semiprofessional, acceptably professional, and unacceptably professional sport. In semipro sport, the representative relationship is genuine; for the individual is a student-athlete—a student first and athlete second. In acceptably pro sport, the representative relationship is still legitimate, for the individual is both student and athlete; but the relative priority of the two roles is blurred as schools recruit and hire individuals to be athletes. The athletic grant-in-aid is the wage the individual receives. In unacceptably pro sport, the representative relationship is broken as schools hire individuals who are athletes first and students not at all, using whatever inducement works.

These stages can be seen in the history of the NCAA. From very early on, college sport contests, particularly in football, were seen as deference challenges— "defending the honor of Alma Mater." The stage of acceptably pro sport was reached when the NCAA formally permitted the granting of financial aid on the basis of athletic ability in the 1950s. The stage of unacceptably professional sport was reached when the NCAA reorganized (1982) and placed the Ivy League colleges, institutions of the first academic order, into Division IAA, the second level for the quintessential college sport, football.

In this line of analysis, the question of eliminating corruption in college sport must be restated. The new question is, How can college sport be moved from its present mode of operation, as unacceptably pro sport, to semipro sport? Does, for example, the NCAA's 1983 decision to tighten academic requirements for athletes (Proposition 48 is discussed elsewhere in this book) move programs in this direction? The answer is no. Why not? Because Proposition 48 does not affect any of the structural constraints at work here. It does not reduce colleges' need to hire great athletes in order to win; it does not improve the quality of secondary education available to the vast majority of urban and rural students, particularly minorities; and it does not alter the relative priority of colleges' commitment to improve athletic ability with colleges' commitment to improve academic ability in the athletes they hire.

If college sport is to exist as semipro sport, that is, as representative sport, two actions must be taken: First, financial aid for talent in athletics should be given only to those individuals who major in (what is now called) physical education, and second, American higher education must be moved away from its present marketplace orientation to where school leaders are no longer predisposed to use sports as a vehicle for promoting institutional growth. This latter point cannot be overemphasized. The corruption of American college athletics is not due primarily to corrupt individuals or to the adverse influences of pro sport or TV or gambling. All these factors merely serve to exacerbate problems inherent in American college athletics because of the relationship between college sport and higher education, that is, because of the nature of American higher education itself.

SUMMARY

1. The present system of college sport is and must be hypocritical.
2. None of the four positions currently prominent in the debate over the nature of college sport is capable of resolving the controversy.
3. To resolve the controversy, one must break with the conventional approach to defining concepts in American sport.
4. If one is willing to break from convention, it is possible to see that college sport is purportedly a form of what has been called here "semiprofessional sport," that is, sport in which teams represent the colleges sponsoring them.
5. College sport is currently not semipro sport; its present mode of operation is unacceptably pro sport—unacceptably professional because the link between the quality of athletic teams and the quality of the university has been broken.

6. If college sport is to exist as semipro sport, financial aid for talent in athletics should be given only to those individuals who major in physical education.

7. For this remedy to be implemented, American higher education must be moved away from its present marketplace orientation so that school leaders are no longer predisposed to use sports as a vehicle for promoting institutional growth.

FOOTNOTES

1. For an early, concise statement of the Establishment position, see Griffith (1931).

2. Almost all debate on college athletics focuses on the NCAA, and primarily on its big-time programs. These are the football and basketball programs which attract the greatest crowds and the most media attention. Reflecting this difference in commercial viability, the NCAA is presently organized into three major subdivisions: Division I (the Big Time), Division II (the Middle Time), and Division III (the Small Time). Division I is further subdivided into IA and IAA; IA contains the major football powers and those aspiring to be major powers. Most of these major powers—with the notable exception of the Big Ten and PAC 10 schools—have joined together to form the College Football Association (CFA). This group has two objectives at present. It wants to restrict Division I membership to those schools who are acknowledged football powers. It also wants to decentralize control of the sale of televising rights for football from the NCAA, where it has resided since 1952, to the individual members and conferences.

3. Reformer positions can be found in physical education as far back as Sargent (1892). An articulate critique of college athletics was given at an early NCAA convention by Savage (1914). The most systematic empirical inquiry into college sport, by the Carnegie Foundation for the Advancement of Teaching, recommended widespread reforms (Savage et al., 1929). In recent years, inquiries intended to lead to reforms have been led by Hanford (1974) and Nyquist (1979a, 1979b). See also Massengale (1979).

4. Since 1938, the NAIA has handled college sport (beginning with basketball) at many of the smaller institutions of higher learning in the U.S. The AIAW was formed in 1971 to administer college sports for women. AIAW effectively ceased operating in 1982. Some observers place much of the responsibility for this demise on AIAW and its leaders. For a different interpretation of the cause of AIAW's death, see Rose and Oglesby (1982).

5. This idea recently received widespread publicity when it was raised in a lawsuit brought against the NCAA by two members of the CFA petitioning the court to invalidate NCAA control over the television rights of big-time college football.

6. A Radical position on sport emerged in the late sixties, inspired by the work and writings of primarily two individuals, Jack Scott (1971) and Harry Edwards (1970, 1973). Also noteworthy here are Hoch (1972) and Shaw (1972).

7. For a more complete discussion evaluating the debate, see Rose (1982).

8. Three lines are typical here: "We are okay because" (a) "we are not big-time," (b) "we finance athletics out of general university funds," or (c) "we administer athletics out of the College of Physical Education."

REFERENCES

EDWARDS, H. (1970). *The revolt of the black athlete*. New York: Free Press.

EDWARDS, H. (1973). *Sociology of sport*. Homewood, IL: Dorsey Press.

GRIFFITH, J. (1931). A philosophy of college athletics. *Athletic Journal*, **11**, 5-30.

HANFORD, G. (1974). *Report on intercollegiate athletics*. Washington, DC: American Council on Education.

HENRY, F. (1978). The academic discipline of physical education. *Quest*, **29**, 13-29.

HOCH, P. (1972). *Rip off the big game: The exploitation of sports by the power elite*. Garden City, NY: Doubleday.

JACKSON, M. (December, 1962). College football has become a losing business. *Fortune*, pp. 119-121.

KOCH, J. (1971). The economics of 'Big Time' intercollegiate athletics. *Social Science Quarterly*, **52**, 248-260.

KOCH, J. (1973). A troubled cartel: The NCAA. *Law and Contemporary Problems*, **38**, 135-150.

LEWIS, G. (1969). Adoption of the sports program, 1906-1939: The role of accommodation in the transformation of physical education. *Quest*, **12**, 34-46.

LUCAS, J., & Smith, R. (1978). *Saga of American sport*. Philadelphia: Lea and Febiger.

MASSENGALE, M. (1979). On collegiate athletics. *Educational Record*, **60**, p. 4.

NYQUIST, E. (Dec. 10, 1979a). Chairman responds to criticisms of Commission on Collegiate Athletics. *Chronicle of Higher Education*, p. 19.

NYQUIST, E. (1979b). Win, women, and money: Collegiate athletics today and tomorrow. *Educational Record*, **60**, 374-393.

ROSE, D. (1980). *Physical culture: A critique of the American sociological study of sport*. Unpublished Ph.D. dissertation, University of Massachusetts.

ROSE, D. (April, 1982). *Recommendations for new directions in intercollegiate athletics*. Paper presented at the pre-convention symposium on sociology of sport at the annual convention of the American Alliance for Health, Physical Education, Recreation and Dance, Houston.

ROSE, D., & Oglesby, C. (November, 1982). *Sociological implications of the NCAA/AIAW dispute over women's sports*. Paper presented at the annual meeting of the North American Society for Sociology of Sport, Toronto.

SACK, A. (1973). Yale 29—Harvard 4: The professionalization of college football. *Quest*, **19**, 24-40.

SACK, A. (1977). Big time college football: Whose free ride? *Quest*, **27**, 87-96.

SARGENT, D. (1892). Regulation and management of athletic sports. *Proceedings of the American Association for the Advancement of Physical Education*, **7**, 97-115.

SAVAGE, C. (1914). The professional versus the educational in college athletics. *Proceedings of the Annual Convention of the NCAA, 9,* 52-59.

SAVAGE, H., Bentley, J., McGovern, J., & Smiley, D. (1929). *American college athletics.* New York: Carnegie Foundation for the Advancement of Teaching.

SCOTT, J. (1971). *The athletic revolution.* New York: Free Press.

SHAW, G. (1972). *Meat on the hoof.* New York: Dell.

SPEARS, B., & Swanson, R. (1978). *History of sport and physical education in the United States.* Dubuque: Wm. C. Brown.

YOUNG, C. (August 10, 1982). College athletics should, and can, be straightened out. *Los Angeles Times,* p. 5.

Part III

GOVERNANCE

Even with the recent establishment of the Department of Education, there is still no "central ministry" of higher education in America to tightly control the operations of the nations' colleges and universities. According to Martin (1982), this lack of systematic educational control is an example of America's pervasive logic and "economy of capitalism," which is our willingness to leave things alone, to let them fail or succeed on their own in response to the demands and competition of the marketplace. The national concept of social pluralism and diversity in American life has contributed to "the national religion": that is, a tolerance of differences in institutions and individuals. This is a tolerance, however, which according to Martin, has all too often eroded into a permissiveness and an unwillingness to define ethical standards. In Martin's view, this overbearing tolerance has contributed to a lack of centralized authority and national standards for appropriate behavior in the institution of higher education.

In place of a central authority, many external agencies such as the American Council on Education have evolved to direct the behavior of the more than 2,000 4-year institutions of higher learning in the United States. The large numbers of these schools and the lack of any one unified "theory" of the purposes appropriate for American higher education has, however, led to a high degree of institutional autonomy—a freedom from direct governance jealously guarded by college and university administrators, and an autonomy which makes national regulation of sport problematic.

It is clear that the diversity of sport forms, the historical autonomy of American higher education, and the pressure to gain money and institutional visibility have made the governance of sport highly problematic. Are rules which apply to NCAA

Division II and III schools appropriate for the Division I powers? For that matter, are the regulations drafted for Division IA schools necessarily right for Division IAA institutions? Clearly, the major football powers that form the bulk of NCAA Division IA and that founded the College Football Association believe that the needs of the big schools are distincly different from schools with less ambitious programs.

Despite the challenge of the CFA and the ACE sponsored president's committee which developed Proposal 35, the traditional NCAA bureaucracy, with its control of championship tournaments and lucrative television contracts, remains, for better or worse, the undisputed policy and rule-making body for college sport. Only time will tell if the NCAA will become an organization truly representative of its constituency or a bureaucracy intent primarily on its own survival—a true advocate for educational sport or an apologist for institutions that will not really govern themselves. Only time will tell if American institutions of higher learning will be able to independently set and maintain appropriate codes of behavior and operating norms consistent with the purposes of higher education. The degree to which our educational organizations mark as deviant unethical behavior and the extent to which they govern themselves according to high standards will also tell us something about the society which withdraws or continues its support of these institutions.

The large number of American schools and the autonomy of these institutions to independently determine appropriate programs is a basic cause of difficulties in the governance of intercollegiate sport. The largest organization overseeing campus sport, the National Collegiate Athletic Association (NCAA) may express consternation concerning the abuses of college sport; however, until relatively recently, the NCAA has had neither the enforcement power or personnel to police the legal proscriptions passed by the membership; furthermore, there has not been an understanding widely held among its member schools of what constitutes educational sport and legitimate ethical behavior.

In his article "The Development of Interorganizational Control Network: The Case of Intercollegiate Athletics," Robert Stern takes a sociohistorical look at the development of the NCAA from a loosely defined structure to its present position as the dominant organization for intercollegiate sport—an organization, which in the minds of some critics "is able to exploit its major labor source—student athletes" (Sage, 1982:131). From its formation in 1906 by the 38 schools responding to public criticism over deaths in football, the original Intercollegiate Athletic Association became the NCAA in 1910. With the increasing numbers of schools and sport conferences, there grew the need for communication and coordination of playing rules, schedules, and championships.

As television's impact expanded from the 1950s to the present day, the NCAA became an increasingly visible speaker on behalf of college sport, a speaker made extremely powerful due to the capacity of the Association to negotiate television contracts for its members. Even with the "enforcement decision" of 1952 which first gave the Association the right to police eligibility, recruitment, and other sport regulations, however, there have been limits to the ability of the NCAA to coerce membership behavior consistent with the original constitutional goal of the organization "to make college sport dignified and ethical." In response to this situation whereby there are inadequate means to enforce organizational decisions, Stern notes the "loose-coupling" of stated organizational goals from actual programs and behaviors in the history of the NCAA.

James Frey considers reasons for the great power of athletic programs. Employing an "open systems perspective," which assumes the importance of external power groups to the decisions and behaviors of an organization, Frey looks at the university athletic department as one of the few academic units able to forge a strong linkage with external groups. Because athletic departments fulfill an entertainment need for the community, and because of the clarity of purpose of the athletic department's objectives, sport programs are highly powerful components of the university. The athletic department's autonomy which results from such favorable relations with important alumni, booster, and public groups makes problematic control of the department by the parent institution.

While the preceding papers by Stern and Frey focus upon external factors important to the governance of intercollegiate sport, the paper by Massengale and Merriman looks directly at the internal bureaucratic structure of sport governance.

John Massengale and John Merriman consider the question of the best administrative housing for the athletic department. Should sport program administrators answer to an academic department head or should the athletic director be immediately responsible to the president of the institution? The answer to this question, according to the authors, is largely dependent upon the view of the institution toward the purposes of the athletic program. If sport is considered a business, and if sport's main purpose is to make money or promote visibility, then the athletic department independent of academic housing might be appropriate; if the "professional service" philosophy is of paramount importance to the athletic department, then some disciplinary affiliation may be necessary. As the governance structure of sport becomes closer to traditional academic forms, then the connection of college athletics to public groups external to the institution becomes even more remote.

Derek Bok's letter to the *Chronicle of Higher Education* is published as the last paper of this section. As President of Harvard University and Chairman of the American Council on Education's Committee on Intercollegiate Athletics, Bok presents background and arguments for Proposition Number 35 presented for consideration before the 1984 NCAA Convention. In its original form, the proposal would have set up a 44-member policy-making group elected by a mail-in ballot of all NCAA member chief executive officers. These policies could only have been overriden by a 2/3 vote of convention delegates. The proposal sought to shift power from the athletic directors, faculty athletic representatives, and the NCAA bureaucracy back to the institutions' leadership. Despite a strong ACE lobbying effort on behalf of Proposition 35, the proposal was ultimately defeated

(328-313) in favor of NCAA sponsored Proposition Number 36—a proposal which set up a Council of Presidents with only advisory capabilities and without the policy-making powers of the ACE inspired proposal.

Bok argues for strong presidential leadership on "important policy issues significantly affecting the academic standards, financial integrity or reputation" of Division I member institutions. While opponents of Proposition 35 have argued that college presidents already exercise control over their institution's voting delegates to the NCAA Conventions, Bok suggests that such presidential control is more theoretical than real. The president who singularly decides to become more directly involved in athletic policy often finds him or herself unapprised of background, issues, and bureaucratic conventions of the annual NCAA policy-making meetings. Extremely busy chief-executive officers typically defer voting responsibilities to the athletic directors or faculty-athletic representatives who are more intimately aware of and concerned with athletic operations. Proposal 35 was an attempt to establish bureaucratically as well as symbolically the supremacy of the chief-executive officer as primarily responsible for athletic policy setting.

REFERENCES

MARTIN, W.B. (1982). *A College of Character*. San Francisco: Jossey Bass.

SAGE, G.H. (1982). "The Intercollegiate Sport Cartel and Its Consequences for Athletes." In James Frey (Ed.) *The Governance of Intercollegiate Athletics* (pp. 131-143). West Point, NY: Leisure Press.

Chapter 11

The Development of an Interorganizational Control Network: The Case of Intercollegiate Athletics

Robert N. Stern
Cornell University

There is renewed interest in the use of network analysis as a tool for the examination of social structure (e.g., Laumann & Pappi, 1976; White, Boorman, & Brieger, 1976; Burt, 1977). Network analysis relies on the assumption that the relationships between social actors in a population can be represented by a set of ties among the actors (Boissevain, 1974). Once the pattern of ties is identified, a researcher can use this network structure as a tool to examine such things as the diffusion of change within a population (Becker, 1970) or the concentration of resources and information among the actors. When the structure of connections is coupled with a description of the processes that maintain the network links, then power relationships, resource mobilization, and coalition formation may be examined.

The majority of network analysts have approached subject populations with quantitative, cross-sectional research strategies and have argued that the representation of ties among actors in mathematical matrix form permits precise prediction and complete description. However, this concentration on mathematical precision has prevented network analysis from reaching its full potential. Researchers have taken measures at only a single point in time, permitting methodological technique to dominate substantive and theoretical interpretation. They have failed to consider how the network reached the state pictured in the quantitative formulation, and they have paid insufficient attention to interaction among network members. Greater attention to developmental processes would show that the variables measured change frequently and require measurement at several points in time. Historical data reveal the arbitrary nature of some of the assumptions made by current network analysts.

159

The intent of this study is to strengthen network analysis, first by showing that network activity is a function of the historical development of relationships as well as current structural characteristics and, second, by showing that the explanatory power of the network approach depends on an analysis of the processes that link network structure to the interests of organizations in the network. An adequate network analysis must specify the environmental context, interaction processes, historical development, and specific structures of the network, not just structural measures. These objectives are accomplished by focusing a case study of the development of the National Collegiate Athletic Association (NCAA) on four structural determinants common in network studies.

CASE BACKGROUND

This study of the intercollegiate athletic network focuses on the period initiated by the founding of the NCAA in 1906 and culminating in the decision by NCAA-member colleges and universities in 1952 to grant the association the right to control athletic programs through rule making and sanctions. This decision, termed the "enforcement decision," marked the complete transformation of the NCAA from a loose confederation designed for mutual support and dissemination of rules into a powerful control agent capable of inflicting serious financial loss on member schools caught violating its rules.

Colleges, universities, conferences, and athletic organizations, together with other related organizations such as government, form the intercollegiate athletic network. Its purpose is the production of athletic competition between representatives of competing schools. At the bases of their interactions are two core problems that emerged immediately after the initiation of intercollegiate competition between the crews of Harvard and Yale in 1852 (Savage, 1929). First, what rules of play should guide such competition? Second, who should be eligible to represent a school in athletic competition? Precision and consensus in answering the first question contrasts sharply with ambiguity and conflict arising over the second. While there has always been mutual benefit in agreement on how to play, the organization that can turn the uncertainty of eligibility criteria to its advantage may dominate on the field.

Recruiting practices are the competitive practices of the industry, and the regulation of intercollegiate athletics has been characterized by continuous conflict over the interpretation and enforcement of these rules. In some schools, the ability to obtain income from admissions receipts and television contracts depends on the quality of athletic talent recruited by the school. The rules of amateur eligibility constrain recruiting practices, but the incentive for stretching or violating these rules is significant. Recruiting and eligibility issues provide much of the political fuel for network development.

In 1906, 38 schools agreed on the constitution for the Intercollegiate Athletic Association (Pierce, 1907), which became the NCAA in 1910. The organization was formed because there was confusion over the rules of play for football and because there was a considerable amount of public displeasure (voiced by newspapers and government officials) over the deaths of several collegiate football players. The members sought mutual support against this public pressure by creating regular rules of play that would eliminate negotiations before each game and protect the players.

At this time, there were already a number of amateur athletic organizations, including a Football Rules Committee, which was merged into the NCAA.[1] In western states (Ohio westward), a number of athletic conferences had been formed in the 1890s to locally promulgate rules of play and eligibility, but in the east, the new association began to carry out this function. Thus, at its founding, the NCAA was not much different from other existing conferences, though it explicitly sought to influence national practices, rather than solely local ones. The incentives for organizations to affiliate were weak because rules published by the group were available to all (Olson, 1965). As a result, the purposive motivation seems less critical than the solidary one of mutual support in explaining the association's initial survival.

By 1906 another organization, the Amateur Athletic Union (AAU), was well established as a coordinating organization for club-affiliated athletes. Though there was a distinction between club-affiliated and college athletes, competition between the AAU and the NCAA was almost immediate. Many athletes were unwilling to restrict their athletic competition solely to collegiate or noncollegiate events, particularly in the international arena, which was controlled by the AAU. The rivalry between the associations significantly influenced network development and continues under current practices.

From its founding through 1952, the NCAA grew both in membership of individual schools and number of conferences. Table 1 shows membership figures

Table 1
NCAA School and Conference Membership*

Year	No. of Schools	No. of Conferences
1906	38	0
1911	79	1
1916	95	6
1921	102	7
1926	148	4
1931	160	16
1936	191	19
1941	220	22
1946	NA	NA
1951	368	24

*Source: *NCAA Proceedings*.
NA—Data not available.

for 5-year intervals. Large increases in school membership occurred initially rather than in the early 1920s and late 1940s. The largest growth in conference membership occurred in the late 1920s.

ENVIRONMENTAL CONTEXT

A variety of social and economic events created the environment for the development of intercollegiate athletics and profoundly influenced network development. The rebirth of the Olympic games, war, depression, and changes in affluence, education, communication, and transportation generally increased public interest in athletic competition and brought new resources, competitors, and a variety of new sports. The economic stakes, accompanied by the creation of divergent interests among schools, vastly increased the pressure to resolve issues raised by environmental events.

Expansion of Programs and Facilities

The rebirth of the Olympics in 1896 stimulated the development of amateur athletic programs in the U.S. The staging of the first modern games brought increased demands for further international competition (Kierman & Daley, 1961). The increased importance of international competition produced conflict between the AAU and the NCAA over team selection procedures and eligibility.

World War I led to increasing concern for physical conditioning in athletic programs. The Secretary of War encouraged NCAA sponsorship of physical training programs in colleges to aid in the development of the physical and leadership qualities needed in young military officers (NCAA, 1917). Military officers continued to participate in NCAA conventions long after the war, emphasizing a link between college athletics and national defense through physical preparation (NCAA, 1927).

College athletic programs paralleled the growth of the American economy in the 1920s (Lewis, 1973). Stadia were built (NCAA, 1922, 1923, 1924, 1926, 1927), attendance at athletic events and gate receipts increased (NCAA, 1920, 1921, 1923-1929), and some schools began to hire coaches on a full-time basis (NCAA, 1921-1924, 1926, 1928, 1929). However, expansion brought a number of unanticipated problems. Building stadia and expanding programs increased indebtedness, putting pressure on schools to raise athletic income by producing exciting teams and soliciting alumni contributions (NCAA, 1926, 1927). Coaches were often hired seasonally with rehiring dependent on winning (NCAA, 1921, 1928). Increased public interest was accompanied by a substantial growth in press coverage of college athletics (NCAA, 1920-1930; *New York Times Index*, 1870-1952), and an increase in the number of zealous alumni pressuring schools and trying to induce young athletes to attend the alma mater (NCAA, 1921-1932). Journalists became concerned about codes of conduct promulgated by the NCAA and produced material condemning the recruiting of students from high schools, the subsidizing of amateur athletes (NCAA, 1915, 1920-1930) and other practices, including summer baseball leagues and free meals at training tables. A report by the Carnegie Foundation showing wide-ranging abuses of the principles of amateurism received considerable press and was attacked by NCAA representatives (Savage, 1929).

Technological Changes—Communication and Transportation

The expansion of facilities and programs collapsed along with the American economy in the early 1930s, but difficulties with gate receipts, subsidies, recruiting, and alumni remained. Technological changes in communications and transportation added to the complexity of amateur athletic control. Decreased attendance during the Depression provoked controversy over the effects of radio broadcasting of football games, with some arguing for the increased interest and good will generated by broadcasts and others noting the loss in gate receipts because of the availability of the game on radio (NCAA, 1931, 1932, 1934).

As radio increased the accessibility of sporting events, improved transportation expanded the distances over which competition could take place. After 1930 long distance travel, and with it long distance competition, became increasingly practical, particularly when combined with radio broadcasts back home.

These changes altered the relationship between schools by increasing competition over two major network resources—athletes and prestige. Though recruiting of high school athletes had been repeatedly condemned (NCAA, 1915), it was an outgrowth of the desire to produce a winning team. Originally recruiting was confined to local high schools or at most to areas only a short distance away, but the decreasing cost of transportation broadened the area a coach or alumnus might expect to survey and increased the distances students were willing to travel to attend school. Competition for athletic talent became more intense as schools invaded one another's protected territories. It expanded considerably in the late 1920s and again during the Depression, when promised subsidies for college attendance became most inviting (NCAA, 1920-1935).

As changes in transportation and communication increased the demand for athletes and created resource competition, competition for athletic prestige intensified. Prior to these technological changes, regional competition and relatively closed schedules produced numerous teams which could claim to be "the best." However, interregional competition, including bowl games in football and national championships in other sports, permitted a comparison of the regional bests, and national prestige emerged. By 1940 national team championships had been established in most sports, and the mythical national champion in football appeared with the Associated Press poll in 1936. As prestige became a scarce resource and the need to maintain gate receipts continued, recruiting competition again intensified.

Technological change in communications presented the colleges with an additional issue. The potential revenue available through television broadcasts was immediately apparent, but the inequality of the likely distribution of revenue was equally obvious (NCAA, 1952). Political conflict emerged between those schools favoring independent negotiation of television contracts and those seeking centralized administration with special revenue-sharing provisions.

Major Effects Created by Environmental Changes

Two general effects on athletic network development arise from changes in the environment. The most obvious is the increased interdependence created by technological changes, increasing affluence, government, and public interest in college athletics. These factors would have altered the nature of intercollegiate athletics even in the absence of the NCAA, but its existence as a forum-facilitating communication and debate determined much of the impact of these changes. The actors in the network used the association as a mechanism for coordinating their interdependence and altered the structure of the network to accommodate their increased need for interaction.

The second, less obvious but equally important, effect of the environment was its differential impact upon particular schools. Not everyone had the resources to construct a new stadium, recruit nationally, and travel outside the local area for games. At least two classes of schools emerged from the growth period of the 1920s. Those which became known as university division schools had more students, more resources, and a greater need to succeed in attracting the revenue brought by fans coming to watch a winning team. Colleges with fewer students and resources certainly wanted to win and hoped to obtain good athletes but wished to participate in athletics for values of competition other than revenue. These two groups developed inherently conflicting interests within the association, particularly with regard to enforcement of the rules of amateurism and distribution of resources accruing to the association. Their investments in athletic facilities differed as well as their espoused views on education and the value of athletic competition.

DETERMINANTS OF NETWORK DEVELOPMENT

The analysis of environmental factors already hints at some of the changes that occurred within the network and promoted the dominance of some organizations over others. The purpose of this section is to reinterpret, from a network perspective, events that occurred among organizations involved in intercollegiate athletic competition. Focusing on the four basic determinants, the description traces changes in the network that ultimately produced the dominance of the NCAA. Table 2 lists the structural changes that occurred during the period and classifies them by the determinant of network characteristics each represents. Each deter-

Table 2

Structural Changes in the NCAA's Emerging Dominance (1906-1952)

A. Administrative structuring

1. Geographic districts
2. Conference membership category
3. Executive board (financial)
4. Council (athletic policy)
5. Paid staff
6. Committee structure

C. Multiplexity of ties

1. Rules of play (1906-1931)
2. Educational material and meetings
3. Administrative recommendations for athletic programs
4. Championship play (1921-1940)
5. Financial incentives
6. U.S. Olympic team participation (1932)

E. The enforcement decision (1948-1952)

1. Chicago conference (1946)
2. Sanity code (1948)
3. Expulsion decision (1950)
4. Public disclosure (1951)
5. Enforcement program (1952)

B. System coupling

1. Local autonomy
2. Nonbinding legislation (1909)
3. Binding legislation (1952)

D. New resource control

1. Representative function
   a. Olympic committee
   b. Government
   c. Press
   d. Television contracts
2. Bowl game certification

minant is discussed in two ways. First, the structures themselves are described; then a process analysis is provided both to explain the origin of particular structures and to reveal the underlying development of the network.

Administrative Structuring

Geographic districts. The initial statement of purpose establishing the NCAA discussed studying college athletics and promoting measures to make college sport dignified and ethical (NCAA Constitution, 1906). Promotion of the association was accomplished by offering standard rules of play along with suggestions for the elimination of professionalism, but studying athletic problems required coordinated information gathering. All schools in the country were divided into geographic districts, each having a representative to maintain the association's presence, consult with member institutions, and persuade unaffiliated schools to join.

Conference membership. The formation of districts added a hierarchical level to the already emerging organization of local conferences. The Intercollegiate Conference (Big Ten), the Chicago Conference on Athletics, and the Southern

Intercollegiate Athletic Conference were well-established pattern setters when the NCAA district representatives arrived (Savage, 1929: 26). Rather than set itself up in competition with these conferences, the NCAA encouraged them as the only mechanism for eliminating improper practices and made special provision for the affiliation of conferences with the association, regardless of the individual membership of conference institutions. The new association grafted itself onto the existing network but retained a mechanism for bringing that network under its influence. In effect, the NCAA developed a method for incorporating existing intermediate-level subsystems of the network under its aegis. The preexistence of these relatively stable subunits probably promoted stability for the new association (Simon, 1962).

The initial division into districts in 1907-1908 was one of the few noncontroversial, but critical, decisions made by the early members. It explicitly recognized the existence of regional interests and legitimized future activity based upon local interests. As conferences developed within districts, schools further separated themselves by size and level of competition, thus creating both political and administrative interest groups that could be used as bases of support in making other decisions.

Executive board, council, and paid staff. As the NCAA developed, its structure became increasingly complex. Initially, three officers and four executive board members were chosen. The size of the executive board had increased to nine by 1921, when a separate council was formed to deal with all nonfinancial matters. The council consisted of the elected representative for each district and five delegates-at-large selected by the council. A second expansion took place in 1928 when the number of delegates-at-large and executive board members was increased, and a third change came in 1949 with the hiring of a full-time staff director.

Committee structure. A second development involved the establishment of committees, whose number varied over time but generally increased as the association approached the 1950s. Standing committees existed for handling rules in each sport, operating championship tournaments as they were established, issuing publications, preparing for the Olympics, and keeping records. These committees further centralized the administration of the NCAA.

Structural implications. The picture provided here is one of cumulative structural development. Administrative structures may be seen as a function of increasing size and task complexity (Blau & Schoenherr, 1971; Meyer, 1972). The number of members affiliated with the NCAA grew steadily and the cumulative effects of increasing size may have provided pressure for administrative structuring. However, the administrative changes did not coincide with extraordinarily large growth; thus the pressure caused by increasing complexity of college athletic programs provides a more inviting explanation for change. The increases in administrative structuring are associated with the expansion of athletic competition which occurred in the 1920s and late 1930s and the enforcement decision of 1952.

Process Perspective

Explaining change. Creating an administrative apparatus was not a simple consensus decision, nor was it a linear function of growth or complexity. Three interest groups competed in the decision process in which a coalition of small colleges opposed the major universities. In 1915 representatives of the universities accused colleges of violating rules that made freshmen ineligible, while a professor from Swarthmore berated the universities for creating a "big-time" athletics image that was drawing attention away from the small private colleges (NCAA, 1915).

A third interest group was composed of association staff and officers. Though they claimed to represent the interests of members, they were meeting with greater frequency than the member delegates, who assembled once each year. The administrative group held independence of action from the membership beyond their policy implementation mandate, a phenomenon often recognized in governmental and voluntary organizations (Michels, 1962; Grodzins, 1966; Wilson, 1973).

Because of conflicting interests among the three groups, there was resistance to administrative change. The periodic debate over hiring a staff director, settled in the 1940s, is particularly illustrative of the conflict. Those involved in administration sought a new position for managing public pressure for information and for supervising the developing rule enforcement effort. Small schools favoring enforcement of rules and provision of services by the association also wanted an expanded staff. The larger universities, however, were engaged in intense competition over gate receipts and athletic talent, and they feared the increasing ability of the association to restrict local autonomy. The small schools were a majority in the association and carried the decision, though the officers and committee members were, ironically, from the larger schools.

Process implications. The initial establishment of administrative mechanisms created a new political force within the network. The administrative interest group gathered information, published documents, and acted on the members' behalf. Its interests became important in debates over changes in association functions and rules. In addition, the emergence of an administrative group created hierarchy and a basis for hierarchical authority, which the association could later rely on to increase the dependence of the membership on services it delivered. Administrative structure became a power base within the association because of the interaction between administrative apparatus and membership demands.

System Coupling

The critical issue with regard to system coupling is the degree to which the NCAA was permitted to monitor and control the athletic programs of member schools.

Coupling varied with the mechanisms through which the association attempted to influence schools' athletic activities.

Structures

Local autonomy. The 38 founding schools that formed the NCAA made rather tenuous commitments. They could not agree upon a strict eligibility code or enforcement procedures, and each school insisted that its program be controlled by its own school faculty (NCAA, 1909; Flath, 1964). Some eligibility rules were adopted, but education of school administrators and the public was chosen as the principal mechanism for reforming athletic practice and image (Pierce, NCAA, 1910).

Nonbinding legislation. The 1906 constitution established local autonomy and faculty control of programs as fundamental principles (NCAA, 1910-1952). These principles were reinforced in the 1909 constitution, which permitted schools to file written objections to any legislation enacted by the delegates. Such a filing made the legislation nonbinding on the institution. This provision established school control of the association at the outset.

Binding legislation. The right of self-governance for constituent members was continually referred to in the rhetoric of association meetings, particularly when the issue of enforcement of NCAA rules of eligibility and conduct was debated (NCAA, 1916, 1921, 1923-1925, 1933, 1935, 1948). In 1948, the membership granted the association the power to pass binding legislation, but without providing viable enforcement powers. Such powers were not voted to the NCAA until 4 years later.

Structural implications. A structural analysis of the relationships between member organizations might be represented by a matrix of interorganizational linkages and counts of organizations with high and low activation of the possible linkages open to them. Such an analysis, if it were taken at several points during the NCAA's history, would no doubt show that the number of organizations and existing connections increased over time and would identify the legislated regulations that accompanied these changes. To be complete, the structural analysis would also specify the frequency with which a given linkage was used. Under current network analysis practices, neither time sampling nor frequency analysis is common.

The structural data show that the principle of local autonomy effectively established a pattern of loose coupling within the association. Unaffiliated schools were linked to the college athletics network only by the practice of following NCAA rules of play. Member conferences often included unaffiliated schools and spread the association's influence by using eligibility and recruiting rules modeled on those proposed by the association (NCAA, 1921). Affiliation brought with it the benefits of information concerning events and innovations in other parts of the network and reduced the burdens of making arrangements for Olympic trials and responding to public inquiries concerning athletic practices.

For example, an innovative attempt at enforcement of a strict eligibility code resulted in the disbanding of the Western Pennsylvania Athletic Conference in 1914. Members refused to follow the rules because they foresaw a decreased ability to maintain teams competitive with schools outside the conference or schools that secretly violated the agreement. The breakdown in the system was isolated by the loosely coupled structure (Weick, 1976:7), and the example demonstrated to others the difficulties of attempts at strong regulation. A 1935 decision by the Southeastern Conference to give scholarships to athletes was in opposition to national association policy, but it proved to be an innovation adopted by other conferences when its costs and benefits became apparent.

Loose coupling due to the policy of local autonomy reduced the cost of administering the association (Weick, 1976:8) because little coordination was needed. The structural analysis suggests, with respect to system coupling, that NCAA power emerged through the tightening of network linkages. The enforcement decision represented extreme tightening of the network and gave the association a formalized dominant position.

Process Perspective

Explaining change. How did dominance and enforcement finally emerge? They certainly were not new ideas, but rather changes based on considerable political debate and several unsuccessful experiments at rule enforcement. The examination of network activity illuminates two related issues. First, the NCAA benefited from the coupling structure within the system, and second, the enforcement issue had a lengthy history within the association.

The association benefited from the loosely coupled system because affiliation was essentially cost free. Rules were not enforced; the association could do only those things which fulfilled perceived member needs and could ask for no more than voluntary compliance. The membership permitted association administrators to meet needs for information, representation, and coordination. These services created reliance on association activities. At the same time, low administrative costs permitted the use of resources in the continuous conflict with the AAU over control of international competition. The loose coupling gave the administrators of the association considerable freedom of action and the appearance of being spokesmen for a large group of affiliated colleges.

The question of establishing enforceable rules was debated frequently, and numerous experiments (representing political compromises) appeared after the 1914 debacle in Pennsylvania. The universities maintained that the association was purely an educational forum permitting discussion of mutual problems and publication of informative pamphlets, while the colleges sought enforceable standards and increased services. Although the small schools dominated numerically, the concerns addressed by the association were largely those of prominent universities seeking financial gain through competition. The administrative interest group also opposed enforcement until the 1930s. Despite the increased power that would have accrued to the administration, the first president of the association, staunchly committed to founding principles, opposed any decision that would compromise local autonomy.

After World War I, news articles on the subsidizing of college athletes and internal debate brought pressure on the association to reform athletic practice. The universities and colleges agreed on the establishment of an arbitration committee to advise on player eligibility and resolve disputes between schools. The committee, with five university and four college members, was consulted only once during its first year (1920-1921), had its structure modified so it could give district level assistance, and was finally abandoned because members did not want third-party influence in their programs. The partisan debate over recruiting and eligibility continued through the twenties and appeared again in 1934 in an unenforceable code of recruiting practices. This code was adopted because universities felt that colleges were offering low cost education to athletes who could not afford to attend larger, more distant schools. The colleges were apparently successful at recruiting during the Depression, and they threatened the resource bases of the universities.

Process implications. A focus on network activity again provides insights beyond the implications of structure alone. First, loose coupling has a reciprocal effect, which organizations may use to enhance their own autonomy while reducing the autonomy of others. In the case of the NCAA, the autonomy demanded by member schools also gave autonomy to the association. The association used this relative independence to provide coordination and services, creating dependence among the members. The process viewpoint shows that lack of enforcement ability was a potential strength, not a weakness.

Second, loose coupling permitted a wide variety of experiments, false starts, and debates over the power of the association. The issue of enforcement of the rules of amateurism was the critical question on which political controversy turned. It had the potential for breaking up the association, but did not do so because the loose structure permitted continued membership without compliance with onerous restrictions. Interaction patterns were influenced by coupling structure and eventually altered that structure.

Multiplexity of Ties

The multiplexity of ties between the NCAA and network institutions increased through the growing number of valued resources and services provided by the association.

Structures

Rules of play (1906-1931). Rules committees governing play were added without controversy following the pattern set by the incorporation of the football rules committee when the NCAA was organized. Groups of members interested in various sports established committees with approval of the executive board, adding basketball in 1909, then track (1910), soccer (1912), baseball (1913), swimming (1914), volleyball (1918), boxing and wrestling (1920), lacrosse (1922), ice hockey (1923), gymnastics (1927), and fencing (1931). Lack of internal opposition was due to the external benefits derived from establishing a rules committee. It provided visible NCAA commitment to the sport and a power base from which to influence sports federations, which were often dominated by the AAU.

Championship play (1921-1940). As participation in a sport grew and prestige started to become a national commodity, some members saw national championship competition as a mechanism for formalizing prestige and increasing revenue. Rules committees carried out feasibility studies and brought proposals to the executive board or council. Again, there was little opposition to the creation of a new source of prestige, and the pattern, set by the national collegiate track and field championship in 1921, was continued in a succession of sports. The benefits of championship play were unequally divided, however, and small colleges began to complain of their inability to compete with university teams. The prohibitive costs of football may have minimized the controversy because schools tended to compete only with those of similar size and resources. In sports such as cross-country running or fencing, where smaller investments were required, competition among schools of varying sizes was balanced.

Financial incentives. Championship competition produced revenue for the association and subsidized transportation costs for competing schools. The executive board, dominated by major university representatives, declared that revenue beyond administrative cost plus a set percentage for the association should be divided between the association and competing institutions (NCAA, executive regulations, 1941). In the early 1950s, the association came to administer contracts for television broadcasts of intercollegiate football games. The substantial revenue available from television provided the strongest financial linkage between the association and its members.

Olympic team participation (1932). An additional tie between the NCAA and its members was established when the NCAA obtained influence in Olympic team and coach selection. College athletes could qualify for the Olympic trials through NCAA competition, and college coaches could be appointed to the American team (Flath, 1964). In principle, the representational role played by the association was on behalf of all members, but in fact it benefited those who recruited high quality athletes with aspirations to participate in international competition. Thus, university competitors received the major benefit, but at the same time these university competitors became more dependent on the association. The ability and authority of the NCAA to influence Olympic participation were dependent on membership need for a power base. Major universities needed access to the AAU-controlled Olympic committee.[2]

Structural implications. The relatively rapid creation of multipurpose linkages between the association and member schools was a critical factor in emerging NCAA dominance of the network, yet it was, aside from the decision concerning television revenue, the least controversial aspect of change. A structural analysis would be effective in examining multiplexity because the accumulation of services is easily measured over time. Weights might be assigned to linkages based upon the number of services provided. In the case of the NCAA, the weighing scheme could show that services provided were more important to universities, which were concerned with national prestige and recruiting, than to colleges.

The accumulation of services designed to fulfill member needs also tied members more firmly to the association. The creation of collegiate championships, for example, effectively linked schools to the association because there was no alternative mechanism for determining college-level champions except participation in AAU open meets.[3] The NCAA held a virtual monopoly on college athletic championships so that athletes from unaffiliated schools found themselves restricted to AAU competitions. As long as services were added without political controversy, the process perspective has less to add here than in the analysis of other determinants.

Process Perspective

Explaining change. Decisions to establish new services required membership approval and were subject to network politics and the resistance of some interest groups. Minor conflicts arose over differential distribution of benefits, but there were no major confrontations over costs, except in the instance of television contracts.

The financial incentive produced by television represented both an increase in the multiplexity of ties and a new system resource. The association emerged as the administrative agent for member television broadcasts because of a confrontation between the colleges and the universities. The numerical majority, composed of colleges and some universities with lesser athletic reputations, fearing lost attendance and seeing the potential revenue from controlled television contracts (NCAA, 1948), enacted a policy establishing a committee through which the association approved and administered network television appearances. NCAA control over the vast revenue available from television coverage reinforced growing member dependence.

Process implications. The activity involved in increasing multiplexity of ties completes the picture that emerged in the structural analysis. Member interests forestalled NCAA control of television contracts until ad hoc committees had reported and political debates had occurred. At the same time, the NCAA had to see whether television networks would bargain with the association rather than individual schools. The result was that the past practice of relying on the association for coordination of network activity was simply extended to the television issue. The process analysis shows that routine addition of services had implications beyond simple accumulation. It created increasing reliance on the association by giving it control over substantial material resources.

A structural contradiction in the network is apparent in this process analysis. The members sought to maintain autonomy through loose coupling but used the association to meet needs generated by increasing interdependence. They added services that tightened coupling and simultaneously reduced their own autonomy. The contradiction is a function of attempts by members to manage interdependence while maintaining discretion.

New System Resources

Network resources included financial rewards, legitimacy, and access to participation. The NCAA was able to discover, create, or control a number of new network resources during the period up to 1952.

Structure

Representational function. Control over access to the Olympics for college athletes exemplifies the ability of the NCAA to capture new resources through its representational role. Similar power was accumulated during World War I, when the Secretary of War came to the association to encourage a coordinated effort to develop physical fitness among college students and a temporary relaxation of the standards of participation (NCAA, 1917; Baker, 1920: 116). Later the government gave the NCAA a seat on the National Advisory Board of the Civilian Fitness Program. This recognition increased the legitimacy of the association's representational function.

Press identification of the NCAA as a symbolic spokesman for college athletics was important. In press coverage of the recruiting, subsidizing, and professionalizing of student athletes, the NCAA became the principal forum for debate and public response. Public acceptance of the NCAA's representational role was reinforced when television networks agreed to arrange telecasts through the association rather than bargain with individual schools. Though this arrangement has weakened with the development of independent television companies, it initially gave the association clear control over television revenue.

Bowl game certification. The NCAA membership granted an association committee the right to set the terms of football bowl game participation. Thus, bowl promoters had to meet association standards regarding rules of play, finances, and sponsorship.

Structural implications. The amateur athletics network broadened over time and many of the new organizations were linked to the network through their connection to the NCAA. Whenever these new linkages contained valued resources, the association increased its power relative to other network members.

Process Perspective

Explaining change. Recognition of the NCAA's representational role by organizations peripheral to the network enhanced the ability of association members to deal with environmental events. Representation through the association removed the burden of negotiating arrangements and handling press inquiries from the individual schools. Conversely, NCAA influence on government committees and international athletic bodies provided a voice for the interests of schools. The question of how that voice was to be used became a subject of discussion within the association. Proposed government legislation regarding athletic programs and physical fitness had different impacts on large and small schools, and a debate over lobbying efforts ensued. Press coverage of public demands for reform in college athletics became ammunition in this debate. Some members, particularly small private colleges, interpreted news reports as a reflection of public attitude and used newspaper coverage as support for their demand that restrictions on professionalism be made enforceable. Larger schools, noting expanding gate receipts and revenues, took news coverage less seriously (NCAA, 1920, 1922, 1930, 1931, 1941, 1948-1952).

Process implications. A structural analysis shows that the association had increased its control over resources but fails to show how the resources became sources of power in some cases (television, bowl games, Olympics) and sources of controversy in others (press coverage, government influence). Member interests in controlling the new resources produced increased tightening of network structures. Thus, political interests modified structural constraints wherever linkages to organizations other than schools were established.

THE ENFORCEMENT DECISION

Analysis of the four determinants and the processes that accompanied them suggest that by 1950, NCAA members were becoming very dependent on the association. An understanding of the history and the political process of the association is critical in developing a complete explanation of the events that occurred between 1948 and 1952. The decision to make the NCAA a sanctioning agent came only after the network had experimented with regulations, member economic and educational interests were threatened, and external pressure increased. The structure-activity interaction is apparent in the series of events which took place during this 4-year period.

The Events

Chicago conference. In the late 1940s, intercollegiate athletics was again confronted with public disclosures of unethical practices in the recruiting and subsidizing of athletes. The schools also recognized that recruiting competition was as costly as it was embarrassing. The major conferences (Big Ten, Pacific Coast, Southwest, and Southeastern) met in Chicago in 1946 to draft yet another program to control payments to athletes. In spite of diverse administrative structures and political interests, they were forced to agree on stringent controls on recruiting and eligibility. A spokesman for the NCAA compliance committee later remarked that the delegates arrived at the meeting thinking, "My institution is all right irrespective of any code, but that fellow over there, you had better go watch out for him. He is the fellow who is taking my athletes" (NCAA, 1950: 164).

The sanity code. The program drafted in Chicago required that scholarships be given only on the basis of need and that they not exceed tuition costs. Athletes were required to work for room and board as well as practice with the team and study. However, the regional conferences themselves were unwilling to enforce the program, arguing that if one conference was strict while another remained loose, the responsible party would face a recruiting disadvantage and lose out in intersectional competitions such as bowl games and national championships. In the face of regional differences, the NCAA membership adopted this program, termed the "sanity code," as a national program in 1948 (Danzig, 1954).

Expulsion decision. Though enforcement of the sanity code occurred in some conferences, many claimed that the scholarship rules were impossible to administer. Southern schools simply refused to comply, challenging the association's ability to enforce regulations (*New York Times*, January 11, 1949: 37; May 24, 1949: 38). Charges against seven schools were brought at the 1950 association meetings, but expulsion was the only remedy available, and a vote to expel the noncomplying schools failed to get the constitutionally required two-thirds vote. An alliance of major universities with southern colleges demonstrated that the membership was not yet prepared to grant the association enforcement power.

Public scandals. The inability of the network to regulate itself became public a short time later. College athletics was accused of losing sight of educational ideals, of being corrupted by alumni, and of victimizing student athletes (Grutzner, 1951: 1). A basketball point-shaving scandal involving Long Island University and City College of New York was revealed (*New York Times*, March 21, 1951: 1), and J. Edgar Hoover condemned college basketball (*New York Times*, April 10, 1951: 18). Ninety West Point cadets were expelled for aiding football players on exams (*New York Times*, August 5, 1951: 1). Two coaches from William and Mary resigned when their tampering with student transcripts was revealed (*New York Times*, August 12, 1951: Section V, 5), and several schools decided to pay athletes full scholarships (*New York Times*, May 12, 1951: 23). Intercollegiate sport was condemned for commercialism, bigness, and hypocrisy (Daley, 1951: 2).[4]

Enforcement program. The revelations led a group of college and university presidents to meet under the auspices of the American Council on Education to recommend changes deemphasizing athletics in college curricula. The threat of outside intervention led the NCAA council, dominated by university representatives, to draft a program through which penalties other than expulsion were available. This program was voted in at the next association meeting, along with a provision making NCAA legislation subject to the penalty system (Daley, 1952: 32). New regulations permitted limited scholarships and forced all schools in an affiliated conference to join the NCAA. The enforcement procedure, coupled with dependence on NCAA-controlled services, secured the association's dominance over intercollegiate athletics.

Environment, structure, and process. The events leading to the enforcement decision involved a complex interaction of the structural determinants of the network, interorganizational process, and the stimulus provided by organizations usually tangential to the network. The interest groups within the network were led to a resolution (albeit temporary, as recent court cases against the NCAA have shown) of their political conflicts. They used structures that had developed in response to conflicting interests as the mechanism for formulating and implementing the regulatory scheme. The association, created to meet constituent needs, was formally granted a large measure of independence.

The positions of the two principal interest groups had been evident throughout the history of the NCAA. The colleges had invariably favored restrictions on recruiting and subsidies, because they lacked the resources to subsidize and hoped that recruiting competition would be equalized. A smaller number of colleges opposed the sanity code because they felt their local autonomy was threatened though they had not violated any standards. They wanted restrictions placed only on the universities.

The universities feared the implications of outside monitoring but were more concerned about cheating by competitors. They each accused others of subsidizing and defended their own practices. Those involved in association administration tended to favor restrictions, arguing that enforcement was necessary to protect intercollegiate athletics from public criticism and outside intervention. When the universities recognized the cost of excessive recruiting competition and the threats of outside intervention, they chose self-regulation rather than imposed controls.

FOOTNOTES

1. An interesting historical debate revolves around the role of Theodore Roosevelt in establishing the Intercollegiate Athletic Association. He apparently used his political position to cause dissension within the existing football rules committee and ultimately got the rules committee to recognize the legitimacy of the new athletic association (Krout, 1929; Flath, 1964; Lewis, 1973).

2. The conflict with the AAU over control of the Olympic movement continues and remains an area in which the AAU has managed to identify the NCAA as the pretender to control (Flath, 1964). An attempt by the NCAA to form a National Amateur Athletic Federation to oversee all activity, including that of the AAU, failed in 1962, and the association has periodically withdrawn from some U.S. Olympic Committee activities.

3. The exception was basketball, where the Metropolitan Invitation (later to become the NIT) was played in Madison Square Garden. The NCAA arranged a playoff game between the NCAA and MIT winners in the 1930s, then later barred schools participating in the NCAA tournament from entering the NIT.

4. There seems to have been an implicit assumption on the part of the schools and the public that athletes were either routinely corruptible or unable to protect themselves from recruiters.

REFERENCES

BAKER, D. (1920). College athletics receive a government o.k. *Literary Digest,* **64**, 116-118.

BECKER, M. (1970). Sociometric location and innovativeness: Reformulation and extension of the diffusion model. *American Sociological Review,* **35**, 267-282.

BLAU, M., & Schoenherr, R.A. (1971). *The Structure of organizations.* New York: Basic Books.

BOISSEVAIN, J. (1974). *Friends of friends.* New York: St. Martin's Press.

BURT, S. (1977). Positions in multiple network systems, part two. *Social Forces,* **56**, 551-575.

DALEY, A. (1951, August 12). Sports of the times. *New York Times,* p. 2.

DALEY, A. (1951, January 15). Sports of the times. *New York Times,* p. 32.

DANZIG, A. (1954, March 23). Ivy agreement is strong force in battle against abuses in college sports. *New York Times,* p. 30.

FLATH, A.W. (1964). *A History of relations between the National Collegiate Athletic Association and the Amateur Athletic Union of the United States.* Champaign, IL: Stipes Publishing.

GRODZINS, M. (1966). *The American system.* Chicago: Rand McNally.

GRUTZNER, C. (1951, November 20). Coaches, colleges blamed in scandal. *New York Times,* p. 26.

KIERNAN, J., & Daley, A. (1961). The story of the Olympic Games, 776 B.C. to 1960 A.D. New York: Lippincott.

LAUMANN, E.O., & Pappi. F.U. (1976). *Networks of collective action.* New York: Academic.

LEWIS, G. (1973). World War I and the emergence of sport for the masses. *The Maryland Historian,* **4**, 109-122.

MEYER, M. (1972). *Bureaucratic structure and authority.* New York: Harper & Row.

MICHELS, R. (1962). *Political parties*. Glencoe, IL: Free Press.

NATIONAL Collegiate Athletic Association. (1906; 1942; 1944-1953). *Proceedings of the Annual Convention of the National Collegiate Athletic Association, 1906-1910*. New York: Intercollegiate Athletic Association.

NEW York Times. (1949, January 11), p. 37; (1949, May 24), p. 38; (1951, March 21), p. 1; (1951, April 10), p. 18; (1951, August 5), p. 1; (1951, August 12), U:5; (1951, May 12), p. 23.

OLSEN, M. (1965). *The logic of collective action: Public goods and the theory of groups*. Cambridge: Harvard University Press.

PIERCE, P. (1910). Speeches delivered to the Annual Convention of the Intercollegiate Athletic Association and the National Collegiate Athletic Association.

SAVAGE, H.J. (1929). *American College Athletics Bulletin Number 23*. New York: Carnegie Foundation for the Advancement of Teaching.

SIMON, H. (1962). The architecture of complexity. *Proceedings of the American Philosophical Society*, **106**, 467-482.

WEICK, K. (1976). Educational organizations as loosely coupled systems. *Administrative Science Quarterly*, **21**, 1-19.

WHITE, H.C., Boorman, S.A., & Breiger R.L. (1976). Social structure from multiple networks I. Block models of roles and positions. *American Journal of Sociology*, **81**, 730-780.

WILSON, J.Q. (1973). *Political organizations*. New York: Basic Books.

Chapter 12

College Athletics: Problems of Institutional Control*

James H. Frey
University of Nevada, Las Vegas

Whenever a new athletic director is hired or a major programmatic change (e.g., move from a "small-time" program to the "big-time" variety) is made in a college athletic program, the president usually presents the athletic administration with the following three guidelines: (a) "Play within the rules," (b) "Don't lose money," and (c) "Be competitive." As simple and direct as these admonitions appear, it is quite apparent that few athletic departments are able to comply.

First, it is evident that history is repeating itself with respect to scandal and controversy within college athletics. The charges of professionalism, academic compromise, and commercialism which promoted the 1929 Carnegie investigation form the basis of widespread contemporary criticism. Although at this time only 22 schools are on probation and 30-40 are being investigated by the enforcement division of the National Collegiate Athletic Association (NCAA), there is a common belief that virtually all athletic programs engage in practices which are in violation of NCAA rules and, in some cases, of federal or state law. Thus, few programs are "playing within the rules."

Second, few athletic departments are making money or even balancing their budgets. The most recent financial analysis conducted by the NCAA (Raiborn, 1982) revealed that average total expenses exceed average total revenues for each category of athletic departments except for the largest group or the Division I category (Raiborn, 1982, p. 40). For the period of 1974-1981, these deficits have increased sharply. The Class A or Division I schools operated with a deficit until

*Preparation of this manuscript was possible only with the assistance of the Research Facilities Office of the Library of Congress, Washington, D.C.

1978 when a lucrative television contract provided large sums to these big-time schools. Even with television revenue, 40% of the top schools lost money in 1981 (Raiborn, 1982, p. 41).

Finally, if being competitive simply means a winning percentage, then many schools were in compliance with the president's directive. However, if it meant winning a national championship, a conference crown, or defeating a traditional cross-state rival, then few teams were competitive.

Despite the conditions of infamy and controversy, of financial gymnastics and red ink, and of marginal competitiveness, college athletic programs continue to operate as if they were true to the rules, making money and winning. That is, athletics operate with relative freedom and independence from institutional control. Why haven't the parent institutions been able to pull in the athletic reins and exercise full institutional control (i.e., demand compliance to the procedures and directives that guide any other department)? The answers do not lie within the unique character of athletics or in the motives of those who command athletics. Institutional control of athletics takes its present form as the result of three factors: (a) the historical features of American colleges and universities, particularly their "public service" appeal; (b) the nature of the modern university as an organization that exhibits loosely coupled parts, many goals, multiple constituencies, and fragmented decision-making; and (c) the unique ability of athletics to forge external community linkages with political and economic elites. The latter is a result of a certain divestiture of athletics by the academic community and of the use of athletics by university administration and external elites to promote institutional and community self-interest.

HISTORICAL DEVELOPMENTS: "GOING NATIVE"

American colleges and universities were modeled originally after the British form which emphasized undergraduate education in the classics. Guided by the principle of *in loco parentis*, the school controlled every aspect of a student's life. Extracurricular activities, particularly games, were viewed as frivolous and unworthy.

The 1850s saw the adoption of the German model of higher education which emphasized science in place of morality, graduate over undergraduate studies, and research over teaching (Kerr, 1963). Furthermore, industrialization, democratization, and frontier expansion in America forced the universities to open their doors to all comers and to expand into areas unrelated to intellectual pursuits but important to the social and emotional development of students (i.e., athletics) (Veysey, 1965). The democratization and diversification of the American university were formalized with the passage of the Morrill Act of 1862 and the land grant movement. In effect, by virtue of this legislation, the federal government was telling American colleges and universities that they must fulfill a public service function.

At the turn of the century, a pragmatic society had demanded a pragmatic curriculum. The basic pattern of the university was that of being a success-oriented enterprise (Veysey, 1965). Its task was to prepare men for competition, not necessarily to promote academic excellence. The schools had "gone native." Their curricula and programs were designed to meet everyone's needs, not just for those of elite backgrounds. Higher education became everybody's right. The result was that institutions became dominated by communities, and their governance responded more to the dictates of external constituencies than to internal preferences. This produced a diversity of institutional forms still retained today: localized control, competitive relations, unstandardized control practices, and undefined or imprecise mission or goal orientation (Carnegie Council on Policy Studies, 1980; Chu, 1982; Shils, 1982; Veysey, 1965).

Because there was no dependable source of support, such as the state, financing higher education was often precarious. Presidents found themselves directing their energies more to fund-raising than to educational development. However, most important, colleges and unversities were put into competition with each other for resources. This developing competition and market orientation forced schools and their boosters to seek avenues to augment their efforts to obtain prestige, visibility, and resources (i.e., the competitive edge). One of these avenues was athletics.

Athletics broadened the appeal of the institution to a new market (Chu, 1982); it assisted in fund-raising and student recruitment; and, it reflected directly upon the competitive position sought by institutions *vis á vis* each other. By the same token, athletic contests sponsored by local schools meant notoriety and money for communities. Justification was not difficult because the sponsorship of athletic programs made good "business sense" for both the school and the community. In addition, public entertainment was a natural extension of a university's public service function.

In summary, America higher education is characterized by diversity in form and curriculum, by a public service ideal, by interinstitutional competition, and by a governance structure which responds to external forces or constituent demands rather than to internal coalitions or pressures. These characteristics continue to exist unabated despite efforts of faculty and administration to make their voices heard in a more meaningful way. These factors produced the peculiar organizational form of the modern university and college.

THE UNIVERSITY AS AN ORGANIZATION: MULTIPLE GOALS AND LOOSE COUPLING

The historical patterns of public service, interinstitutional competition, specialized departmentalization, and external control have created education organizations that can be characterized by multiple goals, fragmented decision-making, and decentralized or *loose coupling* of subunits. Any analysis of this kind of organization must apply a model of governance which views colleges and universities as political systems where decisions are reached via dynamic power coalitions and not by bureaucratic processes or collegial consensus. The goal structure of the university presents the first clue that traditional rational models of organizational analysis do not apply (Baldridge, Curtis, Ecker, & Riley, 1977; Hall, 1982).

Multiple Goals

Universities and colleges, unlike many organizations, can be characterized by goal ambiguity or multiple goals. In a study of the effectiveness (i.e., degree of goal achievement) of universities, Cameron (1978) states that it is difficult to assess effectiveness because goals are "complex, diffuse, ambiguous, and changeable" (p. 609) as well as being difficult to specify in concrete measureable terms. A less reverent view of the university's goal situation was expressed by March and Olson (1976) in their studies of decision-making. They assert "Colleges are 'complex' *garbage cans* into which a striking variety of problems, solutions, and participants have been dumped! Therefore, analysis of effectiveness is impossible because there is only diversity, not singularity of purpose" (p. 176) (italics added). One of the first studies of universities as organizations produced 47 different goals marked as "important" by those surveyed (Gross, 1968). These goals ranged from protecting academic freedom to the character development of students. This same study found that goal change is more likely to be affected by external power shifts than by internal changes (Gross & Grambsch, 1977). It is not surprising that almost any activity on campus can be identified as consistent with one or more institutional goals. Because there is no agreement on goals, and, as we shall see, it is virtually impossible to reach agreement, it is easy to see why athletics were acceptable campus activities. In addition, the multiple goal structure facilitates the university's adaptation to public service demands which are varied and often temporal.

Fragmented Decision Centers

The decision-making pattern of the university reflects its diversity and diffuse goals. The control of the university is in the hands of a federation of collegial groups that is organized around some bureaucratic rules and traditions. Decision-making is often shared and participatory and appears disorderly at times, but it continues to reflect the autonomy of departments and professionals. It is a system with little central coordination or control; it is almost "organized anarchy" where "each individual in the university is seen making autonomous decisions" (Cohen & March, 1974, p. 81). Most recently A. Bartlett Giamatti, president of Yale University (1983), described university decision-making:

> Universities, hierarchical in some ways, are very diffuse, with authority delegated and responsibility widely shared. Thus, a university is a landscape dotted with

pyramids of various sizes. It is not one enormous pyramid, solid and entire. There is constant interplay between centralized authority and localized or individual autonomy; interplay among custom, consultation, and decree. . . .

Universities differ from corporate structures in two essential ways: first, many people participate in the management of the institution; and second, those same people legitimately pursue multiple goals through a variety of means (p. A22).

Earlier, Clark Kerr (1963), noted observer on higher education, asserted that the university is . . . an inconsistent institution. It is not one community, but several . . . (p. 19). Using the United Nations analogy, Kerr states:

There are several 'nations' of students, of faculty, of alumni, of trustees, of public groups. Each has its territory, its jurisdictions, its form of government. Each can declare war on the others; some have the power of veto. Each can settle its own problems by majority vote, but altogether they form no single constituency. It is a pluralistic society with multiple cultures. Coexistence is more likely than unity (p. 36).

Twenty years later Kerr (1982, p. 30) asserted that pluralism was even more pronounced than before and that, as the result of efforts to engage in "participatory democracy" to overcome the obstacles of division, progress was more problematic because special interest groups had the power to veto changes.

Decision-making reflects the variety of goals and the multiplicity of specialized interests of faculty and departments. The apparent lack of control or coordination is not necessarily in deference to academic freedom, but reflects a need to be adaptable to changing and varied public service needs.[1]

Loose Coupling

Diffuse goals, fragmented decision-making, abetted by the norm of public service and the practice of competition, produce an organization which can be described as loosely coupled, or a situation where the various parts are only weakly connected to each other and are therefore free to vary independently (Aldrich, 1979). In this case, the subunits are essentially autonomous where deference is given to the department or division, each of which is oriented to a different part of the environment. Thus, the departments of physics and sociology make decisions independent of other departments and often independent of their division or larger university mission. Each subunit is responsive to institutional needs but only so long as the former is able to preserve its identity and protect its separateness.

The loose coupling of subunits permits adaptation to the environment without the complete restructuring of the organization. Each subunit does not have to respond to every other subunit adaptation. This type of organizational form has been conducive to the survival of universities in the face of varied environmental demands. Subunits will interact or join forces only so far as they share interests or have variables in common (Glassman, 1973); otherwise, they are independent of each other. The independence of athletic departments from academic subunits is the result of the growing perception that academic and athletic subunits do not share any interests. This phenomenon results in the loosening or reduction of the control over athletic departments.

Despite what we may want to believe about educational organizations, particularly universities, these bodies are not rationalized, neat, efficient, coordinated structures (Weick, 1976). Rather, they are complex systems, often held together by tenuous bonds, "muddlng through" rather than acting in a calculated or planned manner. Loose coupling has the advantages of adaptation, of retaining novel solutions, of protecting the organization from demise if one unit fails, and of permitting self-determination (Weick, 1976, pp. 7-8). It is inconceivable that a university could be organized any other way, and survive.[2]

In a study of university decision-making with respect to budgets, Hills and Mahoney (1978) discovered that resource allocation decisions followed a coalition rather than a bureaucratic line. Bargaining, quasi-resolution of conflict and arbitrariness characterized decisions. The relative power of the subunit, rather than logical justification, determined budget decisions. This serves to illustrate the view that the university is a political system characterized by group conflict, group interests, and negotiated outcomes. It is an organization also characterized by loosely coupled subunits and decentralized decision-making. Athletic departments, just as any other department, can act in a relatively autonomous fashion, free of strict organizational constraints. In addition, these departments operate virtually coalition-free internally because athletics and academics share few interests. Thus, the ability of the athletic department to violate organizational guidelines (e.g., play by the rules) is a product of this intraindependence aided by its ability to forge alliances with external constituences with political and economic strength.

THE INDEPENDENCE OF ATHLETICS

The athletic department represents one of the Kerr's independent nations. The autonomy of this subunit is accounted for partially by the historical and organizational factors outlined previously. Just as any other department on campus retains autonomy, athletics have acquired independence, but the latter's autonomy exceeds what is possible for these other subunits. This is largely due to the ability of athletic departments to forge linkages with significant external constituences to an extent beyond what other subunits have been able to do. The creation of these linkages is the result of factors emanating from the university as well as those originating in the constituencies.

University Factors

Market orientation. Earlier I noted that in order to be competitive financially, institutions turned to athletics to aid in efforts to recruit students, to raise money, and to obtain visibility. At the encouragement of administrations, athletic departments were fused with community interests in the hope that the school would ultimately benefit from that association. That is, if persons would establish an initial relation with the institution via athletics, they would eventually support nonathletic, academic programs. In addition, a successful athletic program supported by community groups should also enhance the political, and ultimately financial, position of the university with local and state legislative bodies.

Along this same line, university officials saw athletics as a device whereby the institution could articulate its relationship with the larger community, that is, broaden its appeal and perceived relevance. This was more difficult to establish, say, with physics or psychology. The reverse was also true. That is, the public cannot always justify the presence of a university in its area with lofty and sophisticated rationales; but, it can properly explain the presence by reference to athletics and the latter's personal, economic, and spiritual benefits.

Orphan status. Of all university departments, athletics are viewed as having the least in common with academic endeavors, particularly in big-time programs. Thus, athletics have been "orphaned" or separated operationally and programmatically from normal academic review or responsibility. The faculty have rejected athletics as an unworthy educational activity and, as a result, have avoided asserting themselves in any control measures. Presidents have also tended to avoid athletics, preferring to attend to more important academic matters (Nyquist, 1979). While retaining an organizational link to the institution, athletics have become isolated from academic life and therefore from control measures. Thus, a good portion of the autonomy of athletic departments can be attributed to the organizational nature of universities (i.e., loose coupling).

Resource allocation. Universities have also pushed athletic departments into external partnerships because institutional budgets for athletics have not increased, while athletic costs have doubled in the last 10 years (Raiborn, 1982). Athletic departments have had to seek revenue from external groups, who, in turn, desire control (Atwell, Grimes, & Lopiano, 1980). This financial isolation has reached the point, in some cases, where athletic departments have incorporated separately from the parent institution. These independent entities are responsible for raising their entire budget from nonuniversity sources.

In summary, market orientation of universities, the desire to be visible, inherent interinstitutional competition, and ideological and operational isolation are factors of university organizational life which have pushed athletic departments to establish external linkages or networks. The result has been an inability to con-

trol athletic departments because these units have very powerful network constituencies. However, these linkages were not just the result of university efforts;
the community saw the value of athletics and cultivated profitable linkages.

Community Factors

Ideological congruence. There is a natural ideological congruence between
athletics and business and political life which promotes an easy identification with
college sports programs. The ideological underpinnings of athletics such as hard
work, competition, respect for authority, courage in the face of adversity are
analogous to the components of the American Business Creed. Thus, it was only
natural that community businesses and political elites would be attracted to
athletics; sports provided a vicarious reinforcement of their ideals. No other department on campus could be so attractive.

Boosting the community. More important, however, was the view that a successful college athletic program could reflect positively on the community or
region. First, the area could obtain national recognition or visibility should the
college team be successful. Second, any time a sporting event was conducted,
the business community reaped benefits. Thus, the booster phenomenon was born
in efforts to promote college and university athletic success which, in turn, meant
local and regional business profit (Frey, 1982). Booster groups made up of community businesses and political influentials exist around most every athletic
program. This association permits athletic officials to link or network with the
most important community groups. A coalition of athletic administrators and
booster officials forms the dominant power center of athletics. Furthermore, it
is the most formidable association or network with which college administrators
must deal.

CONCLUSION

As noted above, those subunits with the most significant external network linkages
will be able to maintain their freedom in the face of control efforts by the larger
organization. One explanation of athletic excess lies in the inability of university
administrators to control their athletic departments by normally prescribed institutional means. It is not because accountability is not desired on the part of
the administration, particularly presidents; it is because historical and organizational factors beyond one person's or one institution's control are operating to
promote athletic autonomy or freedom from control.

Colleges and universities have always looked to external groups, voluntarily
or involuntarily, for guidelines and ultimately for stimulus for change. Of course,
the most significant groups in the past have been church denominations, the federal
government, and state legislatures. The situation is no different in athletics. Univer-

sity officials are reluctant to make changes in athletics at their own institution for fear these adjustments will affect the school's competitive standing or national visibility. Therefore, appeals for control have been directed to external, regulatory bodies such as the NCAA. The recent effort to define admission standards for incoming scholarship athletes (Proposition 48) is an example of an external regulatory body setting academic standards, something which should have been done by the institutions themselves.[3] We should expect nothing different because universities are more *reactive* than active, more *conservative* than critical.

Is control possible? I am not sure it can be accomplished without some major redirection. Perhaps some semblance of accountability can be established if efforts are made to reintegrate athletics and academics, to finance athletics through regular channels such as state appropriations, to regionalize schedules and championships, to disassociate with professional sports by refusing to maintain a "farm team" status, and to apply admission and retention standards evenly for all students. The NCAA will not be of much help because its interests are largely those of its members.

Future changes in the organization and operation of college athletics will come about, I predict, as the result of court actions, not as the result of presidential initiatives or NCAA legislation. Student athletes will challenge restrictions on their upward mobility, on eligibility, and on the pursuit of legitimate academic programs while athletes. Constitutional challenges will come in these areas as well as in the areas of NCAA enforcement practices, the allocation of television rights and participants rights. We may even see the unionization of players. Change may come sooner than we think because many of these issues are in the courts at this time.

FOOTNOTES

1. The dualistic approach to decision-making (i.e., professional vs. bureaucratic) is not an accurate model of the university decision-making process because it suggests agreement on the part of bureaucrats and professors. Very often this agreement is impossible to obtain or these two groups cooperate only in some limited way.

2. It is also true that as an organization grows in size, it becomes more complex (i.e., exhibits greater differentiation and requires more information). The more complex an organization, the more likely it is to exhibit a decentralized or loosely coupled structure. Increased size and complexity are distinctive features of modern universities (Shils, 1982).

3. Proposition 48 is an amendment to the NCAA Bylaws adopted at the 1983 NCAA Convention in San Diego. The legislation requires a minimum of 700 of a possible 1600 on the College Board's Scholastic Aptitude Test (SAT) or 15 of a possible 36 on the American College Test (ACT). It also requires a 2.0 grade-point average on a 4.0 scale in a core curriculum of 11 academic courses in high

school, including English, mathematics, and science. The scale becomes effective for the 1986-87 academic year and applies only to incoming freshmen of the 277 Division I schools. If the student-athlete does not meet these requirements, he or she is ineligible for competition or practice for that year.

REFERENCES

ALDRICH, H.E. (1979). *Organizations and environments*. Englewood Cliffs, NJ: Prentice-Hall.

ATWELL, R.H., Grimes, B., & Lopiano, D.A. (1980). *The money game: Financing college athletics*. Washington, DC: American Council on Education.

BALDRIDGE, J.V., Curtis, D.V., Ecker, G.P., & Riley, G.L. (1977). Alternative models of governance in higher education. In G.L. Riley and J.V. Baldridge (Eds.), *Governing academic organizations*. Berkeley: McCutchan Publishing Corporation.

BOORSTIN, D.J. (1973). *The Americans: The democratic experience*. New York: Random House.

CAMERON, K. (1978). Measuring organizational effectiveness in institutions of higher education. *Administrative Science Quarterly, 23*, 604-629.

CARNEGIE Council on Policy Studies. (1980). *Three thousand futures: The next twenty years in higher education*. San Francisco: Jossey-Bass.

CHU, D. (1982). The American conception of higher education and the formal incorporation of intercollegiate sport. *Quest, 34*, 53-71.

COHEN, M.D. & March, J.G. (1974). *Leadership and ambiguity: The American college president*. New York: McGraw-Hill.

FREY, J.H. (1982). Intercollegiate athletics in the future: Booster coalition, institutional control, and the pursuit of scarce resources. In J.H. Frey (Ed.), *The governance of intercollegiate athletics*. West Point, NY: Leisure Press.

GIAMATTI, A.B. (1983). Universities and corporations: Mapping out common ground. *Washington Post*, A22.

GLASSMAN, R. (1973). Persistence and loose coupling in living systems. *Behavioral Science, 18*, 83-98.

GROSS, E. (1968). Universities as organizations: A study of goals. *American Sociological Review, 33*, 518-544.

GROSS, E. & Grambsch, P.V. (1977). Power structures in universities and colleges. In G.L. Riley and J.V. Baldridge (Eds.), *Governing academic organizations*. Berkeley: McCutchan Publishing Corporation.

HALL, R.H. (1982). *Organizations: Structure and process* (3rd ed.). Englewood Cliffs, NJ: Prentice-Hall.

HILLS, F.S. & Mahoney, T.A. (1978). University budgets and organizational decision-making. *Administrative Science Quarterly, 23*, 454-465.

KERR, C. (1963). *The uses of the university*. Cambridge, MA: Harvard University Press.

KERR, C. (1982). The uses of the university: Two decades later. *Change, 14*, 23-31.

LUCAS, J.A. & Smith, R.A. (1978). *Saga of American sport*. Philadelphia: Lea and Febiger.

MARCH, J.G. & Olson, J.P. (1976). *Ambiguity and choice in organizations*. Oslo: Universtes for Lacet.

NYQUIST, E.G. (1979). Win, women, and money: Collegiate athletes today. *Educational Record, 60*, 374-393.

RAIBORN, M.H. (1982). *Revenue and expense of intercollegiate athletic programs: Analysis of financial trends and relationships 1978-1981*. Mission, KS: National Collegiate Athletic Association.

SHILS, E. (1982). The university: A backward glance. *The American Scholar, 50*, 163-179.

VEYSEY, L.R. (1965). *The emergence of the American university*. Chicago: University of Chicago Press.

WEICK, K.E. (1976). Educational organizations as loosely coupled systems. *Administrative Science Quarterly, 21*, 1-9.

Chapter 13

The Administrative Housing of Intercollegiate Athletics: Independent or Affiliated With an Academic Department

John D. Massengale
Eastern Washington University

John W. Merriman
Valdosta State College

This paper presents two general models and rationales for the administrative housing and structure of intercollegiate athletics. One model will be completely independent of any academic department or unit, while the other will feature a strong affiliation with a legitimate academic department or unit.

DEFINITIONS

Independent

An independent athletic department is a conglomerate of smaller units (teams) of varying size which are in competition with each other for limited resources, institutional recognition, and public acclaim. The primary purpose of an independent athletic department is to satisfy many of the external demands placed upon an educational institution. These demands may or may not be compatible with the mission of the institution.

An independent model features an athletic department that is definitely not an academic department. There are no degree programs, and varsity athletic participation does not carry credit toward any degree program or certification. In addition, the independent athletic department does not qualify as a support service because it offers nothing to enhance the scholarly efforts of academic departments.

Intercollegiate athletics in this model is an entertainment enterprise conducted for the purpose of public relations. As such, the institution becomes willing to subsidize athletics for real and/or imagined benefits to the institution, its athletes, and its students.

Because an independent athletic department represents a sizable investment and has extensive potential benefits, it seems prudent that its administrative structure be as efficient and as effective as possible. Even cursory examination of administrative flow charts illustrate that placing athletics under another department compounds the bureaucratic structure, and that such a structure is not motivated by a desire for efficiency (see Figure 1). One can only speculate at what provides the motivation for using such structures. Perhaps it is nothing more than tradition. Or, on closer examination it may be that chief administrators, because of the controversy that often surrounds college athletics, are reluctant to assume the direct control of collegiate athletic programs and prefer the creation of a buffer.

Affiliated

When intercollegiate athletics is affiliated with an academic unit, as shown in Figure 2 or Figure 3, several features became immediately evident. Athletic personnel and programs report directly through normal academic channels regardless of whether departments, divisions, professional schools, or even colleges, become involved. Under this model the athletic department will contain many coaches (sometimes all), who because of their academic affiliation, will be eligible to attain academic rank and tenure; thereby they become more acceptable to the academic community and become more likely to make other academic contributions, such as committee participation, faculty governance, academic advising, and so on. These coaches will have advanced degrees (occasionally earned doctorates), academic interests, and supporting areas of expertise. Most of all, this type of arrangement will feature teacher/coaches that view intercollegiate athletics as an educational service for students and society and not a profit motive corporate business enterprise with economic growth as its top priority.

An affiliated model also features a system where evaluation and worth are determined by the quality of benefits and the total contribution made, and not just by numbers of benefits or by numbers of dollars. Some of the benefits are the improvement of the athletic programs for student/athletes, the promotion and development of educational leadership, physical fitness, recreational participation, and the pursuit of excellence. This situation is a sharp contrast to typical nonaffiliated structures, where the best interests of student/athletes often lose top priority to the purpose of making money or else losing less money, or the simple self-perpetuation of an athletic system.

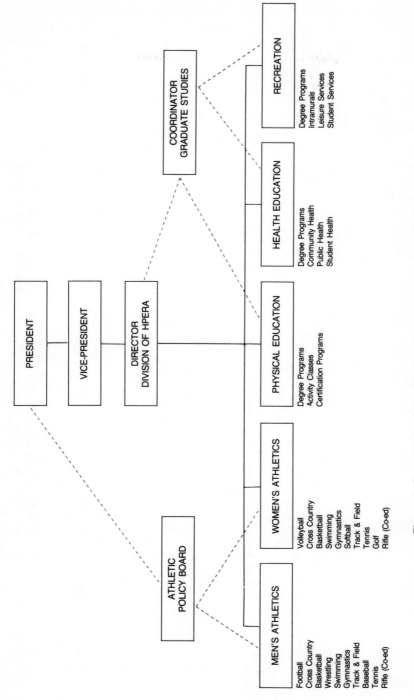

Figure 1. An example of an affiliation with an academic department structure.

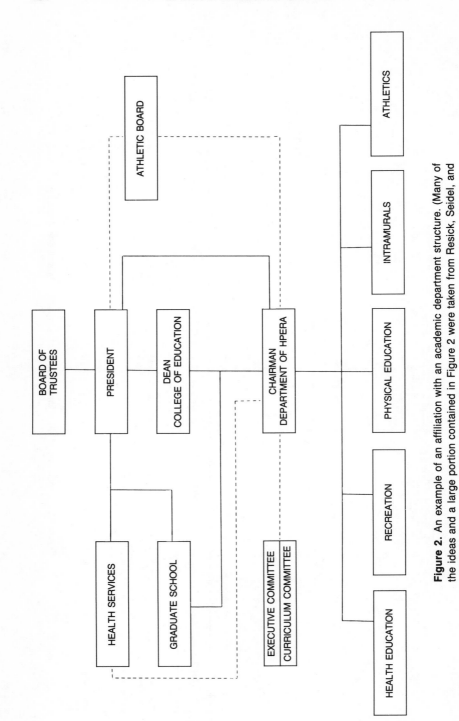

Figure 2. An example of an affiliation with an academic department structure. (Many of the ideas and a large portion contained in Figure 2 were taken from Resick, Seidel, and Mason, 1970, p. 13).

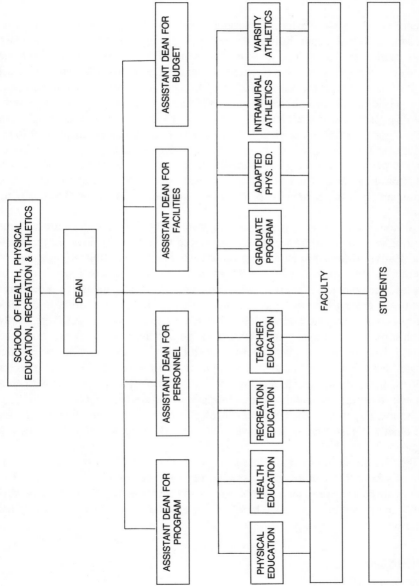

Figure 3. An example of an affiliation with an academic department structure.

ADMINISTRATIVE RESPONSIBILITY

Independent

Because of the dissimilarity of functions among athletic and other departments, the administrative responsibilities of the corresponding department heads are also quite dissimilar. An athletic director's responsibilities focus almost entirely on business concerns as opposed to academic deans or department chairs who direct most of their energies toward academic concerns. An academic administrator is reponsibile for all facets of the learning situation. An athletic director is responsible for providing entertainment. The latter involves tasks that include event scheduling, guarantee negotiation, arranging travel schedules, meals and lodging, ticket sales and promotion, facility and contest management, the hiring of contest officials, assisting with media coverage, and so on. Academic administrators seldom if ever become involved with such tasks and often fail to appreciate their importance, expense, or the amount of time needed to complete them.

Although these concerns are real, they might be considered minor at some institutions. Other differences often considered to be more serious are those administrative responsibilities having far greater potential to impact negatively if intercollegiate athletics is housed in an academic unit. These include type of employment contract, job description, tenure considerations, and hiring procedures that differ among teachers and coaches. Another source of conflict is the disparity between athletic and academic budgets. The athletic budget is generally much higher than the academic budget of the unit in which athletics might be housed. In other words, the budget responsibility of the athletic director is often greater than that of the academic administrator to which the athletic director reports. In addition, the athletic director is responsible for compliance with conference, district, and national rules that can and do effect institutional policy. Consequently, it is in the best interest of the institution if the athletic director and chief admnistrative officer have a direct working relationship, as shown in Figure 4.

Finally, the structure of an athletic department compares to an academic division of school that features many smaller departments, units, or programs. The athletic director has in fact a dean's level responsibilities for a variety of departments and programs (sports). Therefore, an athletic director should receive the same job status as a dean.

Affiliated

According to Etzioni (1964), the most important structural dilemma found in any organization is the inevitable strain imposed upon that organization through the use of knowledge. By "knowledge" it is meant the understanding of truth or reality of some situation which may vary dependent upon the individual and his

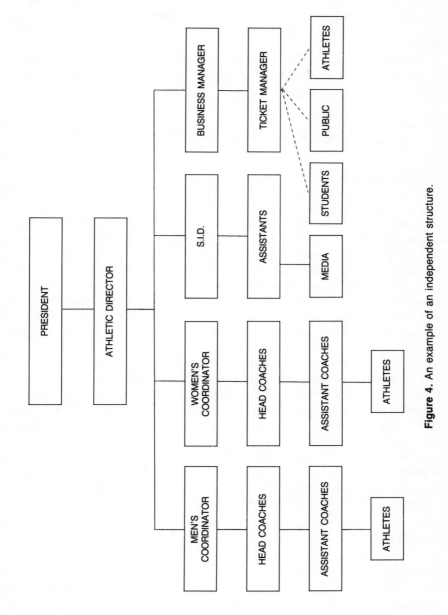

Figure 4. An example of an independent structure.

or her social, cultural, or historical background. Intercollegiate athletics is no exception. Decisions to behave in a certain manner may be contrary to the knowledge held by others in the sport field. The goals which are held in sports are often contrary to knowledge in the field of higher education and athletics. Furthermore, there is often pressure and evaluation from the least knowledgeable in our society.

The dilemma is partially resolved through an organizational structure that places the most knowledgeable people in legitimate positions to make professional decisions. This is best accomplished through academic affiliation.

EXPENDABLE SPORTS AND PROGRAMS

Independent

Under today's economy and with decline in student enrollment, many institutions are faced with elimination decisions and reductions in force. Under such conditions, separation from academic departments seems most sensible. When intercollegiate athletics are an integral part of an academic department, inequality of control exists. This is especially true if the academic department, particularly physical education, is affiliated with athletics when athletics is under control of an athletic policy board. In this situation, physical educators attached to athletics lose control of their own academic programs. In addition, athletic coaches in physical education programs often have a voice in the conduct of those academic programs.

Decisions concerning program expendability should consider several characteristics of intecollegiate athletics. First, athletic departments have greater control of expenses than do academic departments; consequently, they may find alternatives that are more acceptable in meeting budget crises situations than simply eliminating programs. Secondly, athletes come from many different disciplines, and if it becomes necessary to eliminate selected sports and programs, the decision should not be the responsibility of just one academic department. A third consideration is that athletic participation is not generally dependent upon student enrollment; however, it is true that intercollegiate athletics contributes substantially to the total student enrollment.

Affiliated

Affiliation with an academic structure protects all sports and programs, which serves in the best interests of student/athletes, the American athletic system, and our educational process. Affiliation also eliminates the necessity of comparing and contrasting revenue spending versus revenue-producing sports, or spending less and becoming more cost efficient. Evaluation can be made on benefit to participants and spectators. Evaluation need not be made on the basis of dollars.

A pool of up-to-date coaches is created for teacher preparation classes for physical education majors and for activity services classes that function for the entire student body. Affiliation creates a situation where intercollegiate athletics and teacher preparation can supplement one another instead of contaminating one another, and where the careful planning of job descriptions make expendable sports and programs too inexpensive to eliminate.

PHILOSOPHY AND ETHICS

Independent

Everyone and every group follows a standard of behavior, ethics, and philosophy. For cohesiveness of a group, it is important that its members adhere closely to the group's standards of behavior. Sport sociologists (Scott, 1973; Kew, 1978) have identified three such ethics in athletics:

1. The Lombardian Ethic, often viewed as a "win at any cost attitude"
2. The Counter-culture Ethic, featuring a central theme of "it matters not who won or lost but how you played the game"
3. The Radical Ethic, stressing "striving for excellence in performance"

While some individuals might be attempting to create a change, most educators embrace the Lombardian Ethic. It is simply too much a part of our culture. There is an abundance of visible evidence to support it as the dominant ethic in athletics.

The academic world professes to be different. Academically, many educators seem to embrace the Radical Ethic. Professors strive for excellence in themselves and in their students, feeling that if excellence is achieved, winning will not be a concern in itself, but a natural outcome.

As a result of conflict of ethics, a growing number of athletic directors and coaches are caught in a stressful dilemma with growing opposition from both sides. More and more, they tend to blame the problems of athletics on the failure of college and university presidents to assume direct responsibility for control of athletics. The best means of resolving this dilemma is to establish athletics as an independent unit not housed or affiliated with an academic department.

Affiliated

Academic affiliation enhances the chance that those charged with the responsibility of intercollegiate athletics will be of a common philosophy that contains certain characteristics. Athletics will remain the main place in an academic community where a complete commitment to the pursuit of excellence is not only expected and acceptable, but relentlessly promoted. Coaches will be allowed to teach the meaning of excellence and the implications of its pursuit, rather than defining excellence only in terms of winning. Intercollegiate athletics will stress the value of the pursuit, instead of the notion that there can only be one winner. An affiliated athletic program will also be provided the protection and academic respectability necessary to fight off the inevitable dangers that surround the pursuit of excellence. Most importantly, student/athletes will be allowed to experience just how good they can be, while at the same time be provided with the opportunity to fail without fear of retaliation from a system filled with hypocrisy.

FACULTY EVALUATION AND TENURE

Independent

As a general rule, coaching contracts do not contain a provision for tenure. Consequently, it has been the practice to fire coaches on the basis of a win-loss record. In such cases, due process is rather abrupt. On the other hand, it is difficult to dismiss tenured faculty, or to deny tenure to probationary faculty. Due process for negative tenure decisions of faculty can become quite lengthy. It seems extremely inconsistent to have both types of contrasts in the same administrative unit; therefore, it is foolish to expect a spirit of cooperation or cohesiveness to exist under such conditions.

One alternative is to grant coaches tenure. However, this can have a greater negative impact. If coaches by choice or by decree, leave coaching for the classroom, they generally create staffing problems. They are often not current or adequately prepared to meet the needs of an academic unit. In physical education, a faculty can quickly become overloaded with personnel who are not adequately prepared to teach in areas where they are most needed, such as in certain theory courses or scientific foundations. The other pressing problem is that hiring decisions are often based only on coaching qualifications, or specific athletic needs, and not sound academic priorities. The result is that the quality of education suffers, which should be sufficient justification for a completely independent athletic department.

Affiliated

Affiliation with an academic department allows coaches to earn rank and tenure according to the quality and quantity of similar contributions that are normally expected of other members of the academic community; thus rank and tenure will not be determined by win-loss records. Academic affiliation encourages acceptance from within the academic community and lessens the necessity of a coaching occupational subculture (Massengale, 1974), which creates dysfunction in higher education (Massengale, 1981).

Faculty coaching evaluation for merit salary enhancement, promotion in rank, or consideration of tenure, can be assessed by using many traditional factors.

Among those factors are personal and professional attributes that influence coaching, administrative ability, theory and techniques used in coaching, quality and practice of recruiting, public relations skills, coaching effectiveness, professional recognition and growth, promotion and fund raising, and finally, depending on the teaching/coaching portion of the contract job description, an assessment of teaching effectiveness.

BUDGET SOURCES

Independent

At large institutions, the major portion of the athletic budget is self-generated. The administration of that budget and the efforts expended to generate those funds is best conducted by those closest to the situation. In the case of fund raising, the athletic director will minimize duplication of effort and conflict between athletic fund raising and other fund-raising efforts at the institution.

In smaller institutions, the major portion of the athletic budget often originates from the institution itself but generally not from the same budget category as academic budgets. Consequently, linking athletic and academic units together is questionable. Furthermore, in smaller institutions, student services and athletic budgets generally arise from the same budget category, which might make athletics more appropriately aligned with student services rather than an academic department.

If it is necessary to have athletics aligned with another unit of the institution, placing them with student services, as illustrated in Figure 5, would be more appropriate than with an academic department. It is best, however, to have athletics completely independent of other administrative units.

Affiliated

Athletic funding becomes more reasonable when evaluated and analyzed just like any other legitimate program that an educational institution sponsors, and then channeled through an administrative structure similar to other academic programs and functions of a university. Budget decisions should be made by professionals in the field and not by management personnel with a corporate, business, or solely profit-motive perspective. Academic affiliation will maintain the students, the educational system, and our society as the beneficiaries of intercollegiate athletics. After all, beneficiaries of business or corporate concerns are expected to be their owners. One might ask who owns intercollegiate sports anyway? According to Blau and Scott (1962), to convert a university into a business conern that gives the consumers what they want does not serve in the best educational interests of the students. One might also ask if consumerism is the main purpose of intercollegiate sports.

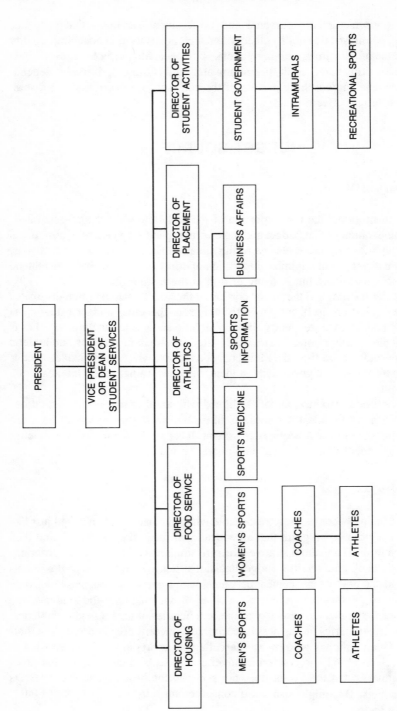

Figure 5. An example of an affiliation with student services.

ACADEMIC MAJORS AND
DEGREE PROGRAMS

Independent

Significant differences between students and athletes further supports an independent organization. In an academic unit, students are all pursuing degrees in the same general discipline which is their common bond. Athletes do not have a common bond other than their specific sport and the institution itself. It is estimated that from institution to institution, no academic unit enrolls more than 20 to 50% of the athletes. It seems strange then to thrust the remaining 50 to 80% into an academic unit simply for the sake of administrative convenience.

It should also be noted that students are buyers and athletes are sellers. Students are buying an education in the form of the collective talent and resources that an institution can provide. Athletes, on the other hand, are sellers of their talents for purposes of entertainment and public relations. As such they are contractural employees, and as athletes, they should be treated as employees and not students.

Affiliated

Affiliation with an academic department, particularly a physical education department, supplements and enhances degree program training in many ways. It provides real working role models. A system of acceptable career sponsorship, career mobility, and working gatekeepers is established. A source of converting educational theory into practice is created.

Affiliated athletic departments provide a source of up-to-date knowledge. There can be a continual source of evidence that good teaching and good coaching are compatible, desirable, and fully attainable. There can also be a continual demonstration that physical education and coaching may be considered an art, a science, a craft, maybe even a calling, and most of all, a legitimate field of academic study.

CONCLUDING STATEMENT

Independent

Harper, Miller, Park, and Davis (1977) attempted to answer the question of what the relationship of physical education and athletics should be. By their own admission, they did not find the answer but did succeed in showing why that relationship is a continuing problem. Their arguments follow a somewhat different rationale than has been raised here, and thereby lend additional support to the idea that intercollegiate athletics should be administered separately from academic departments.

Institutional variability to the rule differences in the purposes of academic and athletic departments and their accompanying administrative responsibilities certainly justifies the total separation of intercollegiate athletics. If it is absolutely necessary to place an additional administrator between the athletic department and the President, the most logical choice would become a vice-president or dean of student services. In addition to the arguments presented, prominent leaders in intercollegiate athletics have been asking, begging, or demanding that college and university presidents assume more direct responsibility for athletics as a necessary step in curing athletic ills. The recommendation then is that athletics should be administered by a director that has a direct line and staff relationship with the president of the institution and that the athletic department be completely independent.

Affiliated

Administering intercollegiate athletics constitutes a special dilemma, a dilemma which is similar to what was best described years ago as "institutionalized role conflict" (Seeman, 1953). Etzioni (1964) has presented various solutions to this dilemma, but by far, the most popular is the rule of the professionally oriented administrator—an administrator who combines a professional education, with managerial practice, experience, and personality.

Only through the credibility derived from legitimate academic department affiliation (with the department administered by a person with a strong professional perspective who has been given legitimate authority) can intercollegiate athletics be appropriately administered in the best interests of the university and its students. Independent athletic departments are far too easily controlled and managed by administrators in higher education who themselves are too easily influenced by sterotypical sports fan mentality.

REFERENCES

BLAU, P.M. & Scott, W.R. (1962). *Formal organizations*. San Francisco: Chandler.

ETZIONI, A. (1964). *Modern organizations*. Englewood Cliffs, NJ: Prentice-Hall.

FROST, R.B. & Marshall, S.J. (1977). *Administration of physical education and athletics*. Dubuque, IA: W.C. Brown.

HARPER, W.A., Miller, D.M., Park, R.J., & Davis, E.C. (1977). *The philosophic process in physical education* (3rd ed.). Philadelphia: Lea and Febiger.

KEW, F.C. (1978). Values in competitive games. *Quest, 29*, 103-112.

MASSENGALE, J.D. (1974). Coaching as an occupational subculture. *Phi Delta Kappan, 54*(2), 140-142.

MASSENGALE, J.D. (1981). Role conflict and the teacher/coach: Some occupational causes and considerations for the sport sociologist. In S.L. Greendorfer (Ed.), *Sociology of sport: Diverse perspectives*. West Point, NY: Leisure Press.

RESICK, N.C., Seidel, B.L., & Mason, J.G. (1970). *Modern administrative practices in physical education and athletics*. Reading, MA: Addison-Wesley.

SCOTT, J. (1973). Sport and the radical ethic. *Quest,* **19,** 71-77.

SEEMAN, M. (1953). Role conflict and ambivalent leadership. *American Sociological Review,* **18,** 373-380.

Chapter 14

Presidents Need Power Within the NCAA to Preserve Academic Standards and Institutional Integrity

Derek Bok
Harvard University

Everyone knows that all is not well with intercollegiate athletics. Newspapers have repeatedly disclosed scandals involving forged transcripts, illegal payments to college athletes, and recruiting violations of various kinds. Much more serious is the evidence of a broad erosion of academic standards. Some universities are admitting more and more athletes whose educational backgrounds and aptitudes are so low that they have little chance of academic success. Graduation rates for athletes in big-time sports reportedly fall below 40% or even below 30% on some campuses.

These statistics reflect the accumulated experience of thousands of young people who are used and eventually cast aside to fulfill the athletic ambitions of their universities. In such circumstances, it is hardly honest to talk of "student-athletes" and "amateur" teams. If colleges have teams in which the vast majority of players never graduate, let alone take a serious academic course load, and if they pay these players thousands of dollars each year for room, board, and incidentals, then their teams are semiprofessional in everything but name.

For educators who wish to do something about this problem, the place to start is the individual campus. A college president can surely take steps to make certain that rules are observed, that only athletes in good academic standing can play, that clearly unqualified students are not admitted, and that special efforts are made to provide tutoring and other forms of educational assistance.

This article originally appeared in *The Chronicle of Higher Education*, December 14, 1983. Reprinted with permission.

Yet we can count on presidents to take such measures only if they can proceed within the framework of reasonable rules to which other colleges must subscribe. If some institutions choose to ignore admissions standards for athletes and are indifferent to whether their athletes ever graduate, other colleges will find it hard to compete with them on the playing field. In a world in which television revenues are so lucrative, alumni and legislators care so much about winning, and gate receipts are so important in meeting athletic costs, many institutions will find it very hard to maintain reasonable academic standards if their competitors refuse to do likewise.

In short, few presidents will make much headway on their own campuses unless they can act within a common framework of collective rules that will maintain adequate minimum academic standards. Making and enforcing such rules is the responsibility of the National Collegiate Athletic Association. Until recently, however, NCAA rules were plainly insufficient for the task. As late as 1982, athletes could remain eligible whether or not they had passed any courses or even taken exams; the only requirement was that they *enroll* in courses carrying a minimum number of credits. No requirements were placed on freshman eligibility save that a student achieve a 2.0 record in high school regardless of what courses were taken or whether they had any academic content.

As evidence of abuse began to mount, voices were increasingly heard urging university presidents to assert themselves. Not only editorial writers but coaches such as Joe Paterno and John Wooden placed the responsibility for reform squarely on the presidents. In the words of James Odenkirk, chairman of physical education at Arizona State University, "There is general agreement that abuses will not be stemmed until university presidents take more responsibility for college sports."

In the past 2 years, an *ad hoc* group of university presidents has formed under the auspices of the American Council on Education (ACE). The first action of this group was to propose rules stiffening academic standards for freshman eligibility so that marginal students would not have to face the pressures of big-time varsity competition before having a year to establish themselves academically. Another proposal required athletes to *complete* a stipulated number of courses each year that counted toward an academic degree in order to stay eligible for varsity play. This rule was designed to create strong incentives for athletes and their institutions to take academic work seriously and to keep up steady progress toward graduation. After strenuous lobbying, both these measures were approved overwhelmingly by the NCAA convention.

This experience persuaded the presidents of several things. Presidents do indeed have an important role to pay. And yet, for the NCAA to function harmoniously and effectively, chief executives must find a way of working within the organization and not go on indefinitely as an outside group. In addition, a body of presidents can continue to be effective and achieve legitimacy only if members are chosen by their peers and armed with at least minimum powers to establish rules to safeguard academic standards. A totally *ad hoc* group can mobilize their fellow presidents occasionally on an informal, grassroots basis, but this is no way to establish sound, workable rules over the long run.

Accordingly, the ACE group has proposed the creation of a board of presidents within the NCAA, elected by the mail ballots of all member presidents. The board would have nothing to do with purely athletic matters; its authority would extend only to important policy issues significantly affecting the academic standards, financial integrity, or reputation of the member institutions. Within this limited jurisdiction, the board could consult with the NCAA staff and council and offer advice and recommendations. If these measures failed, the board could propose new bylaws or suspend existing rules. Such actions would stand unless overruled by two-thirds vote of the NCAA convention. The proposal embodying these provisions is known as Proposition No. 35.

In view of the widespread support for more presidential involvement, the NCAA has also made a proposal—Proposition No. 36—that provides for the creation of a commission of presidents. Although this body bears many superficial resemblances to the board recommended by the ACE presidents in Proposition No. 35, there are two important differences.

First, under the NCAA proposal (Proposition 36), the initial slate of candidates for its commission would be named by 12 chief executive officers chosen by the NCAA council, a body of 44 individuals, only 5 of whom are now college presidents. This slate would then be voted on by the delegates to the NCAA convention, almost all of whom are typically athletic directors and faculty representatives. Once selected, the commission would appoint its own nominating committee to present candidates in future years to be elected by the NCAA convention.

In contrast, under Proposition 35, initial candidates for the board would be nominated by a panel of presidents, the majority of whom are the elected heads of the major presidentially based higher-education associations. The final selection would be made by mail ballot of all member presidents. Thus, the board proposed in Proposition 35 would be clearly determined by the member presidents, while the composition of the NCAA commission would be subject to greater influence from established interests within the NCAA.

Second, under the NCAA proposal, the presidential commission would have minimal powers. It could advise, but the NCAA would be free to ignore its advice. It could call for studies, but presidents can readily arrange studies without creating a board. It could propose rules to the convention, but any group of six presidents can already propose rules to the convention. In short, the NCAA commission would in all significant respects be advisory only. In contrast, the board proposed in Proposition 35 could initiate rules (provided that they were designed to protect the academic standards, financial integrity, or reputation of member institutions). Such actions by the board could be overridden only by a two-thirds vote of the NCAA convention.

In sum, the differences are quite obvious. The NCAA is proposing a presidential commission that can offer advice and make proposals. But the new body will not be given any of the significant powers traditionally exercised by the established organs of the NCAA, even if the most vital academic values are at stake. Not only will the commission lack power, its members will be chosen initially through procedures shaped by the established interests of the NCAA. Proposition 35, on the other hand, would offer university presidents greater power to choose their own representatives and would give the board at least a limited authority to act in defense of academic values and other important institutional concerns.

NCAA representatives reply that presidents already have ultimate power to control the NCAA, because they can attend conventions or instruct their delegates how to vote. But this assertion has no substance in the practical world. Individual presidents are extremely busy. Even if they can spare the time to attend a convention, they have no reason to believe that their presence will make a difference. Because most proposals coming before the convention are technical and involve matters of purely athletic significance, few chief executives take the time to study the proposals with care or to instruct their representatives how to vote. As a result, most decisions at NCAA conventions reflect the wishes of coaches, athletic directors, and faculty athletic representatives rather than the will of the presidents.

The question before us, then, is clear. Recognizing the problems that have beset intercollegiate athletics in the past and the serious difficulties that still persist, are we content to leave all responsibility and power in the hands of the traditional groups and organizations within the NCAA? Or do we wish to insist on a new representative body of presidents, with limited power to create common safeguards to protect the academic standards, financial integrity, and reputations of our institutions? It is for college presidents to choose, for we instruct our delegates to the NCAA convention how to vote on Proposition 35. Let us be sure to exercise our responsibilities and use them in the best interests of our students and our institutions.

Part IV

THE RATIONALIZATION OF INTERCOLLEGIATE ATHLETICS

What in the hell is a commercial entertainment enterprise doing on a university campus? Big-time intercollegiate sport is a business enterprise....Not only are big-time intercollegiate athletic programs a commercial enterprise functioning as part of a cartel and employing athletes, but the programs are operated with employees (athlete) who are being paid slave wages.

Sage (1979:129)

When colleges or universities make decisions about programs, when individuals behave in certain fashions, it is often customary to ask for reasons, for justification for those chosen behaviors. Why should a college start a business school, foreign affairs institute, or big-time intercollegiate sport team for that matter? The need for ''reasons'' has historical roots.

The Enlightenment of 18th century Europe had a sweeping effect on the social institutions of the era. No longer could the leaders of state justify the legitimacy of their rank in society due entirely to supernatural principles such as birthright or power. Rational explanation based upon objectively supported evidence became increasingly necessary as a means to justify the behavior of those involved in the society's institutions.

The effects of the Enlightenment, the perceived need to rationally justify action, strongly influenced the developing European schools of higher learning. Particularly in the German universities of the 19th century, there evolved an ultimate belief in the power of logically presented natural (as opposed to supernatural) evidence. To efficiently discover knowledge, the academic must not be blindly wed to any particular value system or set of beliefs. It was expected that all social institutions should justify their behaviors as most reasonable considering the objectives of that institution.

From this European tradition came the American college and university. Just as the Enlightenment had legitimized the need to rationalize the behaviors of its European models, American schools of higher learning also felt the need to justify the programmatic decisions which were required to suit continental models to the new American condition. Though dependent upon its European ancestors for its origins, definition of the college's legitimate purposes and programs for this native soil was not and is not entrenched by centuries of tradition. The late 19th and early 20th century American college and university which came to embrace sport was an institution relatively free to define and redefine its programs and objectives. Without the stable resources of students and money enjoyed by its continental counterparts, the American school felt the need to pursue its particular vision of the higher learning, altering its substance and stated purpose in response to the needs and desires of those on whom the school was dependent. Unfettered by centuries of traditional understandings of institutional mission, free from restrictive governmental regulation, without a national church to oversee its belief systems, separated by the legal boundaries of statehood and the distance of the new country, the American college of the late 19th and early 20th century came to accept the heretofore alien presence of "sport" within its official programs.

Still there was the need to rationalize, to justify. It was not enough to say that sport seemed to suit the American condition. Why? How did sport serve the purpose of the American college and university?

The Olympic revival of 1896 provided the basis for one justification for sport's inclusion in American college programs. While the classical humanities provided the basis for the English conception of higher education, and the logic of science formed the heart of the German system of higher learning, the 1896 Athens Games once again demonstrated Olympian possibilities of the well-rounded individual. According to the classical Greek philosophy, man should be well-rounded physically and spiritually as well as mentally. This liberal conception of the purpose of education provided popular justification for athletics within the American school.

In the 1980s the fiscal belt-tightening and the dwindling numbers of 18 to 21-year-old youths have made the rationalization of college programs even more important. Scarce resources must be distributed as efficiently as possible. Unnecessary or noncentral programs should be excised, that is, terminated or separated from the formal functions of the institution. The American college and university, with its lay board of trustees, with its very public nature, must constantly be aware of its stated institutional purpose and justification for its programs if it is to consistently receive the support of the public and campus constituencies which provide support for the school.

In this part of the book the following three major justifications for intercollegiate sport's existence will be examined:

1. Intercollegiate sports develop "the individual."
2. There are economic benefits for the colleges and universities that sponsor sport.
3. There are educational benefits for women and blacks who engage in intercollegiate competition.

After review of the sections corresponding to each of these rationales, the problem of big-time sport's justification within the educational institution will be apparent. If college and university programs lose money, do not develop the individual, do not equally benefit women and men, blacks and whites, reform is then clearly called for by a society which demands education and equity from its colleges and universities.

REFERENCE

SAGE, G.H. (1979). The college dilemma of sport and leisure: A sociological perspective. In D. Stanley Eitzen (Ed.), *Sport in contemporary society* (pp. 188-195). St. Martin's.

Section A

Personal Development

Possibly the most popular rationalization for sport in American institutions of higher learning centers about the notion that sport participation is related to the "development of character" or that college athletics somehow enhances the academic and/or occupational attainment of participants. If it can be demonstrated that athletics somehow teach students lessons important for success in life or that it helps them gain success in school or on the job, then sport programs may be justified as an important part of a liberal education.

HISTORICAL ORIGINS

The spread of the personal development rationale for intercollegiate sport was promoted by several historical factors. First was the connection of American education with its roots in England. Though its first colleges were intended to be literal copies of Oxford and Cambridge with their emphasis on the classics, soon the American college and university of the late 19th and early 20th century imported the sporting traditions of the English school system. The Duke of Wellington voiced the popularly held belief that "the Battle of Waterloo was won on the playing fields of Eton." If the character traits and team work necessary for military success could be taught through sport, then it was reasoned that these traits that had made England great (and which might make America great) could and should be inculcated through the American versions of college sport.

The second historical factor behind the popularization of the notion that sport participation develops the individual is related to the revival of the Olympic Games. Paralleling the rise of sport in American colleges and universities of the late 19th and 20th centuries were the efforts of Baron Pierre de Coubertin to return the classical Games of ancient Greece to a position of prominence in contemporary culture. Spurred by the archeological digs at ancient Olympia and successful revivals in the 1896 Athens Games and the 1900 Paris Games, conceptions of the well-rounded sportsman became embodied in the idealized student-athlete. The campus could and should, according to this view of the colleges purpose, develop well-rounded individuals. Intercollegiate sport was to be a primary means for the development of a strong character as well as body.

The third historical factor which promoted the rationale of sport as individual developer was the growing popularity of the liberal arts conception of college purposes. Whereas the first forms of American higher education were steeped in the humanities, and later visions of the university were modeled after German conceptions of the school as scientific workshop, the liberal arts conception of higher learning was less constrained by strictly intellectual objectives. In this view of the legitimate goals of higher education, it was totally appropriate to develop the spirit and emotions as well as the mind and body. With the acceptance of this rationale of college purpose, sport programs became a necessary part of formal college offerings, for here was the "curriculum" to liberally educate the individual.

These three historical factors contributed to the popularization of the "sport as personal developer" rationale for intercollegiate athletics. The legitimacy of sport programs in the English origins of the American college, the revival of the Olympic ideal, and the growing popularity of the liberal arts view of higher learning were all factors promoting the acceptance of the sport in American higher education.

CHARACTER DEVELOPMENT

Upon closer inspection, however, the sport as personal developer rationale is conceptually unclear as well as theoretically questionable. If the assumption that sport participation builds character, for example, is closely inspected, we see that though we may have a feeling for the definition of character, we do not clearly know what it is exactly. While character encompasses certain personality traits such as discipline and perseverance, does it also include values such as the importance of achievement and hard work? How about "spirit"? Is that undefinable spirit to be assumed as part of the character that is developed by sport participation? How about norms, patterns of behavior—are these part of character? How about intellectual skills? One of the primary difficulties with the substantiation of contentions that sport builds character is that it is extremely difficult to define just what character is.

Another problem with validation of the individual development through sport rationale concerns identification of *positive* traits. In the rationale that athletic participation develops favorable traits, it is necessary to define "good" characteristics from "less good" characteristics. If we are to be able to justify sports existence in our schools through its ability to inculcate values, norms of behavior, intellectual skills, and personality traits, inevitably we face the question of which values are important, what norms of behavior are important to teach, which mental skills are significant, and which personality traits should be fostered. All of these decisions involve a subjective value choice. Without knowing what good traits are, we cannot know if sport develops good or bad characteristics.

Another obstacle to substantiation of the sport as personal developer contention is the theoretical problem of the demonstration of causation. While it may be possible to conclusively prove that the "cause" for water formation is the combination of two parts of hydrogen and one part of oxygen under specified lab conditions, the demonstration of conclusive causation in psychology and the social sciences is extremely difficult. Due partly to the immaturity of the field of psychology and sociology (that is the lack of a developed technology to demonstrate causation in human behavior), at this time, it is rarely possible to prove that any human behavior is conclusively caused by some specified set of factors. It is not clearly possible at this time to prove that playing sport *causes* life success or causes higher grades.

Theoretical obstacle to the substantiation of the sport as personal developer rationale stems from the very process through which both sport and higher education affect their participants. While it is commonly believed that youth are rationally taught predetermined skills that better prepare them for success in sport, school, and later life in both settings, this "rational processing" view of how sport and education function stands in stark contrast to a completely different conception of the process through which both sport and higher education do their work. In the "filtering" conception of sport and higher education's process, students are not so much taught the traits important for later success as are these students screened for their possession of certain characteristics. After this screening, students and athletes may then be "allocated" to various roles and positions of differential status and rewards. In this conception of how sport and the schools work, neither may develop personal developer as much as they look for and identify those who already have "it" and those who do not.

PERSONALITY QUALITIES AND SPORT

From this brief overview, it should be apparent that while many believe that sport develops personal qualities, we might suspect that there are actually many problems with the substantiation of this belief. The empirical research in this area verifies our suspicion. In the first paper, Purdy, Eitzen, and Hufnagel examine the relationship between intercollegiate athletic participation and academic achievement. More specifically, the researchers assess "the degree to which college athletes are disadvantaged educationally by their sport participation." Looking at a population of 2,091 men and women athletes at NCAA Division IA Colorado State University between 1970-1980, the following dependent factors were considered: academic preparation for college, college grade-point average, graduation rate in relation to independent variables—athletic/nonathletic status, race, gender, scholarship, and nonscholarship athletes and sport. For this population, it was found that athletes are generally less well prepared for college (relative to high school grade-point average, rank, SAT-ACT score) and that athletes performed less well academically in college (indicated by college grades and graduation rate). These findings were especially pronounced for black, male, scholarship, football, and basketball players. Despite assumptions held by many that athletes should be better students because they are skilled at budgeting their time efficiently and that they are mentally disciplined and motivated to achieve athletic status at this major university actually had a negative relationship to the measures most commonly used to assess educational attainment.

In the next paper, Paul Dubois examines the assumption that sport participation is related to occupational success. The intent of this research on 160 male athletes and a comparison group of 450 male nonathletes was to see if there were any statistically significant relationships between athletic participation or nonparticipation and the dependent variables "occupational prestige" and "earnings." While one might assume that athletics teaches the participant the skills necessary for higher earnings or status, or that an athlete's salience or successful image might lead to sponsored mobility to upper strata of society, apparently neither model for occupational success held for the athlete group. Controlling for the education, age, ethnicity, academic average, work experience and father's occupational prestige, Dubois generally found that athletic participation had no significant effect on the dependent measures. Intercollegiate sport participation seems to have no positive effect on the after-college occupational success of athletes.

In the paper by Christopher Stevenson, the author revisits his classic article on socialization through sport. In what may be the most often quoted review of research on the subject, Stevenson (1975) comprehensively surveys the voluminuous body of research on socialization through sport. After careful consideration, it is concluded that there is little if any scientific substantiation for the belief that sport participation itself *causes* long-lasting changes in athletes. In this new paper, the author builds upon his classical 1975 review originally published in *Research Quarterly*, and considers the new research and continuing problems which have hampered development of the research line. In this intriguing and somewhat personal article, Stevenson illustrates the cultural basis of scientific research. He notes that changes in social concern have altered the focus of "popular" sociological research on sport. Applied research as an aid to athletic performance has become more prevalent as interest in research on the character effects of sport has waned.

Though there has been some new research on the effects of sport involvement on participants, there has been very little progress in the establishment of causal relationships between college athletic participation and the development of positive psychological, behavioral, or attitudinal characteristics. Though some new studies have progressed beyond the methodological problems of test population dissimilarity, inadequate treatments and insensitive or unreliable instrumentation, still far too many suffer these same old flaws. The most striking finding in Stevenson's review of sport socialization research since 1975, however, may be the paucity of research on this once fertile subject. The one important question of "What is the impact of college athletics upon the individual?" has been replaced by "How do people become elite athletes?" Concerns for "civil rights" and "self-actualization" have become secondary to concern for efficient means to produce high-level athletes.

While the previous paper by Stevenson reviews the question of personal development sociologically, the next paper by Ogilvie and Tutko looks at the issue psychologically. The authors, perhaps the two most publicly visible sport psychologists of the 1970s, summarize their years of personal observation and research on competition's effect on personality. Echoing Stevenson's conclusions, Ogilvie and Tutko find "no empirical support for the tradition that sport builds character." Indeed, there is evidence that athletic competition limits growth in some areas. If there is a certain personality type associated with athletics (characterized for example by a high need for achievement, high yet realistic goals, well-organized, orderly, dominant, respectful of authority, trusting, psychological endurance, self-control, a low need for affiliation) the "ideal" personality type is not "molded" from athletic competition but instead "comes out of the ruthless selection process that occurs at all levels of sport."

In the last paper of this section, George Sage considers the question of the sort of personality structure which sport may be promoting. If sport is indeed successful in the modeling of a certain character type, what is that type? Is the personality good or bad? Is that personality conducive to autonomy? Is it consistent with the purposes of education? In response to these questions, Sage notes his observation that sport "conditions (athletes) to the prevailing social structure," a structure which rewards conformity more than autonomy and which ultimately promotes a "bureaucratic personality" which parallels the bureaucratic nature of modern society.

From these papers in Part V, it appears then that there is little proof that intercollegiate sport participation itself causes growth in "character," facilities, occupational, or academic attainment. If, in fact, any changes actually are effected through athletics, these changes may be antithetical to the role of higher education as developer of individual maturity. Justification for sport as a formal part of higher education is apparently not provided by empirical and theoretical research on sport as personal developer. Perhaps rationalization for intercollegiate sport may be found in its effects on the economics of the institution, on women, or on black participants. The remaining chapters in this part of the book will look at these possible justifications.

Chapter 15

Are Athletes Also Students? The Educational Attainment of College Athletes[1]

Dean A. Purdy
Bowling Green State University

D. Stanley Eitzen and Rick Hufnagel
Colorado State University

The foundations of college sports in the United States have been shaken by revelations of academic compromises made in the interests of intercollegiate athletics (Axthelm, 1980; Sanoff, 1980; Underwood, 1980). Among the unethical practices that have been uncovered are falsified transcripts by colleges, athletes receiving credit for courses not taken, and the financial and academic exploitation of athletes. Implicit in the criticisms leveled at college sports is the fundamental issue of their relationship to the educational process (Hanford, 1979:363).

The public is aware of the potential problems regarding the quality of education that college athletes receive through the efforts of muck-raking journalists (Axhelm, 1980; Underwood, 1980) and ex-athletes (Meggysey, 1970; Scott, 1971; Shaw, 1972). The anecdotal evidence they provide suggests that while coaches publicly espouse that their athletes are students first and athletes second, their primary interest is to keep players eligible by whatever means, including credit for phantom courses, surrogates for tests, and counseling on which easy courses do not lead to graduation. These practices are widespread enough to lead some to conclude that the corruption of academic ideals is endemic in universities with major sports programs (Eitzen & Sage, 1982). The organization responsible for policing the athletic programs of major U.S. universities, the National Collegiate Athletic Association (NCAA), has focused on violations of amateurism, such as athletes receiving financial inducements to play, and neglected the investigation of charges that athletes may be receiving inferior educations.

Although educational ethics have been violated by college coaches for some time, they have been exacerbated by the financial climate of contemporary intercollegiate sports programs.[2] Winning programs attract lucrative television money; bowl contracts, alumni donations, and high-attendance figures (Atwell, 1979; Davis, 1979; Grant, 1979; Lopino, 1979; Nyquist, 1979). Society has created "an educational dilemma concerning the lace and mission of athletics within our intellectual estates by mixing 'dollar values with educational ones' " (Hanford, 1978:232).

Studies by universities and social scientists of the educational attainment of college athletes have been few and contradictory. Two variables are commonly used in these studies: graduation rate and grade-point average.

Graduation rate: Several studies indicate that athletes stand a better chance of graduating than nonathletes. Billick (1973) found that 93% of the 1963 University of Pittsburgh football team had graduated, and 46% had received graduate degrees. Pilapil and Stecklein found that 50% of the athletes from the University of Minnesota's class of 1967 had graduated, compared to 41% of nonathletes. Michener (1976:237) studied Stanford University male athletes from the baseball, basketball, football, swimming, and track squads during the academic year 1969-70; he found that 88% of the athletes graduated compared to 82.5% of the total student body.

Other studies yield a different conclusion. Webb's (1968) study of all Michigan State University athletes over a 5-year period revealed that 49% of team sport and 60% of individual sport athletes had graduated. Harrison (1976) found that less than 20% of football players who entered North Texas State University from 1966 to 1971 went on to attain degrees from the university. A study by the University of New Mexico (1980) revealed that only 21% of its football players had graduated since 1970. Other graduation rates cites in this study were track (24%), wrestling (24%), and baseball (28%). Studies conducted by the Southeast and Southwest Conferences have shown similar results (Benagh, 1976:127).

Grade-point average (GPA): Results using this variable are also mixed. Steklein and Dameron (1965) found no significant difference between the grade-point averages of athletes and nonathletes at the University of Minnesota. A later study at the same institution demonstrated that athletes had GPA's of 2.42, compared with 2.40 for nonathletes (Pilapil & Stecklein, 1970). However, Harrison (1976) found that football players at North Texas State University had a mean GPA of 2.00.

THE PROBLEM

Nyquist (1979), in his critique of the exploitation of college athletes, suggested that unethical conduct will continue to embarass educational institutions until they realize the magnitude of the problem and correct the situation. However, research on the relationship between college sport participation, educational attainment, and the possible negative effects on athletes is meager and generally limited to a single indicator of educational success (Hanford, 1974; Hanks & Eckland, 1976;

Harris, 1980; Harrison, 1976; Litchfield & Cope, 1962; Moran, 1980; Pilapil & Stecklein, 1970; Roper & Snow, 1976; Sage, 1967; Stecklein & Dameron, 1965; Webb, 1968). Moreover, the literature lacks empirical studies assessing the general academic preparation and achievement level of college athletics. This is unfortunate in view of Spady's (1970) research which indicated that participation in high school sport may lead to increased educational aspirations but does not necessarily enhance or develop those academic characteristics necessary for success in college.

Our research assesses the degree to which college athletes are disadvantaged educationally by their sports participation. Unlike previous studies, we consider a number of dimensions: academic preparation for college, college grade-point average, and graduation rate. Moreover, we compare athletes with nonathletes, and various categories among the athletes—males and females, whites and nonwhites, scholarship and nonscholarship holders, and participants by sport.

METHOD

We studied the academic achievements of athletes at Colorado State University from the fall of 1970 through to the spring of 1980. The NCAA classifies this university as Division 1A, which means that it is one of the nation's "big-time" sport programs.

The time frame for our study was determined by the fact that computerized educational data from the University's admissions and records department were only available from 1970. This period of 10 years is long enough to determine and include the percentage of athletes who take more than the normal 4 to 5 years to complete their undergraduate education. In 1975, the institution changed from the quarter system, but this had no effect on our analysis.

We identified athletes by the eligibility reports supplied by the athletic department to the Western Athletic Conference. Athletes had to complete one academic term to be included in our sample. These criteria yielded a sample of 2,091 athletes, both men and women.

We obtained grant-in-aid information from the athletic department and transformed it into the percentage of financial aid extended to each of the athletes. The expected cost of an academic term, obtained from the university bulletin, was divided into the amount of financial aid received by an athlete to obtain a percentage. In our analysis, we used the largest percentage of financial aid by athletes during their residence at the university.

We used athletic department records to determine the number of years that an individual played on an athletic team at the university. In cases where the individual participated in several sports, we used the largest number of years of participation in any one sport. Athletic department records also identified students who received an athletic letter and those who participated while classified as seniors.

We obtained educational records from official university records in the department of admissions and records. Variables used in the analysis consisted of cumulative university grade-point averages, American College Test (ACT) and Scholastic Aptitude Test (SAT) scores, high school grade-point average, high school class rank, and the number of years spent at the university to achieve graduation. The official university records also provided information on the demographic variables of sex and race.

RESULTS

This study examines two sets of data: (a) the comparison of athletes to the general student population (GSP) on several variables that measure educational ability and achievement; and (b) an analysis of the same variables within various subcategories of athletes, including sport, letter-winner, and participation as a senior. Both sets of data helped determine whether athletes were substantially different from the GSP and if any significant differences in educational preparation and attainment existed among the athletes by social characteristics.

Athletes and Nonathletes

Table 1 shows the demographic characteristics and mean educational attainment scores for both athletes and the GSP. These data show that athletes in the aggregate differ from the GSP on every dimension. Most significant for our purposes is that the athletes were consistently less prepared than the GSP for college, as shown by lower high school grade-point average, high school class rank (percentile), SAT score, and ACT score. Similarly, the college performance of athletes was lower than the GSP as measured by college grade-point average and

Table 1

Demographic and Academic Information
for Athletes and the General Student Population

	Athletes[a] %	General Student Population (GSP)[b,c] %
Sex:		
Male	79.7	45.5
Female[d]	20.3	54.5
Race:		
Caucasian	88.1	94.3
Black	7.9	1.0
Other	4.0	4.4

Table 1 cont.

	Athletes[a] %	General Student Population (GSP)[b,c] %
College of Last Declared Major:		
Agriculture	5.3	7.2
Business	16.1	12.0
Engineering	5.1	7.1
Natural Resources	7.2	10.7
Home Economics	3.3	10.2
Natural Sciences	11.6	13.5
Professional Studies[e]	17.5	6.3
Arts, Humanities, & Social Sciences	30.7	29.4
Biological Sciences	3.2	6.8
High School GPA[f]	2.99 (743)	3.31 (6,402)[j]
Average Percentile High School Class Standing[g]	69 (1,550)	71
Average SAT Combined Score[h]	949 (1,389)	997 (19,944)
Average ACT Composite Score	20.8 (451)	22.1 (25,529)
Average College GAP	2.56 (2,075)	2.74
Graduate Rate[i]	34.2 (1,457)	46.8 (4,188)

[a] Entire population for the 10-year period: fall 1970 to 1980. N = 2,091.

[b] GSP statistics are from a study completed by the University for the period fall 1973 to 1979. Exceptions to this are the high school class standing (fall 1971 to 1979) and the graduation rate, which is from a study following the freshman class of 1975.

[c] N for sex and race = 25,519. N for college of last declared major = 14,201.

[d] Women do not appear as varsity athletes until 1975.

[e] Professional studies was created in 1975. Before that it was part of the college of arts, humanities, and social sciences. Physical education is included in the college of professional studies.

[f] High school grade-point average was not recorded before 1975.

[g] Class standing is a percentile ranking, calculated as:

$$100 - \frac{\text{Class Rank}}{\text{Class Size}} \times 100$$

[h] Scholastic Aptitude Test (SAT) combined score computed by adding the scores of the verbal and math components.

[i] Because students were given at least 5 years to graduate, the students entering since 1976 were not included in the computation of the graduation rate.

[j] NS (in parentheses) vary because of occasional incomplete data.

the graduation rate. Concerning the latter, we made no attempt to determine whether athletes or members of the GSP had transferred to another institution of higher education and proceeded to graduate because the academic records of the GSP did not contain this information.[3]

Table 2

Indicators of Educational Attainment by Sex for Athletes and the General Student Population

	Athletes[a]		General Student Population (GSP)[b]	
	Male	Female	Male	Female
SAT Combined Score	940 (1,077)	977 (312)**	1,024 (8,943)	979 (10,996)
ACT Composite Score	20.8 (290)	20.7 (161)	22.8 (11,614)	21.3 (13,915)
High School Class Standing	66 (1,181)	79 (369)***	—	—
High School GPA	2.85 (455)	3.21 (288)***	3.23 (2,987)	3.38 (3,415)
College GPA	2.48 (1,651)	2.88 (424)**	2.65	2.84
Graduation Rate	33% (1,270)	41% (189)	—	—

** p < .01
*** p < .001
[a] Significant differences (t-test) refer only to mean differences between male and female athletes.
[b] GSP averages were taken from a university administration study covering the period from fall 1973 to fall 1979. College GPA was computed from yearly averages for the period from fall 1970 to spring 1980.

Table 2 examines more closely the conclusion of Table 1 that athletes score lower than nonathletes on the various measures of educational attainment.[4] Male athletes scored lower on all indicators of academic achievement than their male counterparts from the GSP. Similar, though somewhat smaller, differences were discovered between female athletes and females from the GSP on most indices of educational success. However, female athletes had a slightly higher GPA. Graduation rates factored out by sex were not available for the GSP. Among the athletes, women scored significantly higher than men on all measures of educational achievement except for the ACT score, where men scored one-tenth of a point higher.

Variations Among Athletes

Female athletes differ from male athletes in preparation for college and in college achievement. There are additional characteristics of athletes which indicate that this is not a monolithic category. We consider race, participation as a senior, letterwinner, number of years of athletic participation, and extent of grant-in-aid. Of the athletes studied, 11.9% were nonwhite, 38.9% of those whose entering class had graduated participated as a senior, over half (54.9%) participated for only 1 year, and 39.4% received an athletic letter. Full athletic grants were given to 28.7% of the athletes, while 48.4% received no financial aid.

Table 3 shows black athletes had significantly lower scores on the entire range of educational achievement measures. These results are similar to those found by Spivey and Jones (1975). Comparison data by race were not available for the GSP. However, a study conducted by the university's administration that followed the freshman class of 1975 revealed graduation rates of 40.5% (N=42) for blacks and 48.6% (N=3,986) for Caucasians.

Table 4 shows the results of the mean scores for the educational achievement measures for various athletic subgroups. The first comparison investigates the differences between those athletes who participated as seniors and those who had

Table 3
Indicators of Educational Attainment by Race for Athletes

	Athletes	
	Black	Caucasian
SAT Combined Score	753 (86)	965 (1,247)***
ACT Composite Score	14.9 (22)	21.2 (405)***
High School Class Standing	62 (99)	70 (1,390)***
High School GPA	2.48 (43)	3.04 (658)***
College GPA	2.11 (163)	2.61 (1,830)***
Graduation Rate	21% (118)	35% (1,290)***

*** p<.001

Table 4

Indicators of Educational Attainment by Various Criteria of Athletic Participation

	SAT Combined Scores	ACT Composite Scores	High School GPA	High School Class Standing	College GPA	Graduation Rate
Underclass Participation	959(1,072)	20.8(397)	2.99(661)	69(1,231)	2.51(1,521)	26.2%(991)
Senior Participation	248(317)	21.0(54)	3.02(82)	70(319)	2.69(554)***	51.1%(468)***
Nonletter Winner	958(891)	20.8(339)	3.05(553)	70(1,025)	2.54(1,253)	28.2%(816)
Letter Winner	932(498)**	20.7(112)	2.82(190)***	67(525)**	2.59(822)	41.8%(643)***
Years of Participation						
1 Year	956(769)	20.7(283)	3.01(463)	69(897)	2.48(1,134)	25.5%(774)
2 Years	927(231)	20.8(93)	2.95(134)	67(274)	2.55(401)	35.0%(274)
3 Years	915(190)	20.6(42)	2.92(92)	68(184)	2.67(234)	41.9%(148)
4 Years or More	981(199)***	21.8(33)	3.04(54)	73(195)*	2.78(306)*	54.8%(263)***
Grant-in-Aid:						
No Aid	979(722)	21.5(295)	3.10(489)	73(820)	2.69(1,005)	37.0%(622)
1-33%	949(134)	20.3(58)	2.92(83)	70(151)	2.72(182)	44.6%(112)
34-66%	942(119)	19.2(31)	2.91(54)	66(133)	2.54(205)	37.8%(156)
67-99%	943(53)	19.3(9)	2.76(14)	64(54)	2.54(88)	39.5%(76)
100%	892(361)***	18.3(58)***	2.59(103)***	62(392)**	2.30(595)*	26.4%(493)***
Nongraduate	920(655)	19.7(116)	2.84(223)	63(682)	2.32(945)	
Graduate	988(343)***	21.4(73)*	3.25(28)***	72(350)***	2.86(498)*	

* $p \leqslant .05$

** $p \leqslant .01$

*** $p \leqslant .001$

not yet attained senior status. We included this comparison because some coaches and universities have used only athletes who were seniors to compute graduation rates. This is useful if one who wishes to distort the findings by inflating the graduation rates, because the more education received, the more likely a student is to graduate. We found that almost twice as many athletes who had achieved senior status graduated compared to those who were not yet seniors. However almost half (48.9%) of those athletes who played as seniors did not graduate. This is an important indicator of the potential for athlete exploitation because these athletes had given 4 years to the school yet had not received a diploma.

Table 4 also shows that athletes receiving full grants-in-aid had the lowest mean scores on each of the measures of educational attainment. Scholarship athletes, compared to nonscholarship or partial scholarship athletes, were the least prepared for the academic rigors of college and were the least successful in college, as measured by GPA and graduation rate.

Table 5 presents the educational achievement measures by sport.[5] Athletes in football, basketball, and wrestling had relatively lower mean scores for the educational achievement measures used for university admission. However, those athletes who participated in basketball and wrestling while attaining GPAs similar to those of football players graduated at a higher rate. The data also show that athletes involved in individual sports secured better college grades and were more likely to graduate than those who participated in team sports.

Only 3% of the athletes admitted with a high school GPA under 2.50 graduated. Only 18% of those who scored under 700 on the SAT graduated, as did 24% of those admitted with ACT scores of less than 15. The admission of academically marginal students is primarily a problem of the "revenue" sports of football and basketball. While these two sports accounted for only 29% of the athletes who had taken the SAT exam, they accounted for 47% of those who had scores of under 700. Results for the ACT test are similar. Of the athletes admitted with a high school GPA of under 2.50, basketball and football accounted for 36%, while representing only 18% of the athletes for whom high school GPA records were available. Basketball and football athletes accounted for 33% of the athletes in the sample, while simultaneously accounting for 50% of those athletes whose cumulative college GPA was less than 2.00 and 44% of those under 2.50. The case is even stronger if just football is considered because basketball includes female as well as male athletes, and the women inflate the academic results. Football players were the least prepared of all the athletes for the educational experience of college. They had the lowest college GPA (2.30) and the lowest graduation rate (26.8%) of all athletes by sport.

DISCUSSION

This study demonstrates that college athletes over a 10-year period in one major university scored lower than nonathletes on the measures most commonly used to assess educational attainment: They entered with poorer academic backgrounds,

Table 5

Indicators of Educational Attainment by Sport

	SAT Combined Scores	ACT Composite Scores	High School GPA	High School Class Standing	College GPA	Graduation Rate
Baseball	926 (113)	21.3 (43)	2.90 (62)	68 (123)	2.52 (184)	41.4% (128)
Basketball	893 (100)	19.3 (40)	2.89 (50)	68 (117)	2.49 (165)	39.4% (115)
Field Hockey	992 (34)	20.4 (11)	3.10 (26)	72 (33)	2.81 (44)	47.6% (21)
Football	899 (310)	18.6 (41)	2.60 (81)	61 (336)	2.30 (518)	26.8% (441)
Golf	1,008 (61)	22.0 (23)	3.08 (33)	74 (71)	2.67 (90)	52.2% (67)
Gymnastics	955 (97)	20.4 (45)	3.10 (51)	74 (105)	2.76 (123)	34.1% (88)
Softball	938 (36)	20.6 (20)	3.23 (32)	83 (42)	2.73 (48)	47.6% (21)
Swimming	998 (138)	22.0 (47)	3.04 (86)	69 (153)	2.70 (193)	32.0% (129)
Tennis	993 (63)	22.0 (20)	3.18 (38)	78 (66)	2.77 (89)	33.9% (59)
Track	966 (299)	21.5 (109)	3.08 (201)	71 (341)	2.67 (416)	34.5% (249)
Volleyball	1,001 (30)	21.6 (12)	3.29 (28)	81 (35)	2.95 (40)	36.8% (19)
Wrestling	945 (106)	20.1 (40)	2.79 (53)	65 (126)	2.52 (162)	36.4% (121)

they received lower grades than their nonathletic peers, and fewer of them graduated.

Two findings in particular challenge those who espouse the educational value of college sports:

1. Scholarship athletes fared worse than nonscholarship or partial-scholarship athletes in academic achievement. There are at least two possible explanations for this. First, full scholarship athletes have in a sense become employees of the university. They "owe" their coaches their undivided attention because these coaches are paying the bills. This creates a role conflict for student-athletes, with the student role often being neglected or deemphasized. Second, full-scholarship athletes are likely to be the best athletes. They derive their social status from their athletic endeavors and they may believe that, ultimately, they will have a lucrative professional career in sports (Oates, 1979). Thus, they may overemphasize their sport at the expense of academic pursuits.

2. There is evidence that athletes in the male revenue sports of football and basketball have a relatively low probability of receiving an education compared to nonathletes or athletes in the other sports. Because of the revenue-producing potential of football and basketball, the pressures are intense to win (Odenkirk, 1981; Underwood, 1980). This means that coaches in these sports are likely to be excessive in their demands on the time of their athletes during and between sessions. The serious and far-ranging financial consequences of big-time sports also increase the likelihood that coaches will recruit exceptional athletes who are unqualified for the academic demands of college. To the degree that this occurs, coaches are then faced with keeping these marginal students eligible. At some schools, this has meant obtaining bogus credits for them out of difficult courses leading to graduation, and other tactics. When these practices occur, the goal of higher education has been subverted and the athletes have been exploited (Eitzen & Sage, 1982; Frey, 1979; Moran, 1980; Santomier, Howard, Pilitz, & Romance, 1980; Underwood, 1980; White, 1980).

However, all colleges are not guilty of impeding the educational attainment of athletes. Academic achievement by athletes in the "minor" (nonrevenue) sports is similar to that of the general student population. Female athletes, too, resemble their nonathlete peers in academic accomplishments. There is some evidence, however, that women's college sports programs nationally are moving in the direction of men's programs with scandals, unethical practices, and overemphasis on winning (Eitzen & Sage, 1982:342). If this trend continues, women's sports programs will increasingly interfere with the educational achievement of their athletes.

There appears to be a positive relationship between athletic participation and academic performance at the interscholastic level (Coakley, 1982; Eitzen & Sage,

1982; Loy et al., 1978; Snyder & Spreitzer, 1978), although the research has methodological problems (Stevenson, 1975). Why is the relationship positive in high school and negative at the college level? Loy et al., (1978) have suggested studies at the college level to evaluate whether sport aids or hinders the attainment of the professed goals of the educational system. An explanation of the process dynamics at both levels is urgently needed.

The ideal study would compare several measures of educational attainment for both athletes and nonathletes at all levels of intercollegiate sport—from major universities with huge budgets, national schedules, and full scholarships for athletes to colleges without scholarships playing regional teams and nonscholarship athletes. As Snyder and Spreitzer (1978:76) have suggested: "Valid comparisons between collegiate athletes are difficult because of the variations in institutional quality, degree programs, type of sport and other potentially contaminating factors." These "obstacles" must not deter future efforts to understand the relationship between participation in college sports and educational attainment.

FOOTNOTES

1. An earlier version of this paper was presented at the national convention of the American Alliance for Health, Physical Education, Recreation, and Dance, Boston, April 13-17, 1981. The data for this study were made available through the cooperation of several administrators at Colorado State University: Charles Neidt, George Dennison, James Thomas, Leonard Overturf, Thurman McGraw, and Nancy O'Connor. Correspondence to: Purdy, Department of Sociology, Bowling Green State University, Bowling Green, Ohio 43043.

2. The so-called "revenue" sports of football and basketball frequently lose money, further exacerbating the financial condition of a university's sports program.

3. By "tracking" athletes who transfer to another institution, one may bias the comparative analysis to the general student population, as this information is not included in the university's statistics.

4. Differences of means between athletes and the GSP were not calculated because these groups were not samples but entire populations.

5. Because this is a preliminary report, men and women have not been separated in such sports as gymnastics and basketball.

REFERENCES

ATWELL, R.H. (1979, Fall). Some reflections on collegiate athletics. *Educational Record,* **60,** 367-373.

AXHELM, P. (1980, September 22). The shame of college sports. *Newsweek*, 54-59.

BENAGH, J. (1976). *Making it to No. 1*, New York: Dodd, Mead.

BILLICK, D. (1973). Still winners. *National Collegiate Sports Services Bulletin.*

COAKLEY, J.J. (1982). *Sport in society: Issues and controversies* (2nd edition). St. Louis: C.V. Mosby.

DAVIS, W.E. (1979, Fall). The presidential role in athletics: Leader or figurehead? *Educational Record,* **60**, 420-430.

EITZEN, D.S., & Sage, G.H. (1982). *Sociology of American sport* (2nd edition). Dubuque, IA: William C. Brown.

FREY, H. (1979). The coming demise of intercollegiate athletics. *Arena Review*, **3**(3), 34-43.

GRANT, C.H.B. (1979). Institutional autonomy and intercollegiate athletics. *Educational Record,* **60**(4), 409-419.

HANFORD, G.H. (1974). *The need for and feasibility of a national study of intercollegiate athletics.* Washington, D.C.: American Council of Education.

HANFORD, G.H. (1978, Fall). Intercollegiate athletics today and tomorrow: The President's challenge. *Educational Record,* **59**, 232-235.

HANFORD, G.H. (1979, Fall). Controversies in college sports. *Educational Record,* **60**, 351-366.

HANKS, M.P. & Eckland, B.K. (1976, October). Athletics and social participation in the educational attainment process. *Sociology of Education,* **49**, 272-294.

HARRIS, J.C. (1980, April). *Academic ability and reported adequacy of high school preparation for college of male college freshmen athletes and nonathletes in four states.* Paper presented at the national convention of the American Alliance of Health, Physical Education, and Recreation, Detroit.

HARRISON, J.H. (1976, April). *Intercollegiate football participation and academic achievement.* Paper presented at the annual meeting of the Southwestern Sociological Association, Dallas.

LITCHFIELD, E. & Cope, M. (1962, October 8). Saturday's hero is doing fine. *Sports Illustrated,* **17**, 66-80.

LOPINO, D.A. (1979). Echoing the financial crisis in intercollegiate athletics. *Educational Record,* **60**(4), 394-408.

LOY, J.W., McPherson, B.D. & Kenyon, G. (1978). *Sport and social systems.* Reading, MA: Addison-Wesley.

MEGGYSEY, D. (1970). *Out of their league.* Berkeley: Ramparts.

MICHENER, J.A. (1976). *Sports in America.* New York: Random House.

MORAN, M. (1980, October 16). Former USC president defends policies. *New York Times,* sec. B, p. 5.

NYQUIST, E.B. (1979, Fall). Win, women, and money: Collegiate athletics today and tomorrow. *Educational Record,* **60**, 374-393.

OATES, B. (1979, June 8). The great American tease: Sports as a way out of the ghetto. *New York Times,* sec. A, p. 32.

ODENKIRK, J.E. (1981, April). Intercollegiate athletics: Big business or sport? *Academe,* **67**, 62-66.

PILAPIL, B.J., & Stecklein, H.L. (1970). Intercollegiate athletics and academic progress: A comparison of academic characteristics of athletes and nonathletes at the University of Minnesota. Bureau of Institutional Research, University of Minnesota.

ROPER, L. D. & Snow, K. (1976). Correlation studies of academic excellence and big-time athletics. *International Review of Sport Sociology,* **11**, 57-68.

SAGE, G.H. (1967). *The academic performances of former high school athletes at college.* Unpublished paper, Department of Physical Education, University of Northern Colorado.

SANOFF, A.P. (1980, February 11). Behind scandals in big-time college sports. *U.S. News and World Report*, 61-62.

SANTOMIER, J.P., Howard, W.G., Pilitz, W.L., & Romance, T.J. (1980). White sock crime: Organizational deviance in intercollegiate athletics. *Journal of Sport and Social Issues, 4*, 26-32.

SCOTT, J. (1971). *The athletic revolution*. New York: Free Press.

SHAW, G. (1972). *Meat on the hoof*. New York: St. Martin's Press.

SNYDER, E.E., & Spreitzer, E. (1978). *Social aspects of sport*. Englewood Cliffs, NJ: Prentice-Hall.

SPADY, W.G. (1970). Lament for the letterman: Effects of peer status and extracurricular activities on goals and achievement. *American Journal of Sociology, 75*, 680-702.

SPIVEY, D. & Jones, T.A. (1975). Intercollegiate athletic servitude: A case study of the black Illinois student-athletes, 1931-1967. *Social Science Quarterly, 55*(4), 939-947.

STECKLEIN, J.E. & Dameron, L.D. (1965). Intercollegiate athletics and academic progress: A comparison of academic characteristics of athletes and nonathletes at the University of Minnesota. *Reprint Series No. 3*, Bureau of Institutional Research, University of Minnesota.

STEVENSON, C.L. (1975). Socialization effects of participation in sport: A critical review of the research. *Research Quarterly, 46*(3), 287-301.

UNDERWOOD, J. (1980, May 19). The writing is on the wall. *Sports Illustrated, 52*, 36-71.

UNIVERSITY of New Mexico, (1980). *1970-1979 graduation experience of University of New Mexico student athletes*. Report commissioned by the President and Faculty Athletic Council, University of New Mexico.

WEBB, H. (1968, March). *Social backgrounds of college athletes*. Paper presented at the national convention of the American Alliance for Health, Physical Education and Recreation, St. Louis, Missouri.

WHITE, G.S., Jr. (1980, October 16). Graduates cite USC abuses. *New York Times*, sec. B, p. 11.

Chapter 16

The Occupational Attainment of Former College Athletes: A Comparative Study

Paul E. Dubois
Bridgewater State University

The notion that sport can serve as an effective vehicle for upward social mobility has long been an article of faith accepted *in toto* by many individuals involved in athletics. Indeed, one might reasonably assert that this belief has spread beyond the domain of sport to the American culture as a whole (Annarino, 1953; Miller, 1971; Stevenson & Nixon, 1972; Page, 1973).

Economically disadvantaged individuals in general and ethnic minorities in particular are the most often mentioned beneficiaries of the "upward mobility through sport" belief. However, the belief does not necessarily exclude athletes having other social origins:

> The evidence of sport providing opportunities that lead to other successful careers is convincing. An example may serve to illustrate: In his column, "Dateline America," David Sewell, a senior editor to LIFE, dealt with sports heroes in the business world. He pointed out that "there's nothing like a career in big-time sports to help a fellow succeed in business without really trying." (Miller, 1971:70)

Beliefs are by nature couched in such vague terms that their truth or falsity cannot be tested. Recently, however, scholars have made considerable progress turning the *belief* in question here into a *bona fide* researchable *problem*. The first step in this process was to change what had been generally accepted as "gospel" into an issue. This step was achieved when the belief began to be seriously challenged by athletes and scholars (N.H.B. 1960; Edwards, 1969; Hill & Lowe, 1974).

The second step in the process was to closely scrutinize the evolving issue and then to partition it into a number of researchable problems that readily lent themselves to empirical evaluation. In this writer's opinion, the general issue of sport and social mobility has gradually crystallized into the following three research subcategories:

1. The social mobility of the student-athlete in terms of educational performance, expectations, and goal attainment (Schafer & Armer, 1972); Rehberg & Schafer, 1968; Coleman, 1961; Spady, 1970; Clarke, 1975)
2. The social mobility and attainment opportunities for the professional athlete (Loy & McElvogue, 1970; Rosenblatt, 1967; Yetman & Eitzen, 1972; *Forbes*, 1972)
3. The social mobility and attainment pattern of *former* athletes (Loy, 1972; Luschen, 1969; Litchfield, 1962; Haerle, 1975)

This study was concerned with the third subcategory. Its intent was to investigate whether being a former college athlete can affect one's occupational attainment.

PREVIOUS RESEARCH

Despite the widespread and enduring nature of the sport/upward social mobility belief, little is known about the benefits of sports particiation on subsequent occupational attainment. The paucity of mobility research pertaining specifically to the type of athlete investigated in this study is aptly summed up by Loy (1872):

> There exists little evidence concerning the social origins of collegiate athletes, still less information regarding their social mobility, and *virtually no knowledge concerning the effects of their sports participation upon their post-college career success.*[1] (p. 6)

What little research that *does* exist in this area suffers from a variety of methodological shortcomings. One such shortcoming is the failure to employ a nonathlete comparison group (Litchfield, 1962; Loy, 1972). For example, despite the fact data from Loy's study suggests strongly that former athletes are highly successful in their occupational endeavors, it is not possible to determine if these "findings are especially characteristic of athletic alumni *per se* or more generally apply to all graduates of the particular university from which the athletes were sampled" (Loy, 1972:21).

Other studies (Thisted, 1933; Luschen, 1969; Bowlus, 1975), although comparative in design, fail to employ controls on variables known to have important effects on attainment. Such factors as socioeconomic and ethnic origins, education level, and years of work experience must be considered when attempting to answer questions about a group's occupational attainment. The Luschen study, which investigated the intergenerational mobility of young German sportsmen, suffered from the additional problem of validly assigning these young men into social classes.[2]

A study by Haerle (1975) on the occupational attainment of retired major league baseball players had the most sound research design of all those reviewed by the writer. Haerle used control variables as well as a comparion group. He found that the more skilled athletes in his sample achieved significantly higher ($p < .01$) occupational prestige scores on first jobs than the less skilled ones. Unfortunately, because data were not collected on nonathletes, Haerle's research failed to probe the central issue in this study. On a more pragmatic level, the low return rate (38%) realized from Haerle's mailed questionnaire tends to compromise even his most informative findings.

Most of the aforementioned studies appear to lend at least some support to the sport/upward mobility belief. However, such methodological shortcomings as the failure to gather data on important control variables or on a nonathlete comparison group and, to a lesser extent, poor return rates on mailed survey instruments actually render these studies inconclusive.

RESEARCH HYPOTHESES

Two hypotheses guided this research. Each will be formally stated below and will be accompanied by a theoretical rationale.

Hypothesis I:

Athletes will achieve higher occupational attainment than nonathletes.

Categorizing events, objects, and people helps individuals and social groups bring order, understanding, and efficiency to a highly complex world. Although this categorization process is not intended to be a means of evaluation, such in fact often occurs. For example, employers often differentially *evaluate* prospective employers on the basis of such *categories* as sex and ethnicity. This invidious evaluation by employers of mere categories is so widespread (yet subtle) that we need federally mandated civil rights laws and affirmative action programs to counteract it.

Variables such as sex and ethnicity have been termed *diffuse status characteristic* by Berger and his associates (1966). A diffuse status characteristic can be defined denotatively as any one of several ascriptive (e.g., race, sex, age) or achievement based (e.g., education) properties of an individual that might be used to describe him. Each characteristic is said to consist of two or more "states" (e.g., race contains the states Caucasian, Negro, Oriental, etc.). Associated with each state is a particular set of attributes or personality characteristics. For example, the state of Negro on the diffuse status characteristic "race" is seen by whites to include the following characteristics: lazy, rowdy, strong, and musical (Berger et al., 1966: 32).

According to Berger et al. (1972), a characteristic D is a diffuse status characteristic if and only if the following three criteria are met. I will attempt to demonstrate that "athletic status" meets each of these criteria and this can be classified as a diffuse status characteristic.

1. *The states (in this case "athlete" and "nonathlete") of D are differentially evaluated.*

From the time of the journalistic saga of Frank Merriwell, who embodied "an athletic ideal that was also a social ideal," (Cummings, 1972:107) at the turn of the century, there has always been the normative belief about the superior qualities of the athlete as compared with the rest of the populace. Athletes are sometimes even viewed as legitimate folk heroes (Miller, 1971:58-61; Charnofsky, 1968:41; Ulrich, 1968:73; Andreano, 1973; Browne, 1972). Edwards (1973) further indicates the differential evaluation accorded the states "athlete" and "nonathlete" in our culture:

> Without sport, American youth would have less character, be less physically and mentally fit, less courageous, less disciplined, have less opportunity for achievement and thus America would on the whole experience a decline in its quality of life. (p. 97)

2. *To each of these states there corresponds a distinct set of specific, evaluated characteristics associated with them.*

While some characteristics associated with athletes reflect their physical attributes, athletes are believed to possess substantial amounts of other traits valued in the mainstream culture. In addition to those enumerated above in Edward's quote, the following traits are also believed to be particularly salient in the athlete: competitiveness, independence, initiative (Williams, 1964:168—9), emotional stability, toughmindedness, and conscientiousness (Ogilvie, 1976:350). Implicitly, the nonathlete does not have these characteristics or has them, but in lesser amounts than the athlete.

3. *To each of these states there corresponds a distinct "general performance expectation state" (GES), having the same evaluation as the state to which it corresponds.*

Based on the characteristics mentioned in category 2, the general performance expectation[3] of an athlete is something like the following: a highly competitive, capable, and reliable person who can successfully meet any of life's challenges (see Edwards 1973:97). Conversely, the GES accompanying a nonathlete would be that of a less capable person.

It is reasonable to assume that athletes are aware they are perceived by others as being highly capable, and thus, they (a) *perceive themselves* as capable, and (b) *behave* in such ways to fulfill those perceived capabilities. Therefore, other things being equal, it can be hypothesized that athletes would be expected to realize higher occupational attainment than nonathletes.

Hypothesis II:

The paired characteristics white athlete, white nonathlete, minority athlete, and minority nonathlete will, in the order presented, have an increasingly less positive effect on an individual's occupational attainment.

The reason for including this hypothesis in the study is twofold. First, minorities constitute a very sizable proportion of the college athlete population (see Yetman & Eitzen, 1972:27). Second, despite overwhelming evidence that minorities are generally denied access to the same mobility opportunities as whites, *both in the wider society* (Blau & Duncan, 1967; Featherman & Hauser, 1975) *and in the world of sport* (Rosenblatt, 1967; Yetman & Eitzen, 1972), the sports establishment continues to pat itself on the back for its alleged role as a "Vehicle of Integration, Assimilation, and Status Mobility" (Miller & Aussell, 1971: chap. 4). It would seem appropriate that studies of status attainment in sport begin to rigorously investigate the truth of this message.

The ranking of the paired characteristics in Hypothesis II is based first on the theoretical and empirical evidence that the state "white" on the status characteristic "ethnicity is more highly evaluated than "minority," and second on the rationale presented with Hypothesis I about the higher status accorded the athlete vis-a-vis the nonathlete. Thus, the white athlete (ranked first) has, if you will, two "positive" traits, and the minority nonathlete (ranked last) has two "negative" traits. The ranking of the white nonathlete before the minority athlete (both of whom have one positive and one negative trait) is based on the assumption that ethnicity is a more salient determinant of occupational attainment than athletic status.

PROCEDURES

Sample Selection

The athlete consisted of the entire 1972-73 population (N=160) of senior male intercollegiate athletes from the three San Francisco Bay area state universities. Unless otherwise specific, an athlete was operationally defined as one who used a year of athletic eligibility in his senior year.

An analysis of the athletes' major subjects indicate that one third of them were physical education majors. Consequently, a proportional (one-third physical education majors, two-thirds nonmajors) stratified random sampling procedure was used to select the nonathlete comparison group of 1972−73 senior males (N=450). Each of the three state universities contributed 150 nonathletes to the sample.

Data Collection

Data for the study was gathered primarily by mailed questionnaire.[4] A reminder postcard was set out 1 week after the initial questionnaire mailing. Subjects not responding to the initial mailing and follow-up postcard were mailed second and third questionnaires 3 and 5 weeks after the initial mailing. Each questionnaire mailing included a stamped return addressed envelope and a personalized cover letter. As joint sponsors of the study, the universities' placement centers provided letterhead paper for all questionnaire-related correspondence and agreed to have the completed questionnaires forwarded to their offices (see Dillman et al. 1972, 1974, 1974a).

A total of 24% of the nonathletes could not be located. Of the 339 remaining, completed questionnaires were received from 228 (67%). Only 14 of the athletes were addressee unknowns. Of the 140[5] athletes remaining, 84 (60%) returned completed questionnaires.

Variables

The control variables selected for the study were as follows: father's occupational prestige, level of education, ethnic origins, academic average, work experience, and age. They were chosen because their ability to affect occupational attainment has been clearly established in earlier studies.

The study's dependent variable—occupational attainment—was operationally defined along two dimensions. The *prestige* of the subject's occupation was measured by the NORC/Siegel 0—96 scale of occupational prestige (NORC, 1973). The *privilege* of the subject's occupation was measured by his annual gross earnings. Because it was the purpose of this study to investigate the *early occupational attainment of former college athletes, only occupations held 3 years after the subjects were seniors were investigated.*

Statistical Analyses

Multiple regression was used to analyze the data gathered. The study's variables were added to the regression equation in stepwise fashion, with all control variables included in the first step and "athletic status" added as the second and final step.

FINDINGS

A preliminary analysis of the data did not generally reveal any meaningful differences between the athletes and nonathletes. An exception to this general finding was in the occupational area. For example, it was found that the athletes' earnings are only $7,600 while the nonathletes earn $11,300. One may speculate at this juncture that this earnings differentials is partly due to differences in years of full-time work experience: Nonathletes have worked an average of 3.7 years longer than have the athletes.[6]

Table 1 further reveals the occupational discrepancy between the athletes and nonathletes. As indicated by the chi square statistic, the differences displayed in the table are highly significant. Note that fully 38% of the athletes have worked part-time while only 21% of the nonathletes have done so. For those respondents working full-time, the mismatch is equally striking. Sixty percent of the athletes have worked less than 6 years and only 3% have worked 6 or more years. On the other hand, only 49% of the nonathletes have worked less than 6 years while 31%, a proportion 10 times greater than that of the athletes, have worked 6 or more years.

In summary, the preliminary data analysis clearly indicated that the athletes are at an earlier stage in their occupational careers than the nonathletes. As explained below, this difference had implications for the selection of the sample used in the regression analyses.

Sample Selection for Regression Analyses

Those respondents falling in the "Full-time, less than 6 years of experience" job status category in Table 1 were chosen for the regression analyses that follow. There were two reasons for eliminating other respondents from the regression analyses. First, research that deals with occupational attainment does not usually focus on part-time job holders; part-time jobs are typically short lived and not representative of an individual's career. Second, by looking exclusively at the first 5 years of the respondent's full-time careers, (a) scope condition of the study was sustained (*early* occupational attainment), and (b) the comparability of athletes

Table 1

**Frequency Distribution and Column Percentages
of Job Status by Athletic Status**

Job Status	Athlete	(N = 84)ʸ	Nonathlete	(N = 228)
Part-time student	6	(8%)	11	(6%)
Part-time nonstudent	21	(29%)	23	(15%)
Full-time, less than 6 years experience	44	(60%)	92	(49%)
Full-time, 6 or more years experience	2	(3%)	59	(13%)

$X^2 = 25.57^{***}$ df = 3
$^{***}p < .001$

and nonathletes on variables not of interest in this study was increased (thus enhancing the predictive power of the regression equations).

Regression Analyses—Hypotheses I

Tables 2 and 3 present the effects of the control variables and athletic status on occupational prestige and earnings, respectively. Note that only education affects occupational prestige at the .05 level of significance; academic average is significant at the .10 level. Athletic status has virtually no effect on prestige.

Both age and years of full-time work experience[8] have significant effects ($p < .01$) on earnings. However, as Table 3 indicates, athletic status has no significant effect on this dimension of occupational attainment. In summary, the evidence provided by Tables 2 and 3 leads to a rejection of the hypothesis that athletes will achieve higher occupationat attainment than nonathletes during their early careers.

Regression Analyses—Hypotheses II

Table 4 presents the effects of the control variables and the paired characteristics (interaction terms) on occupational prestige. Note that none of the three paired

Table 2

**Regression Analysis of Occupational Prestige
on Control Variables and Athletic Status,
for Full-Time Workers with Less Than 6 Years Experience**

Independent Variables	Unstandardized Regression Coefficient	Standard Error	Standardized Regression Coefficient
D Minority[9]	1.5	3.0	0.05
Father's occupational prestige (FOCCUP)	−0.0	0.1	−0.03
Academic avenue (ACAV)	0.7*	0.3	0.18*
Education	3.8**	1.5	0.25**
Age	0.3	0.5	0.07
Years full-time work experience (WORKYRS)	−0.2	1.2	−0.02
D athlete	−0.8	2.8	−0.03
Constant	12.6	$R^2 = 14$	$F_{7,103} = 2.38$**

*$p < .10$
**$p < .05$

Table 3
Regression Analysis of Earnings (in Hundreds of Dollars) on Control Variables and Athletic Status, for Full-time Workers with Less Than 6 Years of Work Experience

Independent Variables	Unstandardized Regression Coefficient	Standard Error	Standardized Regression Coefficient
D Minority[9]	7.2	8.0	0.07
(FOCCUP)	− 0.3	0.3	− 0.09
(ACAV)	0.2	0.9	0.02
Education	− 3.8	4.2	− 0.01
Age	6.6***	1.3	0.15***
WORKYRS	9.1***	3.2	0.25***
D athlete	2.1	7.5	0.02
Constant	− 83.0	$R^2 = 0.35$	$F_{7,103} = 8.05$***

*** $p < .01$

characteristics in the regression equation approaches even the 0.10 level of significance. The paired characteristics "white nonathlete" is embedded in the constant term and thus has a "zero effect" (unstandardized coefficient of 0.00) on occupational prestige.

In Table 5 the paired characteristics have been removed from the regression analysis presented in Table 4 and rank ordered according to their effects on oc-

Table 4
Regression Analysis of Occupational Prestige on Control Variables and Selected Interaction Terms, for Full-time Workers with Less Than 6 Years of Work Experience

Independent Variables	Unstandardized Regression Coefficient	Standard Error	Standardized Regression Coefficient
(FOCCUP)	− 0.0	0.1	− 0.04
(ACAV)	0.7**	0.3	0.20**
Education	− 3.5**	1.5	0.23**
Age	0.4	0.5	0.09
WORKYRS	0.6	1.1	− 0.05
Minority Athlete	1.5	4.5	0.03
Minority Nonathlete	− 0.2	3.3	− 0.00
White Athlete	− 1.6	3.0	− 0.05
Constant (White Nonathlete)	13.6	$R^2 = 15$	$F_{8,108} = 2.39$**

** $p < .05$

Table 5

**Rank Order of Effects on Occupational Prestige
of Paired Characteristics Relative to White Nonathlete**

Paired Characteristics	Relative Effects	Hypothesized Rank (1 = highest)
Minority Athlete	1.5	3
White Nonathlete (constant)	0.0	2
Minority Nonathlete	− 0.2	1
White Athlete	− 1.6	1

cupational prestige. Note that only the paired characteristic white nonathlete is in its hypothesized position.

The effects of the control variables and the paired characteristics on earnings are displayed in Table 6. As with prestige, none of the paired characteristics have significant effects on the respondents' earnings.

In Table 7 the paired characteristics are again rank ordered—this time in terms of their effects on earnings. Although the unstandardized regression coefficients indicate rather large differences in earnings between the paired characteristics, it must be reiterated that these differences are not statistically significant. Note that only the paired characteristic minority athlete is in its hypothesized position and that the overall ranking differs substantially from the one presented in Table 5.

Table 6

**Regression Analysis of Earnings (in Hundreds of Dollars)
on Control Variables and Selected Interaction Terms,
for Full-time Workers with Less Than 6 Years of Work Experience**

Independent Variables	Unstandardized Regression Coefficient	Standard Error	Standardized Regression Coefficient
(FOCCUP)	− 0.3	0.2	− 0.12
(ACAV)	0.2	0.9	0.02
Education	− 0.1	4.0	0.00
Age	6.5***	1.3	0.44***
WORKYRS	8.4***	3.1	0.24***
Minority Nonathlete	12.9	8.9	0.12
White Athlete	7.3	8.1	0.08
Nonwhite Athlete	2.4	12.1	0.02
Constant (White Nonathlete)	− 78.0	$R^2 = 36$	$F_{8,108} = 7.54$***

*** $p < .01$

Table 7

**Rank Order of Effects on Earnings (in Hundreds of Dollars)
of Paired Characteristics Relative to White Nonathletes**

Paired Characteristics	Relative Effects	Hypothesized Rank (1 = highest)
Minority Athlete	12.9	4
White Nonathlete	7.3	1
Minority Athlete	2.4	3
White Nonathlete (constant)	0.0	2

In summary, the evidence pertaining to Hypothesis II leads to a rejection of that hypothesis. Based on the data presented here, a ranking of white athlete to white nonathlete and minority athlete to minority nonathlete in terms of their relative occupational attainment cannot be supported.[10]

DISCUSSION

It appears that, for the sample of athletes investigated in this study, the notion of sport as a stepping stone to high status attainment is a myth. None of the regression analyses indicate that athletes are advantaged vis-a-vis nonathletes either in terms of occupational prestige or earnings.

Both the regression analyses and the tables of rank orders demonstrate that in terms of occupational attainment the minority athletes cannot be distinguished from the study's white respondents or from the minority nonathletes. This finding may be discussed from two perspectives. First, one may lament the evidence that minority athletes are not more upwardly mobile than ethnic minorities who are not athletes. On the other hand, it is encouraging to note that this study's— albeit small—sample of minority athletes *fared as well as whites* as concerns their occupational prestige and earnings. This finding may suggest that, for those ethnic minorities who have managed to compete successfully in a white dominated society for as long (i.e., through school and college) as did this sample, participating in an extracurricular activity such as athletics adds no appreciable luster to their many other talents and social "survival skills." Though the minority athlete is skilled in sporting games, perhaps he (and his nonathletic counterpart) is equally skilled in the more important "game" of knowing how to operate successfully as a cultural underdog.

It is hoped that the findings of this research will stimulate further interest in this topic. Although the data presented here do weaken the sport/upward mobility belief, it is still only a single study. As such, it can provide only a tentative and highly qualified refutation of the belief. Perhaps athletes from schools with athletic programs that are provided national exposure by the media enjoy an advantage over their nonathletic peers in the competition for better jobs. Perhaps athletes performing in regions of the country unlike the San Francisco Bay area have job opportunities vastly superior to their nonathletic counterparts. Perhaps athletes and nonathletes demonstrate significantly different occupational attainment levels only at later stages in their careers. In summary, it is recommended that the occupational attainment of former athletes (a) from a wide variety of schools; (b) from geographically diverse areas; and (c) at several career stages be rigorously investigated if the sport/upward mobility issue is to be adequately resolved.

Another important recommendation for future research concerns the model developed here to explain occupational attainment. This model should be improved, particularly as concerns the dependent variable "occupational prestige" where only 14% of the variation in this dependent variable was explained by the model. Variables more appropriate to college educated men must be identified and included in the existing model.

A third recommendation is that worker satisfaction be included with occupational prestige and earnings as a measure of success. This strategy will infuse future research with a sociopsychological measure of success to accompany the purely sociological ones used here. Finally, with more women becoming involved both in sport and in careers outside the home, future studies should investigate how sports participation affects the female athlete's occupational attainment.

REFERENCES

ANDREANO, R. (1973). The affluent baseball player. In J.T. Talamini & C.H. Page (Eds.), *Sport and society*. Boston: Little, Brown and Co.

ANNARINO, A. (1953). *The contributions of athletics to social mobility*. Fifty-Sixth Annual Proceedings of the College Physical Association, New York.

BERGER, J. et al. (1966). Status characteristics and expectation states. In J. Berger et al. (Eds.), *Sociological theories in progress*. I. Boston: Houghton Mifflin Co.

BERGER, J. et al. (1972). Status characteristics and social interaction. *American Sociological Review*, 37(3), 241-255.

BLAU, P.M. & Duncan, O.D. (1967). *The American occupational structure*. New York., John Wiley and Sons.

BOWLUS, W.C. (1975). How well do our college athletes fare? *Journal of Physical Education and Recreation*, 46(6), 25.

BROWNE, R.B. et al. (Eds.). *Heroes of popular culture*. Bowling Green: Bowling Green University Popular Press.

CHARNOFSKY, H. (1963). The major league professional baseball player: Self-conception versus the popular image. *International Review of Sport Sociology*, 3, 39-71.

CLARKE, H.H. (1975). Athletes: Their academic achievement and personal-social status. *Physical Fitness Research Digest*, 5(3).

COLEMAN, J.S. (1961). *The adolescent society*. New York: Free Press.

CUMMINGS, R. (1972). The superbowl society. In R.B. Browne et al. (Eds.), *Heroes of popular culture*. Bowling Green: Bowling Green University Popular Press.

DILLMAN, D.A. (1972). Increasing mail questionnaire response in large samples of the general public. *The Public Opinion Quarterly*, **36**, 254-257.

DILLMAN, D.A. & Christenson, J.A. (1974). Increasing mail questionnaire response: A four state comparison. *American Sociological Review*, **39**, 744-756.

DILLMAN, D.A. & Frey, J.H. (1974). Contribution of personalization on mail questionnaire response as an element of a previously tested method. *Journal of Applied Psychology*, **59**(3), 297-301.

EDWARDS, H. (1969). *Revolt of the black athlete*. New York: Free Press.

EDWARDS, H. (1973). *Sociology of sport*. Homewood, IL: Dorsey Press.

FEATHERMAN, D. & Hauser, R. (1975). Changes in the socioeconomic stratification of the races, 1962-1973, *Working Paper 75-26*. Center for Demography and Ecology, the University of Wisconsin (Madison).

FORBES (1972, September 15). *Superstars! Supermoney!* **110**, pp. 25-32.

HAERLE R., (1975). Education, athletic scholarships and the occupational career of the professional athlete. *Sociology of Work and Occupations*, **4**(2), 373-403.

HILL, P. & Lowe, B. (1974). *The inevitable metathesis of the retiring athlete*. Paper presented at the Annual Conference of the Eastern District Association of the AAHPER, New York.

LITCHFIELD, E.H. & Cope M., (1962). Saturday's hero is doing fine. *Sports Illustrated*, **17**(5), pp. 66-78.

LOY, J. (1972). Social origins and occupational mobility patterns of a selected sample of American athletes. *International Review of Sport Sociology*, **7**, 5-25.

LOY, J., & McElvogue J. (1970). Racial segregation in American sport. *International Review of Sport Sociology*, **5**, 5-24.

LUSCHEN, G. (1969). Social stratification and social mobility among young sportsmen. In Loy, J.W. & Kenyon, G. (Eds.), Sport, culture, and society. New York: Macmillan.

MILLER, D.M., & Russel, K.R.E. (1971). *Sport: A contemporary view*. Philadelphia: Lea and Febiger.

N.H.B. (1960). Round table discussion: The Negro in American sport. *Negro History Bulletin*, **24**(2), 27-31.

N.O.R.C. (1973). *National data program for the social sciences: Spring 1973 general social survey*. Ann Arbor. Inter-University Consortium for Political Research.

OGILVIE, B. (1976). Psychological consistencies within the personality of high-level competitors. In A. Craig Fisher (Ed.), *Psychology of sport*. Palo Alto: Mayfield.

PAGE, C.H. (1973). Introduction: The world of sport and its study. In Talamini, J., & Page, C. (Ed.), *Sport and society: An anthology*. Boston: Little Brown.

REHBERG, R., & Schafer, W. (1968). Participation in interscholastic athletics and college expectations. *American Journal of Sociology*, **73**, 232-240.

ROSENBLATT, A. (1967). Negroes in baseball: The failure of success. *Transaction*, **4**(9), 51-53.

SCHAFER, W., & Armer, J.M., (1972). On scholarship and interscholastic athletics. In Eric Dunning (Ed.), *Sport: Readings from a sociological perspective*. Toronto: University of Toronto Press.

SPADY, W. (1970). Lament for the letterman: Effects of peer status and extracurricular activities on goals and achievement. *American Journal of Sociology*, **75** (4, part 2), 119-132.

STEVENSON, C.L. & Nixon, J.E. (1972). A conceptual scheme of the social functions of sport, *Sportwissenschaft*, **2**(2), 119-132.

THISTED, M.N. (1933). A study of the relationship between participation in college athletics and vocational success. *Research Quarterly*, **4**(3), 5-20.

ULRICH, C., (1968). *The social matrix of physical education*. Englewood Cliffs, NJ: Prentice-Hall.

WILLIAMS, J.F. (1964). *The principles of physical education*. Philadelphia: W.B. Saunders Co.

YETMAN, N. & Eitzen, D.S. (1972). Black Americans in sports: Unequal opportunity for equal ability, *Civil Rights Digest,* 5(2), 20-34.

FOOTNOTES

1. Italics mine.

2. "Social Class" was the indicator used by Luschen to measure his subject's social mobility.

3. It is a general performance expectation because the beliefs about the athlete's performance are not restricted to "specific situations," that is, physical activity situations.

4. All information concerning the athletes was obtained from their athletic departments and or coaches.

5. Six athletes were excluded from data analysis because they were foreign nationals.

6. Predictably, the nonathletes (28,6) were found to be almost 4 years older than the athletes (24,8).

7. There were 11 missing cases (or 13%) in the athlete sample and 39 missing cases (or 17%) in the nonathlete sample.

8. The possibility of the existence of a multicollinearity problem concerning age and work experience was investigated and found not to exist. It was determined that both age and work experience have significant effects on earnings independent of one another.

9. The variables that are preceded by a "D" in this table and all those following are dummy variables coded one if the respondent had the characteristics given by the label and zero otherwise. All other variables are treated as interval scale variables.

10. The reader is cautioned against accepting the rank orders in Tables 5 and 7 at face value. The tables do provide evidence that permits a rejection of Hypothesis II (i.e., that the subsamples cannot be rank ordered as suggested). However, given the fact that none of the paired characteristics significantly affects either measure of occupational attainment, it does not follow that the rank orders presented in Tables 5 and 7 are necessarily the most valid ones. Statistically speaking, all possible permutations of the tables could be argued. At best, Tables 5 and 7 are suggestive of trends.

Chapter 17

College Athletics and "Character": The Decline and Fall of Socialization Research

Christopher L. Stevenson
University of New Brunswick

Nearly 10 years have passed since I last considered "character-building" and participation in college athletics. At that time, in the optimism of youth, I attempted to produce a definitive statement on the matter by means of a review of the research and related literature on the socialization effects of participation in sport (Stevenson, 1975). I will begin this paper by summarizing my 1975 paper and then will indicate the subsequent developments which have occurred over the past decade in the research and in our understanding of the socialization effects of participation in college athletics.

It became clear very quickly that this would not be the relatively straightforward update of the previous review which I had expected. I began by anticipating the possibility of new and significant research on the socialization effects of participation in college athletics; yet I found very little. I was open to the possibility of new conclusions on this relationship; yet I found none. Rather, it appears that the question of the "character-building" effects of college athletics has essentially become moribund as a generator of research. There has, by any estimation, been very little progress. We remain with essentially the same conclusions about the socialization effects of participation in intercollegiate athletics which I reported back in 1975, and with which other authors have subsequently concurred (Coackley, 1982; Eitzeb & Sagem 1982; Loy, McPherson, & Kenyon, 1978; McPherson, 1978, 1981; Snyder & Spreitzer, 1983).

An interesting question, consequently, became, Why is this so? Why are sport sociologists no longer looking at the socialization impact of sport participation upon the athlete? It has been the examination of this development in sport socialization research which I have found fascinating and which will be discussed in detail later in the paper. Let us review the evidence pertaining to the socialization effects of participation in college athletics (essentially, a summary of the 1975 paper updated with the research published since that time and up to 1983).

Although the original review was not concerned exclusively with college athletics but also considered research conducted at the interscholastic level, I have no hesitancy in suggesting that the general conclusions apply to the college level because the majority of studies surveyed did focus specifically at this level of competition. Two major issues emanated from this review: (a) the methodological difficulties which are inherent in research on socialization effects of participation in college athletics; and (b) the demise of "socialization effects" research over the past decade.

THE RESEARCH EVIDENCE[1]

In 1975, I attempted to arrive at some definitive conclusions regarding the socialization affects of participation in sport by means of an extensive, critical review of the literature. This review included 54 studies, the majority published between 1965 and 1973, which were concerned with three major types of potential socialization effects—psychological effects, behavioral effects, and attitudinal effects. In updating the review in 1983, I was able to discover only 12 additional studies focusing upon college athletics; 7 concerned with the psychological effects, 5 with the behavioral effects, and none with the attitudinal effects of participation in college athletics.

Psychological Effects

The research discussed under this heading is that which concentrated upon the personality characteristics of athletes and nonathletes as determined by a variety of personality inventories. In the 1975 review, these studies ($N = 27$) constituted the bulk of the work which may be considered to be concerned with the socialization effects of participation in sport.

There were three main types of investigation. First, there were 18 studies which attempted to compare the personality characteristics of samples with different athletic abilities and from different levels of participation. Eleven of these studies were unable to discern any significant personality factor differences between athletes of different abilities, and between athletes and nonathletes. The remaining 7 studies, on the other hand, were able to conclude that there were some signifi-

---

[1]To summarize the 1975 review, considerable material had to be omitted. In addition, citations are only provided for those articles from the 1975 review which are referred to herein specifically by the name(s) of their author(s). The reader is urged to refer to the original paper.

cant sample differences on certain personality factors; however, there were few instances of multiple support for these factors because each study tended to discover a different set of factors upon which there were sample differences.

Second, there were some studies (N = 4) which focused upon "champion" athletes. In this type of investigation, the personality profiles of the athletes were compared with the "norms" associated with the test instruments which were used. Although the athletes did exhibit some differences from the test norms on some of the factors, there was little consistency in the overall results. The third type of investigation, of which there were 6 representatives, compared participants from different sports. Essentially two types of comparisons were made: Participants in team sports were compared with participants in individual sports, and participants in specific sports were compared with each other. Once again, the results of these comparisons were contradictory; for example, while one study was able to demonstrate differences among, specifically, football players, wrestlers, and gymnasts, other studies were unable to detect any personality differences among the participants in different sports.

In addition to the aforementioned research using specific population comparisons as its fundamental research design, I also considered three other studies which attempted to move closer to the more ideal, longitudinal design. Werner and Gottheil (1966) conducted a 4-year study of cadets (N = 456) at the U.S. Military Academy at West Point. Their results indicated that, despite 4 years of regular athletic participation, the designated "nonparticipant" group did not change in personality structure as measured by the 16 PF test, neither to a greater extent than did the designated "athlete" group, nor in a different pattern than the "athletes," nor so as to become more like the "athletes." They concluded that if socialization effects could not be demonstrated after 4 years of consistent athletic participation, then such effects would be unlikely from the typical pattern of college athletic participation, and indeed as far as they were concerned, "no evidence was found to support the view that college athletics significantly influenced personality structure" (1966, p. 130).

Schendel (1965) compared cross-sections of athletic and nonathletic groups (N = 334) at three different educational levels: Grade 9, Grade 12 and college. The results demonstrated differences among the athlete and nonparticipant groups at each educational level, although the specific differences were not necessarily the same at each level. He concluded that, while both 9th- and 12th-grade athletes generally possessed desirable personal social-psychological characteristics to a greater extent than did the respective nonparticipants, at the college level, this situation was reversed. Schendel (1969) continued this research by means of a longitudinal investigation of 91 athletes and nonathletes from Grade 9 to Grade 12. Once again, he found that there were "clear cut" differences between the athletes and nonparticipants at both grade levels, and that there were "striking differences" among athletes of different ability levels. However, his results also showed that these differences had diminished in number and in degree in the 12th grade as compared with the 9th grade.

In summary, the following conclusions were drawn from this review of the personality research literature: (a) There was a considerable amount of contradictory evidence. Numerically, there was a fairly even dichotomy between those studies (N = 12) which were unable to detect differences among athletes and nonparticipants, among athletes of different ability levels, or among athletes and psychological test "norms," and those studies (N = 11) which were able to demonstrate differences among such groups; and (b) there was little consistency among these latter studies. Each study found evidence of population differences on different personality factors so that little multiple support was present for any particular factor.

In the research published since 1974, we find little reason to challenge these conclusions. The first thing that becomes immediately apparent is that "personality effects" is no longer as popular an area of socialization research. Relatively speaking, very few studies have been published: I was able to discover only seven publications concerned with college athletics (Gruber & Perkins, 1978; Gundersheim, 1982; Konzak & Klavora, 1980; Nation & LeUnes, 1983; Thakur & Ojla, 1981; Thakur & Thakur, 1980; Tyler & Duthie, 1979). What is equally striking, however, is that little has evolved from this research. These studies have been merely replications or modifications of previous research as such are as rife with methodological inadequacies as were the originals. Furthermore, they have also followed the previous pattern in producing ambiguous evidence. The basic conclusion must, therefore, stand that there is no evidence to sustain a claim that participation in college athletics has any effect upon the personality characteristics of the athlete.

Behavioral Effects

The literature which was reviewed under this topic was concerned with the possible relationships between participation in sport and such behavioral features as (a) academic achievement, as indicated by grade point average (GPA) and mental ability as determined by tests of intelligence, and (b) delinquency, which was determined through the examination of court records.

In 1975 the literature in the area of academic achievement was not very extensive, but the evidence suggested that participation in sport was associated with greater academic performance. Using athlete-versus-nonparticipant comparisons, 8 studies were able to demonstrate that the GPA of athletes tended to be significantly higher than that of nonparticipants. Even when indicators of academic achievement other than grades were used, for example, mental ability as determined by intelligence tests and college aspirations, the conclusions remained the same— that a positive correlation existed between participation in sports and academic performance. Two of the studies reviewed made particular efforts to control for a number of confounding variables which had plagued previous research (Edwards, 1967; Schafer & Armer, 1968). They matched their athlete and nonathlete samples on such things as S.E.S., IQ scores as freshmen and as seniors, curriculum type, and so on. In both cases, the GPA of the athletes remained higher than that of the nonathletes, although the difference tended to be much reduced.

There was not, however, a complete consensus: There were at least four disclaimers, two research studies, and two reviews of the literature. Neither research study was able to discover any significant relationship between IQ and athletic ability, on the one hand, or between GPA and athletic participation on the other. The two reviewers, (Cooper, 1969; Ryan, 1969) after considering the available research, were unanimous in concluding that there was no evidence of a causal relationship between participation and academic achievement, and that whatever differences were detectable between athletes and nonathletes were possibly the result of different degrees of "achievement-orientation."

Thus, in 1975 it was concluded that, although a causal relationship had yet to be established, there did appear to be a positive correlation between academic achievement and participation in athletics. It is interesting, therefore, that the research published since 1975 leads one to a different conclusion—that participation in college athletics has at best a slightly negative effect upon GPA (Figler, 1981; Hanks & Eckland, 1976; Messner & Groisser, 1982; Purdy, Eitzen & Hufnagel, 1982; *Scholastic Coach*, 1978). There are a couple of explanations for this situation. First of all, there is the dramatic increase in the sophistication of the research designs which have been used in these latter studies. The research has attempted to control for an ever-encompassing array of variables (see Messner & Groisser, 1982; and Purdy, Eitzen & Hufnagel, 1982). Second, it is possible that the relationship between participation and academic achievement is different at different academic levels. The studies included in the 1975 review were mostly high school-oriented rather than college-oriented, and there does appear to be consistent support for a positive relationship at the high school level. (For an excellent summary, see Snyder & Spreitzer, 1983.)

There are two more points worth mentioning. One concerns the amount of research which is available in this area. It tends to be a consistent complaint that there are but few studies concerned with the academic achievement-participation relationship at the college level (Messner & Groisser, 1982; Purdy, Eitzen & Hufnagel, 1982; Snyder & Spreitzer, 1983). This is certainly an accurate assessment in comparison with the numbers of studies which have been produced at the high school level, but it is quite a misperception when compared with the meager amount published before 1975. However, I should make it clear in this second point that the orientation of the research in the two eras has been quite different. The original concern of the research on this topic was with socialization effects—that is, whether or not participation in the college athletics promoted academic achievement via some effect upon the athlete's intelligence or attitudes, and so on. The recent research has been concerned with using the comparative academic performance of the athlete as a means of determining whether or not the college is meeting its contractual obligations to the athlete, which is quite a different matter.

The research on the relationship between participation in sport and delinquency has basically been investigating the general belief that sport participation produces beneficial effects upon the moral character of the athlete. This area of research has never been overwhelmingly popular; it has always been a rather marginal concern within the socialization repetoire. Most of the research published before 1975 was the work of Schafer and his associates (Phillips & Schafer, 1971; Schafer, 1972) and was concerned almost exclusively with delinquency at the high school level. Their results were clear in demonstrating that indeed athletes were less delinquent than nonathletes, and that this relationship was most significant for that segment of the population—the blue collar, lower achievers—where delinquency was at its highest. These results do, however, have a considerable cloud of doubt hanging over them because of a general failure to control for various influential factors, such as S.E.S., eligibility regulations, and purposive selection factors. To quote Schafer, "the negative relationship between athletic participation and delinquency may not be the result of the deterring influence of athletics at all, but rather to a selection of conformers to the athletic program" (1972, p. 100).

This marginal degree of popularity has continued since 1975. At the high school level there have been a few studies which have looked at delinquency and sport participation (Buhrmann, 1977; Landers & Landers, 1978; Segrave & Chu, 1978; Segrave & Hastad, 1982; Snyder & Spreitzer, 1979). This research continues to support the conclusion that athletes appear to be less delinquent than nonathletes, and does so while demonstrating an increased sophistication in research design as a means of coping with the problem of uncontrolled factors. At the college level, however, little work has been done (Snyder & Spreitzer, 1983). This is, perhaps, a reflection of the effective institutionalized ways that athletic programs have of coping with the "difficult situations" in which some athletes may find themselves. It is possible that more useful work could be done by looking at the behaviors of college athletes after they have left college. It is perhaps unfortunate that those studies which have looked at the postcollege life of athletes have tended to focus upon their occupational patterns (see Dubois in this section, for example) rather than indicators of moral or antisocial behavior.

Attitudinal Effects

A central feature of the character-building assumptions regarding sport participation has been that the sport experience leads to the development of a number of desirable attitudes in the athlete—in particular, those of "sportsmanship" and racial tolerance. It has been upon these attitudes, consequently, that the research has focused. The 1975 review was able to identify six studies concerned with the sportsmanship attitudes of athletes. These studies were consistent in concluding that, contrary to the popular belief, athletes tended to be less sportsmanlike than nonathletes. Furthermore, the research showed that "major" sport athletes were less sportsmanlike than "minor" sport athletes, and that "starters" were less sportsmanlike than "substitutes." It should be pointed out, however, that the methodology used by these studies was not only extremely diverse, but was also extremely questionable. As a consequence, conclusions regarding causality cannot be drawn.

Attitudes towards racial minorities were the subjects of two studies. These were also very different in their methodologies, including, most importantly, the populations which they used. Neither was able to demonstrate any impact upon the attitudes of the participants towards minority groups. One further attitudinal study was reviewed which was concerned with the political attitudes of athletes. Stern was able to conclude that there was a weak, but consistently positive relationship "between sports participation and those variables having to do with perception of authority figures, in this case coaches and politicians, and with the acceptance of rules in both sports and civic contexts" (1972, p. 114).

In 1975, I commented that the "attitudinal effects" topic was a much neglected aspect of socialization research. In 1983, it can best be described as a dead issue. In the pragmatic, business climate of intercollegiate athletics, it is important only that athletes perform well. It is irrelevant whether or not they learn to become sportsmanlike, or whether or not they learn to become more racially tolerant. None of this is critical, as long as the athletes work together to win where it counts—on the field. Therefore, as a consequence, there is no research to discuss.[2]

Conclusions From the Evidence

The research findings which have been described are somewhat confusing and contradictory. In terms of the psychological socialization effects of participation in sport, 50% of the studies suggested that such effects might occur, while the other 50% insisted that they do not. The evidence on academic achievement is also rather confusing—the 1975 review suggesting a positive relationship with athletic participation, and the studies since 1975 suggesting a negative relationship. The research on delinquency was consistent in demonstrating a desirable relationship with participation in athletics; however, causality has yet to be established. The attitudinal studies found some evidence of a relationship between athletic participation and sportsmanship attitudes and political attitudes, but no relationship with attitudes towards racial minorities. In the case of sportsmanship, however, the relationship ran counter to popular beliefs.

The major conclusion I was forced to draw in 1975 on the basis of my evaluation of the evidence itself and of the research methodology underpinning it was that "to date there is no valid evidence that participation in sport causes any verifiable socialization effects" (1975, p. 299). I do not find, in 1984, any reason whatsoever to change my position. To the best of my knowledge, this conclusion

---

[2] I should, however, mention the interesting work done by Chu and Griffey, 1982, at the high school level which refutes the "tolerance-through-contact" hypothesis.

has never been contradicted—at least, in any published form. Indeed, it has been supported and reiterated by a number of other reviewers who have subsequently arrived at essentially the same conclusion (Coakley, 1982; Eitzen & Sage, 1982; Loy, McPherson & Kenyon, 1978; McPherson, 1978, 1981; Snyder & Spreitzer, 1983). McPherson, for example, has concluded that "little empirical evidence exists to substantiate the many claims that have been made for the contribution of sport, physical education and physical activity to the general socialization process" (1981, p. 263). Similarly, Eitzen and Sage state that "the extent to which the attitudes, values, beliefs, and behaviors of American youths are actually influenced by participation (in sport programs) is largely unknown" (1982, p. 90). Loy, McPherson, and Kenyon conclude that "the empirical evidence to date provides little support for the socialization-via-sport hypothesis, at least for institutionalized sport," and that "there is little, if any, valid evidence that participation in sport is an important or essential element of the socialization process, or that involvement in sport teaches or results in the learning of specific outcomes that might not be learned in other social milieu" (1978, p. 244).

It is important to be clear about what we are saying here. We are concluding that the research has not sufficiently demonstrated the existence of effects from participation in sport in general and in college athletes in particular. What we are *not* saying, however, is that the research has demonstrated that such socialization effects do not occur. There is obviously a critical difference. What we find when we look at the research is that, taken overall, the findings are inconsistent, confusing, and often contradictory.

What we are left with, then, is a situation of considerable ambiguity. There have been basically two types of explanations offered to account for it. Either sports in general and college athletics in particular really do not have any socialization effects, and thus we have been fooling ourselves with our beliefs and rhetoric about character-building and so on; or socialization effects do occur but our research methodology has been so woefully inadequate that we have been unable with any acceptable validity to demonstrate their existence. Both of these explanations have their adherents, and it is fairly obvious that reasonably convincing arguments could be proposed for either one. I feel, however, the methodological issue is the most critical. For until the methodological problems are resolved in *all* of the research, it will not be possible to determine in which evidence we should place our faith. The findings of either pro or con, after all, may be spurious.

METHODOLOGICAL DIFFICULTIES INHERENT IN SOCIALIZATION EFFECTS RESEARCH

It has long been accepted that the research on the socialization effects of participation in sport has been riddled with methodological problems (Coakley, 1982; Cooper, 1969; Husman, 1969; McPherson, 1981; Snyder & Spreitzer, 1983). However, let us not condemn it too quickly, for this is not easy research to conduct. Indeed, many of the problems with the research have arisen because of attempts to take an "easy way out" of a tricky theoretical or methodological situation. The complex reality of our social lives and particularly during our developmental stages is that at almost every moment of each day we are surrounded by people and circumstances having the potential to produce socialization effects. The task of sport socialization research is to attempt to isolate out of this morass, the specific consequences of one particular type of socialization experience—participation in college athletics and in sport, in general. An ideal approach to this task would be a longitudinal study. This study would be of sufficient duration that the entirety of the socialization experience (participation in college athletics, plus some anticipatory period, perhaps) may be encompassed, and that socialization effects of measurable magnitude could reasonably be expected to have occurred.

The study would also have a sufficiently sophisticated research design so that as many as possible of the alternative socialization experiences could be controlled or accounted for; it would also have a sufficiently large sample so that the consequent subsamples might be matched as closely as possible. Such a design would permit the direct investigation of the causal relationships between socialization experiences and outcomes. Yet, even when the college athletics question was at the height of its popularity, I know of no accomplished study of this magnitude or sophistication. There are, obviously, many pragmatic reasons why this is so.

Unwilling or unable to take such a direct, longitudinal approach, investigators have turned to other, more indirect research designs from which they have hoped to *infer* causal relationships between socialization experiences and socialization outcomes. The most popular of these alternative approaches has been the use of cross-sectional comparisons of contrasting groups, for example, athletes versus nonathletes, superior athletes versus average athletes, wrestlers versus golfers, and so on. This is an attractive and potentially useful option and at first glance appears to be quite simple and straightforward. There are, however, a number of inherent difficulties which must be accounted for before it is possible to draw inferences of causality from the data.

One of the most critical of these difficulties is the essential, initial assumption of population similarity. The validity of the inferential design rests on the assumption that the two groups which are being compared are in all essential (i.e., socialization) respects exactly the same, except for the single experience of participation in college athletics. If this is so, if the two groups have had completely identical socialization experiences except for the athletic participation experience, then subsequent differences which are discovered between the two groups may confidently be causally attributed to the athletic experience. It is here, of course, that the real world intrudes into the research. The difficulties of creating sufficiently matched samples are immense, and when we are dealing with an athletic population as our primary concern, it becomes virtually impossible to even match subgroups *within* the athletic population (i.e., superior versus average, starters versus substitutes, major sport athletes versus minor sport athletes), let alone to adequately match athletes with nonathletes. In fact, a more accurate assumption in most of the research would be one of population dissimilarity. As a consequence, even if population or subgroup differences are discovered during the course of such an investigation, we cannot confidently say that they are not due to some other uncontrolled-for socialization influence. Thus, our ability to infer causality is much compromised.

This was a critical fault of the research reviewed in 1975. The research designs used were overly simplistic, making little attempt to match samples in even the most basic of forms. Those studies which did make some attempt at this stood out like beacons in darkness—for example, Werner and Gottheil (1966), Edwards (1967), and Schafer and Armer (1968). Fortunately, over the past decade some giant strides have been made in the sophistication of research designs in this area. The work of Messner and Groisser (1982), Purdy, Eitzen, and Hufnagel (1982), and Segrave and Hastad (1982) are some good examples. Yet, sadly, research still appears in which the most basic assumption of population similarity is ignored. There are, for example, the studies of "personality effects" which, in replicating prior research, have also repeated without any apparent concern the often considerable inadequacies of the original methodologies (Gruber & Perkins, 1978; Konzak & Klavora, 1980; Nation & LeUnes, 1983; Thakur & Ojha, 1981; Thaker & Thaker, 1980).

Another difficulty which arises from the cross-sectional approach is the necessity to ensure that the "treatment" experience—i.e., participation in college athletics—has been sufficient to produce measurable socialization consequences. It is necessary for the socialization experience to have been of sufficient duration and of sufficient intensity so that there may be realistic expectations of consequent measurable socialization effects. The investigator is faced with the problem of identifying a sport experience which theoretically has sufficient power to produce discernible effects upon those who participate in it; or alternatively, a sufficiently variable sport experience of sufficient power that differential degrees of exposure (i.e., starters versus substitutes, major sports versus minor sports) will produce discernible differences. This is an extremely problematic endeavor given the complexities of the real world and, once again, the necessity for sufficiently matched samples. Unfortunately, in general, the research has made but token gestures in this regard, making the assumption that it is enough if their subjects have experienced, for example, a physical education class or a game or two of competitive sports. Thus, we see that among the populations studied in sport socialization research have been Little League baseball players, junior high school, senior high school, and college physical education activity classes, youth and adult rugby players, college wrestlers, karate participants, intercollegiate athletes, competitive swimmers, college football players, tennis players, baseball players, fencers, and, of course, the ubiquitous "nonathletes."

A further difficulty is that of adequate instrumentation. This has been one of the major stumbling blocks and criticisms of socialization effects research from the very beginning (Cooper, 1969; Eitzen & Sage, 1982; Husman, 1969, Loy, McPherson, & Kenyon, 1978). The problems relate to both the validity of the instrumentation as well as its sensitivity. When we are interested in detecting socialization changes in a person's "character" and the multitude of diffuse and diverse characteristics which go to make it up—values, attitudes, personality, patterns of behavior, and so on—we are posing ourselves an extremely difficult problem. For example, in order to investigate sportsmanship attitudes, which has been of interest to some investigators, we must develop an instrument which not only *does* measure sportsmanship but does so with sufficient accuracy and sensitivity to allow us to detect differences between, for example, starters and substitutes. This is an incredibly problematic proposition. Even personality studies, which in comparison have a most sophisticated instrumentation, still experience considerable difficulties with sensitivity and, to a lesser extent, validity in this regard, as exemplified by the fact that in the research reviewed, over 12 different psychological instruments were used, ranging from the well known and well tested, such as Catell's 16PF and the MMPI, to the individually developed and the untested. Even that most concrete of indicators, the GPA, is itself problematic as an index of academic achievement.

I have attempted to describe in this section of the paper some of the significant methodological difficulties which face investigators who wish to pursue socialization effects research. At this time, these difficulties have (a) compromised our efforts to determine the socialization effects of participation in college athletics, and (b) doomed our attempts to draw meaningful conclusions from much of the existing research. Furthermore, I would strongly suggest that these inherent difficulties have been significant contributors to the much reduced popularity of socialization effects research.

THE DEMISE OF SOCIALIZATION AFFECTS RESEARCH

If it is difficult to draw any conclusions regarding the effects of participation in college athletics, we can at least conclude with certainty that this area of socialization research is in a very parlous state indeed. Very little work is being done; I was able to identify a total of only 12 studies concerned with college athletics. Even granting the likelihood that a number of publications may have been overlooked, this is still a meager amount of research over a 10-year period. Especially so, when this level of production is contrasted with the relatively enormous explosion which has occurred in sport sociology and sport socialization research over the same decade. Admittedly certain topics within the socialization effects area have done better than others; for example, the topic of academic achievement has seemed to retain its rather marginal status, while the number of personality efforts studies has plummeted and the attitudinal studies have beome virtually nonexistent. Nevertheless, when considered in the context of the general dynamism and expansion of research in the sociology of sport, even maintaining the status quo is to lose considerably in popularity.

Therefore, the key issue is, Why are sport sociologists no longer looking at the socialization impact of sport participation upon the athlete? It is my contention that a shift of emphasis has occurred in sport socialization research, moving from a predominant concern with the socialization effects of participation in sport to an equally predominant concern with the processes of socialization into sport roles. The central question of sport socialization research, which originally was "What is the impact of college athletics upon the individual?" has become replaced by "How do people become elite (college) athletes?" The primary emphasis of the research now is the investigation of the process by which individuals become socialized into sport roles, both general and specific. As the emphasis has changed and as the questions considered to be significant have changed, so research concerned with socialization effects has come to be seen as less important, less exciting, and has consequently become less popular. The result is that the "socialization-into-sport-roles" topic has come to dominate the sport socialization literature to the virtual exclusion of socialization effects research.

This shift in emphasis reflects the changes which have occurred in public social concerns regarding the relationship between the individual and educational institutions, and specifically between the college athlete and the intercollegiate athletic program. We must not ignore, however, the contributions of a number of other factors, such as (a) the previously discussed methodological difficulties which are inherent in socialization effects research; and (b) similar changes in emphasis regarding the populations under investigation—specifically, a dramatically increased concern for the female athlete population, and an age-related shift from a concern with the high school/college population to a concern for the elementary/junior high school population.

It is an interesting exercise to look back over some of the earlier and later sport sociology publications. In the earlier books, which were primarily anthologies (e.g., Sage's first edition in 1970), the primary socialization focus was on articles concerned with socialization effects (Sage included five) rather than with socialization-into-sport roles (Sage had none). Even as recently as 1976, Yiannakis et al., in the collection of articles for their *Sport Sociology: Contemporary Themes* included almost twice as many socialization effects articles. By 1978, however, the emphasis had changed to the extent that Loy, McPherson, and Kenyon devoted over 25 pages of their text to a discussion of the processes of socialization into sport roles, while dismissing the socialization effects issue in a single page. While in 1981, McPherson's review of the sport socialization area for the *Handbook of Social Science of Sport* (Luschen & Sage, 1981) gave over 17 pages to the research on socialization-into-sport roles, but merely 4 pages to the research on socialization effects.

Why has this occurred? The explanation has to do in large part with changes in public social concerns. Research in the social sciences reflects to a surprising extent the social issues and concerns which are considered contemporarily pertinent. Part of the reason for this is financial. Quite often, the sources of financial support for research are sufficiently sensitive to direct the availability of this support to the investigation of these concerns. Equally important is that such social issues create a climate in which any activity concerning them—be it debating, teaching, writing, or research—is seen as important and exciting. The problem with this state of affairs is that as the public social issues and concerns change, so related research follows, leaving behind a body of literature and a series of research questions which are no longer of interest or central concern. This is what has happened to the question of the character-building effects of participation in college athletics—a by-product of a specific social concern. As that concern changed, it was replaced, so different sport socialization questions came to be perceived as more pertinent, and the socialization effects question was left without its underlying dynamism. I should add a qualifying clause here, however: In most instances the relationship between social issue and research activity is not a perfect one, for there usually remains some residual interest in the related research questions and, consequently, some research; however, there has been the additional contribution of certain methodological difficulties inherent in this research which has assisted in its severe decline.

Back in the 1960s and '70s when social idealism was rampant, the most critical concerns of the day were centered on the rights of opportunity and access which were bound up in the civil rights issue, and the more personal rights of the individual to be able to pursue his or her own development as a person, or self-actualization. It is always difficult to determine the pervasiveness of a social issue, the extent to which it really and truly touches the lives and consciousness of a mass of people, but it is clear that the impact of these two issues was real enough upon the patterns of institutional life.

As the philosophers, the libertarians, the dreamers, and the activists became increasingly politicized creatures, the arenas for their actions became the more symbolically significant aspects of our social fabric. Thus, it was that intercollegiate and interscholastic athletics became the focus of the "Athletic Revolution." The concern here was centered around the potential "dehumanization" of the athlete as a consequence of his (there was little concern for the female athlete at this time) athletic experience in a quasimilitaristic, authoritarian, single-minded regime. Two sides quickly became drawn—or perhaps a better analogy would be "the wagons were circled"—on the explosive issue of whether participation in athletics built or destroyed character.

It was during this period that the sociology of sport developed as a legitimate area of research, and a significant part of it was centered on the character-building debate. Although much of this early literature was essentially polemic, very soon research (or what was purported to be research) appeared, to be eagerly grasped and proclaimed by either side depending upon what conclusions (no matter how tenuous or inappropriate, or in some cases even spurious) could be drawn from it.

It is hard to believe, now, the intensity of the time and the significance which the character-building issue was given—to the extent that careers (on both sides of the issue) were destroyed, damaged, and discarded. It is almost totally inconceivable today that such an essentially idealistic, moral-cum-philosophical issue could consume so many people and so many institutions. Today, we appear to be incapable of reaching the level of moral indignation which was aroused then. The expectations which we have of our educational institutions are so different: We are so much more cynical, disillusioned, and pragmatic. We no longer expect, let alone require, that our educational institutions should civilize, citizenize, or in any way develop moral or social characteristics.

As the realities of our economically troubled world press close about us, our expectations are much more pragmatic; we expect educational institutions to train us and to certify us to the point that we may enter the occupational world with some reasonable expectations of success. To be concerned with the moral question of whether athletics builds character is to be out of tune with these pragmatic times. College athletics is now explicitly a business venture whose legitimacy is measured in terms of dollars developed, not characters. The important questions are now pragmatic: From the point of view of the Athletic Department, "How do we get the best athletes?"; then once we have them, "How do we keep them eligible?" and "How do we get the maximum performance out of them?"; and from the point of view of the athlete, "What academic qualifications and career benefits do I get in return for my services?"

It is not surprising then, that research on sport socialization should also reflect these changes in social concerns. From being a burning issue and a vital generator of research, the socialization effects question, born of idealism, has become moribund. It is just not important anymore. On the other hand, research on the processes of socialization into sport roles, essentially pragmatic, has flourished. Important now is to know from where the potentially elite athletes come and how they become elite, as well as how the process can be made more efficient by getting the "right" raw material into the "right" sport career pathways.

Two levels of social concerns operate as driving forces behind this development: one at the college level, the other at the national political level. At the national political level, there has occurred a vastly increased recognition of the political importance of winning international competitions. We are all aware of the impetus given to this concern by the prowess of the Soviet Union, Cuba, and East Germany. It is essential, therefore, for nation states to identify their best potential athletes, to give them the best possible coaching as well as every opportunity to achieve their potential. What has resulted is an overwhelming concern for the age-group athlete, for the earliest possible identification of the potential athlete, and for the provision of the best qualified coaches at the earliest stages. It becomes vital, therefore, to know the processes of socialization which produce elite athletes so that these processes can be used and improved upon. This entirely pragmatic concern provides the socialization-into-sport roles research effort with its dynamism, its legitimacy, and its popularity. What it also does, however, is shift the emphasis of sport socialization research away from the college-age athlete. Thus, it contributes not only to the demise of socialization effects research, but also of socialization research generally on college athletes.

Secondary though it may be to the national age-group concern, there is nevertheless a concern at the college level for the identification of potentially elite athletes and the socialization processes by which they are produced. For the athletic department, the stakes are high. The traditional concern for school spirit and the prestige of the school has been superceded in these economically troubled times by a drive to maximize the available revenues, both by filling the stadium and, where possible, by gaining access to the millions of available TV and radio dollars. It is more critical than ever to win—to win publically and to win significantly. This translates into the necessity to obtain the best athletes—to know where they come from, to know how they get to be so good, and to know what is necessary to maxmize both this production line and their performance.

There are also some other pragmatic concerns at the college level. On the one hand, there is the athlete's concern for whether or not he or she is getting his or her side of the bargain; on the other hand, there is the very visible concern over the ability of female athletes to compete with the same opportunities as male athletes. The new attitude towards women athletes has also been reflected in sport socialization research. Progressively, the focus of research has become modified from an almost exclusive concern with male athletes to an ever-increasing concern with female athletes (although it may be admitted that the increasing numbers of female social scientists has had much to do with this). Also important to note is that this research has been predominantly concerned with sport roles—the documentation of restrictive practices in male-dominated sport, and the processes of socialization into sport roles to which women have been subjected. The purpose is essentially pragmatic: to demonstrate that women are discriminated against, and to ensure that existing and future socialization processes do not hinder women in achieving sport roles. The research has not in the slightest been concerned with the diffuse effects of participation in college athletes upon the character of the female athlete.

A somewhat different line of research has been generated by the pragmatic concerns of the athlete vis-a-vis his or her agreement to participate in the athletic program. The relationship between college and the athlete has increasingly come to be seen in quasicontractual terms: The college gets the athlete's services for 4 years and, in return, the athlete gets an education and a consequent entrée into the occupational structure. What then is the athlete actually getting? Clearly, this is a legitimate concern if the athletic department's prime objective is simply to keep the athlete eligible to compete. Horror stories abound of athletes being kept eligible by means of a string of "bird" courses which do not ultimately count towards a degree, of manipulating grades and outright cheating, and of athletes leaving college after 4 fine athletic years still unable to either read or write. The question is whether such situations are typical or anomalous, and just exactly what is the academic status of college athletes. As Coakley (1982) indicated, athletic departments are extremely resistent to allowing "outsiders" in to look at their internal practices and at "their" athletes. As a consequence, research has turned in a somewhat less sensitive direction and has simply attempted to find out whether athletes do as well academically as nonathletes. Such investigations into the pragmatic effects of participation in college athletics upon the athlete's achieved GPA are clearly qualitatively different from the previously more popular investigations of the diffuse socialization effects of participation upon the athlete's character.

Essentially what has happened to the question of the character-building effects of college athletics is that it has become unimportant. The idealistic social concerns which generated it and gave it pertinence and legitimacy have faded away to be replaced by infinitely more pragmatic concerns to which this question is irrelevant. The relevant research questions now are those related to processes of socialization into sport roles; and as a consequence, it is this research which has come to dominate both the literature and the activities of sport social scientists.

CONCLUSION

It has been a sobering experience to see just how much the sport socialization literature has changed over the past few years. It seems rather sad that all the energy and time and effort that was put into pursuing socialization effects research should now be for nought. Yet, as the social wheel-of-fortune rolls on, it is sometimes the case that anachronisms once again regain favor and become contemporary. There is hope that as our public social issues change, as change they must, perhaps idealism will once again become popular, and socialization effects research will be restored to pertinence and will be pursued with renewed vigor and sophistication. Until that time, however, we much conclude that (a) the socialization effects question has declined considerably as a generator of research activity and little work of significance is being done; and (b) as a consequence, the basic conclusion must remain that there is little valid evidence that participation in college athletics has any effect upon the character of the athlete.

REFERENCES

BUHRMANN, H. (1977). Athletics and deviance: An examination of the relationship between athletic participation and deviant behavior of high school girls. *Review of Sport and Leisure, 2*, 17-34.

CHU, D., & Griffey, D.C. (1982). Sport and racial integration: The relationship of personal contact, attitudes, and behavior. In A.O. Dunleavy, A.W. Miracle, & C.R. Rees (Eds.), *Studies in the sociology of sport*. Fort Worth, TX: T.C.U. Press.

COAKLEY, J.J. (1982). *Sport in society* (2nd ed.). St. Louis: The C.V. Mosby Company.

COLLEGE athletics and graduation. (1978, March). *Scholastic Coach*, p. 163.

COOPER, L. (1969). Athletics, activity, and personality: A review of the literature. *Research Quarterly, 40*, 17-22.

EDWARDS, T.L. (1967). Scholarships and athletics. *Journal of Health, Physical Education and Recreation, 38*, p. 75.

EITZEN, D.S., & Sage, G.H. (1982). *Sociology of American Sport* (2nd ed.). Dubuque, IA: Wm. C. Brown Company.

FIGLER, S.K. (1981). *Sport and play in American life*. Philadelphia, PA: Saunders College.

GRUBER, J., & Perkins, S. (1978). Personality traits of women physical education majors and non-majors at various levels of athletic competition. *International Journal of Sport Psychology, 9*, 40-52.

GUNDERSHEIM, J. (1982). A comparison of male and female athletes and nonathletes on measures of self-actualization. *Journal of Sport Behavior, 5*(4), 186-201.

HANKS, M.P., & Eckland, B.K. (1976). Athletics and social participation in the educational attainment process. *Sociology of Education, 49*, 271-294.

HUSMAN, B. (1969). Sport and personality dynamics. *Proceedings of the 72nd Annual Conference of the National College Physical Education Association for Men, 72,* 56-69.

KONZAK, B., & Klavora, P. (1980). Some social psychological dimensions of karate participation: An examination of personality characteristics within the training context of a traditional martial art. In P. Klavora & K.A.W. Wipper (Eds.), *Psychological and sociological factors in sport.* Toronto: University of Toronto.

LANDERS, D., & Landers, D. (1978). Socialization via interscholastic athletics: Its effects on delinquency. *Sociology of Education, 51,* 299-303.

LOY, J.W., McPherson, B.D., & Kenyon, G. (1978). *Sport and social systems.* Reading, MA: Addison-Wesley.

LUSCHEN, G.R.F., & Sage, G.H. (Eds.). (1981). *Handbook of social science of sport.* Champaign, IL: Stipes.

MCPHERSON, B.D. (1978). Socialization and sport involvement. In G.H. Sage & G.R.F. Luschen (Eds.), *Encyclopedia of physical education (Vol. 5).* Reading, MA: Addison-Wesley.

MCPHERSON, B.D. (1981). Socialization into and through sport. In G.R.F. Luschen & G.H. Sage (Eds.), *Handbook of social science of sport.* Champaign, IL: Stipes.

MESSNER, S., & Groisser, D. (1982). Intercollegiate athletic participation and academic achievement. In A.O. Dunleavy, A.W. Miracle, & C.R. Rees (Eds.), *Studies in the sociology of sport.* Fort Worth, TX: T.C.U. Press.

NATION, J.R., & LeUnes, A.D. (1983). Personality characteristics of intercollegiate football players as determined by position, classification, and redshirt status. *Journal of Sport Behavior, 6*(2), 92-102.

PHILLIPS, J.C., & Schafer, W.E. (1971). Consequences of participation in interscholastic sports. *Pacific Sociological Review, 14,* 328-336.

PURDY, D.A., Eitzen, D.S., & Hufnagel, R. (1982). Are athletes also students? The educational attainment of college athletes. *Social Problems, 29*(4), 439-448.

RYAN, D. (1969). Reaction to "sport and personality dynamics." *Proceedings of the 72nd Annual Conference of the National College Physical Education Association for Men, 72,* 70-75.

SAGE, G.H. (Ed.). (1970). *Sport and American society* (1st ed.). Reading, MA: Addison-Wesley.

SCHAFER, W.E. (1972). Participation in interscholastic athletics and delinquency. In K. Polk & W.E. Schafer (Eds.), *Schools and delinquency.* Englewood Cliffs, NJ: Prentice-Hall.

SCHAFER, W.E., & Armer, M. (1968). Athletes are not inferior students. *Transaction, 6,* 61-62.

SCHENDEL, J.S. (1965). Psychological differences between athletes and nonparticipants in athletics at three educational levels. *Research Quarterly, 36,* 52-67.

SCHENDEL, J.S. (1968). The psychological characteristics of high school athletes and nonparticipants in athletics. *Proceedings of the 2nd International Congress of Sport Psychology,* 79-96.

SEGRAVE, J.O., & Chu, D.G. (1978). Athletics and juvenile delinquency. *Review of Sport and Leisure, 3,* 1-24.

SEGRAVE, J.O., & Hastad, D.M. (1982). Delinquent behavior and interscholastic athletic participation. *Journal of Sport Behavior, 5*(2), 96-111.

SNYDER, E.E. & Spreitzer, E. (1979). High school value climate as related to preferential treatment of athletes. *Research Quarterly, 50*(3), 460-467.

SNYDER, E.E. & Spreitzer, E. (1983). *Social aspects of sport* (2nd ed.). Englewood Cliffs, NJ: Prentice-Hall.

STERN, B.E. (1972). *The relationship between participation in sports and the moral and political socialization of high school youth in Chile.* Unpublished doctoral dissertation, Stanford University.

STEVENSON, C.L. (1975). Socialization effects of participation in sport: A critical review of the research. *Research Quarterly, 46*(3), 287-301.

THAKUR, G.P., & Ojha, M. (1981). Personality differences of Indian table-tennis, badminton and football players on primary source traits in the 16PF. *International Journal of Sport Psychology,* **12**, 196-203.

THAKUR, G.P., & Thakur, M. (1980). Personality differences between the athlete and the nonathlete college males. *International Journal of Sport Psychology,* **11**, 180-188.

TYLER, J.K., & Duthie, J.H. (1979). The effects of ice hockey on social development. *Journal of Sport Behavior,* **2**(1), 49-59.

WERNER, A.C., & Gottheil, E. (1966). Personality development and participation in college athletics. *Research Quarterly,* **37**, 126-31.

YIANNAKIS, A., McIntyre, T.D., Melnick, M.J., & Hart, D.P. (Eds.). (1976). *Sport sociology: Contemporary themes.* Dubuque, IA: Kendall/Hunt.

Chapter 18

Sport: If You Want to Build Character, Try Something Else

Bruce C. Ogilvie and Thomas A. Tutko
San Jose State University

The *Cultural Revolution* has penetrated the last stronghold of the American myth—the locker room. Young athletes, having scaled new levels of consciousness, now challenge a long-standing article of faith—the belief that competition has intrinsic value. They enter sports in search of particular aesthetic experience, essentially personal in nature. They no longer accept the authoritarian structure of sports, nor do they accept the supreme emphasis on winning. Outside critics who see in the sports world a metaphor for the moral deficiencies of American society add to the pressure in the once-sacred precincts.

Coaches and administrators defend organized sport with traditional claims that competition builds character and toughens the young for life in the real world. Coaches in particular do not want to listen to the requests of the young. The stereotype of the ideal athlete is fading fast. Long-haired radicals with life-styles and political beliefs unheard of a few years ago people the uncomfortable dreams of coaches.

COMPETITION AND PERSONALITY

In the midst of the controversy, psychologists find themselves being asked what personal, social, or psychological significance can be attributed to organized sport. For the past 8 years, we have been studying the effects of competition on personality. Our research began with the counseling of problem athletes, but it soon expanded to include athletes from every sport, at every level, from the high school gym to the professional arena. On the evidence gathered in this study, we can make some broad-range value judgments. We found no empirical support for the tradition that sport builds character. Indeed, there is evidence that athletic competition limits growth in some areas. It seems that the personality of the ideal athlete is not the result of any molding process, but comes out of the ruthless selection process that occurs at all levels of sport. Athletic competition has no more beneficial effects than intense endeavor in any other field. Horatio Alger success—in sport or elsewhere—comes only to those who already are mentally fit, resilient, and strong.

The problem athletes who made up our original sample displayed such severe emotional reactions to stress that we had serious doubts about the basic value of athletic competition. The problems associated with sport covered a wide spectrum of behavior, but we were able to isolate major syndromes: the con-man athlete, the hyperanxious athlete, the athlete who resists coaching, the success-phobic athlete, the injury-prone athlete, and the depression-prone athlete.

When we confronted such cases, it became more and more difficult for us to make positive clinical interpretations on the effects of competition. In 1963, we established the Institute for the Study of Athletic Motivation to start research aimed at helping athletes reach their potentials. We wanted to examine normal players as well as problem athletes. To identify sport-specific personality traits, we along with Lee Lyon developed the Athletic Motivation Inventory (AMI) which measures 11 traits common to most successful sports figures. We have since administered the AMI to approximately 15,000 athletes. The results of these tests indicate that general sports personalities do exist.

TRAITS OF THE SUCCESSFUL ATHLETE

Athletes who survive the high attrition rate associated with sports competition are characterized by all or most of the following traits:

1. They have great need for achievement and tend to set high but realistic goals for themselves and others.
2. They are highly organized, orderly, respectful of authority, and dominant.
3. They have large capacity for trust, great psychological endurance, self-control, low-resting levels of anxiety, and slightly greater ability to express aggression.

Most athletes indicate low interest in receiving support and concern from others, low need to take care of others, and low need for affiliation. Such a personality seems necessary to achieve victory over others. There is some question whether these trends are temporary character traits—changing when the athlete gets out of sport—or permanent ones. Using men coaches and women physical educators as reference groups, we would predict that these character trends remain highly stable.

WOMEN COMPETITORS

We discovered subgroupings within the athletic personality. For example, outstanding women competitors show a greater tendency toward introversion, greater autonomy needs, and a combination of qualities suggesting that they are more creative than their male counterparts. They show less need for sensitive and understanding involvement with others. Women competitors are more reserved and cool, more experimental, more independent than male. Interestingly, we found that among women, there was far less trait variation from one sport to another than there was among men. (Exceptions were women fencers, gymnasts, and parachutists.) We attribute this to cultural repression of women: To succeed in *any* field, a woman has to be able to stand up and spit in the eye of those in charge.

INDIVIDUAL AND TEAM PLAYER TRAITS

In addition to sex differences, we were able to distinguish a team-sports personality. Persons in individual competition tend more toward healthy introversion. They are less affiliative than team players, have a higher level of aggression, and tend to be more creative.

For some sports we could even distinguish a particular pesonality type. For example, the data strongly distinguish a race-driver personality. More than participants in any other sport, drivers are tough-minded, hard-headed realists: They are reserved and cool; they override their feelings and are not fanciful; they do not show anxiety or tension and are self-sufficient; and they are tremendously achievement-oriented, far more than the average athlete.

SURVIVAL OF THE FITTEST

Our original hypothesis about the ill effects of high-level competition turned out to be unfounded. When we completed tests on the original teams, we discovered no negative relation between athletic achievement and emotional maturity or control. On the contrary, the higher the achievement, the greater the probability the athlete would have emotional maturity or control. Sport is like most other activities: Those who survive tend to have stronger personalities.

The competitive-sport experience is unique in the way it compresses the selection process into a compact time and space. There are few areas of human endeavor that can match the Olympic trials or a professional training camp for intensity of human stress. A young athlete often must face in hours or days the kind of pressure that occurs over several years in the life of the achievement-oriented man. The potential for laying bare the personality structure of the individual is considerable. When the athlete's ego is deeply invested in sports achievement, very few of the neurotic protective mechanisms provide adequate or sustaining cover. Basically, each must face his moment of truth and live with the consequences. The pro rookie usually gets only three or four chances to demonstrate ability before he is sent home. What sort of personality structure supports the person who can face this blunt reinforcement of reality?

EMOTIONAL SUPPORT SYSTEMS

Beyond brutally rapid and clear evaluation of competence is the stress from the neglect of basic human needs that may accompany athletic success. Take the case of a high draft-choice football player; after tearing up the camp the first few days, he turned morose and sullen. He was experiencing what often happens to men who excel in any area—the withdrawal of emotional support from those outside his field. Persons who were close to this gifted young man had pulled away, assuming that they were no longer important in his life, that he had outgrown his need for them. They anticipated rejection, but rather than live with this threat, they retreated at the first opportunity. Quite often an athlete's wife experiences this reaction. Threatened by her husband's new acclaim, she may withhold love and support from him. When the tension between his success on the field and his crumbling home life gets unbearable, the athlete sometimes manages to get a mild injury. Rare is the man who can make it in sport without the support of his wife.

RESULTS OF THE STRESS OF COMPETITION

Under such intense pressure with threats from so many different directions, personality flaws manifest themselves quickly. We found that personal reactions to the stress of competition remain fairly constant across the sports. Depression, combined with failure due to unconscious fear of success, hyperanxiety (the athlete who burns himself out before the competition begins), and exaggerated sensitivity to failure or criticism accounted for more than half of our referrals. The same telescoping of time and space that uncovers personality deficiencies with such rapidity, however, provides a splendid laboratory for experimentaion with self-change. The rapidity and clarity of feedback in competitive sport provides a fine opportunity for the individual athlete who knows which traits he wants to change and who has the motivation to do so.

By showing the athlete that certain habitual ways of behaving or thinking keep him from reaching his potential, we open a collaborative approach between coach and athlete that may solve the problem. Obviously the motive to change depends on a number of variables, including the extent to which the ego is invested in sports. When we sit down with a young man who has just signed a contract for $250,000 and tell him that on the basis of his test scores he doesn't measure up to his fellow pros in certain traits, he makes only one comment: "How do I change that, Doc?" But the high-school athlete has a motivational conflict of another order when he has to decide whether he will work to support his car so that he can keep his girl friend or spend his time excelling in his sport.

RELATIONSHIP BETWEEN CHARACTER AND SUCCESS

Though we can identify the common traits of successful athletes and counsel a highly motivated youth on how to strengthen particular traits, we cannot tell how much these traits actually contribute to athletic success. Competition does not seem to build character, and it is possible that competition doesn't even *require* much more than a minimally integrated personality.

Innate physical ability is always a contaminating factor when we attempt to make statements about the relationship between character and success. Even using a sample of Olympic competitors and professionals, we find that independent judges' ratings of ability in any given athlete fluctuate considerably. At best, judges can agree on the relative ability of athletes in the top and bottom 6 to 12%.

We are similarly unable to determine the extent to which character contributes to coaching success. In this case, the uncontrolled factor is the degree to which the coach is master of his science. We found that there is no way to compensate for lack of knowledge in one's field, but we do not know the degree to which this skill must be augmented by strong character traits.

We know from our work hundreds of outstanding competitors who possess strong character traits that it was difficult on the basis of personality to account for their success. There were gold-medal Olympic winners in Mexico and Japan whom we would classify as overcompensatory greats. Only magnificent physical gifts enabled them to overcome constant tension, anxiety, and self-doubt. They are unhappy, and when the talent ages and fades, they become derelicts, while someone like Roosevelt Grier just goes on to bigger mountains. We often wonder how much higher some of these great performers might have gone if they had, say, the strong personality structure that characterized our women's Olympic fencing team.

A certain minimum personality development is essential. We once encountered a long-distance runner who was so gifted that, late one night, running in total darkness with only pacers and timers, he broke the NCAA record for his event. The mark would have survived for the next 4 years. But upon achieving this goal, he quit the team, never to compete again. He later explained that he did it to get even with his coach; but our data suggest a different interpretation. It seems that grave personal doubts about his worth as a person impaired his capacity to support the burden of success. He preferred to protect his fragile ego by showing bursts of superior performance then retreating to mediocrity so that others would not depend on him.

SATURATION OF SPORT

We have also seen some indications that there may be an *upper* limit on the character development needed for success in sport. Sometimes we find players who have good physical skills coupled with immense character strengths who do not make it in sports. They seem to be so well put together emotionally that there is no neurotic tie to sport. The rewards of sport are not enough for them any more, and they turn away voluntarily to other, more challenging fields. This is singularly frustrating to their coaches.

We quickly discovered that the coach was the crucial factor—whether we were trying to modify a disturbed athlete's behavior, or measure the influence of competition on the successful athlete's personality. Consequently, we made special efforts to identify the personality traits of coaches. We found that there was indeed a coach personality. It was similar to the competitor's, but the traits tended to be intensified, as with race drivers.

COACHES' PERCEPTIONS

We found that our test data provided a more reliable personality model of athletes than the coaches' observations, that the tests gave better insights into individual differences and allowed for better gauging of individual limitations as well as strengths. Coaches are most reliable in their perception of personality tendencies that are a significant part of their own character structure. They prove to be most reliable in identifying the traits of dominance, psychological endurance, and athletic drive, but are unable to recognize such traits as emotional control, self-confidence, trust, conscience, self-abasement, or tenderness. We also found that coaches tend to be blind to deficiencies in gifted athletes.

We find most coaches uncertain and anxious about the changes taking place in sport. They have shown an overwhelming positive response to our efforts to bring the tools of psychology into their careers. They are crying for new methods, new information. They know that they are not fully prepared for their tasks.

"WINNING ISN'T EVERYTHING—IT'S
THE ONLY THING"

Many of the changes run counter to values deeply rooted in the coach personality. Athletes who ask the basic question—"Is winning all that worthwhile?"—

deny the coach's life's work and his very existence. Most coaches go by the Vince Lombardi dictum that "winning isn't everything—it's the only thing."

Conflict over values manifests itself in struggles over discipline. Hair length comes to mind. The coach sees hair as a problem of authority; he orders the athlete to get it cut and expects his order to be obeyed. In contrast, the athlete sees discipline as a peripheral, frivolous issue compared with his own struggle to find identity in the hair styles of his peers. Coach and hirsute athlete talk past each other. Value changes that involve drugs and politics put the coach under strain. Most coaches believe that a truly good athlete is also, by definition, a red-blooded, clean-living, truth-telling, prepared patriot. A top-notch competitor who disagrees with national policy is a heavy thing for a coach who undoubtedly believes that the wars of England were indeed won on the playing fields of Eton.

Many coaches will not be able to stand the strain. Eventually, the world of sport is going to take the emphasis off winning-at-any-cost. The new direction will be toward helping athletes make personally chosen modifications in behavior; toward the joyous pursuit of aesthetic experience; and toward wide variety of personality types and values. Inevitably, these changes are going to force the least flexible coaches—perhaps as many as a third of them—out of the business.

Chapter 19

American Values and Sport: Formation of a Bureaucratic Personality

George H. Sage
University of Northern Colorado

A recurrent theme of sport sociology is that sport is a microcosm of society. The types of sports played, the way in which sport is organized, who participates, and who does not, all provide clues about the nature of society. In this presentation I shall examine the reciprocal relationship between sport and American values. I say reciprocal because sport promotes and reinforces the American value system as well as reflects it. Adult members of the population who have internalized the value system socialize the younger generation by the way they organize, coach, and administer youth sports programs. Those who are socialized to the value system in this way reach adulthood and enter occupations carrying an internalized version of the value system. They in turn, transmit these values on to the next generation.

CULTURAL VALUE SYSTEMS

Each culture has a distinct value system which can be explored through examination of relevant observation data, concepts, and methods. Functionally, a value system is a set of principles whereby conduct is directed and regulated and is a guide for individuals and the social group. A cultural value system does not describe the values of any single individual: It is a summary construct in which the diverse value sets of individuals and groups are related as complementary elements of a single system (Kluckhohn & Strodtbeck, 1961). One may argue that in any society there are some individuals who have not internalized the cultural values, but there is no society in which most persons have not internalized the values of their culture; indeed, most members accept these values, evaluate their own acts in accordance with them and experience anxiety should they desire to violate them (Spior, 1975). As Emile Dirkheim noted, individuals who together make up a society have a common consciousness, "one part of which is common to our group in its entirety, which, consequently, is not ourself, but society living and acting within us" (Dirkheim, 1947). For the powerful groups of a society, the major problem facing them is the problem of molding a "common consciousness," animating it with the appropriate ethic, and forming attitudes, habits, and lifestyles.

BUREAUCRATIC FORMS OF ORGANIZATION

The fundamental feature of every society is embodied in a characteristic organizational form and for our time it is bureaucracy. It dominates our age, not just in large-scale business but also in government, education, religion, the armed forces, and every other contemporary social institution. Although bureaucratic forms of organization have existed for as far back as the ancient Egyptian civilization, the rise of industrialization, the use of mass production methods, and the formalization of all social institutions into large organizations has brought about a tremendous bureaucratization in both the private and public sectors in the past 75 years. Not bureaucracy, but the bureaucratization of society is unique to modern times. The attitudes and values which are nurtured by it form the cornerstone of the "common consciousness" which we possess.

Bureaucracy is a technical means of administration whose ends are given by those in control, whether they are businesspersons, politicians, clergy, or coaches. According to Max Weber (1968), the German sociologist whose ideas have greatly influenced this field, bureaucratic organization as an ideal type is characterized by a primary orientation toward the attainment of specific goals. For example, the central goal of General Motors is to make profits for its shareholders; thus a central feature of bureaucracy is an acceptance of the priority of the organization and a belief that individuals must subordinate their wills to it.

Hierarchical authority is an indispensable component of bureaucratic organization. Authority must be an attribute of the office and not the person. Moreover, authority is rational; that is, it is based entirely upon understood and accepted rules that have been designed with the efficiency of production or performance uppermost in mind. The subordinate is expected to obey his superior because of the superior's position, regardless of what personal feelings he may have about the person. The interests of the organization are paramount in the development of rules, and the formal aspects of a bureaucracy manifest these interests and rules. Bureaucracy stands in direct opposition to every emotional, unspecialized, personal, and deeply human aspect of personality.

Another feature of the bureaucratic apparatus is that it requires a sharp division of labor, and extensive specialization of employees engaged in semiautomatic, standardized production. They work under fixed rules in a highly disciplined system of control. Indeed, discipline is the watchword of bureaucracy. Rights, duties, privileges, and procedures are specified by the organization and its internal laws. People come and go, policies change, whole administrations succeed each other, but the well-built bureaucracy stands fast through it all. It is the harbinger of standardization, mass production, objectivity, and impersonality in complex organizations.

INTERNALIZATION OF THE BUREAUCRATIC ETHIC

Bureaucracy is designed only as a technical system of administration, but its influence goes beyond the organizations that employ this form of administrative process. Bureaucracy is connected with everything else that gives our culture its distinctiveness. It is a source of norms regulating a large number of activities both within and beyond large-scale organization boundaries. So powerful and so pervasive are the organizations that employ bureaucratic methods that the value orientations engendered by this form of organization constitute the core of the value system salient in American society. It permeates the fabric of every social institution, and the American socialization process is largely devoted to conditioning the youth of the nation to this orientation.

THE BUREAUCRATIC INFLUENCE IN SPORT

It is not appropriate for me to divulge the main theme of this presentation. My major thesis is that organized sport—from youth programs to the pros—has nothing at all to do with playfulness—fun, joy, self-satisfaction—but is, instead, a social agent for the deliberate socialization of people into the acceptance of our most salient organization form. This is not to say that sports participants and spectators do not occasionally experience fun and joy, but the main point is that those emotions are irrelevant to the real purpose of our sports programs. They are not organized to provide an outlet for human expression and self-fulfillment. They are programs for the formation of a common consciousness—the internalization of the bureaucratic ethic.

As organized sport has grown prominent and powerful in the past 60 years, it has clearly adopted the assumptions and values of bureaucratic organizations. Sociologist Charles Page (1973) has persuasively argued that sport has been greatly influenced by the powerful thrust of bureaucracy:

> The social revolution of sport, viewed in historical perspective, has been in large
> part the transition from both folkrooted informal contests and the agonistic recre-

ation of elites to its bureaucratization—or, in simple terms, from player-controlled "games" to the management-controlled "big-time."

This transition has been two-sided. On the one hand, there has been the ever-growing rationalization and formalization of sport, with the aim of maximizing athletic "output," abetted by consistently improved techniques and equipment and measured by victory, record breaking, and, of fundamental importance, sheer economic profit—on this count, sport has become big business with all of its familiar features. On the other hand, there has been the decreasing degree of autonomy of the athlete himself, whose onetime position as a more or less independent participant has been largely replaced by the status of skilled athletic worker under the strict discipline of coaches, managers, and, in the case of the pro, the "front office." This large-scale bureaucratization of sport, it should be stressed, is by no means confined to its professional version: rules and routine, the ascendancy of work over play, and the rise of the coach's authority within and beyond the athletic realm have penetrated deeply into collegiate and high school sports and even into the adult-controlled, highly organized "little leagues" in baseball and football.

EMERGENCE OF A BUREAUCRATIC MENTALITY IN SPORT

Bureaucracy has been transplanted from public and private organizations, to which it was largely confined at first, to the affairs of sport, and the emergence of a bureaucratic mentality in sport has been dependent upon many of the same factors which were responsible for the growth of bureaucracy in other areas of organizational life, for example, the expansion of a money economy, the increased size of administrative units, the growth of occupational specialization, and the prominence of the profit motive (Ingham, 1975).

The growth in organized sport has witnessed an acceptance of the priority of sports organizations and a belief that the individual must subordinate his will to them. Established hierarchy and efficiency procedures are seen as necessary and inviolable. The basic concern is with athletes' subjecting themselves to the will of the coach whose primary concern is with winning athletic contests. The rise of increasingly institutionalized and codified sports teams has caused many coaches to view team members as objects in a machine-like environment who need to be conditioned to perform prescribed, fragmented tasks as instrumental to team performance. Thus, the players become another person's (the coach's) instrument and are used to reach the objectives and goals of the organization; they are reduced to cogs in the organization's machinery. In this respect, Paul Hoch (1972), in his book *Rip Off the Big Game*, noted:

> In football, like business. . .every pattern of movement on the field is increasingly being brought under the control of a group of nonplaying managerial technocrats who sit up in the stands. . .with their headphones and dictate offenses, defenses, special plays, substitutions, and so forth to the players below.

Individual players are expected to do their best to fit themselves into functions which are needed by the organization. This is vividly exemplified in popular locker room slogans, such as "There is no I in team," "A player doesn't make the team, the team makes the player." A system of incentives and rewards, for example, letter awards and helmet decals are instituted to "motivate" athletes to perform. It may be seen that in this approach decisions are made by management (the coaches), after a thorough cost efficiency analysis and the players are expected to carry out the will of the coach for accomplishment of organizational goals (Sage, 1973). The extent to which this attitude is found in sport is aptly illustrated by this story from a recent issue of *Sports Illustrated* (1977).

> With a base hit his last time at the plate, Sid Davis of Bear Creek High School, Tremonton, Utah, would have ended his three-year varsity career with a batting average of 1.000. As it was, Davis finished as one of the most productive members of this team—despite a career average of .000.
>
> Sparking more rallies than any other Bear, Davis went to the plate 24 times and drew 24 walks. Davis stands 3'9", and crouching at the plate in a stance developed by his coach. . .he offered opposing pitchers a strike zone about the size of a milk carton.
>
> "He's given us maybe 10 victories over the past three years," [the coach] said of his disciplined pinch hitter.
>
> "Sometimes I'd like to smack it," Davis admits, "but I know that wouldn't help the team."

ORGANIZATIONAL GOALS ABOVE ALL

In most cases, athletes are not consulted about the organizational goals. (It is assumed that they want to be champions and that they are willing to "pay the price" to be winners.) They are not consulted about team membership, practice methods, team strategy, or any of the other dynamic functions of a team. The assumption has been made that they have nothing to contribute toward identifying group goals and the means for achieving them. The situation is eloquently captured by Bob Morford (1973) as follows:

> The modern coach, instead of being the man who encourages and guides others to struggle to do their thing, has instead become the person who manipulates and controls others and their environment so as to do his thing. Thus, the individual loses his chance to struggle himself, to seek his own experience.

Habermas (1972) has argued that "sport has long since become a sector for the rationalization of work." The training process is analyzed, dissected, calculated and synthesized just like the production process. "Sport is a copy of the world of work. And individuals become substrata of units of measurement in it." What do coaches say when they want to praise an athlete? They say he is a hard worker! According to Plessner (1972), "two worlds of work" stand opposite to each other: Sport being "a copy of the world of industry" with the same formal functional rules and standards of valuation.

COACHING AS AN OCCUPATION

Of course, coaches themselves are as much a victim of the bureaucratization of sport as are the athletes. Until the beginning of this century, sports were basically pastimes people engaged in during their leisure time. However, by the early years of the 20th century, the control of sports programs were taken away from the participants, for all intents and purposes, and became vested in various non-participants who wished to use sports for entertainment or the promotion of some product or organization.

Once the entertainment and public relations functions of sports became dominant, the need for experienced coaches arose. Whereas previously coaching functions were performed by older players or by adults in their spare time, now coaching became a serious business, and coaches were employed to direct the destinies of athletic teams. There were several consequences of employing coaches and using sports for entertainment and publicity. Once teams became part of a bureaucratic structure, such as intercollegiate and professional teams are, and once coaching became an occupation, bureaucratic criteria became associated with competence. Objective rational criteria became the only measure of coaching ability and "win" became as synonymous with success as "lose" became associated with failure. Prestige in coaching is basd on won-loss records. A coach, according to all accepted standards, must win in order to have coached well. One college coach recently proclaimed: "I'd give anything—my house, my bank account, anything but my wife and family—to get an undefeated season" (*Newsweek*, 1974). Another coach, when asked to what lengths he would go to win said: "I'd lie, cheat, and steal" (*Sports Illustrated*, 1977).

I think that it is easy to see how this system may produce coaching behavior which emphasizes the treatment of athletes for what they can do for the coach and the team—win—rather than the treatment of athletes based upon what coaches can do for the personal-social growth of athletes as persons. But coaches are not immoral; they merely adapt personal morality to the social norm in order to be "successful." Faced with the "system," coaches acquiesce because the evaluation they receive will be important to their careers and their futures.

EFFECTS OF RATIONALIZATION

A major effect of rationalization is an increase in centralization and consequent elitism. The consequences of increased rationality consists of high levels of institutional centralization and elitist control, for example, institutional domination. The consequences of these processes at the individual level consist of a decline in freedom and an undermining of the development of responsible, politically active citizens. Sociologist Harold Laski (1960) maintains that internalization of the bureaucratic ethic produces cautious, security-oriented persons who would not try to stop or redirect the bureaucratic machine as it slowly dehumanizes and restricts personal liberties. Rationalization thus results in psychological as well as institutional control, the result of which is the decline of freedom on all levels of society. Anyone who is familiar with the various organizations which control organized sports—high school athletic association, NCAA, U.S. Olympic Committee, AAU—are well aware of how they restrict the individual freedoms of the athletes. But, of course, most athletes and coaches are so well indoctrinated to the priority of the organization that they do not object to its treatment of them.

EVOLUTION OF THE BUREAUCRATIC PERSONALITY

You may think that I have been too critical of bureaucratic organization, that I am somehow advocating its abolition. This is not true, of course. It has many social benefits, and to a certain extent, bureaucracy is inescapable and here to stay for quite a while. As society is more and more dominated by largeness, bureaucracy's share of our total life will probably grow with it. The argument here is not about the goodness or badness of bureaucratic organization, but rather to show how it is related to sport.

What I am suggesting here is that participation by America's youth in the world of sport is substantially influential in producing that final result, the bureaucratic personality. The real achievement of organized sports programs consists of their ability to train participants to accept the prevailing social structure and their fate as workers within bureaucratic organizations. Contrary to the myths propounded by promoters, sports are instruments not for human expression, but of social stasis. Although there are many agents and agencies applying pressures and forces to socialize young persons, there is perhaps no social agency that is more salient and powerful for socializing youth to the bureaucratic mentality. To continue the sophomoric insistence on sports contribution to physical health, mental and emotional well-being, joy in movement and other sweetheart characteristics, is to ignore its structural and ethical similarities to the social structure dominating our institutional life, and to the substantial contribution that participation in sport makes to committed and effective participation in the larger society (Webb, 1969).

While you may not like the notion that organized sports programs are fundamentally social agents for the development of the American common consciousness, basically it is true. Moreover, it serves to illustrate that sport is a microcosm of American society.

REFERENCES

DURKHEIM, E. (1947). *Division of labor in society*, [trans.]. New York: Free Press.

HABERMAS, J. (1972). In O. Grupe, D. Kruz, & J.M. Teipel (Eds.), *The scientific view of sport*. Berlin: Springer-Verlag.

HOCH, P. (1972). *Rip off the big game*. Garden City, NY: Doubleday.

INGHAM, A.G. (1975). Occupational subcultures in the work world of sport. In Donald W. Ball & John W. Loy (Eds.), *Sport and social order* (pp. 333-390). Reading, MA: Addison-Wesley.

KLUCKHOHN, F.R. & Strodtbeck, F.L. (1961). *Variations in value orientations*. Evanston, IL: Row, Peterson.

LASKI, H.J. (1960). The limitations of the expert. In George B. deHuszar (Ed.), *The intellectuals*. Glencoe, IL: Free Press.

MORFORD, W.R. (1973, January). Is sport the struggle or the triumph? *Quest, 19*, 83-86.

NEWSWEEK (1974, November 25).

PAGE, C.H. (1973). Pervasive sociological themes in the study of sport. In John T. Talamini and Charles H. Page (Eds.). *Sport and Society* (pp. 14-36). Boston: Little, Brown Co.

PLESSNER, H. (1972). In O. Grupe, D. Kruz, & J.M. Teipel (Eds.), *The scientific view of sport*. Berlin: Springer-Verlag.

SAGE, G.H. (1973, January). The coach as management: Organizational leadership in American sport. *Quest, 19*, 35-40.

SCORECARD (1977, March 21). *Sports Illustrated, 46*, p. 17.

SCORECARD (1977, June 20). *Sports Illustrated, 46*, p. 11.

SPIOR, M. (1975). *Children of the Kubbutz*. Cambridge, MA: Harvard University Press.

WEBB, H. (1969). Professionalization of attitudes toward play among adolescents. In Gerald S. Kenyon (Ed.), *Aspects of contemporary sport sociology* (pp. 161-178). Chicago: The Athletic Institute.

WEBER, M. (1968). *Economy and society*. New York: Bedminster Press. (Originally published 1922).

Section B

The Economics of Intercollegiate Sport

While financial difficulties have been recognized as endemic to many athletic programs it is often assumed that highly visible traditionally successful sport programs earn sufficient revenue to maintain athletic excellence. Financial insecurity has become so widespread, however, that even the Fighting Irish of Notre Dame are no longer immune to the hard realities of economic times. The University of Notre Dame, with 1980-81 revenues of greater than $4 million from football and basketball concessions and ticket sales, showed an income over expenses of only $29,000. Although the university showed a profit of almost $1 million as late as 1975, increasing costs and the expenses of women's sport have reduced revenues to the point that consideration must be given to the cutback of sport offerings (Middleton, 1982).

Traditional views of the economics of intercollegiate sport have been dominated by the "doctrine of good works." In its most expansive form, it is suggested that revenues generated by intercollegiate athletics are so much greater than the cost of sport that the entire college benefits financially. Buildings may be erected and scholarship monies may grow. A less radical claim for the benefits which may accrue from campus sport contends that "major" sports such as football and basketball generate revenue sufficient to fund their own expenses as well as the costs of most other sport and recreation programs. Not only would traditionally nonrevenue-producing sport such as tennis and water polo be funded, but the expenses of intramurals and recreational equipment and facilities might be covered by football and basketball profits. Finally, the most conservative interpretation of the doctrine of good works contends that football and basketball revenues are sufficient to cover their own costs. Other athletic and recreational activities must themselves find sufficient funding.

With the introduction of athletics to the already economically hard-pressed colleges and universities of late 19th and early 20th century America, the doctrine of good works offered some hope of relief from further financial hardships. Along with claims concerning the educational value of athletics—that sport participation builds character and that it helps student grades—the financial rationale for sport programs eased the entry onto campus of athleticism, a program previously foreign to the cognitively oriented college and university of the era.

Though few other self-proclaimed educational programs of the institution were required to be self-supporting, intercollegiate sport found greater justification for its place on campus with the doctrine of good works rationale. Controversy remains, however, concerning the validity of this rationale. Questions center about the following themes:

- Is ''winning'' athletics necessary for attendance at events and contributions by alumni and boosters? Does the need to win subvert the moral base of academe?
- What is the actual level of financial gain generated by athletics? Are legislative and public monies increased? Are students attracted or retained who would otherwise not attend the institution? What is the value of publicity?
- Considering the cost of athletic teams, are they cost-effective? Do they promote the primary educational objectives of the college or university efficiently given their level of funding?
- Should men's revenue-producing sports (football and/or basketball) be required to cover the expenses of other nonrevenue producing men's sports? Should the men's athletic program be required to cover the expenses of deficit-producing women's athletic teams?
- What is the effect of outside monies on the autonomy of the campus—given levels of funding derived from booster groups, television revenues, and promotion sales? Is the college/university becoming too dependent on these financial sources, and is it thus losing control of its own governance to these outside groups?

Though avid proponents and scathing critics might have us believe otherwise, clearly there are few simple answers to any of these questions. Given the availability of financial data, many of these questions require sophisticated longitudinal investigation employing multivariate techniques which take into account the various levels of play and types of costs and revenues. Validation of the economic claims for intercollegiate sport are further complicated by the many different types of colleges and universities in America. Among the over 2,000 4-year colleges and universities in the United States, there are many distinctive visions of the mission of higher education and the value of programs such as athletics for men and women in the educational and financial scheme of the institution. There cannot be simple answers to the question of the validity of the doctrine of good works.

The complicated economic nature of intercollegiate sport is illustrated in Glenn Begly's overview of the current economic status of campus athletics. Given the multiple levels of play and the types of sport played, conclusions concerning the economic status of intercollegiate sport must be specific and not overly generalized. Though the biggest level of football playing institutions seem to make money, schools competing at other levels of play lose more money through sport than they generate. While deficits are expected to increase in almost all types of schools, varying sources of intercollegiate sport deficits will have a differential impact on each institution's athletic offerings and internal governance.

In their article "Winning and Giving: Another Look" Sack and Watkins review conceptually and empirically the notion that athletic success stimulates alumni contributions to the institution. Should large athletic expenditures be justified as an economic investment that will return dividends to the institution? Given the degree to which sport is capable of building community pride and identification with the institution it might seem reasonable to expect symbolic identification with a winning school through increased alumni donations.

REFERENCES

CHU, D. (1979). Origins of the connection of sport and physical education. *Journal of Sport and Social Issues,* **3**, 22-32.

MIDDLETON, L. (1982, March 3). Large expenses for sports programs lead more colleges to seek funds from honors. *Chronicle of Higher Education,* **24**, 5-6.

RAIBORN, M.H. (1982). *Revenues and expenses of intercollegiate athletic programs.* Mission, KS: National Collegiate Athletic Association.

STEVENSON, C. (1985). College athletics and "character": The decline and fall of socialization research. In D. Chu & J. Seagrave (Eds.), *Sport and Higher Education* (pp. 247-264). Champaign, IL: Human Kinetics.

Chapter 20

The Current Economic Status of Intercollegiate Sport

Glenn Begly
Skidmore College

Harsh economic realities have influenced nearly all aspects of American society, including the affairs of colleges and universities. Chu (1983) has suggested that because of "economic and enrollment difficulties, the derived organizational goal of survival is *the primary* (author's emphasis) consideration of American higher education."

Despite these concerns, intercollegiate athletics have maintained and even increased their national visibility (NCAA, 1983). Athletics are an important component of the public image of higher education. A recent survey of college presidents by *The Chronicle of Higher Education* indicated that 86% of the respondents felt that success in sport facilitated the fund-raising programs of their institutions (Crowl, 1983). This rather imposing figure is even more remarkable in light of the fact that 67% of the same subject pool reported that *none* of their athletic programs produced *any* revenue whatsoever. Based on these results, it would appear that intercollegiate athletics are currently occupying a crucial—in the eyes of university leaders—and yet ambiguous—in terms of their own viability—position.

CURRENT ECONOMIC STATUS

Raiborn's (1982) study of the revenues and expenses of National Collegiate Athletic Association (NCAA) programs provides a foundation for assessing the current economic status of intercollegiate sport. The major purposes of Raiborn's investigation were to (a) describe the revenue and expense categories of athletic programs; (b) define trends in revenues and expenses from 1977-1981; (c) identify factors underlying such trends; and (d) discover how sources of revenue and revenue contribution to total expenses have changed over the duration of the study. The investigation utilized a questionnaire mailed to all NCAA members. The respondents were classified into six groups "based upon the criteria of dominance of particular sports within the program and relative strength of athletic programs according to level of competition" (Raiborn, 1982, p. 7).

Table 1 indicates that expenses have exceeded revenues in all categories except for Division I schools with football. Raiborn (1982) noted that this data provide substantial support for the opinion expressed in the survey that rising costs of athletics are a serious problem which need to be controlled.

Table 1
Financial Operational Highlights for Men's Athletics
Fiscal years 1977, 1978, and 1981
(Dollar Amounts in Thousands)

Financial and Operational Measures*	Class A**	Class B	Class C	Class D	Class E	Class F
Average Total Revenues						
Fiscal year 1981 (1980-81)	$3,391	$248	$ 56	$426	$102	$ 30
Fiscal year 1978 (1977-78)	2,368	164	40	277	74	24
Percentage increase	43%	51%	40%	72%	38%	25%
Average Total Expenses						
Fiscal year 1981	$3,243	$392	$249	$631	$232	$144
Fiscal year 1978	2,238	287	188	410	163	106
Percentage increase	45%	37%	32%	54%	42%	36%
Average Number of Sports						
Fiscal year 1981	12	10	11	9	8	9
Fiscal year 1977	10	10	11	9	8	8
Average Number of Athletes						
Fiscal year 1981	343	305	294	150	147	169
Fiscal year 1977	337	303	308	145	135	159

*Unless indicated otherwise, all information reported in this study involves only men's athletic programs.

**Class A: Division I schools with football
Class B: Division II schools with football
Class C: Division III schools with football
Class D: Division I schools in basketball without football
Class E: Division II schools in basketball without football
Class F: Division III schools in basketball without football

Note. From Mitchell H. Raiborn, *Revenues and expenses of intercollegiate athletic programs.* Mission, Kansas: National Collegiate Athletic Association, 1982, p. 9. Reprinted with permission.

The analysis of revenues revealed a number of trends. First, a dramatic disparity in revenues existed among athletic programs classified as Division I. That is, while a relatively few of the elite athletic programs generated considerable income, far more produced vastly smaller amounts. This funding would seem to corroborate the Crowl (1983) survey of Division I institutions, in which only 6% reported that both football and basketball produce a surplus, 19% football only, and 20% basketball only. Second, all categories showed real revenue growth consistent with inflation. Third, the sources of intercollegiate athletic support underwent a marked change during the period of the study. Sources of revenue related specifically to athletic events displayed a decline while "unearned revenue sources, such as contributions from alumni and government" increased (Raiborn, 1982, p. 22). As the total revenue related to intercollegiate athletics increased, so did revenue from the unearned sources.

Expenses of intercollegiate athletics were also analyzed by Raiborn (1982). Generally, expenses increased across all levels of competition, with a wide range within each group. Table 2 indicates that expenses for each category of institu-

Table 2

Analysis of Trends in Total Expenses
Fiscal Years 1970-1981
(Dollar Amounts in Thousands)

Expense Measures by Respondent Category	1970	1973	1977	1981
Class A Institutions				
Average total expenses	$1,263	$1,614	$2,213	$3,243
Ratio to 1970 expenses	100	128	175	257
Class B Institutions				
Average total expenses	$ 265	$ 339	$ 460	$ 392
Ratio to 1970 expenses	100	128	174	148
Class C Institutions				
Average total expenses	$ 125	$ 136	$ 171	$ 249
Ratio to 1970 expenses	100	109	137	199
Class D Institutions				
Average total expenses	$ 216	$ 235	$ 317	$ 631
Ratio to 1970 expenses	100	109	147	292
Class E Institutions				
Average total expenses	$ 80	$ 134	$ 146	$ 232
Ratio to 1970 expenses	100	167	182	290
Class F Institutions				
Average total expenses	$ 48	$ 59	$ 83	$ 144
Ratio to 1970 expenses	100	123	173	300

Note. From Mitchell H. Raiborn, *Revenues and expenses of intercollegiate athletic programs*. Mission, Kansas: National Collegiate Athletic Association, 1982, p. 24. Reprinted with permission.

Table 3
Operating Expenses Classified by Object of Expenditure
Fiscal Years 1977 and 1981
(Dollar Amounts in Thousands)

Average Expense and Percentage of Total Expenses by Respondent Category	Grants in Aid		Guarantees and Options		Salaries and Wages		Team and Other Travel		Equipment and Supplies		All Other Expenses		Total Expenses
	Mean	Percent	Mean	Percent	Mean	Percent	Mean	Percent	Mean	Percent	Mean	Percent	
Class A Institutions													
Fiscal Year 1981	$556	16%	$408	11%	$1,012	30%	$436	13%	$157	5%	$844	25%	100%
Fiscal year 1977	432	18	315	12	652	28	264	12	116	5	560	25	100
Class B Institutions													
Fiscal Year 1981	$148	26%	34	5%	$ 148	23%	$ 69	15%	$ 37	8%	$108	23%	100%
Fiscal Year 1977	161	29	16	2	180	32	70	14	44	9	85	14	100
Class C Institutions													
Fiscal Year 1981	$223	10%	$ 10	1%	$ 160	38%	$ 51	18%	$ 30	10%	$ 68	23%	100%
Fiscal Year 1977	97	14	15	2	104	39	31	15	30	15	42	15	100
Class D Institutions													
Fiscal Year 1981	$184	25%	$ 23	3%	$ 233	32%	$122	17%	$ 47	6%	$131	17%	100%
Fiscal Year 1977	126	27	21	4	116	27	50	13	24	6	89	23	100
Class E Institutions													
Fiscal Year 1981	$ 82	26%	$ 6	1%	$ 91	30%	$ 45	16%	$ 25	9%	$ 53	18%	100%
Fiscal Year 1977	57	28	6	1	68	34	23	14	14	8	30	15	100
Class F Institutions													
Fiscal Year 1981	$ 13	*	$ 2	*	$ 126	52%	$ 28	16%	$ 22	14%	$ 31	18%	100%
Fiscal Year 1977	65	9	4	*	111	44	28	12	21	11	58	24	100

*Less than 1%

Note. From Mitchell H. Raiborn, Revenues and expenses of intercollegiate athletic programs. Mission, Kansas: National Collegiate Athletic Association, 1982, p. 29. Reprinted with permission.

tion increased in each of the years sampled, with four of the six categories increasing 50% or more over the duration of the study. Specific expenses for each group were analyzed as a percentage of total revenues. Table 3 shows that the most common trend across the classifications was a decrease in grants-in-aid and an increase in salaries and wages. These two factors combined accounted for the bulk of expenses.

RELATIONSHIPS BETWEEN EXPENSES AND REVENUES

Based on the data produced in his discussion of revenues and expenses, Raiborn (1982) was able to draw a number of conclusions regarding expense and revenue relationships. Most of the institutions surveyed indicated that either operating expenses (travel, etc.) or sports which were not self-supporting were sustained by institutional resources. Given that many institutions operate athletics under a deficit, it is not surprising that the least common policy regarding revenue and expenses was to run a self-sustaining sports program without using institutional resources. The report also concluded that the "general trend indicates that revenue growth was not sufficient to match the increase in total operating expenses" (Raiborn, 1982, p. 40). Additionally, while the number of upper level (Class A) institutions reporting deficits dropped 7% in 1980-81, the average deficit increased. It may be implied that although some programs are getting richer, many more are getting poorer. Moreover, economic difficulties are apparently one source of a trend which indicates a decrease in the number of opportunities for participation across the classes of institutions surveyed.

When examining Raiborn's (1982) report, it is important to recall that the data on women's athletics are relegated to a separate section. Raiborn (1982) supports this method of discussion in order to "maintain comparability with prior financial trends" (p. 47). While this treatment of the data may in some sense be logical, it does little to illuminate the current economic status of intercollegiate sport as a whole. The majority of women's athletic programs presently exist under the same organizational umbrella as men's programs (Carpenter & Acosta, 1983). Therefore, these data should be considered along with that associated with men's intercollegiate athletics.

Table 4 shows that revenues produced by women's athletics fell short of expenses in all categories. As the average total expenses of women's programs increased, so did the percentage of women's expenses paid by men's programs.

If the financial picture of men's and women's intercollegiate athletics is discouraging when the two are considered independently, a combination of the two sources of data is even more dismal. Chu (1983) tabulated total revenues and expenses for men's and women's athletics for 1981. Table 5 displays a deficit in every category. As Chu (1983) concludes, "while there are specific institu-

Table 4

Total Revenues and Expenses of Women's Athletic Programs
Fiscal Years 1978-1981)
(Dollar Amounts in Thousands)

Average Financial Results by Respondent Category	1978	1979	1980	1981
Class A*Institutions				
Average total revenues (a)	$ 70	$ 93	$109	$124
Average total expenses	161	244	339	392
Expenses paid by men's program	40%	44%	46%	44%
Class B Institutions				
Average total revenues	$ 25	$ 24	$ 17	$ 19
Average total expenses	62	68	89	101
Expenses paid by men's program	26%	24%	21%	32%
Class C Institutions				
Average total revenues	$ 10	$ 8	$ 8	$ 7
Average total expenses	28	33	40	48
Expenses paid by men's program	15%	12%	13%	16%
Class D Institutions				
Average total revenues	$ 8	$ 13	$ 15	$ 44
Average total expenses	95	151	167	188
Expenses paid by men's program	7%	18%	19%	19%
Class E Institutions				
Average total revenues	$ 10	$ 16	$ 25	$ 27
Average total expenses	36	45	56	72
Expenses paid by men's program	1%	10%	9%	12%
Class F Institutions				
Average total revenues	$ 17	$ 19	$ 17	$ 15
Average total expenses	26	31	36	37
Expenses paid by men's program	0%	0%	0%	2%

*Class A: Division I schools with football
Class B: Division II schools with football
Class C: Division III schools with football
Class D: Division I schools in basketball without football
Class E: Division II schools in basketball without football
Class F: Division III schools in basketball without football

Note. From Mitchell H. Raiborn, Revenues and expenses of intercollegiate athletic programs. Mission, Kansas: National Collegiate Athletic Association, 1982, p. 9. Reprinted with permission.

tional exceptions to the deficit rule, these representations of economic tendencies demonstrate the financial difficulties generally facing intercollegiate athletics.''

Clearly, inclusion of women's data would seem to be essential in future analyses. Raiborn's (1982) study indicated that the expense of women's athletics

Table 5

**Total Revenues and Expenses for Men's and Women's Athletics Fiscal Year 1981
(Thousands of Dollars)**

Average Financial Results by Respondent Category	Men's Athletics	Women's Athletics	Total	Average Deficit
Class A Institutions				
Average revenues	$3,391	$124	$3,515	$120
Average expenses	3,243	392	3,625	
Class B Institutions				
Average revenues	248	19	267	226
Average expenses	392	101	493	
Class C Institutions				
Average revenues	56	7	63	234
Average expenses	249	48	297	
Class D Institutions				
Average revenues	476	44	520	299
Average expenses	631	188	819	
Class E Institutions				
Average revenues	102	27	129	175
Average expenses	232	72	304	
Class F Institutions				
Average revenues	30	15	45	136
Average expenses	144	37	181	

Note. From Chu, D. Economics and intercollegiate sport. In *Sport and higher education: Strange bedfellows.* Unpublished manuscript, Skidmore College, 1983. Reprinted with permission.

programs was ranked as the primary cause for increased expenses in six of the eight respondent categories and second in the other two.

What, then, are the economic prospects for intercollegiate sport? Tables 6 and 7 project an ever-widening gap between expenses and revenues across most categories of men's competition. Inclusion of finances from women's athletics would undoubtedly increase the disparity. Obviously, if revenues cannot meet expenses, programs must either be sustained with monies from other sources or curtailed. Table 8 depicts the increase in passive or unearned revenues and the decrease in revenues directly associated with athletic events, such as tickets, activity fees, guarantees, and options.

One major source of passive revenue has been donations from boosters and alumni. A national survey (*New York Times*, 1983) found that athletic donations have grown rapidly despite a weak national economy. The six major conferences surveyed (58/59 institutions responded) averaged $1.74 million per institution in donations, with one university garnering $3.14 million. The report cited Andy

Table 6

Forecasts of Average Total Expenses
Fiscal Years 1982-1985
(Dollar Amounts in Thousands)

Respondent Category	Actual Expenses 1981	Forecast of Average Total Expenses			
		1982	1983	1984	1985
Class A Institutions	$3,243	$3,404	$3,674	$3,944	$4,214
Class B Institutions	392	425	460	495	530
Class C Institutions	249	262	281	300	319
Class D Institutions	631	713	791	868	946
Class E Institutions	232	233	252	270	289
Class F Institutions	144	159	174	188	203

Note. From Mitchell H. Raiborn, *Revenues and expenses of intercollegiate athletic programs.* Mission, Kansas: National Collegiate Athletic Association, 1982, p. 25. Reprinted with permission.

Table 7

Forecasts of Average Total Revenues
Fiscal Years 1982-1985
(Dollar Amounts in Thousands)

Respondent Category	Actual Expenses 1981	Forecast of Average Total Expenses			
		1982	1983	1984	1985
Class A Institutions	$3,391	$3,598	$3,898	$4,199	$4,499
Class B Institutions	248	271	299	327	355
Class C Institutions	56	60	65	70	75
Class D Institutions	476	529	593	657	720
Class E Institutions	102	104	112	120	127
Class F Institutions	30	32	35	37	40

Note. From Mitchell H. Raiborn, *Revenues and expenses of intercollegiate athletic programs.* Mission, Kansas: National Collegiate Athletic Association, 1982, p. 15, 28. Reprinted with permission.

Miller, director of Florida State University's fund raising, on the economic lure of college athletics during such lean times: "Sports are such a part of the American way of life, people will give up a lot for a winner" (*New York Times*, 1983, p. 20). *The Wall Street Journal* (Klein, 1982) reported that donations represented the fastest rising component of funding, increasing from 5% of the total revenues in 1962 to 11% in 1981. In the same article, Mitchell Raiborn, author of the

Table 8
Revenue Sources: Passive and Active

Combined Percentage of Total Revenues for	Unearned or Passive Revenues*		
	1973	1977	1981
Class A	12%	14%	69%
Class B	39	40	46
Class C	36	47	35
Class D	19	16	29
Class E	18	35	71
Class F	21	30	74

Combined Percentage of Total Revenues for	Revenues Related to Athletic Events (Active Sources)**		
	1973	1977	1981
Class A	75%	76%	69%
Class B	54	42	50
Class C	52	37	54
Class D	70	60	60
Class E	80	57	27
Class F	78	68	18

*Passive Sources: Student assessments, contributions, government support.

**Active Sources: Ticket sales, guarantees, activity fees, options.

Note. From Chu, D. Economics and intercollegiate sport. In Sport and higher education: Strange bedfellows. Unpublished manuscript, Skidmore College, 1983. Reprinted with permission.

NCAA (1982) study cited previously, noted that if donations were deleted from athletic programs "relatively few schools would break even on sports. That's how expensive and competitive they've become" (Klein, 1982, p. 1). As the financial impact of booster clubs and alumni increase in intercollegiate sport, so does the possibility that special interest groups might compromise the conduct of intercollegiate athletics.

Stanley Ward, counsel for the University of Oklahoma, said, "If money is the root of all evil, it's also the mother's milk of college athletics" (Vance, 1982a, p. 16). The money Ward specifically refers to is television revenue. Monies provided the NCAA from television networks are of substantial importance to the schools and conferences whose games are televised and currently support many athletic programs whose teams never appear on the screen (Vance, 1982).

Not surprisingly, some universities whose teams make frequent television appearances have sought to wrest television control from the NCAA. In a 1982 court decision, NCAA television pacts were found to violate antitrust laws (Vance, 1982b). The NCAA held the position that membership in the organization was voluntary, thereby circumventing an antitrust violation. The court, however, ruled that although NCAA membership was theoretically voluntary, no school could feasibly operate an intercollegiate program outside NCAA membership, particularly as related to sports programs which might be attractive television properties.

The stakes in this confrontation are high, $263.5 million for televising college football alone. As the final ruling will undoubtedly be subject to a lengthy appeal process, the outcome is far from certain. It is, however, certain that the final decision will have a profound and lasting impact on collegiate sport. The issue is likely to be complicated by the emergence of cable television as a lucrative source of income. Some universities have already sold cable rights of basketball games (Vance, 1982b). Cable broadcast of 24 of the 1983 NCAA basketball playoff games alone grossed $607,000 (NCAA, 1983). Because of its relatively recent rise in media popularity, intercollegiate basketball may be open to greater institutional and less NCAA control. Any institutional dispensation of basketball in avenues which diverge from football could have powerful ramifications on court decisions on the economic control of college sport.

CONCLUSIONS

Based on the current available data and trends, it is possible to draw a number of conclusions about the current economic status of intercollegiate sport:

1. Total expenses currently exceed revenues generated at almost all levels of men's intercollegiate sport.
2. Costs are increasing despite a decrease in grants-in-aid.
3. Women's intercollegiate sports programs are rarely, if ever, self-sustaining.
4. If men's and women's programs are analyzed together, deficits exist at every level.
5. The cost of intercollegiate programs cannot typically be sustained by income generated through ticket sales.
6. Opportunities for participation may be curtailed by rising costs.
7. An increased reliance on revenue generated by special interest groups could compromise the administration of intercollegiate athletics.
8. Current legislation over television rights may have a drastic and far-reaching impact on intercollegiate athletics.
9. Despite financial problems, there is no reason to believe that big-time intercollegiate sport will be less visible or important in the public eye.

REFERENCES

ATHLETIC donations rise. (1983, February 2). *The New York Times*, p. 20.

CARPENTER, L.J., & Acosta, R.V. (1985). The status of women in intercollegiate athletics: A five year national study. In D. Chu, J. Segrave, & B. Becker, (Eds.), *Sport and higher education.* Champaign, IL: Human Kinetics Publishers.

CHU, D. (1983). Economics and intercollegiate sport. In *Sport and higher education: Strange bedfellows.* Unpublished manuscript, Skidmore College, Saratoga Springs, NY.

CROWL, J.A. (1983, January 5). NCAA can prevent abuses, many college chiefs say. *The Chronicle of Higher Education,* p. 21.

KLEIN, F.C. (1982, October 29). Money plays. *The Wall Street Journal,* p. 1.

NORTH Carolina State. (1983, April 13). Houston game basketball's biggest TV draw ever. *The NCAA News,* p. 1.

RAIBORN, M.H. (1982). *Revenues and expenses of intercollegiate athletic programs.* Mission, KS: National Collegiate Athletic Association.

VANCE, N.S. (1982a, September 8). Colleges, NCAA clash over how to split increasingly big money for TV sports. *The Chronicle of Higher Education,* pp. 13, 16.

VANCE, N.S. (1982b, September 22). Judge rules NCAA television pacts violate anti-trust laws, says colleges own TV rights. *The Chronicle of Higher Education,* pp. 1, 10.

Chapter 21

Winning and Giving

Allen L. Sack and Charles Watkins
University of New Haven

Academically, it is difficult to justify the existence of highly commercialized sport on America's college campuses. In fact, evidence accumulated over the years (Hanford, 1974; Savage, 1929; Underwood, 1980) suggests that college sport, in the form of mass commercial entertainment, subverts many cherished academic values. Thus, various rationalizations for big-time college sport have tended to focus on important nonacademic functions it performs for universities, surrounding communities, and the nation as a whole.

One of the most widely held beliefs about big-time college sports is that it generates alumni contributions. Some have argued (Sack, 1977) that even if a school cannot cover its athletic expenses with gate receipts and television revenue, a successful sports program can bring in revenue indirectly through increased alumni contributions. Sigelman and Carter (1979) document that a wide variety of people, including sportswriters, athletic directors, college fund raisers, and college presidents are convinced that athletic success is a major factor affecting alumni giving. The major purpose of this study will be to review some of the arguments for and against the notion that athletic success stimulates alumni giving and to examine this supposed relationshnip empirically.

There are good theoretical reasons for expecting alumni support to be affected by a school's athletic performance. Studies of collectivities as large as nations (Mandell, 1971) and as small as high schools and universities (Albonico, 1967; Coleman, 1960; Stein, 1977) have demonstrated that sport can generate intense group loyalties, and can affect the degree to which individual members are willing to put group interests above their own. According to Anderson and Stone (1980) this is especially true in modern industrial societies where family, religion, and other traditional sources of solidarity are declining in importance. Given sport's capacity to build community pride and the incredible emphasis Americans place on winning, it seems reasonable to hypothesize that success in college sport will increase alumni identity with and financial support for their alma maters.

A number of studies suggest, however, that athletics are not uppermost in the minds of the majority of alumni. Frey (1979) found that Washington State University alumni rank expenditures for athletics fairly low on their university's list of financial priorities. Far more important than sports, in their view, were expenditures on academic programs, salary increases for faculty, maintenance of classroom facilities and so forth. Frey did find, however, that the 32 members of the Board of Directors of the Alumni Association were far more likely than average alumni to rank athletic expenditures as a high priority. Frey concludes that this small group of influential alumni, because they work closely with top administrators, are able to create the false impression that most alumni share their enthusiasm for college sports.

Conklin's (1976) survey of Notre Dame alumni adds support to Frey's findings. When asked about their motivation for contributing to the alumni fund, Notre Dame Alumni ranked the following as most important: alleviating the university's financial need, keeping private higher education viable, and recognizing Notre Dame's academic promise. At the bottom of the motivational scale were obtaining an income deduction, gratitude for financial aid received as a student, and endorsement of Notre Dame's athletic success. Both Frey's and Conklin's studies lend support to the argument that athletic success is not as important a determinant of alumni giving as is often assumed. Frey even suggests that "if college and university presidents were to act to curtail and even eliminate athletic programs the reaction would not be as severe as anticipated" (Frey, 1972, p. 12).

Sack's 1978 survey of 529 Notre Dame alumni indicates that Frey and Conklin may be underestimating the zeal with which alumni follow their school's athletic fortunes.[1] When asked to respond to the statement "I would be less likely to give financial support to Notre Dame if football were sharply deemphasized," 50% of the respondents agreed, 40% disagreed and 6% were undecided. Importantly, agreement with this statement was found to be related to the respondent's income. While 65% of those making more $50,000 a year or more said they would withdraw support, this was true of only 47% of those in the $30-49,000 category and 45% of those making less than $30,000.

What these findings suggest is that alumni may place a lower priority on college sport relative to other university concerns as long as athletics are not under attack. However, effort by administrators to severely curtail or eliminate a program might well produce hostile reactions from large numbers of alumni, especially wealthy and influential ones. The following comment written on the back of a questionnaire returned by a very wealthy Notre Dame alumnus in Sack's survey is informative in this regard:

Not only would I be less likely to contribute to the university if they deemphasized football, I would cease contributing altogether which would also lose for the University the matching contribution of my company. In addition, I would feel that I had been deprived of part of my academic, social and intellectual heritage from the University. If he (Father Hesburgh) makes this move I am no longer going to affiliated with him in the University or in the government or anywhere else. Tell Father Hesburgh that by commissioning this survey he is not messing with football!—he's messing with a part of my life and I resent it deeply.

It is clear that some alumni do take sport very seriously and base their financial support on their school's athletic policies. Whether there are enough such people to have a significant impact on overall alumni giving is not clear. Nor has there been much research to determine under what conditions alumni give and withdraw their support. Sigelman and Carter (1979) attempt to address both of these questions, at least in part. On the basis of an analysis of financial data compiled by the Council for Financial Aid to Education, the authors attempted to test the hypothesis that total alumni giving rises and falls with the fortunes of big-time intercollegiate athletic programs.

Although the methods used by the authors were an improvement over earlier studies in this area (Budig, 1976; Springer, 1974), they were still not adequate to justify their sweeping conclusions. Regardless of what they set out to do, Sigelman and Carter ended up subjecting the following questions to empirical investigation: Is a school's won-loss record in a given year a good predictor of yearly percentage increases and decreases in alumni contributions? Given the author's operational definition of the independent variable, in example, percentage of games won in a given year, one might argue that their finding of no relationship was guaranteed from the outset.

If a perennial football power like Alabama goes 11-1 in 1980, there is no good reason to expect a percentage increase in alumni contributions over the previous year. Rather, one would predict a continuation of the same high level of alumni giving that has characterized their 10 or so previous successful seasons. The real issue, and one Sigelman and Carter fail to address empirically, is what happens when a perennial power like Notre Dame, Ohio State, or Alabama suddenly has a losing season. Conversely, what happens when a consistent loser like Pitt in the 1960s suddenly becomes a winner?

The most convincing evidence linking winning and giving is derived from that handful of cases where schools have had dramatic changes in won-loss records. Sigleman and Carter themselves cite examples like Ohio State in 1966, the University of Georgia in 1961, the University of Missouri in 1960, and Amherst and Wilkes College in the 1960s. In each case, alumni contributions seemed to vary considerably with changes in the school's athletic fortunes. By ignoring the issue of continuity and change in won-loss records from year to year, the authors could not test their major hypothesis. Thus their study, while important in terms of suggesting methods future researchers might use, produced findings that were less than convincing.

METHODS

The approach taken in the present study was to borrow heavily from Sigelman and Carter's methodology while at the same time redefining the athletic success variable in terms of yearly changes in the percentage of games won. It should be noted that the hypothesis to be tested here addresses only one dimension of the winning and giving question. That is, Do yearly fluctuations in games won in football produce concommitant changes in alumni contributions?

The 166 schools included in this study were taken from a list of teams playing Division I football in the fall of 1978.[2] For each of these schools, won-loss records were compiled for the 1969 through 1978 football seasons from *NCAA Football Guides*. Data alumni giving during this same period were derived from a Council of Financial Aid to Education publication entitled *Voluntary Support for Higher Education*. Alumni data gathered by CFAE by means of a questionnaire sent to all institutions of higher education on a yearly basis. Although data for some schools are incomplete and in some instances of questionable reliability, the CFAE data are the best available for practical purposes.[3]

The independent variable, change in games won, was operationalized as the change in the percentage of games won by a team from one year to the next. The dependent variable, percentage change in alumni giving, was measured in three ways. First, yearly percentage changes in total alumni giving were determined by the following formula:

$$\%\text{change in total alumni giving} = \frac{\text{total giving (most recent year)} - \text{total giving (year before)}}{\text{total giving (year before)}}$$

It was also possible using CFAE data to determine the proportion of alumni who were solicited in the annual fund drive who actually sent in contributions. The change in this proportion from one year to the next was calculated for each school. Finally, the percentage change in the size of the average gift to the annual fund was calculated as follows:

$$\%\text{ change in the \$ value of average gift from year to year} = \frac{\text{\$ value of average gift (most recent year)} - \text{\$ value of average gift (year before)}}{\text{\$ value of average gift (year before)}}$$

Because data were gathered for a 10-year period, it was possible to calculate 9 separate year-to-year changes in games won and alumni giving for each school. This yielded a total of 9 x 166, or 1,494 possible observations. This large number of observations made it possible to examine the relationship between winning and giving, not only by year (as was done by Sigelman and Carter) but by conference and for public, private, and church-related institutions as well. It can be hypothesized that while alumni in football-oriented conferences like the Big 8 might be influenced by athletic performance, such would not be the case in the Ivy League.

Another reason for using as many observations as possible was that there appears to be a great deal of continuity in won-loss records at a given school over the years. In the 1974-75, 1975-76 comparison years, for instance, only 9 of the 166 schools had a change in total games won of 5 or more. Sixty-eight percent of the schools changed by 2 or less, 17% by 3 and only 9% by 4. One would hardly expect very small changes to have a significant impact on alumni giving. By expanding the number of cases to 1,494, it was hoped that there would be a sufficient variation on the independent variable to test the major hypothesis.

FINDINGS

The results of the correlation analysis of the relationship between athletic success and the three measures of alumni financial support are summarized in Table 1. It is clear that there is no relationship between winning and giving when all possible cases are included in the analysis. The same is true when the analysis is limited to public, private, or church-related institutions. In none of these cases, regardless of the measure of alumni giving used, do the resulting correlation coefficients approach accepted levels of statistical significance.

Breaking the schools down by conference produced a few statistically significant, albeit weak, correlations. In the Atlantic Coast Conference, comprised of schools like Clemson, Duke, Maryland, and North Carolina, there was a modest positive relationship between yearly changes in games won and total alumni giving. Athletic success was not significantly related, however, to increase in the proportion of alumni contributing or to changes in the size of the average gifts to the alumni fund.

The schools in the Big 10 were among the most conscientious in providing early data to the CFAE. On the basis of 80 observations of Big 10 schools, it was determined that winning and total giving were significantly related. Surprisingly, the relationship was negative. That is, while the percentage of games won increased, alumni contributions decreased. Another statistically significant inverse relationship was found in the Yankee Conference where winning was negatively related to changes in the proportion of alumni contributing to the Annual Fund. Overall, these statistically significant r values were anomalies. Of the 54 correlation coefficients calculated, only 3 were significant at least at the .05 level.

Table 1

Zero Order Correlations Between Change in Percentage of Games Won and 3 Measures of Percentage Change in Alumni Financial Support[a]

	% Change in Total Alumni Contributions	Change in $ of Alumni Who Gave	% Change in The Average Gift
Total	.02 (980)	.05 (894)	−.03 (891)
Public	.01 (848)	.06 (781)	−.03 (775)
Private	−.11 (228)	.05 (214)	.00 (216)
Church-Related	.07 (86)	−.01 (86)	.06 (84)
Conference[b]			
Atlantic Coast	.32 (58) *	.09 (62)	.21 (60)
Big 8	.01 (46)	.02 (46)	−14 (46)
Big Ten	−.39 (80) *	−.06 (75)	−.19 (78)
Independents	.02 (228)	.09 (229)	−.07 (226)
Ivy League	−.09 (71)	−.07 (64)	.16 (64)
Mid-American	.11 (79)	−.09 (75)	−.05 (74)
Missouri Valley	.08 (46)	.17 (33)	−.13 (33)
Ohio Valley	.01 (26)	.15 (20)	−.26 (18)
Pacific 10	−.03 (75)	.23 (63)	.05 (59)
Southeastern	−.11 (66)	.11 (61)	−.01 (59)
Southern	.22 (39)	.25 (38)	−20 (38)
Southwest	−.21 (48)	−.20 (45)	.18 (45)
Western Atlantic	.27 (41)	.09 (24)	.13 (27)
Yankee	.26 (30)	−.39 (30) *	.26 (32)

[a] The number of observation is in parentheses.

[b] Five conferences were omitted because missing data created extremely low-cell frequencies.

*Statistically significant at .01

DISCUSSION

This study has established fairly conclusively that yearly fluctuations in a school's football performances have little or no impact on yearly changes in alumni contributions. However, these findings should not be interpreted to mean that an athletic program cannot affect alumni contributions in a variety of other ways. Perhaps the very fact that a school has a visible sports program, regardless of changes in won-loss records, stimulates alumni giving. College sport is often the center of campus social life. Around it has grown homecomings, football weekends, and a wide variety of collegiate rituals which keep alumni in touch with their schools. A losing season may not affect alumni giving, but an attempt to eliminate college sport at a school with a strong athletic tradition might well lead to financial disaster.

Notre Dame is a good case in point. In the 10 years covered in this study, an average of 47% of Notre Dame alumni solicited in the Annual Fund campaign actually contributed, and the average gift was about $150. Few schools outside the Ivy League have that kind of commitment from their alumni. It is difficult to believe, given Notre Dame's history, that football could be downgraded to the level of intramurals without very serious reductions in alumni financial support. This would be true of most schools with a tradition of athletic excellence.

It should be noted that alumni response to a losing season or to an attempt to deemphasize sport need not take the form of an immediate withdrawal of alumni contributions. First would come letters and phone calls to college presidents and governing boards threatening the withdrawal of support. Usually, this would be enough to have a coach fired or to force antiathletic administrators to rethink their positions. If a school continued to pursue a policy of deemphasis, or if it continued to produce losing teams one would then predict a withdrawal of alumni contributions as a strategy of last resort. Obviously, the methods used in this study as well as the methods used by Sigelman and Carter are not adequate to investigate this complex process.

Perhaps a series of in-depth interviews with college presidents who have tried to deemphasize sports but have met considerable opposition from alumni would shed light on the way sportsminded alumni shape athletic policy. The case of Yale's President Giammati is one that comes to mind. Surveys of alumni attitudes toward sport and giving on the lines of Frey and Conklin might also be useful if care is taken to ask the right questions. Whatever the method, it is clear that the role of athletics in generating alumni financial support remains a topic need of further empirical research. At present, many issues remain unresolved.

REFERENCES

ALBONICO, R. (1967). Modern university sport as a contribution to social integration. *International Review of Sport Sociology, 2, 155-162.*

ANDERSON & Stone, G. (1980, October 18). *A search for community.* Paper presented at the First Annual Conference of The North American Society of Sport Sociology, Denver, CO.

BUDIG, J.E. (1976). The relationships among intercollegiate athletics, enrollment, and voluntary support for public higher education. Unpublished doctoral, Illinois State University.

COLEMAN, J.S. (1961). *The adolescent society.* New York: Free Press.

CONKLIN, R. (1976). Unmasking the Notre Dame alumnus. *Notre Dame Magazine.*

COUNCIL for Financial Aid to Education. Voluntary Support for Higher Education. New York: CFAE (1969-79).

FREY, J.H. (1977). *The place of athletics in the educational priorities of university alumni.* Paper presented at the Pacific Sociological Society Meetings.

HANFORD, G.H. (1974). An inquiry into the need for the feasibility of a national study of intercollegiate athletics. Washington, DC: American Council on Education.

MANDELL, R. (1971). *The Nazi Olympics.* New York: Ballantine Books.

NATIONAL Collegiate Athletic Association. *NCAA Official Football Guide*. Shawnee Mission, KS: NCAA (1969-79).

SACK, A. (1977). Big-time college football: Whose free ride? *Quest,* **27**, 87-96.

SACK, A. & Thiel, R. (1979). College football and social mobility. *Sociology of Education,* **52**.

SAVAGE, H. (1929). *American college athletics*. New York: The Carnegie Foundation.

SIGELMAN, L. & Carter, R. (1979). Win one for the giver? Alumni giving and big-time college sports. *Social Sciences Quarterly,* **60**, 284-294.

SPRINGER, F. (1974). The experience of senior colleges that have discontinued football. In Hanford (Ed.), *An inquiry in the feasibility of a national study of intercollegiate athletics*. Washington, DC: American Council on Education.

STEIN, M. (1980). Cult and sport: The case of big red. *Mid-American Review of Sociology,* **2**.

UNDERWOOD, J. (1980) Student athletes: The sham, the shame. *Sports Illustrated,* **52** (21), 36-72.

FOOTNOTES

1. Results of this survey pertaining to social mobility were published in Sack and Theil (1979). Other findings are available on request.

2. Although basketball is very important at many schools, it is football that is the major revenue producer and the game most closely associated with college life and traditions.

3. Discussions with a number of alumni directors revealed that there was some confusion as to the meaning of certain categories listed in the CFAE questionnaire. Such confusion undoubtedly reduced the reliability of their instrument.

Section C

Benefits for Women?

In an era of economic instability (about the turn of the 20th century), college administrators who advocated expansion of sports' foothold on the academic campus, saw athletic programs as a means of dealing with the resource requirements of the college or university. Leaders of struggling institutions, faced with the continual search for students, money, and the prestige which would in the long-run supply both human and financial resources, saw in sport an untapped means of gaining that support. Similarly faced with the need to legitimize athletic programs to concerned faculty and educational critics, sport was deemed both the purveyor of "good works" and of educational benefits (Chu, 1979). Examination of the reality of these two rationales for sport's place on campus becomes all the more important with the growth of women's intercollegiate athletics in an economic climate today which is similar to that about the beginning of the century.

Demographic realities of the 1980s in general have been highly unfavorable to American higher education. Reduced numbers of potential students and the economic scarcities of recession have given college administrators the unenviable task of evaluating the importance of school programs and personnel relative to their cost to the institution. Educational philosophy must be translated into concrete programs in the most efficient manner possible.

Concurrent with the constraints of demography has been a greater societal acceptance of physical activity for girls and women. New athletic ideals of the vigorous female have challenged traditional American normative expectations for female frailty and passivity. With research evidence demonstrating the invalidity of physiological myths concerning the "danger" of sport for women, there has developed among the college age and general population a more favorable view of the sporting woman.

The unfortunate timing of expanding demand for women's sport during this period of economic "belt-tightening" has placed the entire system of American intercollegiate athletics under tremendous strain. Responding to questions concerning the major factors explaining increasing operating costs, athletic directors at all sizes of institutions identified the "expansion of women's programs" as the major cause of increased costs, a factor considered more important than higher costs for scholarships, additional sports, higher salaries, or recruiting expenses. In the minds of most respondents, the economic situation is so worrisome that "serious methods" are deemed immediately needed to control expenses (Raiborn, 1982).

Given the solemnity with which the "burden" of women's intercollegiate sport costs are often viewed by athletic directors, the actual scope of women's sport in American higher education may come as some surprise. Table 1 indicates the level of female participation for the years 1977 and 1981 in NCAA affiliated schools.

As may be seen from this table the relative proportion of women athletes playing intercollegiate sport has risen only slightly during the 4-year span of this study. More importantly, the absolute level of women's participation ranges from 22% to 31% of male participation rates. Well less than one third of all participants in intercollegiate sport are female.

Table 2 provides another perspective on the scope of women's athletics revenues and expenses for the years 1977 and 1981. Figures in parentheses indicate women's costs and income relative to male figures.

A number of interesting findings are evident in this table. Like men's athletics, in almost all cases, women's sport loses money. The only exception to this rule is in "Class A" Division I football playing schools where men's program revenues exceed expenses. Female intercollegiate sport generally does not generate the revenues of men's athletics, but at the same time, neither does it consume as much expense money as does male athletics. Women's athletic expenses range from 12.1% to 31% of male athletic expenses. During the 4-year span of this table's statistics, trends generally indicate the growing proportional cost of women's sport. In the six classes of intercollegiate sport surveyed, four (A, B, C, E) show a general increase relative to male athletic costs. In sum, however, it cannot be said that there has been a significant growth in the cost of women's sport relative to men's sport during the time period 1978 to 1981. During this timeframe in Class A football playing Division I schools, the cost of women's sport has increased $231,000 while the cost of men's programs has increased by $1,005,000. Relative expense changes for all classes are listed in Table 3. As is evident from these figures, while it is indisputable that monies allocated to women's athletics have significantly increased, the rate of increase for monies allocated to men's athletics have risen much more. Dependent upon the class surveyed men's expenses have risen at a rate of almost 2 times (Class E) to 4 times (Class A) the rate of increase for women's athletics. In sum then, while athletic administrators

Table 1

Participating Athletes and Opportunities for Intercollegiate Sport

	1977			1981		
	Men	Women	# Women to All Athletes	Men	Women	# Women to All Athletes
Class A	337 (10)	114 (8)	25%	343 (12)	123 (8)	26%
Class B	303 (10)	75 (6)	20%	305 (10)	86 (6)	22%
Class C	308 (11)	100 (6)	25%	294 (11)	102 (8)	26%
Class D	145 (8)	50 (4)	26%	150 (9)	67 (5)	31%
Class E	135 (8)	46 (4)	25%	147 (8)	60 (6)	29%
Class F	159 (8)	52 (4)	25%	169 (9)	80 (5)	31%

( ) = number of intercollegiate teams available to men or women

Class A = Division I football playing schools, Class B = Division II football playing schools, Class C = Division III football playing schools, Class D = Division I nonfootball playing schools, Class E = Division II nonfootball playing schools, Class F = Division III nonfootball playing schools.

Note: From Mitchell H. Raiborn (1982). *Revenues and expenses of intercollegiate athletic programs.* Mission, KS: National Collegiate Athletic Association. Adapted from Table 4.10, page 48, Tables 4.12-4.17, pages 52-57.

Table 2

Total Revenues and Expenses of Men's and Women's Athletic Programs
(Dollar Amounts in Thousands)

	1978		1979		1980		1981	
	Men's	Women's	Men's	Women's	Men's	Women's	Men's	Women's
Class A								
Average Revenues	2,368 (3.0)	70	2,581 (3.6)	109	2,959 (3.7)	109	3,391 (3.7)	124
Average Expenses	2,238 (7.2)	161	2,460 (9.9)	244	2,875 (11.8)	339	3,242 (12.1)	392
Class B								
Average Revenues	164 (15.2)	25	182 (13.2)	24	212 (8.0)	17	248 (7.7)	19
Average Expenses	287 (21.7)	62	322 (21.1)	68	353 (25.1)	89	392 (25.8)	101
Class C								
Average Revenues	40 (25.0)	10	45 (17.8)	8	51 (15.7)	8	56 (12.5)	7
Average Expenses	188 (14.9)	28	201 (16.4)	33	221 (18.1)	40	249 (19.3)	48
Class D								
Average Revenues	277 (2.9)	8	343 (3.8)	13	384 (3.9)	15	476 (9.3)	44
Average Expenses	410 (23.2)	95	476 (31.8)	151	563 (29.7)	167	631 (29.8)	188
Class E								
Average Revenues	74 (13.5)	10	77 (20.1)	16	86 (29.1)	25	102 (26.5)	27
Average Expenses	163 (22.1)	36	166 (27.1)	45	180 (31.1)	56	232 (31.0)	72
Class F								
Average Revenues	24 (70.8)	17	26 (73.0)	19	29 (58.6)	17	30 (50.0)	15
Average Expenses	106 (24.5)	26	121 (25.6)	36	129 (27.9)	36	144 (25.7)	37

( ) indicate percentage of women's revenues and expenses relative to men's revenues and expenses

Class A = Division I football playing schools, Class B = Division II football playing schools, Class C = Division III football playing schools, Class D = Division I nonfootball playing schools, Class E = Division II nonfootball playing schools, Class F = Division III nonfootball playing schools.

Note: From Table 4.1, page 41 and Table 4.8, page 46, Mitchell H. Raiborn (1982). *Revenues and expenses of intercollegiate athletic programs,* Mission, KS: National Collegiate Athletic Association.

Table 3

Relative Change in Revenues and Expenses
for Men's and Women's Athletics Between the Years 1978-1981 (Figures in Thousands)

	Men's Athletics	Women's Athletics
Class A		
Expense Change	+ 1,005	+ 231
Class B		
Expense Change	+ 105	+ 39
Class C		
Expense Change	+ 61	+ 20
Class D		
Expense Change	+ 221	+ 93
Class E		
Expense Change	+ 69	+ 36
Classs F		
Expense Change	+ 38	+ 11

Note: Adapted from Table 4.1, page 41 and Table 4.9, page 46, Mitchell H. Raiborn (1982). *Revenues and expenses of intercollegiate athletic programs*, Mission, KS: National Collegiate Athletic Association.

may cite women's athletics as the primary cause for increased athletic costs, male athletic programs have actually contributed more to absolute costs than have women's athletic expenses.

With increasing costs, a seemingly inevitable component of intercollegiate athletics, it becomes all the more imperative to rationalize sport programs on other than economic grounds. If the vast majority of men's and women's athletic programs do not make money for their institutions and do not fulfill the "doctrine of good works," then possible educational benefits to athletes and/or spectators grow in significance as a criteria of program legitimacy.

While controversy exists concerning the validity of notions that sport "causes positive value and attitude changes (Stevenson, 1985), it seems reasonable to suggest that the educational benefits which might be gained through sport should be as available for women as they are for men. If indeed sport "builds character" or develops positive norms of behavior then there should be approximately equal access to such growth opportunities offered to female and male students at the college or university. As we have seen from the tables, however, women's athletic budgets are generally less than one third of male athletic budgets (Table 2), and there are fewer sport teams available to women than men (Table 1). The papers in this section look at the current stage of women's athletics and assess the validity of egalitarian notions concerning the availability of sport opportunity and the governance of women's intercollegiate athletics.

In their first paper of this section, R. Vivian Acosta and Linda Carpenter trace the organizational structures of women's college sport in America from the 1920s and the concomitant attitudes of the organizations concerning competition, commercialism, athlete autonomy, and education. Attempts by the National College Athletic Association to envelop women's sport within its traditional domain of men's athletics are also viewed in light of the NCAA's attempts to overturn or reinterpret Title IX legislation.

In their second paper, "The Status of Women in Intercollegiate Athletics—A Five-Year National Study," Carpenter and Acosta provide empirical data to assess the popular assumption that substantial sport opportunities are available given the "burgeoning" of women's intercollegiate athletics. Looking at the year immediately preceding and the 4 years after compliance to Title IX regulations first became mandatory, the authors chronicle the growth and then restriction of participation opportunities for women in sport. In addition, Carpenter and Acosta first substantiate and then raise questions concerning the possible effects that decreasing female placement in coaching and administrative positions may have on women's sport.

REFERENCES

CHU, D. (1979). Origins of the connection of physical education and athletics at the American university: An organizational interpretation. *Journal of Sport and Social Issues, 3*, 22-32.

RAIBORN, M.H. (1982). Revenues and expenses of intercollegiate athletic programs. Mission, KS: National Collegiate Athletic Association.

STEVENSON, C. (1985). College athletics and character: The decline and fall of research. In D. Chu, J.O. Segrave, & B.J. Becker (Eds.), *Sport and higher education* (pp. 247-264). Champaign, IL: Human Kinetics.

Chapter 22

Women in Sport

R. Vivian Acosta and Linda Jean Carpenter
Brooklyn College

In order to fully understand the role sport plays in women's lives, one must first look to the past. The development of the current level of participation by women in sport did not begin from a void, but rather had a slow metamorphosis which developed in stages. This discussion takes a concentrated look at the historical development of women in sport beginning with the 1920s and quickly proceeds to the viewpoints of today.

1920-1971: ORGANIZATIONAL ONTOGENY

The 1920s brought great wealth and prosperity to America. With this came an avid pursuit of leisure activities and the appearance of women in advertising campaigns. As advertising tools, women were shown in abbreviated sports clothing and bathing suits. Women were not participants but frills, accompanying men who actually participated in athletic endeavors.

The main thrust of the attitude toward women as actual participants in sport was one of protectionism. Women physical educators held the belief that women should not involve themselves in high-level athletics because doing so could easily lead to corruption as evidenced by the scandals which seemed to permeate men's competitive sports. As a result of this attitude, women's sports turned toward a program of activities which would serve the needs of *all* women participants. Forms of competition were devised to meet the needs of women who did desire to compete however.

In a search for inter-institutional competition which would not lead to commercialization and professionalization, playdays and sportsdays were devised. Playday teams were picked at random from the schools participating. If six schools participated in a playday, each team would include a player from each school....At a sportsday, the institution played as a team, but usually in a modified form of competition such as a round robin tournament. (Oglesby, 1978, p. 10)

Other forms of competition were used, but the playday and sportsday were the mode and continued to be so until the 1960s.

No governance organization for women similar to the National Collegiate Athletic Association (NCAA) existed until the creation of the Commission on Intercollegiate Athletics for Women (CIAW) in 1971, the forerunner of the Association for Intercollegiate Athletics for Women (AIAW). However, even before the advent of the CIAW/AIAW, there were organizations which did concern themselves with policies and guidelines for girls' and women's sports. The following were among these organizations:

1. The Committee on Women's Athletics (CWA) of the American Association for Health, Physical Education, and Recreation (AAHPER) now American Alliance for Health, Physical Education, Recreation, and Dance (AAHPERD)
2. The National Association for Physical Education for College Women (NAPECW)
3. The Women's Division of the National Amateur Athletic Federation (NAAF)

These organizations, which had their beginnings in the 1920s and continued to be guiding forces until the 1960s, consisted of women physical educators whose purposes were to protect women and girls from the negative connotations of sports activities and of the participants themselves. In some ways it could be said that because of the protective nature of these organizations, "competition" in its highest sense was suppressed rather than encouraged.

A detailed, 16-point platform[1] concerning the conduct of varsity athletic competition for women was adopted at a 1923 conference. The platform was to be used by almost all colleges and universities until the mid-1940s.

In the main the creed [platform] expressed the physical educators' beliefs that their role should be protective, guarding against situations which they deemed potentially injurious to women athletes. The underlying assumption throughout the creed [platform] was that athletic competition *would* take place. That was why they set forth in considerable detail the conditions under which it should be conducted. Unfortunately, the creed and resolutions upon which it was based were widely interpreted as embodying negative attitudes toward competition. (Gerber, Felshin, & Wyrick, 1974, p. 73)

During the early stages of women's athletics, a concept unique to women's athletics was established: student involvement in the establishment of policies and guidelines which would determine the path of women's athletics. Thus, in addition to the professional organizations such as the CWA, NAPECW, and NAAF, there were student organizations on most university and college campuses. Among them were the Women's Athletic Association (WAA) and the Women's Recreation Association (WRA). This concept of student involvement was continued when the AIAW was established, although the WAA and WRA programs from which it was born slowly died. The WRAs and WAAs were under the direct supervision of the women's physical education department and always had faculty leaders as advisors and followed their leaders' philosophical viewpoints.

The student organization which played a national role in the governance of women's athletics until the 1960s was the Athletic and Recreation Federation of College Women (ARFCW). Student representatives from the WAAs and WRAs attended national conventions of the ARFCW to exchange ideas and to conduct business. The ARFCW, and thus the WAAs and WRAs, adhered closely to the 1923 16-point platform published by the NAAF and CWA. The adherence to the platform by ARFCW reinforced the appearance that highly competitive experiences for women athletes were to be avoided.

As time passed and organizations went through name changes, the Division for Girls' and Women's Sports (DGWS) of AAHPER became the most prominent organization in the governance of sport for both girls and women. DGWS acknowledged the fact that more and more women were fulfilling the role of Olympic competitor, and so in 1956 it requested and received representation on the United States Olympic Sport Committees. Thus, DGWS expressed the philosophy that there was indeed a place for competition by the highly-skilled female student athlete, but added the caveat that the competitive experience should not supersede the instructional or recreative programs of the general student.

A year later, in 1957, DGWS, ARFCW, and NAPECW approved the inclusion of women's intercollegiate athletics in their areas of concern. The three organizations attempted to jointly govern the conduct of athletic competitions between institutions, but the group governance plan was deemed unworkable and impractical. Thus, in 1965, the joint governance plan was discarded, and DGWS assumed the solitary governance position (Lopiano, 1981, p. 21).

The DGWS, under the larger umbrella of AAHPER, seemed the logical choice to assume the governance position for interscholastic competitions because its philosophical viewpoint was one which supported the belief that the educational activities of women should be protected from commercial exploitation to benefit athletic endeavors. However, it became clear that with the increasing participation of women in high-level athletics, a governance body with a different viewpoint on the intercollegiate competitive experience might be necessary.

The establishment of CIAW took place in 1966 with the full backing of DGWS and AAHPER. Its purpose was to sanction women's intercollegiate athletic events and to establish, conduct, and promote national championships. The CIAW existed until October 1971, when its replacement by AIAW was approved by AAHPER.

The change from a commission to an association was approved by DGWS/AAHPER in the belief that to best serve women's *intercollegiate* sport, it was necessary to have a strong financial base. Such a financial base could only come from institutional membership dues. Additionally, it was believed that institutions would be more apt to comply with policies and regulations which they themselves had helped establish. The rationale of DGWS/AAHPER appears to have been well founded because the membership of AIAW grew from its charter year membership of 278 in 1971-72 to 973 in 1979-80 (AIAW, 1979-80).

The "participation first/competition second" philosophy (greatest good for greatest number) to which the majority of women physical educators adhered as the cornerstone and underlying basis for the design of women's participation in sport during the major part of this century was apparently losing its hold on intercollegiate athletics. Society was becoming more willing to accept women as skillful competitors. As a result, more programs were developed and new opportunities for participation by women in sport evolved. However, not all obstacles had been removed. For example, sex stereotyping of women in sport still existed, and the public had not yet developed an interest in watching women play competitively. Furthermore, many believed that women lacked the interest to compete and/or compete as intensely as men. These myths have been difficult to overcome by a society that has been conditioned to accept the notion that the sportswoman is a social anomaly.

In spite of the continued existence of myths and stereotypes, the half century prologue for women in sport was concluding, and the body of the story was beginning to come into view. By 1972, women's athletics had indeed crossed the threshold. A national governing association (AIAW) which supported high-level competitive experiences for collegiate women was in place. national competitions were being held and more were being planned. Coincident with the emergence of women's intercollegiate athletics as national entity in 1972 was the passage of federal legislation which was to have a greater impact on women's athletics than any event in its 50-year prologue. The legislation was known as Title IX.

1972-1978: TURMOIL AND TRANSITION

In 1972, Title IX was put into law. Title IX of the Education Amendment provides that

> No person in the United States shall, on the basis of sex, be excluded from participation in, be denied the benefits of, or be subjected to discrimination under any education program or activity receiving Federal financial assistance....(U.S. Commission on Civil Rights, 1980, Section 1681-1686)

All secondary and postsecondary schools were given the next 6 years to put in place programs and procedures which would bring the schools into compliance with Title IX by 1978. Long before the mandatory compliance date, Title IX was having an effect on women's sports.

This 6-year period of turmoil and transition was one of great financial growth for the governance of women's sports. The 1975 AIAW Division I Basketball and Gymnastics Championships represented the first major network television contract entered into by AIAW. Thirteen percent (over $15,000) of the AIAW's 1975-76 operating budget was garnered from such television contracts (Lopiano, 1981, p. 31). By 1978 (compliance), the figure had grown to almost $110,000 (21% of the budget) (Lopiano, 1981, p. 31). Thus, in these years of transition, the budget of AIAW as well as the amount contributed to the budget by television contracts had grown markedly.

Similar growth between Title IX enactment and compliance was seen in participation opportunities for women. In 1973, an average of 2.5 sports per college campus were offered for women (7.3 for men). Six years later the number for women had grown to 6.48 (Acosta & Carpenter, 1980), (7.4 for men) (U.S. Commission on Civil Rights, 1980) and the number continued to grow through 1982—however, at a much lower rate.

Thus, a citation of the positive effects of Title IX must include the notation that the number of participation opportunities and, therefore, the number of participants in women's sports has increased. It is not so certain though, nor perhaps is it even important, whether the increase was due to intentional efforts to comply with the perceived requirements of Title IX, or rather merely a relaxation of the limitations placed on women sports participants and their programs, resulting from the sensitization of society to the problem. Whatever the cause or interacting causes, it cannot be denied that the decade in which Title IX's enactment and compliance may have had an influence is the same decade in which women's sports opportunities grew more than any other.

It is good that Title IX has had a positive impact on women's sports which may be independent of its ability to be implemented and enforced effectively. The legal strength and ability of Title IX to affect athletics has been frequently assaulted. Men, fearful of its financial impact on men's programs and power bases, individually and as represented by the NCAA, were quick to launch an attack on its applicability to athletics. For example, the 1973-1974 NCAA Annual Report includes several references to and resolutions about the financial inability of many colleges and universities to support intercollegiate athletic programs for both men and women. The NCAA Executive Director, Walter Byers, was quoted as saying that Title IX would mean the "possible doom of intercollegiate sports" (Barnes & Scannell, 1974, p. A-14). The NCAA issued opinions, papers, and formal comments on the developing regulations for Title IX. The efforts of the NCAA were temporarily realized when the Tower Amendment passed the Senate. The Tower Amendment excluded revenue sports from the concerns of Title IX. However, although the Tower Amendment passed the Senate, it died in the House Senate Conference Committee.

The assault on the application of Title IX to athletics was not abated by the defeat of the Tower Amendment. For instance, in *NCAA v. Califano* (1980) the

NCAA asserted that HEW, in issuing Title IX regulations, exceeded its authority under Title IX and that portions of the regulations were arbitrary and capricious, unconstitutionally vague, and that portions of the regulations created a sex-based quota system in violation of Title IX and the Fifth Amendment. Another, perhaps stronger, argument against the imposition of Title IX requirements on intercollegiate athletic programs found its way to the Supreme Court (*Grove City College v. Bell*, 1980) and was decided in the fall of 1984. The argument that Title IX applies only to *programs* receiving federal funds was successful. Although a college or university receives such funds, its athletic program does not. Bills and resolutions now on the floor of Congress have been proposed to overcome the very narrow interpretation of Title IX imposed by the Supreme Court in *Grove City*.

IMPACT OF TITLE IX ON WOMEN'S SPORT

Whatever the final disposition of the legal arguments concerning Title IX, Title IX has had a massive impact on women's sport. The impact has been both positive and negative. The positive is reflected numerically in the increased participation opportunities for women athletes. The negative is reflected numerically in the declining representation of women in the coaching and administering of women's sports (Acosta & Carpenter, 1980, note 5).

The nonnumerical impact of Title IX also has positive and negative aspects. Society seems to be more ready to accept the role of sports in women's lives. The awareness of the limitations placed on women's sports participants has become broader. A greater segment of the population is interested in having those limitations either removed or reduced.

In spite of the gains in participation and in societal interest in women's sports, Title IX has had far-reaching negative effects on the design, autonomy, and governance structure of women's intercollegiate athletics. Even though the NCAA has fought diligently to remove athletics from Title IX, Title IX has been used as the reason for merging athletic departments as well as physical education departments. In over 80% of the cases where women administered women's programs and men administered men's programs, the merger resulted in a male assuming the administrative role for both programs.[2] Thus, the underrepresented female in administration became even more scarce with the apparent support of federal legislation intended to end sex discrimination.

The same double-bind logic prevailed to prevent the insistence of some women coaches and administrators that women should coach and administer women's teams. Although it was unclear until recently whether Title IX applied to employment, the double-bind logic was nonetheless successful, and over 6% of the female coaches of women's teams have been replaced by males from 1978 to 1982 (Acosta & Carpenter, 1980). Furthermore, an evergrowing number of women's programs are administered by males.

Nor did the design of women's athletics escape the impact of Title IX. For instance, in 1973, the emerging AIAW which had developed a philosophy for women's sports which did not include the use of scholarships changed its position and followed the men's traditional mode of granting scholarships. The threat of a Title IX lawsuit against AIAW by women athletes (Minutes, AIAW Delegate Assembly, 1973) desirous of scholarship support was a strong catalyst in inducing this fundamental change in the design of women's athletics. The development of recruitment procedures in response to the decision to permit scholarships was the next logical step for women's athletics. The AIAW designed a set of recruitment procedures peculiar to women's athletics.[3] The procedures acknowledged the desire for women's athletics to avoid some of the abuses which have long beset men's athletics. It is not difficult to believe that this design will change[4] now that women's athletics has lost the AIAW and, thus, the chance to be autonomous and the designer of its own future (*Chronicle of Higher Education*, 1980).

1983: THE DEATH OF THE AIAW

Women's athletics will survive the potential setbacks that have recently developed if, and only if, women continue to 'play the game'—fairly, justly, and with determination to win. (Thomas & Sheldon-Wildgren, 1982, p. 330)

The encouragement available from the previous statement made in 1982 had little warmth in 1983. The conflict between AIAW and NCAA born in the early 1970s reached its conclusion in February of 1983 when the AIAW lost its antitrust suit against the NCAA.[5] Without the ability to realistically compete in the offering of championships in women's athletics, the AIAW has no membership and thus no reason to exist. Less than 5 years after the compliance date of Title IX, the nation's governance of women's intercollegiate athletics is solely in the hands of the male-dominated NCAA. How did it happen?

Soon after the 1974 defeat of the Tower Amendment (proposing the exclusion of revenue sports from Title IX), the NCAA's staff prepared a recommendation that the NCAA "take 'affirmative action' in meeting the anticipated Title IX guidelines by offering Championship Competition for women immediately" (NCAA Annual Report 1974-75, p. 63). The rationale that antisex discrimination legislation mandated such an intrusion into women's sports was also used in this instance. The recommendation was made at the same time that NCAA continued its apparently contradictory efforts to exclude athletics from Title IX.

The presentation of the recommendation involved a degree of drama. After abortive attempts by the AIAW to shape a representative organization for the governance of both men's and women's intercollegiate sports, and while the AIAW was led to believe it was still negotiating for some sort of joint governance with the NCAA, the NCAA, contrary to its normal procedures, presented its previously unannounced recommendations[6] to its 1975 convention. The 1975 NCAA Convention, held almost concurrently with the AIAW Convention, however did not accept the proposal. Despite the membership's lack of acceptance, the NCAA's leadership continued to seek both the exclusion of athletics from Title IX and membership approval of NCAA's entrance into the governance of women's intercollegiate athletics. It appears that NCAA wanted to be certain to have control whichever way Title IX went with regard to women's athletics. "It appear[ed] to remain the [NCAA] Council's view that usurpation is preferable to cooperation" (Morrison, 1975, p. 2).

By July 1975 when the final Title IX regulations were issued with the inclusion of athletics, the NCAA supported the resurfacing of the proposal to exempt revenue sports via the Tower Bill. Following testimony by AIAW and NCAA, the Tower Bill failed to be enacted however.

The following months saw a number of acrimonious exchanges and political manipulations between AIAW and NCAA. Attempts were made by the NCAA, both surrepticious and overt, to bring women athletes under the rules of NCAA.[7] Joint AIAW/NCAA committees were formed, altered, and disbanded unilaterally. Accusations of bad faith were frequently heard.

As late as February 1978, the AIAW was still hoping for constructive, good faith meetings with the NCAA[8] for the development of appropriate governance structures. However, by the 1980 NCAA Convention, it became clear that there was no longer any vestige of interorganization cooperation left.

> At the January 1980 NCAA Council meeting held just prior to the commencement of the 1980 Convention, the Council considered its response to AIAW's request for a five-year moratorium on the establishment of NCAA women's championships; the officers explained that....AIAW's request was moot. In retrospect, it seems clear that prior to the 1980 Convention the NCAA had decided to drop any facade of mutuality or cooperation with AIAW and to 'go-it-alone' with respect to expanding into women's intercollegiate athletics. (Lopiano, 1981, p. 134)

The 1980 NCAA Convention established 10 women's championships in two competitive divisions. NCAA's ability to offer financial assistance which included travel expenses to those women's teams participating in its championships was irresistible to many schools and might have played a major role in the exodus of schools from membership in AIAW to membership in NCAA. The condition of AIAW following the NCAA 1980 Convention could be described as terminal.

The entrance of NCAA into the world of women's championships produced not only a loss of AIAW membership, but also the loss of commercial sponsorship of AIAW's awards programs, loss of television exposure, and income for AIAW, and the development of increased confusion and distrust. With the loss of the antitrust suit in February 1983 came the ultimate loss: The demise of a governance voice for women's intercollegiate athletics which had a female identity.

The future of intercollegiate athletics in America is most likely going to be unidimensional in character, and that dimension will continue to be designed by male architects. The passing of the opportunity for the involvement of female architects in the future of women's intercollegiate athletics is to be lamented.

REFERENCES

ACOSTA, V., & Carpenter, L. (1980, June). *Administrative structure and gender of personnel in intercollegiate athletics for women.* Unpublished research report, Brooklyn College.

AIAW membership directory, 1979-80.

AIAW Minutes, 1973 Delegate Assembly.

BARNES, B., & Scannell, N. (1974, May 12). No sporting chance: The girls in the locker room. *The Washington Post*, p. A-14.

CHRONICLE of Higher Education (1980, December 8), p. 9.

GERBER, E., Felshin, J., Berlin, R., & Wyrick, W. (1974). *The American woman in sport.* Reading, MA: Addison-Wesley.

HEW News (1979, December 4), p. 5.

LOPIANO, D. (1981). Brief filed in *AIAW v. NCAA* antitrust case.

MORRISON, L. (1975, April 29). *Memorandum to AIAW voting representatives.*

NCAA Annual Report 1974-75.

NCAA Convention Proceedings, 1981, 1975.

NCAA v. Califano, 622 F 2d 1382 (10th Circuit, 1980).

OGELSBY, C. (1978). (Ed.). *Women in sport: From myth to reality.* Philadelphia: Lea and Febiger.

THOMAS, A. & Sheldon-Wildgen, J. (1981-82). Women in athletics: Winning the game but losing the support. *Journal of College and University Law,* **8**, 295-330.

UNITED States Commission of Civil Rights. (1980, July). *More hurdles to clear: Women and girls in competitive athletics.* Clearinghouse Publication #63.

FOOTNOTES

1. The 16-point platform reads:

The Women's Division believes in the spirit of play for its own sake and works for the promotion of physical activity for the largest possible proportion of persons in any given group, in forms suitable to individual needs and capacities, under leadership and environmental conditions that foster health, physical efficiency, and the development of good citizenship.

To accomplish this ideal for women and girls, it aims

- To promote programs of physical activities for all members of given social groups rather than for a limited number chosen for their physical prowess.

- To protect athletics from exploitation for the enjoyment of the spectators or for the athletic reputation or commercial advantage of any institution or organization.
- To stress enjoyment of the sport and the development of sportsmanship, and to minimize the emphasis placed on individual accomplishment and the wining of championships.
- To restrict recognition for athletic accomplishment to awards which are symbolic and which have the least possible intrinsic value.
- To discourage sensational publicity, to guide publicity along educational lines and to stress through it the sport rather than the individual or group competitors.
- To put well-trained and properly qualified women in immediate charge of athletics and other physical education activities.
- To work toward placing the administration as well as the immediate leadership of all physical education activities for girls and women in the hands of well-trained and properly qualified women.
- To secure adequate medical examination and medical follow-up advice as a basis for participation in physical activities.
- To work for such adequate time allotment for a physical education program as shall meet the need of the various age groups for growth, development, and maintenance of physical fitness.
- To promote a reasonable and sane attitude toward certain physiological conditions which may occasion temporary unfitness for vigorous athletes in order that effective safeguards should be maintained.
- To avoid countenancing the sacrifice of an individual's health for the sake of her participation in athletic competition.
- To promote the adoption of appropriate costumes for the various athletic activities.
- To eliminate gate receipts.
- To discourage athletic competition which involves travel.
- To eliminate types and systems of competition which put the emphasis upon individual accomplishment and winning rather than upon stressing the enjoyment of the sport and the development of sportsmanship among many.

From L. Schoedler (1921, June). Report of Progress, Women's Division, National Amateur Athletic Federation of America, *APER, 29*, pp. 308-309 as reprinted in Gerber, Felshin, Berlin & Wyrick, 1974.

2. Mattison, M. (1980, February). A selective study of women's athletic administrative settings involving AIAW Division I Institutions. University of Pittsburgh.

See also, Acosta, V. & Carpenter, L. (1980). Status of women in intercollegiate athletics—a five-year national study. Brooklyn College; Homan, M. & Parkhouse, B. (1981). Trends in the selection of coaches for female athletes: A demographic inquiry. *Research Quarterly for Exercise and Sport, 52*, 9-18.

HEW's concern for the problem was expressed by its Secretary, Patricia Harris,

We would expect that as schools amend their programs, they would do so with sensitivity and with recognition that such changes should result in enhancing—not minimizing—the role of women coaches and athletic directors, as well as women athletes, in sport programs. (*HEW News*, December 4, 1979, p. 5)

3. *Chronicle of Higher Education*, December 8, 1980, p. 9. The *Chronicle* article reiterates the statement of the AIAW stressing its founding principles which included the goal to provide a national championship program for female athletes and to develop a governance system that would serve rather than exploit student-athletes while avoiding the excesses that were typical of the men's programs. The AIAW stressed that it followed much less expensive recruitment rules, flexible competitive structures (unlike the division structure faced by women under the NCAA which basically will require women's teams to compete in the division in which the men's teams hold membership unless a petition to do otherwise is granted each school).

4. The recruitment problem was expressed by a male athletic director at the 1981 NCAA Convention:

I have watched a power play I would like to have had when I was playing and coaching football. I have never seen such a blitzkreig against a group of people who have worked hard to develop their own organization. My women happen to be happy in the AIAW and, you have understood here, many have said that I have a choice. Let me assure you, and make it clear once and for all (and every athletic director in this room knows), that we have no choice when we talk about national championships.

My women are going to want to compete for the national championships. That is fine in the NCAA. If they do this, they have a good time. If they are going to have a good team, they have to meet competition. Any coach knows he has to meet competition. If any neighbor can go out and talk to a prospect in their home and pay their way to the campus, and I choose to stay in the AIAW rule and I can't, how can I compete for the national championships? So let's make it clear.

There is no option. There is no option for any athletic director in this room. When you get back to your campus, there will be no option; you will be recruiting.

Let me just say I don't envy the women. We have reflected a certain philosophy in recruiting. I have resigned from coaching and many others my age have resigned from coaching. We like to believe that we coached for nothing and we are paid to recruit. You are asking the women to join a method of recruiting that is forcing people out of the profession. That is, going into the homes and recruiting. You will have to get another investigative staff, maybe double the size we have now. (*1981 NCAA Convention Proceedings*, p. 163)

5. The antitrust suit filed by the AIAW against the NCAA was unsuccessful at the U.S. District Court level. An appeal has been filed and disposition of the case is expected sometime late in 1983 or early 1984. The District Court held that although the AIAW had proven the probability of NCAA's success as a monopolist in obtaining complete dominion of the women's market, they failed

to prove the specific intent to develop a monopoly on the part of the NCAA which the court required. The court further held that the evidence failed to prove that the NCAA tied its television rights to the women's basketball championships to the men's in its negotiations with the networks. Such tying would be illegal even if the tying existed only in the minds of the buyer and seller. Proving state of mind is always a difficult task and yet here the court ruled that even if the AIAW had been successful in proving anti-competitive intent, the court believed that the results were only the product of direct competition. Some might hasten to add that the relative financial strengths of the two organizations were so unequal as to make 'direct competition' in this sense impossible. (*AIAW v. NCAA* 558 F. Supp. 487, 1983)

6. The proposal to authorize women's championships as a pilot program in 1976-77 read:

Whereas, this Association [NCAA] has taken an active interest in the development of women's intercollegiate athletics since 1963; and,

Whereas, developments in the field of equal rights—as to legal requirements and society's needs—now pose serious demands upon the NCAA as an organization; and

Whereas, the Association's legal counsel has consistently reminded the NCAA Council that

1. The Association's rules and the obligations of institutional membership relate to all varsity intercollegiate sports and do not differentiate between men and women; and
2. The Association is facing legal obligations to offer services and programs to women student-athletes as they do for men; and

Whereas, each member institution has had these influences and requirements visited upon it at the institutional level and now the Association, itself, must move to adjust its concepts and programs to meet the demands of today's society and today's law;

Now, Therefore, Be It Resolved, that the NCAA Council prepare a comprehensive report and plan on the several issues involved in the administration of women's intercollegiate athletics at the national level in light of existing court decisions, anticipated regulations implementing Title IX of the Educational Amendments of 1972 and present developments in women's intercollegiate athletics.....

Be It Further Resolved, that the Council include in its report whether the Council believes it would be desirable or legally necessary for national championships to be conducted by the Association for female student-athletes either on an integrated or segregated basis, and that the Council direct its Special Committee on Women's Intercollegiate Athletics to determine if it is advisable to conduct pilot programs for women's national championships as a part of development of a final proposal for consideration by the membership, it being understood that no such pilot program shall be conducted during this academic year. (*1975 NCAA Convention Proceedings*, p. A-28)

7. For an interesting and complete discussion of NCAA's attempt to bring women athletes under NCAA rules, see brief of Donna Lopiano, President of AIAW, filed as part of the AIAW-NCAA antitrust suit in Federal District Court, Washington, DC, p. 99.

8. Charlotte West, AIAW President in 1978 wrote to AIAW institutions:

In its seven-year existence, AIAW's program has grown to the point where it is currently serving over 100,000 female student-athletes. AIAW offers seventeen national championships in twelve different sports. Perhaps of even greater significance is the fact that AIAW has demonstrated that a progressive, humanistic concept of sport in an educational framework is workable and viable. Student representation, due process for students and institutions and a commitment to broad based institutionally oriented athletic programs are the cornerstones upon which AIAW has built an organization of 823 active members.

Against this background, it is difficult to justify the NCAA's repeated attempts to develop a competing program which would undermine this viable organization at a time when women's intercollegiate athletic programs are in an emerging state. Neither basic equity nor the legal requirements of equal opportunity call for the NCAA to start programs for women. Indeed both would be disserved thereby, since as a practical matter, the existence of such a competing program would inhibit the efforts of women to fashion a program which best serves the needs of female student-athletes.

AIAW remains hopeful that NCAA will join with it in seeking positive, constructive solutions to the problems faced by many intercollegiate athletic programs. However, we believe that a conducive climate for mutual endeavor can only exist if the NCAA ceases its efforts to duplicate AIAW's program. We therefore seek your support in informing the NCAA that your institution does not wish the NCAA to initiate women's championship programs. (*Memorandum to Presidents of AIAW Member Institutions*, February 21, 1978)

Chapter 23

The Status of Women in Intercollegiate Athletics— A Five-Year National Study*

Linda Jean Carpenter and R. Vivian Acosta
Brooklyn College

I had not realized until the comment period that athletics is the single most important thing in the United States.

Caspar Weinberger[1]

The nature of intercollegiate athletic programs has been the source of much controversy during the last decade. The subject of the most heated controversy and discussion has been the role of women in those programs. This is due at least in part to the emergence of a societal sensitivity to the activities of women as well as to such governmental actions as Title IX.[2]

The literature is generously supplied with unsupported statements predicting both massive increases and decreases in the role of women in athletic programs. Institutions of higher education are making financial plans based on their unsupported perceptions of the impact of those changes. Government agencies are designing Title IX implementation procedures as well as questioning the functional value of Title IX[3] based on interpretations of the size and direction of those

---

*Since the 1981 presentation of this paper at Skidmore College's Conference on Sport in Higher Education, several significant events have occurred. Among these are (a) the loss of AIAW's anti-trust suit against the NCAA and the subsequent demise of the AIAW, (b) the Supreme Court's decision in *Grove City College v. Bell* which interprets Title IX as "program specific," and (c) the gathering of 2 more years of data in the study described here. Summaries of the 7 years (9 years by Winter, 1986) of data are available from the authors.

changes founded on largely unsupported "best guess" and secondary sources. Academic departments which train and educate personnel hoping to enter the field of coaching and administering women's intercollegiate athletics are planning for and encouraging their students concerning a job market for which little data exist.

It was the purpose of this 5-year[4] national study to provide substantive data concerning the role of women in intercollegiate athletics and to trace any changes in that role. The half decade for which data have been obtained covers the time from one year preceding the mandatory compliance date of Title IX to a point 4 years past compliance (1977-1982).[5]

BACKGROUND

A review of the attempts which have been made to gather data upon which to base supportable predictions, statements, and implementation procedures will highlight the need for the information sought in the present research.

In July 1980 the United States Commission on Civil Rights issued *More Hurdles to Clear* which attempted to gather together data which would reflect the status of women in sport as it existed in the 2 years following Title IX's compliance date. Unfortunately, the Commission was forced to base its conclusions on an intuitive combination and interrelation of data from secondary sources. The secondary sources dealt only with small areas of the larger question which is the topic of this paper. In fact, the commission never addressed the question directly.

The role of minorities in sport was considered in an unpublished master's thesis entitled "Status of Minority Women in the Association of Intercollegiate Athletics for Women."[6,7] Contrary to the title of the thesis, the gender of the subjects was not obtained. This was due to a potentially inaccurate assumption that the administrators and coaches of women's athletics were, in fact, women. Although the thesis provides interesting information concernig the ethnicity of the coaches and administrators of women's intercollegiate athletics, it provides no basis for determining gender.

A small study sampling less than a third of the AIAW member colleges and universities concerning the gender of coaches of women's teams demonstrated an apparent trend toward an increase in the percentage of women's teams being coached by males.[8] In addition to involving a small sample, no data were collected concerning administrative structure or gender of administrative personnel.[9] Because budget, schedules, selection, and retention of coaches and the type of sports offered are decisions all generally controlled by the program administrators, data concerning administrative structure and gender of personnel would be of great interest.

SIGNIFICANCE OF THIS STUDY

This study provides data which are crucial to the evaluation of trends in gender-related aspects of the female interested in the intercollegiate sports experience.

The significance of this project lies particularly in two areas: (a) in the generation of comparative and longitudinal data on the role of women in intercollegiate athletics; and (b) in the determination of the extent to which the spirit of Title IX has been incorporated into intercollegiate athletics. Such information, although of great value, is not available elsewhere.

RESEARCH DESIGN

The primary purposes of this study were to (a) determine if, with the advent of Title IX, there are women coaching and administering women's intercollegiate athletic programs; and (b) develop a longitudinal view of the role of women in intercollegiate athletics by comparing and adding data to the original 3-year base study.

In order to accomplish these primary purposes, the following specific purposes were formulated:

1. To determine what sports opportunities were being offered to women in all 4-year colleges and universities providing an athletic program for women under the sponsorship of either the AIAW or the NCAA.
2. To determine the number of teams available to the potential woman athlete and to note trends if they exist.
3. To determine if there are varsity and/or junior varsity teams offered in each sport and to note trends if they exist.
4. To determine the gender of the coach(es) for each of the women's teams at the respondent's school and to note trends if they exist.
5. To determine the administrative structure of the women's athletic program at each responding school and to note trends if they exist.
6. To determine the gender of those individuals who are serving in an administrative capacity in the women's athletic program at each responding school and to note trends if they exist.

PROCEDURES

Data have been gathered in two phases. The vehicle for data gathering consisted of a three-page questionnaire sent to all member schools of the AIAW (915 members in 1980 when the first data collection took place, and 780 members in 1982 when the second data collection took place). During the second data gathering phase, questionnaires were also sent to all NCAA members schools which fielded women's athletic teams (120 schools). Thus, for a period of 5 years, data have been sought from all colleges and universities fielding women's intercollegiate teams regardless of their affiliation with either NCAA or AIAW. In both data-gathering phases, return rates of 66% or over were obtained. The researchers did not use follow-up letters and thus believe that the high rate of return is an indication of the interest in the topic of the questionnaire.

The second phase data have special importance because they cover the period of time in which the AIAW-NCAA conflict born of Title IX 6 years ago reached the courts. As of this writing, the AIAW has filed an antitrust suit against the NCAA. Recognizing that failure of the suit means the demise of the AIAW, the AIAW has suspended its activities in the administration of women's sports until the suit is decided.[10] Will this action of the AIAW and the potential total governance of women's sports by the male dominated NCAA affect the gender composition of the coaching and administering of women's intercollegiate sports? It seems likely that it will be based on the trends established in the first two phases of data collection. The third phase planned for 1984 will be more definitive however.

THEORETICAL BASE

Based on trends apparent in the data gathered during Phases 1 and 2 of this study, there seems to be a strong increase in the number of sports opportunities for the female athlete (see Table 1), while at the same time, the representation of females among the coaching and administrative staff is declining (see Table 2). Intuition leads one to believe that this decline is due to an alteration in the hiring and retention of female professionals which was either generated by Title IX (contrary to its intended purpose) or has been unabated by Title IX. Causality is difficult to establish nor was this study intended to strongly examine such cause and effect relationships. Instead, this study was a correlative one.

Thus, it might be said that the essential dimension being investigated is that of males coaching and administering women's intercollegiate athletics. For instance, why does the percentage of male coaches for female teams seem to be increasing? Is it a budgetary decision? Are adequately trained female coaches available? Does the gender of the hiring administrator affect the gender make-up in women's athletics?

STATISTICAL ANALYSIS

Upon receipt of the completed questionnaires, the data were transferred to a coding form permitting computer analysis. The SPSS package was used to provide the treatment of the data. Cross tab, Chi square, and frequency determinations were among the manipulations of the data performed to obtain descriptive statistics and to set up contingency tables.

RESULTS

The numerical opportunity for women athletes to participate in intercollegiate sports is increasing. For instance, the number of teams offered women in the academic year of 1977-78 was 5.61 per school. In 1980 the number had grown to 6.48 per school and continues to grow although at a lesser rate through 1982. Through 1982 no women's team (of those governed by either AIAW or NCAA) or sports activity demonstrated a decrease. However, by 1982 there was a degree of consolidation taking place with some sports such as archery and tennis demonstrating a decrease in the number of schools offering them for women. (See Table 1 for a fuller itemization.) Even though the number of teams being offered is on the increase since Title IX, the percentage of those teams having a female coach is decreasing (see Table 2).

It is interesting to note that in those specific sports where traditionally men have no participation interest in the United States such as field hockey, the representation of women among the coaching staffs remains relatively constant. This seems to indicate that there is no mass exodus of women from the ranks of coaching because of their disinterest in coaching. Rather, it may indicate a replacement of women coaches with male coaches in those areas where men have some experience.

Table 1
Sport Offerings for Women Intercollegiate Athletes

Sport	1979/80 Percentage of schools with teams	1979/80 # of teams	1978/79 # of teams	1977/78 # of teams
Archery	2.8	17	20	18
Badminton	5.4	33	37	36
Basketball	97.5	594	587	550
Bowling	3.6	22	22	21
Crew	7.2	44	42	42
Cross-Country	46.6	284	241	179
Fencing	9.6	59	58	60
Field Hockey	37.1	226	233	221
Golf	24.1	147	127	121
Gymnastics	25.6	156	172	158
Ice Hockey	1.8	11	9	8
Lacrosse	13.9	85	84	79
Riding	3.1	19	15	12
Riflery	3.4	21	20	23
Sailing	1.9	12	15	14
Skiing	5.2	32	28	22
Soccer	8.2	50	28	17
Softball	62.3	380	359	297
Squash	2.8	17	15	14
Swimming/Diving	46.9	286	273	250
Synch. Swimming	3.2	20	21	20
Tennis	88.6	540	527	487
Track	58.6	357	331	281
Volleyball	87.8	535	523	488

Table 2

Percentage of Women's Teams Coached by Females

Sport	1979/80	1978/79	1977/78
*Archery	76.5	75.0	83.4
*Badminton	72.7	73.0	75.0
*Basketball	76.5	77.7	79.4
*Bowling	40.9	36.4	42.9
Crew	18.2	19.1	11.9
*Cross-Country	25.0	29.9	35.2
*Fencing	37.3	46.6	51.7
*Field Hockey	98.3	97.4	99.1
*Golf	46.3	55.1	54.6
*Gymnastics	66.6	68.0	69.7
*Ice Hockey	18.2	11.1	37.5
Lacrosse	100.0	100.0	98.7
*Riding	73.7	73.4	75.0
Riflery	19.0	10.0	17.4
Sailing	8.3	13.3	7.1
Skiing	25.0	25.0	22.7
*Soccer	28.0	35.7	29.4
*Softball	82.9	83.1	83.5
*Squash	53.0	73.3	71.4
*Swimming/Div.	44.8	50.9	53.6
Synch. Swim	95.0	90.5	85.0
*Tennis	68.9	71.6	72.9
*Track	43.1	46.5	52.3
*Volleyball	83.7	83.6	86.6

* % decline from 1977 to 1980
Total % of women coaching women's teams:
1977/78 - 58.2
1978/79 - 56.1
1979/80 - 54.2

Although this study was not intended to determine cause and effect relationships, it might be intuitively hypothesized that the gender make-up of the administration might have some effect on the gender make-up of the coaching staffs. Both phases of data gathering have indicated that more than 80% of women's intercollegiate athletic programs are under the supervision of a male head athletic director. This figure is perhaps more shocking when it is realized that the trend analysis of the data shows an increasing movement to more head athletic directors being male.

Even more striking is the fact that no female at all is involved in the administration of over 30% of women's athletics programs, and the percentage is growing as we increase the distance from Title IX compliance dates. Thirty-four percent of colleges and universities having women's intercollegiate athletic programs have only one administrator of the programs. A greater number (36.6%) have two while only 16.0% have three. It seems logical to assume that many colleges select an administrative structure involving only one or two individuals in response to budgetary considerations. However, while over 36% of the institutions have two administrators, less than 20% of all institutions have a female administering the women's program. This means that even where institutions have two administrators, the women's program is still often not supervised by a woman.

CONCLUSIONS

The opportunities for women to participate in intercollegiate sports have been increasing in the last 5 years. The last 2 years see some change and restricting of the choice of those opportunities however.

Although the opportunity for participation is growing, the opportunity for placement in either coaching or administering those sports is decreasing on a percentage basis. Thus, at a time when women are developing an affection for competitive sport (perhaps the affection has always been present but the opportunity was lacking), these same women will find it more and more difficult to market their experience as coaches and administrators.

The change in sport offerings away from some of the "minor sports" to those more traditionally coachable by men, may be an indication of the impending demise of the variety which has long marked women's sport participation. It is difficult to support the notion that such a contraction of offerings is good.

Similarly, the decreased percentage of women serving as coaches and administrators seems to remove some of the support for the profession's current development of coaching curricula for physical education majors of both sexes. Intuition tells us that the movement toward a male dominated national governing body as well as the significant increase in male controlled women's programs is likely to only expand the exclusion of women in the roles of coaches and administrators.

FOOTNOTES

1. *New York Times*, June 27, 1975, at 16, column 4.

2. Title IX provides that "no person. . .shall, on the basis of sex, be excluded from participation in, be denied the benefits of, or be subject to discrimination under any education program or activity receiving federal financial assistance . . ." 20 USC section 1681 (Supp V 1975).

3. "Title IX Under Attack," *Update*, American Alliance for Health, Physical Education, Recreation and Dance, October, 1981, page, 1.

4. The study is continuing through 1983 and beyond and is supported in part by a grant from the Professional Staff Congress/Research Foundation of the City University of New York Faculty Research Grant Program.

5. Post secondary schools were required to be in compliance with the provisions of Title IX by July 21, 1978.

6. Alfa Alexander, Temple University, 1978.

7. AIAW is the governing body for the majority of women's intercollegiate sports programs in the United States. A comparison could be drawn to the NCAA which governs men's intercollegiate sports. It is important to note, however, that as of this writing, the AIAW and the NCAA are involved in litigation to determine which group will govern women's sports in the future.

8. Milton G. Homan and Bonnie L. Parkhouse. "Trends in the Selection of Coaches for Female Athletes: A Demographic Inquiry." *Research Quarterly for Exercise and Sport*, Vol. 52, Number 1, March, 1981, page, 9.

9. The impact of Title IX is not limited to students.

10. A ruling on the case is expected in spring, 1983.

Section D

The Racial Question

There are fewer than 1,000 blacks making a living playing professional sports, while every black kid is busting his butt so he can make it, too...perhaps three million black youths between 13 and 22 are out there dreaming of careers as professional athletes...The odds against them are worse than 20,000 to 1.

Harry Edwards in John Underwood
(1980:60)

Let's name some of the most important college athletes of our time—Ralph Sampson and Kareem Abdul Jabbar in basketball, Herschel Walker and O.J. Simpson in football. It is obvious, then, that black athletes capture a good deal of the sporting public's attention. Yet as Edwards' quotation clearly tells us, chances are any particular individual will probably not become a professional athlete. Yet the myth persists—the myth that you can make it if you try hard enough regardless of racial or ethnic background, or of social class. As Brower (1972) has noted, blacks are stereotypically expected not to have the leadership abilities and mental skills required for the important central leadership positions in sport. Blacks apparently have to perform better in baseball, batting almost 20 points better than white players (Rosenblatt, 1967), and are only kept on sport teams if their performance is clearly superior to white players (Brower, 1972; Pascal & Rapping, 1970).

While one might expect racism to rear its ugly head in the money-chasing world of professional sports, one might hope the idealistic tower of ivy will not exhibit such discrimination. As the papers in this section demonstrate, however, differential treatment relative to an athlete or coach's skin color may very well be found at the American college and university. As sport reflects the dominant American belief system, so do the higher educational institutions which are dependent upon society for their survival.

In the first article Adolph Grundman looks at the relationship of the premises of the civil rights movement and sport, and the racial frustrations of the 1960s. In the '50s it was assumed that blacks could enter the American marketplace having had the obstacles of racial discrimination removed. After all, had not America fought World War II for the principles of freedom and against Nazi claims of the superiority/inferiority of races? After all, had not America seen Jackie Robinson rise to stardom? It was assumed in the '50s that removal of racial barriers was inevitable and was proceeding inexorably. Criticisms of sport as insensitive to the needs of the blacks came, then, as a great surprise to most Americans. To critics such as Harry Edwards and Jack Olsen, the sporting establishment was patently racist: a system which used athletes at both the professional and collegiate level; a system which recruited black athletes poorly prepared for college coursework, used up their athletic eligibility, and then discarded the young black, often without an education. The white power structure of this nation was shocked to hear this critique of one of their most sacred institutions.

In Grundman's view, the reasons for white society's shock rests on the exaggerated picture of the integrative powers of college sport because of the liberal's belief in the inevitable "triumph of egalitarianism" in American society and in the assumption that blacks would want to, could, and should gain acceptance in white society by acting and thinking like whites. Romantic images of sport as an instrument to build sportsmanship and character held fast in the '50s and did not yield easily to charges of tokenism—the use of a few highly skilled black athletes to promote winning and images of institutional liberalism.

The racism historically discussed in Grundman's article is researched empirically by Chu and Segrave in their article "Leadership Recruitment and Ethnic Stratification in Basketball." In this piece, the sport of college and professional basketball is examined relative to the race of players and coaches, the positions in which they played, and the assumption of leadership positions in the sport. With the apparent domination of black players in basketball, observers have suggested that blacks may be less often "stacked" (i.e., assigned to only a limited number of playing positions) in basketball and have more of an opportunity to gain coaching positions.

Based upon a sample drawn from 1978-79 college and professional basketball teams, it was found, however, that though blacks comprised 33% of all college players, only 9% of all coaches at that level were black. In addition, it was found that white players are disproportionately found at the guard position, the position most highly related to leadership opportunities, and that white players are most often selected as head or assistant coaches. Furthermore, in comparing whites and blacks who played the guard position, the white player is more than 15 times as likely to be selected for a coaching position.

Though proponents of intercollegiate sport might want to justify its costly existence on the campus because of its utility as an instrument of racial integration, the articles in this section suggest the invalidity of this argument. Black athletes, though highly visible on campus, may be too often token racial representatives still answerable to the dominant white standards of those controlling higher education and sport. Even when given the opportunity to play at the big-time sport level, the black athlete may not be afforded the opportunity to progress into leadership positions.

In the previous section, the limits of opportunity for women in intercollegiate sport were pointed out. In much the same way, the record of black participation in campus sport forces the observer to recognize the limits of intercollegiate athletics as a means of providing opportunities for advancement for the black athlete.

REFERENCES

BROWER, J.J. (1972) *The racial basis of the division of labor among players in the national football league as function of stereotypes*. Paper presented at the annual meetings of the Pacific Sociological Association, Portland.

PASCAL, A.M., & Rapping, L.A. (1970). *Racial discrimination in organized baseball*. Santa Monica, CA: The Rand Corporation.

ROSENBLATT, A. (1967, September). The shame of American education: The student-athlete hoax. *Sports Illustrated*, 38-44, 47-48, 52-54, 57, 60, 62, 65-66, 71-72.

Chapter 24

The Image
of Intercollegiate Sports
and the Civil Rights Movement:
A Historian's View

Adolph H. Grundman
Metropolitan State College

HISTORICAL OVERVIEW
OF THE SPORT/RACISM RELATIONSHIP

In the late 1960s, the American view of the relationship of sport and racism received a severe jolt. Until that time conventional wisdom held that sport treated blacks fairly and that it contributed mightily to good race relations. The *New York Times* captured the spirit of the latter ideal when it wrote that "there has been no one channel of understanding that has been better than that of sports. It has proved that most problems can be solved in the right spirit."[1] John Lardner, the sophisticated sports columnist of *Newsweek* in the 1950s, wrote that "race equality in baseball and in jazz music had done more than anything else to improve the climate for integration in America."[2]

Thus, it came as a shock, in 1967, when 200 participants to the Black Youth Conference, including some of America's foremost black collegiate athletes, voted to boycott the 1968 Olympics.[3] The essence of the protest was that blacks served as America's athletic "spear carriers" while the larger society remained insensitive to the condition of black America. *Life* magazine spoke for middle-America and conventional wisdom when it observed, "The athletic achievements of individual Negroes have been a source of great pride for all Negroes. The more young Negro athletes add to these powerful examples, the more they will do for their race."[4] Nonetheless, the organizer of the conference, sociologist Harry Edwards, emerged as a leading critic of the sport, especially as it applied to the

black athlete. In 1968 Jack Olsen explored the shortcomings of sport in its treatment of black athletes in a *Sports Illustrated* series which later appeared in book
form.[5] At the collegiate level, Olsen described a very sordid story. His portrait
of the black athlete depicted a young person poorly prepared for college, directed
toward the easiest courses, and upon using up his eligiblity, left with neither an
education nor a degree.

The Edwards-Olsen critique and related events were an expression of the black
militancy and the general reexamination of American culture that peaked in the
second half of the decade. Stokely Carmichael, remember, introduced the phrase
"black power" in Greenwood, Mississippi, in the summer of 1966. As blacks
sought ways of influencing society, they naturally turned to the world of sports
where they participated in numbers which far exceeded their proportion in
American society. In fact, given the mood of the mid-1960s, it would have been
strange indeed if sport had remained unaffected. Although one might dispute parts
of the Edwards-Olsen indictment, their work brought a new level of sophistication to the study of sport and established the new parameters of the debate regarding blacks and sport. Yet a review of their work and other secondary literature
revealed that most authors focused on exposing or detailing the racism of the
sports establishment. Perhaps, because they were engaged in much needed
muckraking, they avoided a full exploration of the reasons for the failure of racial
integration in sport; or, to be more exact, they simply used their examples as
further proof of racism in American society. They neglected to examine the relationship of the premises of the civil rights movement and sport to the frustrations
of the 1960s which is the purpose of this paper. In fact, the integration of sports
has some very close parallels to the civil rights movement.

The foundation of the civil rights movement of the 1950s was simply that all
barriers to equal opportunity should be removed. As white liberal America and
middle-class blacks envisioned the future, blacks, without the handicap of past
prejudice, would enter the marketplace where they would rise or fall according
to their abilities. Although industrialization, urbanization, and a technological
revolution had made the individual in the marketplace or the self-made man a
myth, its attraction was and remains powerful. This was especially so in the '50s
when America's booming economy suggested that blacks could be propelled into
the economic mainstream of American society without hurting whites. In addition, liberals shared the view that America must act, in its fashion, against racism
in America. The idealistic rhetoric of World War II, the decolonization of the
Third World, and the Cold War confrontation with the Soviet Union required
some action on the part of the United States. This was the background to the
famous school desegregation decision, *Brown versus Board of Education*, and
it was also the backdrop to an important transition for the black collegiate athlete.

Prior to World War II, blacks competed with distinction for white colleges
and universities in football, basketball, baseball, and track. Paul Robeson,
Frederick "Fritz" Pollard, Fred "Duke" Slater, De Hart Hubbard, Eddie Tolan,
Ralph Metcalfe, Jackie Robinson, and Kenny Washington were among the
notables. Nonetheless, white colleges provided spots for only a token black athlete,

and, of course, in the South and Southwest, there were no blacks attending white colleges or universities. As a result, black colleges provided competition for hundreds of skilled performers known only to those in the black community.[6] The galloping professionalization of collegiate sports after World War II, particularly football and basketball, made the recuitment of black athletes especially enticing. Many athletic programs saw this untapped source of talent as a shortcut to national recognition. Consequently, universities outside the South were in the enviable position where they could build their athletic programs and claim that they were advancing the cause of race relations in America. The media, in turn, pointed with pride to collegiate sports (as well as professional) as a model for race relations in American society.

SCHOLARSHIP OPPORTUNITIES

In the beginning, the black athletes offered scholarships were selected with care. The impression given by the media was that integration would not jeopardize the mythic tradition of the scholar athlete. As in the first examples of school integration in the South, the first black athletes were super-blacks who were admitted on white terms. To cite an example, the University of Illinois' J.C. Caroline received much publicity during the early 1950s as he broke many of the offensive records of the legendary Harold "Red" Grange. The media portrayed Caroline, a native of South Carolina, as a black Horatio Alger. With no steady home until the age of 14, Caroline's football skills were the ticket to Illinois. Although Caroline flunked two courses in his sophomore year, he was described as a serious student. The sports publicity director observed that "I never saw a boy work so hard. He hardly took time off from his books all summer." Caroline hinted at the real problem when he said

> If they would just leave you alone around exam time. I am up here to get an education. I'm not just going to play football. A man has to improve himself. The only way to do it is to get an education.

In addition to stressing this interest in education, Caroline was described as a person with simple tastes and meager wants who did not smoke or drink.[7] Finally, Caroline avoided civil rights controversies. Although the campus barbershop excluded blacks, Caroline refused to join a campus organization's protest of this policy on the theory that "one person in particular is not going to stop anything like that."[8] Given this portrait of Caroline, it was not surprising and probably obligatory for a journalist to comment "Caroline's teammates say that there is absolutely no racial prejudice on the team."[9]

Several years later Prentice Gautt, Oklahoma's first black football player, was described the same way. Gautt rejected other scholarships offered to enroll at Oklahoma where his education was financed by a "group of doctors, dentists, and pharmacists." Although his football exploits received much attention, *Look* magazine did not fail to add that he was carrying a "B" average. *Look* credited Bud Wilkinson, the Oklahoma coach, with exercising "soft-spoken moral guidance." Wilkinson, in turn, thought that "A person less fine than Prentice would not have made his contribution." In reflecting upon his career at Oklahoma, Gautt admitted that the first year had been tough, but added, "It was my fault. I held back." Again, Gautt's career was a civil rights moral because *Look* noted that the freshman team had walked out of a restaurant which refused to serve him.[10]

INTEGRATION PROBLEMS

The Caroline-Gautt examples showed that integration in sport as in public schools was a one-way street in which it was incumbent upon blacks to demonstrate their ability to assimilate the white value system. Although 1960s revisionists rightly criticized the unfairness of their process, they forgot, because history had moved so rapidly, how enlightened the Caroline-Gautt road appeared to the '50s generation. After all, when historian Kenneth Stampp wrote in his preface to *The Peculiar Institution* that "Negroes are, after all, only white men with black skins, nothing more, nothing less," this was considered a statement of model liberal enlightenment.[11] When local black leaders sent the Carolines and Gautts to white schools, it was to prove that Stampp was correct. The prestige of the universities and the eminence of the United States made it difficult to buck the one-way street to integration. After all, it was not until 1962 that James Baldwin asked, "Do I really want to be integrated into a burning house?"[12]

In addition to identifying models for integration in sport, the media pointed to other civil rights victories in the athletic arena. Following the 1954 school desegregation ruling, the South responded by announcing that it would resist any measures that compromised racial segregation. For intercollegiate sports, this meant that some states and universities passed laws or adopted policies which prohibited competition in the South with institutions that had black players on their athletic teams. One example of the intermingling of sport and politics came in December of 1955 when the segregationist Governor of Georgia, Marvin Griffin, asked Georgia Tech to reject its Sugar Bowl bid because its opponent, the University of Pittsburgh, had a black player, Bobby Grier. Although 2000 students protested at the Georgia State capital and the *Atlanta Journal* thought the recommendation "ill considered," these reservations had little to do with civil rights or Georgia Tech's decision to remain in the Sugar Bowl. As one unhappy segregationist regent observed, principles were easily sacrificed "when there is money involved." David Rice, a Georgia Tech regent who favored Sugar Bowl participation, described Griffin's request as "ridiculous and asinine" because it would limit future bowl bids and hurt recruiting. The Georgia Board of Regents genuflected in the direction of "principle" by banning Georgia schools from future bowl bids in the South which did not follow segregation laws and customs.[13]

In assessing these events, the *New York Times* not only observed that the students were not motivated by principle, but agreed with them that "The issue is not discrimination but a good football game." In formulating the dominant liberal position of the moment, the *Times* argued, "The test in any question of race is not one of pigmentation but of performance." In underscoring its commitment to equality of opportunty, the *Times* observed that "The person who is really interested in human achievement...doesn't care about racial origins when he sees the results." Significantly, it was in the sports arena that the *Times* saw color blindness at its best. In its estimate of race relations, it thought that at "no point has this struggle been better and more happily carrried out than in the world of sport." The reason for this, the *Times* later wrote, was that this "is the one field in which individual human performance can be accurately measured." Expanding upon this idea in a subsequent editorial, the *Times* stressed that performance was the basis upon which "our whole (race) problem must eventually be solved. Judgments must be made on the basis of worth, not prejudice."[14]

From the liberal vantage point, collegiate sport seemed to mark the triumph of equalitarian ideals in American society. The refusal of some southern schools to play racially integrated teams in the South was occasionally met by a decision of a northern school to withdraw from a basketball tournament or cancel a southern trip. The *New York Times*, for one, applauded these boycotts as a way of "simply making it plain that concepts that they have long discarded shall not be enforced upon them."[15] Some major football powers from the North did refuse to cancel games with southern teams. The University of Syracuse thought it "unsportsmanlike" to refuse to play a worthy opponent. It told protesting alumni "that fielding a team dedicated to the best ideals is a good example for others to follow." When three Michigan State legislators asked the University of Michigan to cancel a game with the University of Georgia, the University of Michigan Board of Control of Intercollegiate Athletics thought it "legally, morally, and socially unjustifiable."[16]

Despite these setbacks, from an integrationist point of view, collegiate sport was heading in the right direction. In 1963 the University of Kentucky announced that it would open its athletic program to all races. In 1964 Billy Jones was the first black basketball player to sign a letter of intent at the University of Maryland and the first in Atlantic Coast Conference. When Warren McVea signed with the University of Houston, he and the university received national attention. The *New York Times*, once again, capsulized the liberal view of these events when it observed,

A few outfielders like Willie Mays, a few centers like Bill Russell, a few fullbacks like Jim Brown—who knows what tremendous champions might come out of the Southeast, with such recruits to build upon, and what miracles might be worked in better race relations?[17]

The passage of time demonstrated that black achievement in sport did not have a significant spillover effect in other aspects of American social, political, and economic life. Advancements in these areas were and are the result of hard fought political and legal action.

THE ALL-AMERICAN—
A MODEL FOR RACE RELATIONS

The 1950s' faith in sports as a model for race relations did not rest solely upon the belief that this was an arena where talent prevailed. Many Americans also held a romantic view of sports. They believed that sports built character and mandated good sportsmanship. Perhaps the concept of an All-American best captured the spirit of this ideal. As late as 1960 *Look* prefaced the selection of its All-American football team by stating that

> Sportsmanship and good behavior carried more weight than ever...Walter Camp, Casper Whitney, and Grantland Rice intended that the team reflect not only physical skill, but chivalry as well. The football writers cherish this image and intend to preserve it.

The All-America players, *Look* concluded, were unselfish, avoided brutality, never violated the rules and found that "the true reward of football is the communal-effort experience, climaxed by victory or at least by the sure knowledge that their effort is complete."[18]

This ideal was tested with the integration of collegiate sport and stauchly defended, especially when it was breached. In 1951, for example, when Johnny Bright, a record-breaking black back at Drake University, had his jaw broken by an illegal forearm, the Oklahoma A&M coach, J.B. Whitworth, denied that his players ganged up on Bright. In the face of overwhelming photographic evidence, Whitworth apologized for the offender, Wilbanks Smith, but did not discipline him. Whitworth described Smith as "not the dirty type of football player. He just lost his head for a few minutes." Nine years later, to cite another example, the Syracuse football team charged that Texas players had barked racial slurs at them during the former's Cotton Bowl victory. Although Texas coach, Darrel Royal, refused to comment, the University of Texas president, Logan Wilson, branded the charges as irresponsible. "They have damaged the reputation of this university, of a fine football team and of intercollegiate athletics generally."[19]

The '50s' romantic view of sport also helped that generation to overlook the fact that racial integration in sports was limited to the superstar. In 1958, *Life* magazine predicted that

> on the basis of performance over the last season it is possible—and many coaches think it very probable that this year will see a unique All-America: every player will be a Negro.

The players were Oscar Robertson, Wilt Chamberlain, Bob Boozer, Elgin Baylor, and Guy Rodgers. The *New York Times* also observed that the 1957-58 season marked the first time that more than "two Negroes" were named to the first team basketball All-America.[20] This evidence of racial progress hid another significant reality: Black representation at white universities was limited to star athletes.

Another example of making much out of tokenism was the celebrated recruiting race for Wilt Chamberlain.[21] The effort to attract Chamberlain to the University of Kansas involved an elaborate strategy headed by Coach Forrest "Phog" Allen. In explaining the intensity of this recruiting effort, the KU president, Franklin D. Murphy, said that he was eager to improve racial integration in Kansas and that he had thought earlier about attracting a top Negro athlete to the campus. Coach Allen outdid Murphy by explaining that Kansas succeeded in getting Chamberlain because "we showed him how successful the Negro in Kansas was." Because Kansas had fought school desegregation before the Supreme Court between 1952 and 1955, Allen's statement contained more than a little historic irony.

The record of recruiting excesses in the name of civil rights showed that black middle class uncritically entered into this game. *Ebony* magazine, the voice of the black middle class, boasted that five black high school stars—Warren McVea, Vernon Payne, Mile Warren, Westley Unseld, and James Dugan were worth $5 million. *Ebony* based this exaggerated statement of financial worth on their "firm offers of athletic grants-in-aid to attend nearly every major college in the country." Black athletes, from *Ebony*'s perspective, were symbols of racial and economic progress. The popular literature also suggested that the black middle class was also the medium between the athlete and the recruiting institution. In pursuing Chamberlain, the University of Kansas utilized a black concert singer, a black publisher, and a black businessman to sing the praises of KU. In recruiting Warren McVea, described as the first Negro to receive a football scholarship to a major previously all-white conference, Houston coach, Bill Yeoman, worked through the leadership of Houston's black community. All of this suggested that white institutions devoted some time to stroking the ego of the black middle class.[22]

By the end of 1967 racial integration passed another watershed. *Ebony* carried an article which reported that blacks were breaking into the schools of the "Old South." In reporting that Glen Page had died in a freakish accident at Kentucky, *Ebony* eulogized that "Page was credited with having made an outstanding contribution to race relations in Kentucky." The only sour note struck from Florida A&M's famous football coach, Jake Gaither, who noted that the Old South's new recruiting policies hurt black colleges. He added that black athletes were exploited by white schools and would be until there is complete integration into every phase of college life.[23]

Another watershed in 1967 was the emergence of numerical superiority of blacks on the 1966-67 *Look* All-America basketball team. Six of the ten All-Americans were black, and the following year eight black basketball players were named to *Look*'s top 10. The domination of basketball by blacks was not accompanied by any fanfare on behalf of race relations. Beneath this apparent color blindness lurked a concern, often expressed indirectly, about black domination of this game. This concern was expressed in several ways. For example, in the early '60s, *Look* commented upon the return of "a patterned ball-control offense, which seeks the good percentage shot....the game (as) it is meant to be—one of balanced skills." *Look* also emphasized that an All-American "must be a team player." Was *Look* saying, in effect, that basketball was still played according to white principles? Whatever the answer, the virtuosity of black players caused a ferment in college basketball where the blending of individualism and the team concept were more difficult than in football.[24]

In addition to style, the influx of black college stars led to a search for "white hopes." *Look*'s effusiveness over Princeton's Bill Bradley was unmatched in the history of its All-America. According to *Look*,

> Bradley's skills are matched by his dedication and his team attitude. Nothing he might do with a basketball would surprise. He might even convert those few who regard the sport as anathema.

Oscar Robertson, in *Look*'s opinion, was the only collegiate player to top Bradley. *Look* seemed relieved when it wrote:

> Whether the Tiger nobody holds could go on to match or surpass Robertson as a pro never will be known because Bradley has rejected a career with the New York Knickerbockers to accept a Rhodes Scholarship at Oxford.[25]

Bradley's appeal rested on his skill, his color, and his ability to confirm middle-class values. His play was a perfect blend of individualism and cooperation; his skills derived from "dedication" as much as natural ability; and his Rhodes Scholarship saved him from the sin of overemphasis.

It was ironic that black domination of the All-American basketball teams and the extension of scholarships to black athletes by the universities of the Old South came in 1967. After all, as discussed earlier, this was also the year that some black athletes made a serious effort to boycott the Olympics.[26] The black indictment of sports surprisingly came at the very moment when black athletes seemed to have broken all intercollegiate color barriers. Significantly, this paralleled the larger civil rights movement. Black nationalism, violence in American cities, and second thoughts about integration followed or paralleled the Civil Rights Act of 1964, the Voting Rights Act of 1965, and the Supreme Court decisions ordering busing to integrate public schools. The linkage between intercollegiate sports and society seemed almost perfect. Intercollegiate sports were not merely reflecting society, they were part of it. Their failure to serve as a model of equality of opportunity and race relations was due to the fact that intercollegiate sports were closely connected with the symbols and economics of America. The belief so widely held in the early '50s and encouraged by the media that intercollegiate sports were different from the rest of society was less easily held in the late '60s. Thus, by 1968, as black and white civil rights activists advocated equality of result through affirmative action, intercollegiate sports stood as one more example of the limitations of equality of opportunity.

FOOTNOTES

1. Editorial, *New York Times*, May 31, 1959, IV, 8.

2. John Lardner, "The Old Emancipator—1," *Newsweek*, April 2, 1956, p. 85.

3. *New York Times*, November 24, 2967, p. 8.

4. Editorial, *Life*, December 8, 1967, p. 4.

5. Jack Olsen, *The Black Athlete, A Shameful Story: The Myth of Integration in American Sport* (New York: Time-Life Books, 1968). The *Sports Illustrated* series began on July 1, 1968. See also Harry Edwards, *The Revolt of the Black Athlete* (New York: The Free Press, 1969).

6. Ocania Chalk, *Black College Sport* (New York: Dodd, Mead and Company, 1976).

7. Fred Parker, "The Skinny Terror of Illinois," *Saturday Evening Post*, October 9, 1954, pp. 31, 117-120.

8. Letter to the Editor, *Saturday Evening Post*, November 27, 1954, p. 4.

9. Parker, "The Skinny Terror," p. 119.

10. "Oklahoma's Quiet Powerhouse," *Look*, October 13, 1959, p. 54.

11. Kenneth M. Stamp, *That Peculiar Institution: Slavery in the Ante-Bellum South* (New York: Vintage Books, 1956), p. vii.

12. James Baldwin, *The Fire Next Time* (New York: Dell Publishing, 1962), p. 127.

13. *New York Times*, December 4, 1955, p. 1; December 3, 1955, p. 1; and December 6, 1955, p. 1.

14. Editorials, Ibid., December 4, 1955, E, p. 10; July 22, 1956, E, p. 8; and May 31, 1959, IV, p. 8.

15. Editorial, Ibid., October 6, 1956, p. 20.

16. *New York Times*, February 18, 1964, p. 20, and February 16, 1957, p. 10.

17. Ibid., May 30, 1963, p. 13; April 9, 1964, p. 37; Mickey Herskowitz, "Warren goes this away and that away," *Sports Illustrated*, November 9, 1964, pp. 48-49; and Editorial, *New York Times*, April 21, 1963, IV, p. 8.

18. Tim Cohane, "Football All-America—1960," *Look*, December 20, 1960, pp. 130-36.

19. *New York Times*, October 22, 1951, p. 28; October 23, 1951, p. 39; January 2, 1960, p. 8; and January 12, 1960, p. 24.

20. "New Look for the All-America," *Life*, March 10, 1958, pp. 99, and *New York Times*, March 6, 1958, p. 34.

21. "What It Took To Get Wilt," *Life*, January 28, 1957, pp. 113-17.

22. "Athletes—500 Scholarships," *Ebony*, October, 1964, pp. 57-61; "Wilt," *Life*, p. 114; and Herkowitz, "Warren goes this away," p. 48.

23. Louie Robinson, "New Football Stars in the Old South," *Ebony*, December, 1967, pp. 75-78.

24. "Basketball All-America—1966-67," *Look*, March 21, 1967, pp. 71-75; "Basketball All-America—1967-68," *Look*, March 19, 1968, pp. 91-93; "Basketball All-America—1962-63," *Look*, March 26, 1963, pp. 109-12; and "Basketball All-America," *Look*, March 27, 1962, pp. 111-14.

25. "Basketball All-America—1964-65," *Look*, March 23, 1965, pp. 87-91.

26. This was not the first time that black athletes advocated an Olympic boycott. See Mal Whitfield, "Let's Boycott the Olympics," *Ebony*, March 1964, pp. 95-100.

Chapter 25

Leadership Recruitment and Ethnic Stratification in Basketball

Donald B. Chu and Jeffrey O. Segrave
Skidmore College

Considerable empirical evidence has suggested that patterns of leadership and group composition in American team sports may be accounted for in terms of organizational structure. This body of literature has indicated that leadership recruitment and ethnic stratification may be viewed as a function of the occupation of position of high interaction (i.e., positions of centrality within the formal organizational structure of certain team sports). These findings are based largely on the theories originally posited by Blalock (1962) and Grusky (1963). Blalock (1962) proposed that occupational discrimination is positively associated with the degree of social interaction required on the job. Grusky (1963) hypothesized that

> All else being equal, the more central one's spatial location: (1) the greater the likelihood dependent or coordinative tasks will be performed and (2) the greater the rate of interaction with the occupants of other positions. Also the performance of dependent tasks is positively related to frequency of interaction. (p. 346)

Based on the rationale underlying Blalock's and Grusky's model, several studies have indicated a positive relationship between centrality of playing position and the occupation of positions of team leadership (i.e., captain and co-captain) in a variety of team sports, including baseball (Loy & Sage, 1970; Loy, Sage & Ingham, 1970), football (Sage, 1974), and hockey (Roy, 1974). Similarly, positive

The authors express their gratitude to Norma Unczer and Kim Alger for their research assistance. Special thanks must also be extended to J. Ray Cooley for his unflagging support.

relationships have also been found between centrality of playing position and leadership recruitment (e.g., leading to the role of coach and manager) in various team sport settings such as hockey (Roy, 1974), football (Massengale & Farrington, 1977; Roland 1977), baseball (Grusky, 1963; Loy, Sage, & Ingham, 1970) and basketball (Klonsky, 1975).

Combining the theoretical propositions of Blalock and Grusky, Loy and McElvogue (1970) extended the research on centrality to account for patterns of racial segregation in football and baseball. Specifically, they demonstrated that whites were overrepresented in the central, high-interactive playing positions, while blacks were overrepresented in the peripheral (noncentral) positions. The overrepresentation of certain groups by playing position, commonly referred to as "stacking" has been well substantiated in football (Madison & Landers, 1971; Brower, 1972; Ball, 1973), baseball (Rosenblatt, 1967; Loy & McElvogue, 1920; Henderson, 1975; Dougherty, 1976; Leonard, 1977), and basketball (Eitzen & Tessendorf, 1978). With the relegation of minority groups to peripheral playing positions, it is hardly surprising that members of racial or ethnic groups are underrepresented in decision-making positions at both management and coaching levels.

THE SPECIAL CASE OF BASKETBALL

Although the consequences of racial segregation for the process of leadership recruitment has been empirically substantiated for football, baseball, and hockey, this line of research was not, until recently, extended to the sport of basketball largely on the grounds that it somehow represented a "special case." It was Edwards (1973) who indicated that basketball may be the exception to the stacking phenomenon when he stated that

> ...in basketball there is no positional certainty as in the case in football and baseball, because there are no fixed zones of role responsibility attached to specific positions. (p. 213)

Arguing to the contrary, however, Eitzen and Tessendorf (1978) found support for their hypothesis that "blacks would be overly represented at the forward position, while underrepresented at the center and guard positions" (p. 119). From a survey of 274 integrated college basketball teams from the 1970-71 season, they concluded that the role responsibilities attached to specific positions tended to

> ...apportion whites to those positions most responsible for the outcome of games because they require decision-making leadership and dependability while blacks are shunted by coaches (either intentionally or unintentionally) to those positions where the requisite characteristics are quickness, jumping ability, and other physical attributes. (p. 125)

After reviewing the collegiate baskeball data for the years 1974-75, however, research seemed to indicate a modification of the 1970-71 findings. In their 1977 study, Eitzen and Yetman concluded that for basketball

> The pattern of stacking detected in 1970-71 has not persisted. Thus although stacking has remained in football and baseball, the situation in basketball (most heavily black in racial composition of the three major sports) would appear to have undergone substantial change during the first half of the 1970s. (pp. 395-396)

According to Eitzen and Yetman (1977), accompanying the steady decline in the stacking of black collegiate basketball players, there has also been a corresponding increase in the percentages of blacks coaching the sport. Whereas in 1970 there were but two, in 1973 there were 21 black head basketball coaches. Eitzen and Yetman optimistically note an appreciable change in the percentage of black head basketball coaches at the major colleges, with blacks comprising but 0.64% in 1970 as opposed to 5.1% in 1975.

From this brief review of the literature, it appears that though there may exist patterns of stacking in the sport of basketball, there appears to be considerable change. Blacks are less often stacked at the forward position and more often allowed to play the guard position.

It is the purpose of the present study to extend the centrality hypothesis to account for patterns of leadership recruitment and racial discrimination in the sport of basketball. For the purpose of this study, the guard is considered as the position of greatest centrality. Although the center is clearly the most centrally located playing position, it is, as others have pointed out, (Klonsky, 1975; Loy, McPherson, & Kenyon, 1978) in fact a low interaction position which does not require the high rate of interaction and the performance of dependent and coordinative tasks which typifies the role responsibilites of the guard.

Based upon the previous research which relates the concept of centrality to leadership recruitment and ethnic stratification, it is hypothesized that for the sport of basketball

1. Players occupying the position of guard are more likely than forwards and centers to have access to the positions of head and assistant coach.
2. Because white players are disproportionately found at the guard position (Eitzen & Tessendorf, 1978), whites are more likely than blacks to be selected as head and assistant coaches.

In order to evaluate these hypotheses, data were collected from both collegiate (NCAA) and professional (NBA) coaches. Collegiate data was further broken down to Divisions I, II, and III. This was done to investigate the contention that disparities in leadership opportunities are most evident at the "big-time" sport level.

Methods

The study covered the 1978-79 collegiate and professional basketball season. Drawing from the *NCAA Official Basketball Guide* listing 726 member institutions, questionnaires were mailed to the athletic directors of 380 schools. The sample was stratified as follows: 125 out of 254 Division I, 108 out of 173 Division II, and 147 out of 299 Division III institutions. A total of 271 questionnaires were returned, representing a response rate of 71%. Of the 271 questionnaires received, 12 were discarded due to incomplete information. The final usable sample was 259 schools of which 89 were Divison I, 80 were Division II, and 88 were Division III.

Professional ranks were surveyed by telephone. Information concerning the professional coaches was gleaned from conversations with franchise spokesmen including the coaches themselves, team secretaries, and public relations personnel. Complete responses were collected from all 22 NBA teams. In all, the total number of basketball organizations used was 281.

Findings

When viewing the present data, it should be remembered that each basketball team is made up of two guards, two forwards, and one center, and that the expected proportions would be 40% and 20%, respectively.

The data presented in Tables 1 and 2 clearly support the first hypothesis:

Hypothesis 1: Players occupying the position of guard are more likely than forwards and centers to have access to the positions of head and assistant coach.

Guards are overrepresented as both head and assistant coaches at all levels. The data, in fact, reveal that 66% of all head coaches and 67% of all assistant coaches

Table 1

**Playing Positions of Head Coaches
in Professional and Collegiate Basketball**

Playing Position	NBA	NCAA Division I	NCAA Division II	NCAA Division III	Totals
Guard	68% (15)	65% (58)	59% (47)	73% (64)	66% (184)
Forward	18% (4)	28% (25)	26% (21)	19% (17)	24% (67)
Center	5% (1)	2% (2)	5% (4)	5% (4)	4% (11)
Other*	9% (2)	5% (4)	10% (8)	3% (3)	6% (17)
Totals	100% (22)	100% (89)	100% (80)	100% (88)	100% (279)*

*Incomplete data for two institutions.

Table 2

**Playing Positions of Assistant Coaches
in Professional and Collegiate Basketball**

Playing Position	NBA	NCAA Division I	NCAA Division II	NCAA Division III	Totals
Guard	52% (14)	68% (23)	66% (27)	77% (39)	67% (103)
Forward	22% (6)	24% (8)	27% (11)	14% (7)	21% (32)
Center	4% (1)	6% (2)	5% (2)	8% (4)	6% (9)
Other*	22% (6)	3% (1)	2% (1)	2% (1)	6% (9)
Totals	100% (27)	101% (34)	100% (41)	101% (51)	100% (153)

*Includes "swing-men" who did not exclusively play one position and coaches who did not play intercollegiate basketball.

are recruited from the guard position. Moreover, all the other percentages reported in Tables 1 and 2 are remarkably consistent across every playing level (i.e., professional and collegidate divisions). These findings also show that both forwards and centers are underrepresented as head and assistant coaches at both the collegiate and professional level. Overall, these data offer further support for the centrality hypothesis:

Hypothesis 2: Because white players are disproportionately found at the guard position, whites are more likely than blacks to be selected as head and assistant coaches.

Results of the present survey concerning the racial composition of head and assistant coaches are presented in Tables 3 and 4. The data clearly indicate that the coaching ranks at all levels of competition are still predominantly manned by whites. However, it seems that blacks may indeed have made significant strides in this respect. The present study shows that 9% of the head basketball coaches at the collegiate level were recruited from the minority group compared to the 5.1% reported in 1975 (Eitzen & Yetman, 1977). Gross underrepresentations

Table 3

**Racial Composition of Head Coaches
in Professional and Collegiate Basketball**

Race	NBA	NCAA Division I	NCAA Division II	NCAA Division III	Totals
White	86% (19)	92% (82)	86% (69)	95% (84)	91% (254)
Black	14% (3)	8% (7)	14% (11)	5% (4)	9% (25)
Totals	100% (22)	100% (89)	100% (80)	100% (88)	100% (279)

Table 4

**Racial Composition of Assistant Coaches
in Professional and Collegiate Basketball**

Race	NBA	NCAA Division I	NCAA Division II	NCAA Division III	Totals
White	81% (22)	74% (25)	76% (31)	86% (43)	80% (121)
Black	19% (5)	26% (9)	24% (10)	14% (7)	20% (31)
Totals	100% (27)	101% (34)	100% (41)	100% (50)	100% (152)

are apparent, however, when comparing these figures with the total percentage of players who are black, both at the professional (63%) and collegiate (33%) levels (Eitzen & Yetman, 1977).

Among assistant coaches, the situation appears slightly different. Table 4 shows that blacks represent 20% of assistant coaches, while whites comprise 80%. This proportion is once again relatively stable across the professional and collegiate ranks. It seems that the chances of a black becoming an assistant coach are greater than his chances of becoming a head coach.

Tables 5, 6, 7, and 8 classify the present sample of head and assistant coaches by race and playing position.

The data clearly indicate that white guards predominate in the coaching ranks at both professional and collegiate levels. Moreover, these percentages are once again relatively stable across all levels of collegiate competition. The data in Table 7 may be further interpreted through a comparison with the total proportion of college players by position and race as reported by Eitzen and Tessendorf in their Table 9 (1978:120). Reinterpreting the figures in this table, it can be seen that white guards comprised 30%, white forwards 24%, black forwards 17%, white centers 14%, black guards 10%, and black centers 5% of the college basketball player population. Though blacks are most often represented at the playing posi-

Table 5

NBA Head Coaches By Race and Playing Position

Race	Guard	Forward	Center	Other*	Totals
White	59% (13)	14 % (3)	4.5% (1)	9% (2)	85.5% (19)
Black	9% (2)	6.5% (1)	0% (0)	0% (0)	13.5% (3)
Totals	68% (15)	18.5% (4)	4.6% (1)	9% (2)	100% (22)

*Includes "swing-men" who did not exclusively play one position and coaches who did not play intercollegiate basketball.

Table 6
NBA Assistant Coaches by Race and Playing Position

Race	Guard	Forward	Center	Other	Totals
White	41% (11)	15% (6)	4% (1)	22% (6)	82% (22)
Black	11% (3)	7% (2)	0% (0)	0% (0)	18% (5)
Totals	52% (14)	22% (6)	4% (1)	22% (6)	100% (27)

Table 7
NBA Head Basketball Coaches By Race and Playing Position

Race	Guard	Forward	Center	Other	Totals
White	62% (159)	21% (55)	3% (8)	5% (13)	91% (235)
Black	4% (10)	3% (8)	1% (2)	1% (2)	9% (22)
Totals	66% (169)	24% (63)	4% (10)	6% (15)	100% (257)

Table 8
NBA Assistant Basketball Coaches by Race and Playing Position

Race	Guard	Forward	Center	Other*	Totals
White	60% (75)	13% (16)	5% (7)	0.5% (1)	78.5% (99)
Black	11% (14)	8% (10)	0.5% (1)	2% (2)	21.5% (27)
Totals	71% (89)	21% (26)	5.5% (8)	2.5% (3)	100 % (126)

*Includes "swing-men" who did not exclusively play one position and coaches who did not play intercollegiate basketball.

tion of forward, the present study shows that only 3% of college head coaches and 8% of college assistant coaches were previously black forwards. These are also over 15 times as many white coaches who were guards than there are black coaches who previously played the guard position.

Overall, these findings support the second hypothesis and suggest that, because white players are disproportionately found at the guard position, they are more likely than blacks to be selected as head and assistant coaches. The present data indicate that this is true at all levels of competition.

As further evidence of racial discrimination in the selection process of coaches, Table 9 provides a breakdown of inter- and intraracial coaching staffs in professional and collegiate basketball.

Most striking here are the relative numbers of interracial coaching staffs at the collegiate level. Though there are 20 cases of white head coaches with black assistants, there are but 2 black head coaches with white assistants in the sample of 117 coaching staffs included in this table.

DISCUSSION

The evidence presented in this study shows that the central playing position of guard is overrepresented in both the head and assistant coaching ranks at all levels of the sport of basketball. It may be that the high interaction position of guard leads to coaching positions because it (a) attracts individuals with leadership qualities, (b) may be a role into which certain types of players are channeled by their coaches, (c) may develop abilities useful in future leadership roles and (d) may facilitate leadership opportunities due to the affiliative nature of the coordinative and dependent tasks requisite of the guard position.

At the same time that guards are overrepresented in leadership positions, blacks are clearly underrepresented. Although blacks comprise 63% of NBA and 33% of college players, only 14% of professional and 9% of collegiate head basketball coaches are black. The present data suggest that these discriminatory patterns may be accounted for by the relegation of blacks to the peripheral position of forward where leadership opportunities are clearly limited.

Assuming that the star professional basketball player is blessed with a playing career of anywhere from 10-15 years, we could expect his availability as a coach somewhere between 10-15 years after entrance into the league. Whereas in 1966 almost 51% of all NBA players were black, 13 years later, only 14% of head coaches in the professional ranks were black. In the college ranks the situation is a bit different. Because most college coaches have not played professional basketball, they are available as coaches sooner than their professional colleagues. If

Table 9
Intra- and Interracial Coaching Staffs
in Professional and Collegiate Basketball

Level	White Head White Ass't	Black Head Black Ass't	White Head Black Ass't	Black Head White Ass't	Totals
NBA	70% (15.5)*	5% (1)	16% (3.5)*	9% (2)	100% (22)
NCAA	77% (90)	4% (5)	17% (20)	2% (2)	100% (177)

*Fractional representations indicate one white coach with one white and one black assistant coach.

Table 10
The Historical Proportion of Blacks Playing College and Professional Basketball

Year	College Black Players As % of Total Players	Professional Black Players As % of Total Players
1948	1.4	0
1954	4.5	4.6
1958	9.1	11.8
1962	10.1	30.4
1966	16.2	50.9
1970	27.1	55.6
1975	33.4	63.3

Note: From Eitzen & Yetman, 1977.

we compare the 1978-1979 percentage of college basketball coaches (9%) to the proportion of black players in 1966, then it appears as if discrimination is not great. Comparing our 9% proportion to the 1970 data (27.1%), however, indicates a great deal of discrimination (see Table 10).

It is also apparent from the present data that overrepresentation of white guards and the underrepresentation of blacks in coaching positions are not only observable at the big time levels of competition, for example, professional and NCAA Division I basketball. Such patterns of discrimination are also evident at smaller institutions, for example, NCAA Division II and Division III colleges. Though strides appear to have been made across all levels of competition, it still remains that blacks are underrepresented in leadership roles relative to their population in professional and collegiate basketball. It is perhaps less surprising that the possibility of a black becoming an assistant coach is greater than his chances of becoming a head coach (20% vs. 9%, respectively). To engage a black in assistant capacities serves to "co-opt" this potential source of conflict and external pressure. However, the ten-fold greater proportion of white head coaches with black assistants as opposed to black head coaches with white assistants is a figure worth future monitoring as an indicator of egalitarianism in the sport of basketball.

CONCLUSION

The results of this study offer further support for the centrality hypothesis in terms of accounting for patterns of leadership recruitment and racial discrimination in the sport of basketball. Based on the sample of professional and collegiate coaches we may conclude that

1. Players occupying the position of guard are more likely than forwards and centers to have access to the positions of head and assistant coach.

2. Because white players are disproportionately found at the guard position, whites are more likely than blacks to be selected as head and assistant coaches.

REFERENCES

BALL, D.W. (1973, May). Ascription and position A comparative analysis of "stacking" in professional football. *Canadian Review of Sociology and Anthropology,* **10**, 97-133.

BLALOCK, H.M., Jr. (1972, Winter). Occupational discrimination: Some theoretical prepositions. *Social Problems,* **9**, 240-247.

BROWER, J.J. (1972, April). *The racial basis of the division of labor among players in the National Football League as a function of racial stereotypes.* Paper presented at the Pacific Sociological Association, Portland, Oregon.

DOUGHERTY, J. (1976, Spring). Race and sport: A follow up study. *Sport Sociology Bulletin,* **5**, 1-2.

EDWARDS, H. (1973). *Sociology of Sport.* Homewood, IL: Dorsey Press.

EITZEN, D.S. & Tessendorf, I. (1978, June). Racial segregation by position in sports: The special case of basketball. *Review of Sport and Leisure,* **2**, 109-128.

EITZEN, D.S. & Yetman, N.R. (1977, Winter). Immune from racism? Blacks still suffer from discrimination in sport. *Civil Rights Digest,* **9**, 3-13.

GRUSKY, O. (1963, September). The effects of formal structure on managerial recruitment: A study of baseball organization. *Sociometry,* **26**, 345-353.

HENDERSON, F. (1975). *Latin Americans in baseball: The absence of stacking.* Unpublished paper, Department of Sport Studies, University of Massachusetts, Amherst.

KLONSKY, B. (1975). *The effects of formal structure and role skills on coaching recruitment and longevity: A study of professional basketball teams.* Unpublished paper, Department of Psychology, Fordham University.

LEONARD, W.M. (1977, June). Stacking and performance differentials of whites, blacks and Latins in professional baseball. *Review of Sport and Leisure,* **2**, 77-106.

LOY, J.W. & McElvogue, J.F. (1970). Racial segregation in American sports. *International Review of Sport Sociology,* **5**, 5-23.

LOY, J.W., McPherson, B., & Kenyon, G.S. (1978). *Sport and social system,* Reading, MA: Addison-Wesley.

LOY, J.W., & Sage, J. (1970). The effects of formal structure on organizational leadership: An investigation of interscholastic baseball teams. In G.S. Kenyon & T. Grogg (Eds.), *Contemporary Psychology of Sport* (pp. 363-373). Chicago: The Athletic Institute.

LOY, J.W., Sage, J., & Ingham, A. (1970). *The effects of formal structure on organizational leadership: An investigation of varsity baseball teams.* Unpublished paper. Department of Sport Studies, University of Massachusetts, Amherst.

MADISON, D., & Landers, D. (1971, December). *Racial discrimination in football: A test of the "stacking" of playing positions hypothesis.* Paper presented at the Conference on Sport and Social Deviancy. Brockport, New York.

MASSENGALE, J., & Farrington, S. (1977, June). The influence of playing position centrality on the careers of college football coaches. *Review of Sport and Leisure,* **2**, 107-115.

ROLAND, P. (1977). *Ascription and position: A comparative analysis of the influence of playing position on the careers of professional football coaches.* Unpublished paper, Department of Sport Studies, University of Massachusetts, Amherst.

ROSENBLATT, A. (1976, September). Negroes in baseball: The failure of success. *Transaction*, 5, 51-53.

ROY, G. (1974). *The relationship between centrality and mobility: The case of the National Hockey League*. M.S. thesis, Department of Kinesiology, University of Waterloo.

SAGE, J. (1974, March). *The relationship of formal structure on organizational leadership: An investigation of collegiate football teams*. Paper presented at the National AAHPER Convention, Anaheim, California.

Part V

REFORM

Efforts to reform intercollegiate sport's abuses have paralleled the record of their improprieties. Rules governing play, recruiting, and eligibility have been adopted with the express purpose of promoting fair and equal playing opportunities within the educational setting.

Generally reform efforts have taken place within an extraorganizational setting. Colleges and universities have not, for the most part, been able to autonomously make the changes perceived as necessary for intercollegiate sport. The nation's schools have instead relied upon athletic organizations such as the NCAA to determine rules of play, recruiting, and eligibility. This is especially interesting considering the record of academic autonomy so jealously guarded by the diverse institutions in America.

A recent example of the historical reform process in intercollegiate sport is Rule 48 which was proposed, debated, and accepted by the delegates to the 1982 annual meeting of the National Collegiate Athletic Association. Originally designed by a panel of college presidents working under the auspices of the American Council on Education (ACE), Rule 48 seeks to tighten eligibility standards by requiring Division I freshman athletic scholarship recipients to have a 2.0 core curriculum high school average and a minimum combined math and verbal score on the Scholastic Aptitude Test (SAT) of 700. Student-athletes not fulfilling these minimum requirements may still receive athletic scholarships, but they would not be eligible for varsity participation during their freshman year. Rule 48 seeks to remedy abuses in the recruitment of secondary school athletes who will be unable to do college level work.

While the intent of Rule 48 is applauded by the first author in this section, serious problems are perceived to exist with this legislation. In the view of George Hanford, President of the College Board which administers the SAT, designation of one minimum test score violates many of the scientific and philosophical principles upon which the SAT is based. Designation of 700 as the minimum standard, for example, does not take into account the SAT's standard deviation of 50 points. While it may be, therefore, statistically impossible to tell the difference between SAT scores of 650 and 750, if present regulations remain in effect, students scoring 650 will be ineligible for freshman play, while the 750 scorer will be eligible as the student-athlete who scores 1200 on the SAT. This holds true regardless of the statistical conventions which regard both the 650 and 750 scores as the same and the predicted academic competence of the test takers as equal.

According to Hanford, the SAT should never be used as the sole predictor of college academic success. The expected academic ability of entering student athletes in college must be evaluated relative to many factors. The SAT is designed to be used only in conjunction with other predictors such as class rank, graduating school, grade point average, and secondary school curriculum. Furthermore, the correlation of SAT and predicted academic success of student test takers varies per institution. Low SAT scores may historically be highly correlated with good student college work at one school but much less correlated with demonstrations of student academic performance at another school.

Echoing the strident criticisms voiced by presidents of many of the nation's predominantly black colleges, Hanford also decries use of this one SAT standard for the determination of eligibility as a disservice to minority athletes. Although college academic performance and SAT scores may be less highly correlated for black students, Rule 48 in the form originally adopted at the 1983 NCAA convention does not take this into account. Minority athletes who may suffer from cultural biases in their education and in the SAT testing process itself are still to be judged according to the same 700 cut-off score as white athletes. Implementation of the 700 cut-off minimum as proposed for 1986 may make athletically ineligible the majority of black athletes entering colleges and universities at that time.

Critics have also found fault with Rule 48 on other accounts. The 700 minimum SAT score is criticized as too low, and the rule is criticized as too easily circumvented because of inadequate policing and implementation procedures. Some see junior colleges as a potential "dumping ground" for athletes who would otherwise not be eligible to play. Critics contend that after a freshman year at some junior college and with the first year eligibility "problem" no longer a concern, the sophomore could now enter the university ready to play ball, having been taught by a cooperating junior college coach the tactical "system" to be used for the remaining 3 years of university eligibility. Still other critics see Rule 48 as an attempt to deal with the problems of college sport by inappropriately placing responsibility for eligibility on the secondary school. In its originally adopted version, Rule 48 requires high school personnel to oversee the academic progress of students who may recieve scholarships to play Division I sports. To some critics, this is asking the high school counselor, teacher, and coach to do the work which should more appropriately be performed by college personnel as they screen and only select athletes able to perform academically and athletically at the college level. To George Hanford and others, serious effort to curb abuses should take the form of freshman ineligibility—a remedy appropriately within the responsibilities of the college and university itself.

Radical sociologist Harry Edwards then presents an overview of the black collegiate athlete before providing his view of Rule 48. Despite the large numbers of athletically gifted blacks, an estimated 25 to 35% of these athletes cannot qualify for sport scholarships due to academic insufficiencies. As many as 65 to 75% of those accepting scholarships may then never graduate from college. At the end of the black collegiate athlete's career, then there is often no professional career and no good job prospects without a degree.

While Edwards agrees with other black leaders that the 700 SAT minimum is arbitrary, he differs with them in that he feels these standards are too low. In his view predominantly white colleges and universities will continue to enroll athletically gifted black athletes—after all they have the "loopholes" in Rule 48 to exploit and too much at stake to allow this major source of personnel to dissipate. Edwards goes on to further suggest that the root cause for outcries from predominantly black college leadership is that Rule 48 puts these institutions at a financial disadvantage in the competition for black athletic talent. Generally while Rule 48 may be "a very small and perhaps even inept step," in Edwards' view it is a message to young high school athletes that certain standards of academic as well as athletic achievement are expected.

In the next chapter, Robert Atwell, Executive Vice-President for the American Council on Education, clarifies and defends the actions of the ACE sponsored college president's group which recommended Rule 48. While recognizing that the rule by itself does not ensure academic progress for athletes enrolled on campus and acknowledging the concerns of black college leaders, Atwell sees Rule 48 as a very encouraging step toward the reform of campus sport—a step with 3 years to make necessary modifications before implementation in 1986. While a majority of the 40 presidents on the ACE Athletic Committee preferred recommendation of freshman ineligibility, the current legislation was seen as more immediately workable. Rule 48 is described not as an admission standard but as an initial eligibility standard. It is contended that marginal students must concentrate a year on their studies before being immersed in the often overwhelming demands of big-time sport. In the face of criticism concerning the lack of action on the part of college leadership, Atwell sees Rule 48 as a sincere effort on the part of college presidents to strengthen amateurism. More importantly, Rule 48 is a demonstration that college and university presidents can work against the sometimes pernicious influence of boosters and local business interests when college leadership is organized and unified.

In their paper "Controlling Deviance in Intercollegiate Athletics" James Santomier and Peter Cautilli cogently argue that problems of abuse in intercollegiate sport are the result not of the transgressions of a deviant few individuals such as boosters or coaches or due to "loopholes" in otherwise sound athletic regulations. Instead the authors suggest that the fundamental issue at the heart of these problems is the "incongruence that exists between the values of higher education and the values of big-time intercollegiate athletics." In their view much of the unethical behavior attributed to individuals may be the surface manifestation of deviance whose source is the organization itself. Unethical behavior may contribute to organizational goals—winning athletics promotes college visibility. In other words, deviance is "often facilitated, if not engendered" by the athletic organization. Santomier and Cautilli suggest that common athletic behavior fits the conditions of organizational deviance (the situation where unethical behavior by individuals is promoted by the organization). These conditions are (a) unethical or deviant behavior violates the norms outside of the organization, (b) deviant behavior is supported in the norms of the organization, (c) deviant behavior must be known to the dominant coalition of the organization, and (d) new members must be socialized into the norms of the organization. According to the authors, university and college organizations must not look to outside regulating organizations for leadership to control deviance. Because the site of primary problems is within the institution, American schools should raise their own ethical standards.

To Ernest Boyer, President of the Carnegie Foundation for the Advancement of Teaching, however, more fundamental changes are required to reform campus sport. Changes not only in rules are required, but more importantly, an alteration of attitude toward sport and campus governance is necessary. According to Boyer, "more than rule changing and tinkering is needed. Reduction of sports' abuses will come only when a wave of moral indignation sweeps the campus." This indignation could take specific form as faculty protest, college accreditation revocation for serious violations, or revocation of NCAA eligibility. Attitudes of college presidents and board members must be altered from the passive inaction of the recent past to a renewal of leadership, from within the individual college or university. Drawing from the Carnegie Foundation paper "The Control of the Campus: A Report on the Governance of Higher Education (1983), Boyer asserts that "the academy must have full authority over the essential function on the campus." Just as corporations and vested political interests may impinge on free speech, research, and academic freedom, so may boosters and athletic donors subvert the educational principles of the university. In Boyer's view, presidential leadership must define academic standards for their own institutions "rather than wait passively for such standards to be imposed by others."

The final paper in this section by Barbara Uehling looks at two questions concerning the governance of intercollegiate sport—"can athletics remain a part of an academic institution . . ." and secondly "how can (athletics) be controlled?" After consideration of the arguments for the separation of athletics from the university and college Uehling calls for efforts to integrate athletic and academic programs so that athletics can contribute "value" to the institution. Echoing Boyer's sentiments, Uehling contends that institutions must take charge of athletics and not leave governance up to conferences or external organizations. The academic progress of athletes must be more closely monitored, the pressure to produce revenue through sport must be reduced and schools must arrange cooperative agreements to reduce spending on intercollegiate sport.

REFERENCE

CARNEGIE Foundation for the Advancement of Teaching. (1983). *The control of the campus: A report on the governance of higher education.* Washington, DC:USPGO.

Chapter 26

Proposition 48

George H. Hanford
President of the College Board

The College Board sympathizes with, applauds, and supports the declared intent of the ACE's ad hoc committee of college presidents to refurbish the image of higher education tarnished by revelations of the substandard performance and pampering of some college athletes. It would be refurbished in part by ensuring that participants in college sports, like other students, are able to do the college-level academic work expected of all. In so criticizing one aspect of the mechanism chosen to reach that goal (rigid 700 cut-offs), the College Board is not, and does not want to be, perceived as being critical of the proclaimed objectives.

By the same token, the College Board sympathizes and agrees with those who observe that the aspect of the mechanism which the College Board questions will, in the absence of explicit actions to improve the lot of minority students generally, have a disproportionately severe effect on minority athletes. In offering the following commentary, the College Board seeks to illuminate the problem in the hope that illumination will help achieve the goal of restoring integrity to athletics in higher education without having the practical effect of working against minority students.

A BRIEF REVIEW

Recent action by the NCAA requires that for a freshman to be eligible in 1986 to compete in intercollegiate sports at a Division I institution, he or she must meet three standards: have studied a prescribed core curriculum in high school; have achieved a 2.0 grade point average in high school; *and* have earned a combined Verbal and Mathematical score of 700 on the Scholastic Aptitude Test. The issue from the Board's point of view is the SAT score requirement. Such use of the SAT in the process of selecting students for admission to college would be contrary to the guidelines for test use published by the College Board. Two points apply here: First, the SAT is designed solely to help predict how well students will do academically in college; and second, the College Board guidelines indicate that test scores should be used only as one factor (i.e., used only in combination with other factors such as grade-point average or class rank) in making admissions decisions. In other words, test scores should never be used alone in determining admission to college. The NCAA's action violates that principle by establishing a minimum 700 combined SAT score as a necessary, though not sufficient, requirement for freshman athletic eligibility. In summary, under the NCAA rule, the SAT would be used for a purpose which it was neither intended nor designed to serve—determining athletic eligibility rather than college admissions; and, much more important, the way SAT scores are being used in establishing athletic eligibility is contrary to the College Board's guidelines with respect to the use of test scores in making college admissions decision.

THE VALUE OF SAT SCORES

Colleges are advised by the College Board that they should conduct validity studies to determine how well SAT scores do their intended job of predicting academic performance in college; that is, what weight should be given to them relative to the other factors used in making admissions decisions. This advice reflects two other principles of proper test use: First, test scores should be used uniquely by each college according to its experience with respect to their utility; and second, each institution should have a rationale for making admissions decisions based on the scores' predictive power in relation to other admissions criteria at that institution. The new NCAA regulation applies a national rather than an institutional standard and its 700 minimum combined SAT Verbal and Mathematical score requirement has no declared or demonstrated rationale. Thus, the new NCAA regulation for determining freshman eligibility violates the principles of proper test use by being national and not institutional in application and by not having a validated rationale.

The principles of proper use of test scores are not the only principles being violated by Proposition 48. The rules for the conduct of intercollegiate sports both on and off the field have been promulgated to balance competition and insure fairness. On the surface, employing the same 700 number to all institutions would appear to be even-handed, but it is not. Some institutions attract and enroll literally no students who score that low. These institution and their students will not be affected by the new regulation; all freshmen at such institutions attract and enroll a significant number of students with combined SAT scores below 700. They will be affected; freshmen who meet the institution's admissions requirements but score below 700 will not be eligible. In this instance, we wonder if the goal of balancing out the competition is really going to be served.

Higher education in the United States is self-regulating, and in the regulating takes into account the important diversity and pluralism of the system which recognized as one of its greatest strengths. Six regional accrediting associations conduct periodic peer reviews of colleges and universities. These reviews are undertaken to determine whether institutions of higher learning are fulfilling their stated missions and maintaining academic standards—but not the *same* mission or the *same* standard. The recent NCAA action by establishing a single standard, defies the principle of diversity.

In this regard, one observation is in order: Diversity in academic standards and diversity in athletic eligibility standards will always lead to uneven contests on the playing field. The most effective way to balance the competition, of course, is for colleges and universities of like standards to play each other, but that topic comes later.

Then put the single freshman eligibility standard next to the NCAA's companion requirement that to maintain eligibility an athlete must make satisfactory progress toward a degree in a regular degree program. This regulation was instituted because once in higher education, students can be kept eligible by being enrolled in undemanding courses not necessarily leading to a degree. The establishment of a cut-off score for freshman eligibility suggests an assumption that a student with a 700 combined SAT score at any institution is capable of successfully, if minimally, pursuing a degree program. Yet, neither is there evidence to support this assumption nor do the regional accrediting agencies make it about the institutions they accredit.

In these circumstances, why then did the NCAA choose the route it did? Why did it not accept an earlier proposal involving the core curriculum with *either* a 2.0 grade-point average *or* a combined SAT score of 700? Why *and*? The answer appears to be that the college and university presidents advising the NCAA membership were concerned about the reliability of the 2.0 grade-point average as the sole determinant of ability to do college level work—concerned, as their admissions officers are, about the lack of uniformity in secondary school curriculums and in the grading standards within and among secondary schools. Because you cannot always trust a grade-point average and you can trust an SAT score, they seem to have reasoned, you should use the latter to confirm the former.

The College Board is pleased that its SAT is held in such high regard but believes that this application in intercollegiate athletics to validate the secondary school record is as inappropriate in that context as it would be in college admissions. It is inappropriate not only for the reasons already noted with respect to use in combination with other criteria and with respect to its validity, but also because the problems people are trying to overcome should be dealt with directly and openly and not through a test.

The situation is further complicated by the fact that a compelling consideration in the implementation of any NCAA regulation is the ease with which it can be enforced. The more complicated or complex a regulation is, the easier it is for a designing coach, athletic director, or institution to find ways around it. One of the attractive features of the 700 combined SAT score criterion appears to be its simplicity. A 700 is a 700, is it not? The fact is, it is not, as all informed admissions officers know. For an individual student it means that, because of the standard error of measurement, the chances are two out of three that the combined score he or she might get on a given edition of the test would be within 50 points one way or the other of the "true score" that he or she would display if he or she took the SAT an infinite number of times. That obviously is one of the major reasons it should not be used as a sole or necessary criterion. Nevertheless, it can be helpful because (a) it has been generated by a disinterested third party, and (b) it is attractive because data in a statistically derived formula involving factors in addition to the SAT can provide opportunities for individual or institutional chicanery and produce numbers that are difficult for outsiders to verify.

However, this is not sufficient justification for using the score alone. In college admissions, and just as surely in determining athletic eligibility, there is no *simple* procedure that is both valid and fair. Educators above all should know this and should be willing to invest the care and professional expertise it takes to do the job correctly. Whereas those who proposed the new regulation saw the application of the SAT as even-handed and easy to enforce, the presidents of some predominantly black institutions have criticized the recent action for being unfair to black athletes. They based that criticism, in part, on the charge that the SAT and ACT are biased against minority students. The criticism of the effect of the regulation is justified; the charge of bias in the SAT is not!

It is an undisputed fact that minority candidates on the average earn significantly lower scores on the SAT than do whites on the average. However, as confirmed by a recent 2-year study by the prestigious and unbiased National Academy of Science, this circumstance exists not because the SAT does its job less well for them than for whites. Indeed, it predicts equally well for minority and majority. Rather, black students display lower scores on the average because many of them are less privileged educationally and socioeconomically than whites. The new regulation will have a differentially severe impact on the aspiring athletes among blacks, but not because of bias in the SAT, but because of the educational deficit that exists in this nation. In the view of the College Board this should be addressed and overcome through activities like our Educational EQuality Project—capital *E*, capital *Q*.

The contrast between the way the NCAA deals with freshman eligibility and the way it deals with maintaining eligibility during the sophomore, junior, senior, and red shirt years is curious. The latter require that an athlete make satisfactory progress toward a degree in a recognized degree program. Recognized, that is, by some authority external to the athletic department, such as as a regional accrediting association, state board of higher education, or simply the teaching faculty of the institution itself.

This inconsistency between freshmen eligibility determined by a national standard (singular) and later eligibility determined by institutional standards (plural) could be eliminated simply by returning to the former practice of not permitting freshmen to participate in intercollegiate varsity sports. Indeed, such an action would have the effect of leaving unviolated, all of the principles that are now violated by the new regulation. Such a change would also get the question of athletic eligibility for college freshmen off the shoulders of the secondary school, where the new regulation puts it, and put it squarely where it belongs, in the hands of the colleges. For all these reasons, the College Board favors an end to freshman participation on varsity teams at Division I institutions.

If those are not reasons enough, one could argue quite convincingly that, athletic eligibility aside, freshmen should not be expected to handle the all-too-often difficult and sometimes perilous transition from high school to college. They are not only dealing with the academic, social, and personal demands inherent in that first college year, but also playing, practicing, living, eating, and thinking football or basketball for 40 or more hours per week—not to mention the effects of travel requirements, missed lectures, and the like associated with big-time athletic endeavors. There are, in other words, sound intellectual and academic reasons why freshmen should not engage in big-time college sports in addition to the ones that make it all but impossible to regulate eligibility in the freshman year. Let the student with a 750 have the same privilege as the one with a 650: not having to compete his or her freshman year.

REFORMS IN FRESHMAN ELIGIBILTIY

Do away then with freshman eligibility. It would be nice simply to leave the matter at that and walk away from it, but some allege that doing away with freshman eligibility is economically unfeasible at this time. If that is indeed so, then the question becomes, Which principles should be sacrificed, and to what degree, in order to satisfy the economic "practicalities" of big-time college sports? Some possibilities emerge.

For instance, if one were to sacrifice the principles of individuality and diversity of institutions, but not the principles of validated and combined use of test scores, one could presumably conduct a group validity study of some sort for constellations of like-minded institutions. The Big Ten, Big Eight, Pac Ten, and the Southeast Conference, for instance, could each have a standard for its conference, but that approach would leave out, among other independent big-time football powers, Notre Dame, Penn State, and Pittsburgh. Or perhaps a single Division IA validity study might be developed. However, the same generality could not be applied to Division IAA, which includes institutions with such diverse admissions standards as the Ivy League and the large predominantly black colleges in the South. Or one could try to develop some kind of national formula that would somehow combine test scores and school records in ways that would let a low score be offset by a high grade-point average or vice-versa.

Or, as some others are suggesting, complicated formulas could be derived which would match the characteristics of entering athletes on some kind of relativistic basis either with the characteristics of the class with which they are entering or with those of a recent graduating class. The College Board intends to take a look at and to offer advice about these and similar options but does so in the belief that they will all be found to be so complicated that wisdom will ultimately prevail and freshman eligibility will become a thing of the past.

Against this background, I conclude with the caveat that the only principled way in which the elements in Proposition 48 should be employed as freshman eligibility criteria would be if they are validated *in combination* as reasonable predictors of freshman academic success. Institutions could be held responsible for conducting such validation research and for subjecting the results to impartial third party verification tests. (They do this now, in a sense, when they provide student eligibility reports to NCAA and various athletic conferences.)

As noted earlier, the criteria against which predictive indexes might be compared include the following:

- All freshmen admitted by an institution
- All freshmen admitted by a group of institutions in the same league
- All letter-winning athletes who actually graduated from the institution within a specified prior period

The basic point is that higher institutions must recognize and respect the differences among themselves with regard to educational mission, goals for student accomplishment, and the like. Accordingly, they must also extend the same consideration with regard to differences in admissions standards and in freshman eligibility requirements. What is imperative in such a scheme is that the standards colleges apply to students who are athletes be no lower than those they apply for all students in the institution. If this test is met, then all that is left for institutions to decide is whether they want to compete in sports against institutions whose standards are markedly different.

If someone says, "But that concept is too idealistic and complex for the world of big-time, big dollar sports," our answer has to be that you cannot have it both ways. The devising of a simple-to-administer, impersonal, arbitrary, and insensitive mechanism pertaining to freshman eligibility is at best temporizing with the serious matters of educational principle and practice, and probably to the detriment of educational opportunity for student athletes. Thus, we return to our basic recommendation: that freshman eligibility in Division I intercollegiate sports, and at least in football and basketball, be eliminated.

Chapter 27

Educating Black Athletes

Harry Edwards
University of California at Berkeley

For decades, student athletes, usually 17-to-19-year-old freshmen, have informally agreed to a contract with the universities they attend: athletic performance in exchange for an education. The athletes have kept their part of the bargain; the universities have not. Universities and athletic departments have gained huge gate receipts, television revenues, national visibility, donors to university programs, and more as a result of the performances of gifted basketball and football players, of whom a disproportionate number of the most gifted and most exploited have been black.

While blacks are not the only student athletes exploited, the abuses usually happen to them first and worst. To understand why, we must understand sports' impact upon black society: How the popular beliefs that blacks are innately superior athletes, and that sports are "inherently" beneficial combine with the life circumstances of young blacks and with the aspirations of black student athletes to make those student athletes especially vulnerable to victimization.

Sports at all levels are widely believed to have achieved extraordinary, if not exemplary, advances in the realm of interracial relations since the time when Jackie Robinson became the first black to play major-league baseball. To some extent, this reputation has been deliberately fostered by skilled sports propagandists eager to project "patriotic" views consistent with America's professed ideals of racial justice and equality of opportunity. To a much greater extent, however, this view of sports has been encouraged by observers of the sporting scene who have simply been naive about the dynamics of sports as an institution, about their relationship to society generally, and about the race-related realities of American sports in particular.

Many misconcpetions about race and sports can be traced to developments in sports that would appear on the surface to represent significant racial progress. For instance, although blacks constitute only 11.7% of the U.S. population, in 1982 more than 55% of the players in the National Football League were black, and, in 1981, 24 of the 28 first-round NFL draft choices were black. As for the two other major professional team sports, 70% of the players making National Basketball Association rosters during the 1982-1983 season, and 80% of the starters that same season, were black, while 19% of America's major-league baseball players at the beginning of the 1982 season were black.

Black representation on sports honor rolls has been even more disproportionate. For example, the past nine Heisman trophies, awarded each year to the "best" collegiate football player in the land, have gone to blacks. In the final rushing statistics of the 1982 NFL season, 36 of the top running backs were black. In 1982, not a single white athlete was named to the first team of a major Division I All-American basketball roster. Similarly, 21 of the 24 athletes selected for the 1982 NBA All-Star game were black. Since 1955, whites have won the NBA's "most valuable player" award only 5 times, as opposed to 23 times for blacks. And, of course, boxing championships in the heavier weight divisions have been dominated by black athletes since the 1960s. But a judicious interpretation of these and related figures points toward conclusions quite different from what one might expect.

Patterns of opportunity for blacks in American sports, like those in the society at large, are shaped by racial discrimination; this phenomenon explains the disproportionately high number of talented black athletes in certain sports and the utter exclusion of blacks from most other American sports, as well as from decision-making and authority positions in virtually all sports.

Most educated people today accept the idea that the level of black representation and the quality of black performance in sports have no demonstrable relationship to race-linked genetic characteristics. Every study purporting to demonstrate such a relationship has exhibited critical deficiencies in methodological, theoretical, or conceptual design. Moreover, the factors determining the caliber of sports performances are so complex and disparate as to render ludicrous any attempt to trace athletic excellence to a single biological feature.

Thus, despite a popular view that blacks are "natural" athletes, physically superior to athletes from other groups, the evidence tends to support the following cultural and social—rather than biological—explanations of their athletic success:

• Thanks to the mass media and to long-standing traditions of racial discrimination limiting blacks' access to many high-prestige occupational opportunities, the black athlete is much more visible to black youths than, say, black doctors or black lawyers. Therefore, unlike white children, who see many different potential role models in the media, black children tend to model themselves after, or to admire as symbolically masculine, the black athlete—the one prevalent and positive black success figure they are exposed to regularly, year in and year out, in America's white-dominated mass media.

- The black family and the black community tend to reward athletic achievement much more and earlier than any other activity. This also lures more young blacks into sports-career aspirations than the actual opportunities for sports success would warrant.
- Because most American sports activities are still devoid of any significant black presence, the overwhelming majority of aspiring black athletes emulate established black role models and seek careers in only four or five sports—basketball, football, baseball, boxing, and track. The brutally competitive selection process that ensues eliminates all but the most skilled black athletes by the time they reach the collegiate and advanced amateur ranks. The competition is made all the more intense because even in these sports, some positions (such as quarterback, center, and middle linebacker in football, and catcher in baseball) are relatively closed to blacks.
- Finally, sports are seen by many black male youths as a means of proving their manhood. This tends to be extraordinarily important to blacks because the black male in American society has been systematically cut off from mainstream routes of masculine expression such as economic success, authority positions, and so forth.

SCHOLARSHIP AWARDS

Despite the great pool of athletic talent generated in black society, black athletes still get fewer than 1 in 10 of the athletic scholarships given out in the United States. And, at least partially as a result of the emphasis placed upon developing their athletic talents from early childhood, an estimated 25 to 35% of male black high school athletes qualifying for athletic scholarships cannot accept those scholarships because of accumulated academic deficiencies. Many of these young men eventually end up in what is called, appropriately enough, the "slave trade"—a nationwide phenomenon involving independent scouts who, for a fee (usually paid by a 4-year college), search out talented but academically "high-risk" black athletes and place them in accommodating junior colleges, where their athletic skills are further honed while they earn the grades they need to transfer to the sponsoring 4-year schools.

Of those who are eventully awarded collegiate athletic scholarships, studies indicate, as many as 65 to 75% may never graduate from college. Of the 25 to 35% who do eventually graduate from the schools they play for, an estimated 75% graduate either with physical education degrees or in majors created specifically for athletes and generally held in low repute. The problem with these "jock majors," and increasingly with the physical education major as well, is that they make poor credentials in the job market. One might assume that ample occupational opportunities would be available to outstanding black former athletes, at least within the sports world. The reality, however, is quite different. To begin with, the overwhelming majority of black athletes, whether scholarship-holders or professionals, have *no* post-career occupational plans or formal preparation for any type of post-career employment either inside or outside sports. These blacks are unemployed more often and earn less when they do have jobs than their nonathletic college peers; they are also likely to switch jobs more often, to hold a wider variety of jobs, and to be less satisfied with the jobs they hold—primarily because the jobs tend to be dull, dead-end, or minimally rewarding.

Few Americans appreciate the extent to which the overwhelming majority of young males seeking affluence and stardom through sports are foredoomed to fail. The three major team sports provide approximately 2,663 jobs for professional athletes, regardless of color, in a nation of 226 million people, roughly half of whom are male. This means that only one American male in about 42,000 is a professional football, basketball, or baseball player.

While the proportion of blacks in professional basketball is 70%, in professional football 55%, and in professional baseball 19%, only about 1,400 black people (up from about 1,100 since the establishment of the United States Football League) are making a living as professional athletes in these three major sports today. If one adds to this number all the black professional athletes in all other American sports, all the blacks in minor and semiprofessional sports leagues, and all the black trainers, coaches, and doctors in professional sports, one sees that fewer than 2,400 black Americans can be said to be making a living in professional athletics today.

This situation, considered in combination with the black athlete's educational underdevelopment, helps explain why so many black athletes not only fail to achieve their expectations of life-long affluence, but also frequently fall far short of the levels achieved by their nonathletic peers.

Despite the fact, then, that American basketball, boxing, football, and baseball competitions have come more and more to look like Ghana playing Nigeria, sport continues to loom like a fog-shrouded minefield for the overwhelming majority of black athletes. It has been a treadmill to oblivion rather than the escalator to wealth and glory it was believed to be. The black athlete who blindly sets out today to fill the shoes of Dr. J., Reggie J., Magic J., Kareem Abdul-J., or O.J. may well end up with "No J."—no job that he is qualified to do in our modern, technologically sophisticated society. At the end of his sports career, the black athlete is not likely to be running or flying through airports like O.J. He is much more likely to be sweeping up airports—if he has the good fortune to land even that job.

RULE 48

These are the tragic circumstances that prompted Joe Paterno, 1982 Division I football "Coach of the Year" of the New York Football Writers' Association, to exclaim in January from the floor of the 1983 NCAA convention in San Diego: "For fifteen years we have had a race problem. We have taken kids and sold them on bouncing a ball and running with a football and that being able to do certain things athletically was going to be an end in itself. We cannot afford to do that to another generation." With that statement, Coach Paterno gave impetus to the passage of the NCAA's "Rule 48," which set off what is probably the most heated race-related controversy within the NCAA since the onset of widespread racial integration in major college sports programs during the 1950s and 1960s.

Put most simply, Rule 48 stipulates that beginning in 1986, freshman athletes who want to participate in sports in any of the nation's 277 Division I colleges and universities must have attained a minimum score of 700 (out of a possible 1,600) on the Scholastic Aptitude Test (SAT) or a score of 15 (out of a possible 36) on the American College Test (ACT), and must have achieved a C average in eleven designated high school courses, including English, mathematics, social sciences, and physical sciences. Further, as *The N.C.A.A. News* reported, Rule 48

> does not interfere with the admissions policies of any Division I institution. Nonqualifiers under this legislation may be admitted and attend class. Such a student could compete as a sophomore if he or she satisfies the satisfactory progress rules and would have four varsity seasons starting as a sophomore if he or she continues to make satisfactory progress.

> Further, under related Proposal No. 49-B, any student who achieves at least 2.0 in all high school courses but does not meet the new terms of No. 48 can receive athletically related financial aid in his or her first year, but cannot practice or compete in intercollegiate athletics. This student would have three varsity years of participation remaining.

The outcry in response to the passage of Rule 48 was immediate. Ironically, the most heated opposition to the rule came from black civil-rights leaders and black college presidents and educators—the very groups one might have expected to be most supportive of the action. Their concern was over those provisions of Rule 48 specifying minimum test scores as a condition for sports participation, particularly the 700 score on the SAT. Leading the black criticism of the NCAA's new academic standards were the National Association For Equal Opportunity in Higher Education (NAFEO), representing 114 traditionally black colleges and universities; the National Alliance of Black School Educators (NABSE); Rev. Jesse Jackson, president of People United to Serve Humanity (Operation PUSH); Rev. Benjamin Hooks, executive director of the National Association for the Advancement of Colored People (NAACP); and Rev. Joseph Lowery, president of the Southern Christian Leadership Conference (SCLC). They argued first, that blacks were not consulted in the formulation of Rule 48; second, that the minimum SAT score requirement was arbitrary; and, finally, that the SAT and the ACT are racist diagnostic tests, which reflect a cultural bias favoring whites. They believed that the 700 SAT and 15 ACT score requirements would unfairly penalize black student athletes, given that 55% of black students generally score lower than 700 on the SAT and 69% score lower than 15 on the ACT. Why would the majority of NCAA Division I institutions vote to support a rule that would reduce participation opportunities for black athletes? For NAFEO and its supporters, the answer was clear. The most outspoken among the critics of Rule 48 was Dr. Jesse N. Stone, Jr., the president of the Southern University System of Louisiana, who said:

> The end result of all this is the black athlete has been too good. If it [Rule 48] is followed to its logical conclusion, we say to our youngsters, "Let the white boy win once in a while." This has set the black athlete back twenty-five or thirty years. The message is that white schools no longer want black athletes.

Members of the American Council on Education (ACE) committee charged with developing Rule 48 vehemently denied claims that no blacks were involved in the process. Whatever the truth of the matter, the majority of black NCAA delegates felt that their interests and views had not been represented.

I could not agree more with NAFEO, Jackson, Hooks, Lower et al. on their contention that the minimum SAT and ACT test scores are arbitrary. Neither the ACE nor the NCAA has yet provided any reason or logical basis for setting the minimum scores. But whereas NAFEO and others say that the scores are arbitrary and too high, I contend that they are arbitrary and so *low* as to constitute virtually no standards at all. I have other, more fundamental disagreements with the NAFEO position.

One need not survey very much literature on the racist abuse of diagnostic testing in this country to appreciate the historical basis of NAFEO's concerns about rigidly applied test standards. But the demand that Rule 48 be repealed on the grounds that its test score requirements are racist and will unfairly affect blacks is both factually contestable and strategically regrettable. The evidence is overwhelming that the SAT and the ACT discriminate principally on the basis of class, rather than race. The greater discrepancy between black and white scores occurs on the math section of the SAT, where cultural differences between the races logically would have the least impact. Even on the verbal sections of these diagnostic tests, differences in black and white scores are at least partially explained as class-related phenomena. As Dr. Mary Frances Berry, a NAFEO supporter, asserts:

> A major differential [among test scores] was *not* between black and white students, but between students from well-off families and students from poor families. The better-off the family, the higher the score—for whites *and* blacks.

Dr. Norman C. Francis, president of the traditionally black Xavier University of Louisiana and immediate past chairman of the College Board, agrees:

> The SAT is not merely a measure of potential aptitude, as many believe, but is also an achievement test which accurately measures what students have learned to

that point. Most students do poorly on the test simply because they have never been taught the concepts that will help them to understand what testing and test-taking is all about. It is an educational disadvantage, not an inability to learn....The plain truth is that students in poorer schools are never taught to deal with word problems and...critical analysis. The problem therefore is not with the students, nor with the test, but rather with an educational system which fails to teach youngsters what they need to know.

Rule 48, therefore, involves far more than a simple black-white controversy, as 1981 SAT test statistics bear out. While 49% of black male students in 1981 failed to achieve at least a 700 on the combined SAT, as compared with 14% of the whites and 27% of other minorities, far more whites (31,140) and other minorities (27,145) than blacks (15,330) would have been affected under Rule 48.

Furthermore, between 1981 and 1982, blacks' verbal scores rose 9 points and mathematics scores rose 4 points, compared with a 2-point gain in verbal and a 1-point gain in math for the white majority.

NAFEO claims that black athletes would have less access to traditionally white Division I institutions in the wake of Rule 48. But even though proportionately more blacks score below Rule 48's minimum score requirements, it is unlikely that significant numbers of blacks would be deprived of opportunities to attend traditionally white schools on athletic scholarships. Indeed, if the enrollment of black athletes falls off at any Division I schools for this reason, I submit that the schools most likely to suffer will be the traditionally black colleges. NCAA disciplinary records show that traditionally white institutions have led the way in amateur-athletic rules infractions and in exploiting black athletes. Why? Because they have the largest financial investment in their athletic programs, and because they and their athletic personnel stand to reap the greatest rewards from athletic success. With so much at stake, why would schools that for so long have stretched, bent, and broken rules to enroll black athletes no longer want them?

The loopholes in Rule 48 are sufficient to allow any school to recruit any athlete it really wants. Junior colleges are not covered under the rule, so schools could still secure and develop athletes not eligible for freshman sports participation at 4-year Division I colleges. Furthermore, Rule 48 allows Division I schools to recruit freshman athletes who are academically ineligible to participate, and even to provide them with financial support. After several meetings with NAFEO representatives, Rev. Jesse Jackson, and others, I am strongly convinced that for many within the ranks of Rule 48's detractors, fiscal rather than educational issues are the priority concern. The overwhelming majority of athletes recruited by traditionally black Division I schools are black, score below Rule 48 minimum test score requirements, and tend to need financial support in order to attend college. However, because they have far more modest athletic budgets than traditionally white schools, traditionally black schools are not nearly so able to provide financial support for both a roster of active athletes and a long roster of newly recruited athletes ineligible for athletic participation under Rule 48. Traditionally, black Division I schools, already at a recruiting disadvantage, owing to smaller budgets and less access to lucrative TV exposure, would be placed at an even more critical recruiting disadvantage because they would not be able to afford even those athletes they would orginarily be able to get.

Thus, the core issue in the Rule 48 controversy is not racist academic standards or alleged efforts by whites to resegregate major college sports, so much as parity between black and white institutions in the collegiate athletic arms race.

Strategically, the position of NAFEO, the NABSE, and the black civil-rights leaders vis-à-vis Rule 48 poses two problems. First, they have missed the greatest opportunity since the *Brown* v. *Board of Education of Topeka* case 30 years ago to make an impressive statement about quality and equality in education. Because they had the attention of the nation, they also squandered a rare opportunity to direct a national dialogue on restructuring the role and stipulating the rights of athletes in the academy. Second, with no real evidence to support their claims of racist motives on the part of Rule 48's white supporters, or of simple race bias in the rule's stipulations, these black educators and civil-rights leaders left the unfortunate and unintended impression that they were against *all* academic standards because they believed that black students are unable to achieve even the moderate standards established under Rule 48.

THE REALITIES OF RULE 48

Notwithstanding the transparent criticisms leveled by Rule 48's detractors, the measure does contain some real flaws relative to its proposed goal of shoring up the academic integrity of Division I athletic programs. First, the standards stipulated in Rule 48 are *too low*. A score of 700 on the SAT, for example, projects less than a 50-50 chance of graduating from most Division schools.

Second, Rule 48 does not address in any way the educational problems of students once they have matriculated, which is where the real educational rip-off of collegiate student athletes has occurred. Rather, it establishes standards of high school preparation and scholastic achievement necessary for students who wish to participate in college sports as freshmen.

Nonetheless, the NCAA action is worthy of support, not as a satisfactory solution to the educational problems of big-time collegiate sports, but as a step—a very small and perhaps even inept step—toward dealing with these problems. Rule 48 communicates to young athletes, beginning with those who are sophomores in high school, that we expect them to develop academically as well as athletically. In California, 320,000 students each year participate in California Interscholastic Federation athletic programs and most undoubtedly aspire to win athletic scholarships to Division I institutions. However, only 5% of these students will ever participate in college sports at any level (including junior college), and the overwhelming majority will never even enroll at a 4-year school. If Rule 48 does indeed encourage greater academic seriousness among high school athletes, the vast majority of high school student athletes who are *not* going on to college may benefit most from the NCAA's action because they face the realities of life after sports immediately upon graduation from high school.

Furthermore, were I not to support Rule 48, I would risk communicating to black youth in particular that I, a nationally known black educator, do not believe that they have the capacity to achieve a 700 score on the SAT with 3 years to prepare for the test, when they are given a total of 400 points simply for answering a single question in each of the two sections of the test, and when they have a significant chance of scoring 460 by a purely random marking of the test. Finally, I support the NCAA's action because I believe that black parents, black educators, and the black community must insist that black children be taught and that they learn whatever subject matter is necessary to excel on diagnostic and all other skills tests.

Outcries of "racism," and calls for black boycotts of or exemptions from such tests seem to me neither rational nor constructive long-term responses to the problem of black students' low test scores. Culture can be learned and taught. Class-specific values and perspectives can be learned and taught. Preparing our young people to meet the challenges they face on these tests and, by extension, in this society is what we should be about as black educators.

I believe that (a) student athletes and nonathletes alike should be given diagnostic tests on a recurrent basis to assure skills achievement; (b) test-score standards should and must be raised, based upon the skill demands and challenges of our contemporary world; and (c) the test standards set should be established as post enrollment goals and not preenrollment obstacles.

In the case of scholarship athletes, every institution should have the right to set its own academic enrollment standards. But those same institutions *must* acknowledge a binding corollary obligation and responsibility to develop and to implement support programs sufficiently effective to fulfill their implied contracts with the athletes recruited.

For all of its divisive impact, the debate over Rule 48 has illuminated a much larger crisis involving the failure of this nation to properly educate its young, athletes and nonathletes. In 1967, the national average on the SAT was 958; by 1982, it had dropped to 893. Furthermore, even students who score well on diagnostic tests frequently require remedial work to handle college-level course work. From 1975 to 1980, the number of remedial math courses in public 4-year colleges increased by 72%; they now constitute a quarter of all math courses offered by those institutions. At 2-year colleges, 42% of math courses are below the level of college algebra.

In high school transcripts, according to a study done for the National Commission on Excellence in Education, credit value for American history has declined by 11% over the past 15 years, for chemistry by 6%, for algebra by 7%, and for French by 9%. In the same period, credit value for remedial English has risen by 39% and for driver education by 75%. Only 31% of recent high school graduates took intermediate algebra, only 16% took geography, and only 13% took French. High school students have abandoned college-preparatory and vocational-education "tracks" in droves, so that between 1964 and 1979, the number who chose the "general" track rose from 12 to 42%. About 25% of all credits earned by general-track graduates were in physical and health education, driver education, home management, food and cooking, training for adulthood and marriage, remedial courses, and for work experience outside school.

Part of the problem is with our teachers: the way they are recruited, their low status, and their even lower rewards. According to a recent article in *U.S. News & World Report*,

> A study conducted for the National Institute of Education, which looked at college graduates who entered teaching in the late '70s, found that those with the highest academic ability were much more likely to leave their jobs than those who were lower achievers. Among high-achieving students, only 26% intended to teach at age 30, as compared with approximately 60% of those with the lowest academic ability.

In yet another study, one third of the nearly 7,000 prospective teachers who took the California minimum-competency test failed to meet the most basic skills requirements. And in 1982, the average SAT score of students indicating teaching as their field of study ranked 26th among average scores achieved by students declaring 29 different fields of interest.

Black colleges are not blameless with respect to inadequate teacher preparation. Currently, at least 20 states require teacher candidates to pass a state qualifying exam. In Florida, 79% of white teacher-college graduates achieved a passing rate, compared with 35% for black test-takers. The two black schools that produce the largest number of black teacher candidates in that same state had the worst passing rates—37% and 16%.

That state's Association of Black Psychologists held a press conference and denounced the tests as "instruments of European cultural imperialism," and urged the black community—as a front—to resist the tests. But there is really only one legitimate concern relative to such tests: Do they measure what should be taught in schools of education if teachers are to be competent?

The majority of black students today come from schools in which blacks either predominate or make up the entire student body. And much—if not most—of the failure to educate black youths has occurred under black educators. In the 1960s, from Ocean Hill-Brownsville, in New York, to Watts, in California, blacks quite rightly criticized inner-city schools where white teachers and white superintendents were indifferent to the learning abilities of black students. Many of these school systems now have a majority of black teachers and black superintendents, and many black students still do not learn. Can we afford to be any less critical when white incompetence is replaced by black incompetence? Given what is at stake, the answer must be an emphatic and resounding *NO!* We must let all of our educators know that if they are not competent to do their jobs, they have no business in our schools.

AMERICAN EDUCATION

Pointing out teachers' inadequacies is not enough. For all of its modernity, education still advances on "four legs." Though formal instruction takes place in the classroom, education is the result of coordinated effort on the part of parents, the school, the community, and the larger society. Parents who do not participate in school activities, who do not attend parent-teacher conferences to review their children's academic progress, who generally show little or no interest in school-related issues—indeed, who do not know, and have never even asked, the name of the teacher charged with instructing their children—over the years communicate to those children the idea that education does not matter. The community that undercuts the solvency of its libraries and schools communicates the idea that education does not matter. The school that emphasizes and revels in the glories of sports, while fighting efforts to set academic standards for sports participation, communicates the idea that education does not matter.

Current national policy which calls for severe cuts in educational funding and defense expenditures of $1.6 trillion over the next 4 years, is both contradictory and shortsighted. Education *is* a national-defense issue. As Jefferson pointed out at this nation's birth, an educated, informed populace is necessary to the operation of a viable democracy. As the world's leading democracy, we simply cannot afford the current burden of 26 million adults who are functionally illiterate and 46 million who are only marginally literate. Since the late 1970s, the U.S. military has found that it must print comic-book versions of some of its manuals in order to accommodate the educational deficiencies of troops charged with operating and maintaining some of the most sophisticated weapons in history. Along with greater emphasis upon parental involvement in schools, insistence upon teacher competence, and greater academic expectations of our students, we must put more, not less, money into education.

The National Center for Education Statistics estimates that the average 1980-1981 salary for classroom teachers was $17,602—up from $9,269 in 1971. However, in constant 1981 dollars, teachers have lost money because their 1971 average salary translates to roughly $20,212. The outlook for the future is equally bleak. Education cannot attract and hold the best-trained and most competent people without offering competitive salaries. Particularly in the more technologically applicable disciplines, education is suffering a severe "brain-drain." Thus, in 1981, nationwide, half the teachers hired to teach high school math and science were not certified to teach those subjects, while more than 40 states reported shortages of qualified teachers in those areas.

Compared with other national school systems, American education comes up short. The American school year is 180 days, and the average student misses roughly 18 of those, but Japan, Germany, and most other industrial nations require at least 220 days a year. In the Soviet Union, students from the first grade on attend school 6 days a week. About 35% of their classwork is in science. They take 5 years of arithmetic, then are introduced to algebra and geometry, followed by calculus. The national minimum curriculum also calls for 1 year each of astronomy and mechanical drawing, 4 years of chemistry, 5 years of physics, and 6 years of biology.

In sum, education must be put at the very top of the U.S. domestic agenda. Clearly, we must demonstrate greater concern for and commitment to educational quality for all American youths—athletes as well as nonathletes. I am confident that with adequate support and proper encouragement, American youths can achieve whatever levels of performance are necessitated by the challenges they face. In today's world, neither they nor we have any other choice.

Chapter 28

It's Only A Game

Robert Atwell
American Council on Education

Athletics is deeply rooted in our national life and, indeed, in our Western heritage. While an excessive preoccupation with athletics can be a way of avoiding the real world, the Greeks taught us that life and all valuable things are to be seen as contests. President Giammati of Yale University recently reminded us that by the 5th Century B.C. (about 25 centuries before George Allen and Vince Lombardi) the athletes and the artists were inseparable in the intensity of competition and the importance attributed to their activities by society. Athletics was not seen by the Greeks as simply pleasurable but rather as contributing to the formation of the shapely and balanced soul and as enabling the city/state to defend itself against it enemies.

From the Anglo-Saxon tradition we have inherited a concept of athletics as building character and developing fair play and team spirit. This part of our heritage stresses fellowship, sacrifice for the common good, and the idea that how one plays is emblematic of how one will later behave. Victory is less important than the experience of struggle.

Our task as educators is to reconcile these rather different views—the one stressing the individual and the other stressing the self-effacing participant. Both share the concept of discipline, and both can be accommodated within the belief that athletics is a worthy part of education in the same manner as art. Indeed, athletics is viewed as an art form, but it is a worthy contributor to undergraduate education for a number of reasons.

First, athletics teaches us that excellence comes only through discipline. Excellence in athletics is very measurable. Most of us go through life without being seriously tested, able to cover up most of our mistakes, and measure our performance against generally rather obscure criteria. Furthermore, athletics teaches us not simply how to test our ability but also how to develop and rely on our own individual strengths in pursuit of excellence. We live in an enormously competitive society, and we become socialized to all that competition at a very early stage. To help our children compete, we make often unseemly efforts to provide them with the advantageous inside lanes in the race of life. We enroll them in the best classes and the best schools so that they will get into the best Wall Street law firms or corporations. The pervasive parental nudging or shoving, as the case may be, can help young people to compensate for weaknesses for a time, and, indeed, for some there are so many advantages inherent in social status that there is never any moment of truth in the great game of getting ahead in America.

While there is a great deal of room in this country for the overachiever, that observation does not hold true in athletics. Certainly, there are advantages accrued during all those years of parental pushing in lessons, but without native athletic ability, they will have limited effect. When a tennis player faces an opposing player across the net, or a batter faces the pitcher, the contest is immediate, measurable, and unmitigated by externalities. Concentration and capability are far more important than the advantages provided by birth and status. Thus, athletics provides sobering and an inherently equalizing introduction to the realities of a competitive society. At the same time that athletics teaches inner reliance, it also ideally requires that our competitive fires be tempered for the common good, particularly in the team sports where the individual urge should be sublimated to the requirements of the group.

Athletics fulfills yet another important role in our society: Vicariously experienced athletics provides an escape. If Karl Marx were alive today, he would probably observe that it is no longer religion but televised sports that is the "opiate of the people." If we ever doubted that, a review of the $2 billion television contracts between the NFL and the major networks should convince us. It is probably no accident that star athletes are most idolized by persons who themselves lead the most humdrum of existences in steel mills, coal mines, or the office bull pens of large corporations. Athletics is a surrogate way of raising our spirits as we trudge through a thoroughly dull life. Roger Angell, writing about Bob Gibson, the great St. Louis Cardinals pitcher said,

> Even those of us who have not been spoiled by an athletic triumph of our own and the fulfillment of the wild expectations of our early youth, are aware of the humdrum, twilight quality to all our doings of middle life. There is a loss of light and ease and early joy and we look to other exemplars to sustain us in that loss.

ATHLETICS AS AN ART FORM

Returning to the topic of undergraduate education, I must comment on athletics as an art form. Similarities between ballet and gymnastics, for example, are self-evident. We have observed these similarities in the pursuits of our own children. Less obvious but equally strong are the artistic elements of seemingly less aesthetic sports. Lynn Swan (even the name is graceful) is in every sense a ballet dancer in the beauty and timing of his leaps into the sky to pull down a pass. By the same token, think of the physical strength, concentration, and courage required of Rudolf Nureyev. In figure skating, too, we see art and athletics mysteriously and magically combined. From both art and athletics, we learn the importance of concentration, of ceaseless discipline and practice, and the ultimate and beautiful test of raw talent.

That test of talent makes one of the most important contributions of athletics to the development of the individual athlete—the lesson of defeat. For every winner, there is a loser. A 1981 movie, *Chariots of Fire*, fully and movingly captured the intensity of the athlete and the price of excellence. The movie ends happily with the good guys winning as our American ideals would wish it, but the film had a significant flaw: It dealt with defeat rather inadequately. Most young people will suffer some defeat, as painful as it is to know, and from that defeat, they will have matured. Indeed, one of the hallmarks of a mature person is having endured a kick in the butt and weathered the experience. A graceful loser is more admirable than a boastful winner, but much of that is lost in a world where losing is dying.

SPORTSMANSHIP

Sportsmanship—we don't even hear the term much anymore. Whatever happened to fair play? Somehow it got lost on the way to the Rose Bowl, lost in the myth that everyone can be a winner if he or she just tries hard enough, or, more cynically, cheat enough. The cliches of fair play and sportsmanship have been ousted all too frequently in the cliché-ridden world of sports in which you do whatever you have to do to win.

One of the worst manifestations of the obsession of winning is the baiting of officials by athletes and by coaches (and particularly, though not exclusively, in basketball). McEnroe has developed the intimidation of officials to a science. The idea is that you harass and intimidate the officials, yelling at them constantly and protesting every call that goes against you so that they will relent and call the next close one in your favor. The theory is that nice guys finish last and the well-mannered coach will not be heard.

One of the more insidious realities of big-time college athletics today is that the relationship between money and success has become an economic necessity, as well as a public relations one, so that coaches and administrators are driven to downright indecent behavior simply to survive economically. The message to the athlete is perfectly clear. Winning is very literally everything. The injuries in terms of broken bodies, broken spirits, broken character, in the almost total lack of an educational context are around us every day.

ATHLETE EXPLOITATION

I have been slow to accept a notion that the big-time college athletes are out-rageously exploited. The persuasive case can be made that they are overly pampered, excessively tutored, and often living in better accommodations, eating better food, and having much more financial aid than is available to most students. They have the opportunity to obtain a first-class education in colleges and univer-sities to which some of them might not have been admitted had they not been athletes.

However, there is a clear validity to the exploitation argument, and none of the advantages I just cited are incompatible with the notion that athletes are ex-ploited. Exploitation takes many forms: some subtle, others dramatic. Occasion-ally, it means that a young person is induced to take pain-killing drugs to play through short-run pain at considerable long-term risk. More frequently, there is no truth in advertising which if practiced would compel the institution to inform the athlete of the miniscule chances he has of ever playing in the NBA or the NFL. Or exploitation may take the corrupting form of gifts or outright payments, clear violations of NCAA rules; or most subtle of all, it may take the form of messages given off by many coaches that the real purpose of being in school is to play football or basketball rather than to get an education. There are many conscientious coaches and ethical institutions that stress the student role of the student-athlete. They include and go well beyond Joe Paterno and the impressive Notre Dame graduation rate. Unfortunately, there are all too many illustrations that go the other way. To deny these forms of exploitation, even in the face of the exemplary practices of most that do exist, is to seriously misunderstand or to deliberately distort the realities of big-time collegiate athletics.

SEXISM

In discussing the seamier side of a much loved enterprise, we must include the historical and scandalously sexist dimension of athletics. There have long been sports in which women excel and receive the recognition their excellence deserves. Ice skating and swimming are prominent examples, with gymnastics and tennis coming along more recently, thanks to Nadia Comaneci and Billie Jean King. There has long been women's basketball with great crowd appeal in some parts of the Midwest, and I can recall being in a crowd of mostly men watching women's slow pitch softball on a lazy summer afternoon in Aspen. Colleges and univer-sities only started paying attention to women's athletics under the Title IX gun, although they have in many cases performed admirably under that gun. When it looked as if the women had something going in terms of its own governance structure, the NCAA, aided and abetted by the political mistakes of the AIAW, simply exercised their power, which is deeply rooted in money, and gobbled them up in one of the most blatant exercises of male chauvinism academia has ever witnessed.

COACHES' DILEMMA

As Bill Walton so eloquently stated, "It's only a game, man." I wonder how many coaches have been called in by the college president and told something like

> I know you'll be judged by many of our supporters entirely in terms of your won and loss record. But I want you to know that I will be looking at how you conduct yourself as a coach and as a human being and how your athletes conduct themselves. If they are dirty players or if you throw tantrums and harass officials, I will fire you regardless of your wins and on the other hand, if I believe that you are a good example of character and fair play for your athletes and you haven't cheated or violated any of the NCAA rules and have generally conducted yourself in a manner which brings credit to this institution, then I'll defend you against your adversaries. In short, as long as I'm the chief executive you aren't going to be fired because you lose too many games.

All that is required are long-term contracts for coaches to dilute some of the pressures for instant gratification.

MONEY AND ATHLETICS

Much of the sordid behavior we increasingly see associated with intercollegiate athletics can be traced to the almighty dollar. That is a supreme irony considering intercollegiate athletics is supposed to be amateur, that is, no one is supposed to be in it for profit. What we have to say on that subject applies to approximately 80 institutions that play semiprofessional football and to maybe 150 semiprofessional basketball powers. Most of the athletes and most of the institutions involved in intercollegiate athletics are not in it for money, and the fierce pressures to win it at all costs simply do not exist. What we read about in the sports pages over the breakfast table applies largely to two sports affecting maybe 5 or 6,000 young people out of 250,000 who participate in intercollegiate athletics every year in 1,000 4-year institutions. Let us keep it all in some kind of perspective.

The world of big-time collegiate football and basketball is one in which filling seats is necessary, not to support that particular sport (football actually generates a profit in at least half of those 80 schools), but to support the rest of the athletic program which in total is supposed to be self-supporting. Seats get filled only if you win, so you have got to win. You not only have to fill seats, but you have to get on television, and you have to get a bowl bid in order to live the life-style which befits the company you keep or to which you aspire. California State University at Long Beach President Steve Horn, a president who cares deeply about athletics and who has had the courage in speaking out in some rather hostile environment, has stated, "We want more money to do more things in order to generate more money to do more things." It is not only money, but let us not forget those "more things." With a college president there is a supreme temptation to try to put his or her institution on the map via a big-time basketball program. After all, with just one blue-chip 7-footer you might make it to the final four, and that amounts to 700 grand. So you declare yourself in Division I and try to find institutions with which to compete and then try to sell the university to blue-chip athletes as a place where they can play immediately in hopes of getting the national visibility that will lead to a future big pro contract.

Meanwhile, that basketball program is a unifying factor against what Steve Horn has correctly identified as the increasingly fragmented quality of college life. Would the University of Southern California, a predominantly commuter school, really be a university as distinct from a multiuniversity, if everyone did not come together as a community on five or six Saturdays in the fall over at the coliseum? Thus, big-time athletics holds out the hope of building a community and putting the institution on the map. That means more students, more athletes, better support from the legislature, better relations with the local business community, and somehow, like supply-side economics, some of the goodies will trickle down to the students and to the faculty members in the trenches. It is truly surprising how many otherwise mature adults, supposedly educational leaders pointing a way to a richer cultural intellectual life, actually believe this scenario of wishful thinking and act on it. Sadly, it sometimes works, but you only read about the winners, not about the disillusioned losers.

SCANDALS

Some of us used to say that big-time college football and basketball were scandals not waiting to happen, only waiting to be revealed—but we have now seen both the happening and the revelation. There is considerable evidence the public does not care and that, ironically enough, gives us some hope. A year or so ago, I got in trouble by writing a short piece meant exclusively for college presidents which somehow found its way into the hands of the sports press. I argued then, and I would still contend, that we really have three choices confronting the vast wasteland of collegiate athletics. The first is a sincere effort to strengthen and to return to the amateur student-athletic model—student first, athlete second. This is the regulatory route. The NCAA rule book will inevitably get thicker and the enforcement machinery larger and more expensive.

The second choice for those 80 football and 150 basketball programs is to drop the pretense of amateurism. If the athletes want to be students—fine, but they need not be. They would be paid whatever it takes to have them play for a college team. The institutions would be acknowledging that they are in the entertainment business and doing so for public relations purposes and for money. In a few years there would be far less than 80 major football powers and 150 major basketball powers as players drifted toward the consistent winners and as television did the same things with no NCAA Robin Hood schemes as we now have. NCAA could go its way as the amateur athletic association for the other institutions and for sports other than football and basketball in those schools which went pro in those two sports.

The third choice is to do nothing at all, in which case we will most surely drift toward my second choice. Let us be clear that unless we tighten academic standards, reduce the intensity and the demanding aspects of recruiting, build messages other than winning into the employment condition of the coaches, get serious about regulation, and unless college presidents assert leadership roles in the NCAA, then the present quasi-regulatory structure will become a hollow and thoroughly hypocritical shell behind which we will have essentially an unregulated industrial jungle.

While I favor an effort to strengthen the amateur model, I want to assert respect for the deregulation model—professionalism. I see nothing inherently wrong with it, in view it is a much more honest approach than the triumph of form over substance which the present regulatory structure represents. Deregulation interferes far less with the lives and choices of gifted young athletes. It permits institutions to continue to strive for the highest levels of athletic excellence. It recognizes and does not try to buck the American mania for spectator sports and simply tries to differentiate that from the educational role of the college or university.

RULE 48

For the past 8 months, it has been my pleasure to be associated with a very serious effort on the part of a group of chief executives at institutions with major athletic programs to strengthen the amateur model. Had I given this speech a year ago I would have argued that a return to amateurism was probably beyond the internal fortitude or even the convictions of most college presidents, not to mention the governing boards. I would have said that the pervasive and pernicious influence of alumni, booster clubs, and ubiquitous local business interests were far too powerful. But I am pleased to report today that it is now simply a matter of fact that the college presidents are on the move, and that there is a track record proving when they unite and get organized, they can accomplish a great deal. The heartening message of the past year is not so much the tightening of academic standards through the passage of Motions #48 and #56 (landmark pieces of legislation regardless of the particular details of each), but the display of presidential leadership.

There were 100 Division I presidents at the 1983 NCAA convention in San Diego, which represents more than one third of the 277 institutions in that division. They not only attended but did a tremendous amount of homework—extensive lobbying in advance of that meeting and speaking and participating at the meeting. Many of those who did not attend instructed their delegates on how to vote on certain key measures. All those presidents did not favor Motions #48 and #56, but they were all committed to the principles of presidential leadership and to the tightening of academic standards.

Because their greatest accomplishments are Motions #48 and #56 and the defeat of Motion #71 for a smaller Division I, I want to address the first two of these three motions. Until last January, a young person could be initially eligible to participate in intercollegiate athletics by having a high school grade-point average of 2.0. As an academic standard that is a travesty because something like 95% of American high school graduates exceed that standard. There are many examples of marginal high school students who are gifted athletes being counseled into the easy courses to assure college eligibility. In short, students major in eligibility at the high school level, let alone college.

Furthermore, the quality of American high schools, not to mention colleges, differs widely so that a 2.0 grade-point average in a good suburban high school is something very different from a 2.0 grade-point average in a financially starved and deprived intercity high school. Sadly enough, many gifted athletes graduate from bad high schools with a 3.0 grade-point average or higher and turn up with combined SAT scores of 550. The scandals of the last 2 years have caused many college presidents to review personally athletes' high school and college transcripts. Many have been embarrassed and even sickened by what they saw: Too many young people are being taken into institutions because they are gifted athletes with very little hope of graduating from these institutions—really no hope of graduating without a great deal of tutoring and counseling, and very little hope if they are immediately dropped into the 30 or 40 hours-week maelstrom (not to mention the psychic demands of big-time football and basketball).

A majority of the college presidents with whom I have worked in the ACE Committee on Division I Intercollegiate Athletics (there are 40 college presidents on that committee) would have preferred to recommend freshmen ineligibility to the last NCAA convention. They were, however, aware of unanswered questions such as, Could the freshmen practice but not play and Would there be three seasons or four of eligibility after the freshmen year? Furthermore, if freshmen were to receive grants-in-aid, would there need to be more grants-in-aid authorized and what would this cost be? Would there have to be freshmen programs and what would these programs cost?

Recognizing these difficulties but not wanting to wait until 1984 to take a dramatic step toward the tightening of standards, the presidents came up with Motions #48 and #56 as significant first steps toward the tightening process. Motion #48 with four amendments tightens eligibility standards for Division I as follows: First, in addition to the continuation of the present 2.0 high school grade-point average, initial eligibility would be conditioned on the completion of a core curriculum of 11 academic courses in high school of which 9 were specified in the legislation. Second, in addition to the core curriculum and the grade-point average, a student would have to have a combined Verbal and Math SAT score of 700 or a ACT score of 15. A student not meeting the standard could still receive athletic aid, but if that student did receive such aid he or she would be limited to three seasons of eligibility after that initial year. Nonqualifying students who did not receive athletic aid in the initial year would have four seasons of eligibility.

Rule 56 simply reinforced the present satisfactory progress standard. That standard was strengthened for the first time in recent years at the 1982 NCAA convention, calling for an athlete to satisfactorily complete 24 semester hours or the quarter-hour equivalent of credit in the year preceding competition. In order to attack the phenomenon of majoring in eligibility—Football 101 and 102 followed by Golf 304—Rule 56 adds the requirement that the student be pursuing a regular baccalaureate degree.

Rule 48 has been attacked by presidents of historically black institutions; there are 17 such institutions in Division I, the only Division to which Rule 48 will apply. Though the opposition to the rule is by no means limited to historically black institutions, it has also been attacked by some representatives of the testing community. About one half of the blacks taking the SAT score below 700, and on the average, blacks score about 250 points below whites. This does not mean that the test is discriminatory, for it is not. It predicts equally well for blacks and whites. The test is simply the messenger of the historic discrimination which exists and has existed in our society. The testing community's problem is that a device intended to be used in combination with high school performance and other factors (high school grade-point average, the greatest predictor of college success) has been made into a cut-off—a cut-off not for admission, but for initial eligibility.

I have yet to meet anyone who does not agree that a young person with a 700 SAT score will have considerable trouble graduating from most of our colleges and universities. I have yet to meet anyone familiar with big-time collegiate athletics who quarrels with the assertion that the previous nonstandard created a situation in which young people are thrown up on the beach after their eligibility is completed with no education and no means of earning a living in professional sports. In my judgment, that is exploitation.

In reply to the critics Rule 48, far from being discriminatory, is designed to provide equal opportunity and to assure a set of conditions in which the marginal students have a better possibility of getting an education. It is not an admission standard and I doubt that a single president would have supported it as an admission standard. It is, however, an initial eligibility standard. It simply means that a marginal student (precisely defined) must concentrate a year on studies before becoming embroiled in the pressures of big-time sports. While there may be athletic deprivation involved, Rule 48 is without question in the academic interest of the student. The student can achieve eligibility in the second year by meeting the newly tightened satisfactory progress standard and at that point, the test score is irrelevant.

While believing firmly in Rule 48, the sponsoring college presidents have acknowledged that other reasonable people have differed. They are anxious to heal the racial divisions which Rule 48 has caused, although as already indicated, opposition to Rule 48 is not limited to the black community, nor is the black community totally unified in opposing it. As a result, we are hoping to arrange through the National Association for Equal Opportunity In Higher Education, representing 114 historically black colleges and universities, a meeting later this spring among some of those 17 Division I black college presidents and with people on the ACE Committee to discuss options for the tightening of academic standards. Rule 48 is not yet the last word from presidents on academic standards and there are 3 years in which to modify it before it becomes effective in 1986. Many people have seen universal freshman ineligibility as a probable compromise; however, although I personally support it, it would present many difficulties. Furthermore, it would certainly be opposed by the swimmers, gymnasts, and others representing sports that are not overwhelmed with scandal but consist of performers who peak in their late teens and for whom freshman ineligibility may bring an even earlier end to their athletic days.

As emphasized earlier, the message is not so much the details of the particular proposal which the presidents succeeded in persuading the NCAA Convention to adopt (and I do not mean to make light of that very substantial accomplishment on their part)—the real message is their own growing strength and interest. The ACE Committee on Division I Intercollegiate Athletics will continue to exist and will, through subcomittees comprised of Division I presidents, give attention to and develop 1984 legislative proposals in several additional areas which include further refining of academic standards; affording more presidential participation in and leadership of the NCAA; reorganizing Division I; strengthening the rules of recruiting and enforcement machinery; and examining the impact of television and television revenue in shaping athletic programs. With their energy and commitment, these Division I presidents comprising the subcommittees have the attention span and the staying power to achieve their goals.

REFORMING COLLEGIATE ATHLETICS

Much of the work of reforming collegiate athletics has to start in the elementary and secondary schools. The core curriculum required for initial eligibility is a loud message to our nation's high schools that colleges are serious about the academic preparation of athletes. However, we must go further. The fact is that we have a system that leads too many young people to accept the exploitation of their bodies at the expense of their education. They accept it because they are led to believe that their future, their escape from the inner city in many instances, is professional football or basketball. The facts are otherwise, but we do little to disabuse them of the myth because it is in the best interest of the athletic establishment to perpetuate the myth.

Every young athlete should be confronted with these following facts: There are about 40,000 college football players every year, 12,000 of them estimated as seniors. Between 300 and 350 are drafted by the NFL each year and about 200 of them make squads that play for less than 4 years. That means that about 1.5% of those completing eligibility have any hope of making the pros. Furthermore, there are about 14,000 men's basketball players in colleges and universities. The NBA drafts about 300 and only 50 make NBA squads. If 3,000 of the 14,000 are seniors, that means again that something like 1.5% of those completing eligibility make the pros and have average NBA careers of about 3 years. The message to youngsters out of all these facts is that they had better get an education because the odds against a pro career are absolutely overwhelming.

There is much to be learned from athletics: Its place in the educational enterprise is not simply legitimate, but essential. It is essential not only because it develops a sound body to accompany a sound mind, but because of what it teaches the young people about the life which awaits them. In his fifth discourse on *The Idea of a University*, John Henry Newman helps us understand the role of athletics in liberal education. In that discourse, Newman attempts to distinguish liberal education from servile or useful education as he called it. Parenthetically, these days I have observed that many of us are uncomfortable with the polarity between liberal and useful education because we do not like to appear useless. Newman notes that liberal education

> stands on its own pretentions which, independent of sequel, expect no complement, refuses to be informed by any end or absorbed into any art, in order to duly present itself to our contemplation. The most ordinary pursuits have this specific character if they are self-sufficient and complete; the highest lose it when they administer to something beyond them.

He continues to argue that there are bodily exercises which are liberal and mental exercises which are not. So we can accept athletics into liberal education when the discrete character of the activity is the essence—where there is no consequence beyond the playing of the game as well as possible and where the object is not conquest or winning or money or the NCAA championship. We should no more encourage a professionalism of spirit in our athletic programs than we should encourage a professional view of such education. Athletics have an important role to play in undergraduate education—a role that is liberating and liberal. Athletics partakes of art, teaches courage, informs us of and disciplines us to the price and rewards of excellence. It gives us high pleasure, helps us to shape our ideals and our values, and is not incidentally good for our bodies. Let us keep athletics in that perspective.

Chapter 29

Controlling Deviance in Intercollegiate Athletics

James Santomier and Peter Cautilli
New York University

The regulations passed at the recent National Collegiate Athletic Association (NCAA) convention represent an attempt to restore academic credibility to intercollegiate athletics; the expansion of the NCAA's enforcement division represents an attempt to control deviance in intercollegiate athletics. The effectiveness of both these measures may be limited because the leaders of intercollegiatge athletics failed to address the fundamental issue: the incongruence that exists between the values of higher education and the values of big-time intercollegiate athletics. Increased NCAA regulation and expanded NCAA enforcement, without a concomitant change in the value structure of big-time intercollegiate athletics, may actually increase deviance in intercollegiate athletics rather than deter it.

In order to control effectively unethical and deviant behavior, the leaders of intercollegiate athletics at all levels of management must understand the nature and conditions of deviance, and the potential result of increased regulation and enforcement. They must also take an active role in implementing strategies to reinforce ethical behavior among athletic personnel (Coaches, athletic directors, etc.) at their respective universities.

NATURE AND CONDITIONS OF DEVIANCE

Much of the unethical and deviant behavior in intercollegiate athletics may be considered organizational deviance because it contributes primarily to achieving organizational goals and objectives, for example, winning intercollegiate athletic contests (Santomier, Howard, Piltz, & Romance, 1980). Although specific individuals (e.g., specific coaches, assistant coaches, or athletic directors) within intercollegiate athletics commit deviant acts, their deviance is often facilitated, if not engendered, by a deviant athletic organization. Individuals who commit deviant acts violate the norms governing appropriate occupational endeavors in intercollegiate athletics. Occupational deviance in intercollegiate athletics has been referred to as "white sock crime" (Santomier et al., 1980).

An examination of four specific conditions of organizational deviance (Ermann & Lundman, 1978) and of how each relates to deviance in intercollegiate athletics will provide a systematic and comprehensive understanding of organizational deviance in intercollegiate athletics. The first condition stipulates that unethical or deviant behavior violates the norms outside of the organization. Specific deviant behaviors such as falsifying academic transcripts, awarding academic credit to athletes who neither completed coursework nor attended classes, and other academic abuses are neither condoned by those outside of intercollegiate athletics nor, generally, by those within intercollegiate athletics.

The second condition stipulates that the deviant behavior must find support in the norms of a given level or division of the organization. It is naive to consider that deviance in intercollegiate athletics is the result of individual aberrations or personal inadequacies, and that others within the athletic organization do not, at least passively, support it. Unethical and deviant behavior is learned and reinforced within informal social systems whose norms and practices are at variance with academic standards and NCAA regulations. Deviance in intercollegiate athletics is socially prescribed and patterned through an informal "code," and is a natural result of increased institutional pressure and societal demand for professional quality intercollegiate athletic teams.

The third condition stipulates the deviant behavior must be known to the dominant coalition of the organization. It seems unreasonable to assume that certain university presidents, faculty athletic representatives, and athletic directors were totally unaware of any unethical or deviant behavior occurring within their respective administrative units. Some leaders accept unethical and deviant behavior because it may appear necessary for survival in the highly competitive intercollegiate athletic system. Leaders are often involved in attempting to rationalize or neutralize definitions of behaviors that are considered undesirable. As an example, Louis G. McCullough, Director of Athletics at Iowa State University, stated,

> I've talked to several college presidents who agree that probably the easiest thing to do is go ahead and cheat, because the NCAA isn't going to do anything meaningful to you. (Vance, 1982, p. 16)

The fourth condition stipulates that new members must be socialized to participate in the deviant behavior. Big-time intercollegiate athletic programs, by their nature, are work organizations. As work organizations they are goal-oriented systems designed to insure that one's livelihood is contingent upon one's adequate performance as defined by one's superiors in the organization (Santomier et al., 1980). Ingham (1975, p. 358) states that within athletic organizations "formal socialization agents...facilitate the internalization of the performance principle necessary for organizational efficiency." Thus through professional socialization, new members in the athletic fraternity are socialized into occupationally related role-specific deviant behaviors.

More specifically, individuals become deviant through differential association with peers and through exposure to opportunities to engage in deviant behaviors. (Zey-Ferrell & Ferrell, 1982). Individuals (e.g., coaches) in intercollegiate athletics are socialized into deviant roles through close association within informal systems (e.g., coaching staffs) which have the power to sanction the individuals. Whether or not the socialization process results in unethical or deviant behavior is contingent upon the ratio of contacts with unethical patterns of behavior to ethical patterns. Zey-Ferrell and Ferrell (1982) suggest that an individual's referent other group predicting ethical/unethical behavior is actually the peer group rather than top management. When individuals perceive their peers to be unethical in behavior, they are more likely to be unethical. This is more significant when there exists little interaction between the individual and top management, and when peer interaction is frequent.

Organizational and occupational deviance "is regulated by informally established normative consensus of the informal system or work group" (Hollinger & Clark, 1982, p. 335). Thus deviance in intercollegiate athletics may be "more constrained by informal social control present in the primary work-group relationship than by the formal reactions to deviance by those in positions of authority within the formal organization" (Hollinger & Clark, 1982, p. 342). In intercollegiate athletics the reaction of one's fellow coaches, not management, appears to be more significant in establishing appropriate limits on the acceptable range of behaviors (Hollinger & Clark, 1982).

If leaders are going to control deviance in intercollegiate athletics effectively, they must realize that the primary source of social control comes about through the internalization of group norms "wherein conformity to norms comes about through...socialization" (Hollinger & Clark, 1982, p. 334). The secondary source of social control comes from external pressure in the form of sanctions in order to encourage conformity with its regulations. This approach, without a major effort aimed at the primary source of social control—the informal work-group (e.g., coaching staff), will have limited effectiveness.

In summary, it can be determined that much of the unethical and deviant behavior in intercollegiate athletics is related to achieving organizational goals and objectives, and that the rationalized actions required to achieve these goals and objectives violate the normative expectations surrounding the organization. In addition, these actions are peer and elite supported.

INCREASED REGULATION
AND EXPANDED ENFORCEMENT:
TOWARD ESCALATION

Officials of the National Collegiate Athletic Association, under heavy pressure to curb abuses in college sport, say a bigger more efficient "police force" is needed to deter rule breakers. They do not think that tougher penalties for proven cheaters, as proposed by many reformers, will do the job.

To that end, the NCAA has expanded its enforcement department staff from two full time investigators in 1972 to 3 supervisors, 10 full time field investigators, and..., 25 private detectives, some with experience at the Federal Bureau of Investigation. (Vance, 1982, p. 15)

The NCAA, by expanding its enforcement capabilities, may actually contribute to rather than deter rule breaking. According to Marx (1981), the presence of social control may act as an important variable in the production of deviance. There exists interdependence between social control and deviance and some infractions are "shaped or induced by prior or concomitant actions of authorities" (Marx, 1981, p. 222). By taking expanded enforcement actions, the NCAA may unintentionally encourage rule breaking because increased social control may result in additional violations—in effect, a snowballing or mushrooming of deviance. Marx (1982, p. 223) has identified five major analytic elements of escalation:

1. An increase in the frequency of the original violation
2. An increase in the seriousness of the violations
3. The appearance of new categories of violators and/or victims
4. An increase in the commitment and/or skill and effectiveness of those engaged in the violation
5. The appearance of violations whose very definition is tied to social control intervention

One consequence of increased regulation and expanded enforcement in intercollegiate athletics is, for example, to change the personnel and social organization of those involved in deviance. Regulation by the NCAA has now placed the athletic booster and the university alumni in potentially deviant roles. Previously, athletic boosters and alumni may have played a large role in recruiting. By voting to limit recruiting to only "institutional staff members" (*New York Times*, 1983), the NCAA has created a potential new category of deviance—a category which now requires control by the NCAA.

Social control actions may unintentionally generate functional alternatives. The relationship between controllers and controlled may often be characterized as a movable equilibrium. As in sports, or any competitive endeavor, new strategies, techniques and resources may give one side a temporary advantage, but the other side tends to find ways to neutralize, avoid, or counter them. The action may be altered—but the game does not stop. (Marx, 1982, p. 226)

Intercollegiate athletics are linked to the National Collegiate Athletic Association, an organization established to, ostensibly, label and control deviance in intercollegiate athletics. However, this agency may also be responsible for creating and encouraging deviance.

STRATEGIES FOR CONTROLLING DEVIANCE

In big-time intercollegiate athletics, competition for athletic victories and concomitant profits may push ethical and moral considerations into the background. Although some responsibility for unethical and deviant behavior must be placed upon society, the bulk of the responsibility must be placed upon the leadership of intercollegiate athletics. University presidents, faculty, athletic directors, and coaches have failed to reinforce ethical values and have, at least passively, supported unethical and deviant behavior within their respective athletic organizations. University presidents and other leaders must now take an active role in order to raise the ethical standards upon which their athletic programs are operating. The leadership to raise ethical standards, however, must not come only from the top, but from every level within the athletic organization. Rein (1980, p. 740) in an article titled "Is Your (Ethical) Slippage Showing?" has provided a number of strategies for raising ethical standards. The following strategies, adapted from Rein (1980), may be implemented by intercollegiate athletic leaders at all levels of management.

1. The leaders should reexamine what has gone wrong with their intercollegiate athletic program and attempt to determine to what extent the program had created on-campus and/or community hostility. William Atcheley, president of Clemson University,

   > in examining the Clemson athletic program...found its growth over the past 15 years had far outstripped its management structure. Like a business that suddenly is hit with a best-selling product and finds its product distribution system inadequate, the organization was not in place to run dozens of major and minor sports programs, and negotiate television contracts, and plan facilities expansion, and so forth. It was as if a small-town, mom and pop operation had awakened one day to find itself facing the problems of a corporate conglomerate.

   > We experienced growing pains, and the potential was there for abuse, whether through ignorance or intent. (Atcheley, 1982, Sec. 5-2)

   With respect to the feeling among community members generated by the Clemson situation, Atcheley stated, "I heard expressions of shock, disappointment and disillusionment, from Clemson people and from those outside of the university family'' (1982, Sec. 5-2).

2. They should identify their specific responsibilities and management decisions related to intercollegiate athletics and determine if they would feel comfortable telling their superiors, or other leaders of intercollegiate athletics, about their actions and decisions. If they would not feel comfortable in doing that, then they should reevaluate those actions and decisions in light of ethical and moral considerations.

3. They should take an active role in speaking out on questions involving ethical and moral considerations in intercollegiate athletics. The leaders of intercollegiate athletics should not assume that reinforcing ethical behavior should be someone else's responsibility, but should assert their program's concerns and policies in all matters related to unethical and deviant behavior, and address the critical issues facing intercollegiate athletics generally and facing their programs specifically.

4. They should assure faculty, community constituencies, athletic boosters, and so forth, that ethical considerations are important to the way that their athletic programs are managed. However, athletic leaders must be committed to ensure that the conduct of the entire program reflects those high standards.

5. They should evaluate their athletic policies and operating procedures in terms of ethics. Are the established goals of the intercollegiate athletic program realistic? Athletic leaders should avoid establishing goals that are unrealistic because they engender the attitude that ''anything goes— the end justifies the means.''

6. They should promote the concept of honesty over expediency. They should encourage an accurate representation of their universities by athletic recruiters, and encourage a policy to manage with integrity the academic programs of athletes.

7. They should involve all levels of athletic management and athletic personnel in ethical concerns. Delegate authority to establish ethical guidelines for various dimensions of the athletic program and, if feasible, ''establish quality circles on codes of conduct and ethical behavior'' (Rein, 1980, p. 742).

8. They should hold ''ethics workshops'' for athletic personnel, management, and athletes. The objective should be to examine the need for the development of a comprehensive athletic program code of ethics to help reverse the trend toward unethical behavior. The growing negative attitudes among the public toward intercollegiate athletics should be examined and discussed.

9. They should send athletic leaders, coaches, and athletes to represent their universities in speaking out on ethical questions and topics. Intercollegiate athletic leaders should reinforce ethical values that relate to matters vital to the intercollegiate athletic program.

10. They should publicize and reinforce positive examples of ethical con-

duct. They should hold seminars with media to inform the university community and the public of the appropriate and ethical behaviors within their respective athletic programs.

11. They should coordinate the intercollegiate athletic department's efforts to speak out and to answer false or unjust media or public criticism of the program.

12. They should specifically include ethical behavior, conduct, and goals as an integral part of the athletic program's management-by-objectives and/or performance appraisal system.

13. They should integrate athletic personnel into the mainstream of academic life. When appropriate and relevant, athletic personnel, especially coaches, should be encouraged to and given the opportunity to serve on university committees concerned with admissions policies and standards, and academic regulations and standards.

In summary, if intercollegiate athletic leaders are going to effectively control deviance within their collegiate athletic programs, they must not depend upon increased NCAA regulations and expanded NCAA enforcement, but they must implement strategies designed to reinforce ethical values within all levels of the intercollegiate athletic organization.

REFERENCES

AKERS, R.L. (1977). *Defiant behavior: A social learning approach*, (2nd ed.). Belmont, CA: Wadsworth.

ALUMNI Recruiting Curtailed. *New York Times*. (1983, January 13).

ATCHELEY, B.L. (1982, December 12). Restore integrity to college sports. *New York Times*.

ERMANN, M.D., & Lundman, R.J. (1978). Deviant acts by complex organizations: Deviance and social control at the organizational level of analysis. *The Sociological Quarterly, 19*, 55-67.

HOLLINGER, R.C., & Clark, J.P. (1982). Formal and informal social controls of employee deviance. *The Sociological Quarterly, 23*, 333-343.

INGHAM, A.G. (1975). Occupational subcultures in the world of work. In D.W. Ball & J.W. Loy (Eds.), *Sport and social order: Contributions to the sociology of sport*. Menlo Park, CA: Addison-Wesley.

MARX, G.T. (1981). Ironies of social control: Authorities as contributors deviance through escalation, nonenforcement and covert facilitation. *Social Problems, 28*(3), 221-143.

REIN, L.G. (1980, September). Is your (ethical) slippage showing? *Personnel Journal*.

SANTOMIER, J.P., Howard, W.G., Piltz, W.L., & Romance, T.J. (1980). White sock crime: Organizational deviance in intercollegiate athletics. *Journal of Sport and Social Issues, 4*(2).

VANCE, N.S. (1982). Deterring cheaters in college sports: Tougher penalties vs. better policing. *The Chronical of Higher Education, 25*(8), 15-16.

ZEY-FERRELL, M., & Ferrell, O.C. (1982). Role-set configuration and opportunity as predictors of unethical behavior in organizations. *Human Relations, 35*(7), 587-604.

Chapter 30

College Athletics: The Control of the Campus

Ernest L. Boyer
The Carnegie Foundation for the Advancement of Teaching

November 22, 1938. One of America's most popular publications, *Look* magazine (newstand price 10¢), featured Claudette Colbert on the cover doing the can-can. Another eye-catcher was a bold headline

EXPOSED—College Football is a Racket

Inside, the article said:

> Back in the days when the season ended on Thanksgiving there was a college sport called football....But only old alumni remember it as a sport....Today, it has become a big business. Hypocritical as Snow White's stepmother—a $50 million racket that wears out turnstiles, amateur rules and educational standards. (p. 6)

That was more than 45 years ago.

About 10 years before *Look* magazine exposé—in 1929, to be exact—the Carnegie Foundation for the Advancement of Teaching prepared a massive report: Bulletin No. 23, entitled *American College Athletics* (Savage, 1929). The report, while quaint sounding, still has a familiar ring. A few key quotations from that 1929 report are as follows:

> The extreme development of competitive games in the colleges has reached into secondary schools. The college athlete begins his career before he gets to college.

> Once in college the student who goes in for competitive sports, finds himself under a pressure, hard to resist, to give full time to his athletic career. No college boy training for a major team can have much time for thought and study.

The college athlete finds himself suddenly an important man on campus. He begins to live on a scale never before imagined. A special table is provided. Sport clothes and expensive trips are furnished him out of the athletic chest.

He works under paid professional coaches. Any father who has listened to the professional coaching a college team will have some misgivings as to the cultural value of the process.

A system of recruiting and subsidizing has grown up, under which boys are offered pecuniary and other inducements to enter a particular college.

For many games the strict organization and the tendency to commercialize the sport has taken the joy out of the game.

Finally, it is said that the blaze of publicity in which the college athlete lives is a demoralizing influence.

The irony is that what the Carnegie Foundation called a "demoralizing influence" in 1929 looks like the age of innocence today. Today, college coaches become folk heroes on campuses and across the state. They are more powerful than presidents, they operate private fiefdoms on the campus and earn more than two or three professors or more than the president himself. Today, scandalous offers of multimillion dollar contracts are offered to young students. Also, it is estimated that today colleges spend about $500 million each year to recruit athletes.

Today, big-time sports has become the slave of two powerful corrupting masters—professional athletics and TV. As far back as 1969, William Johnson said in *Sports Illustrated*,

In the past ten years sports in America has come to be the stepchild of television and, in a sense, handmaiden to the vicissitudes of Madison Avenue...the impact of television in these last ten years has produced more revolutionary—and irrevocable—changes in sports than anything since mankind began to play organized games.

In that same article, the late Bear Bryant is quoted as saying, "We think TV exposure is so important to our program and so important to this university that we will schedule ourselves to fit the medium. I'll play at midnight if that's what TV wants" (Johnson, 1969).

Hovering over the twin industries of professional sports and television is the "industry" of gambling. The goal is to field the teams, keep television ratings high and the gambling coffers full. Recently, the *Chronicle of Higher Education* (Paul, 1983) had a page 1 article headlined "Gambling on College Games Said To Be Up Dramatically." The *Chronicle* story estimated that wagering on college sports annually has topped $1 billion.

Today, gambling, TV, and professional sports have their own agenda—and it is money. Students are simply "used" as raw material for the profit-makers. The nation's campuses have become the "farm clubs" of pro football and basketball and the situation can only get worse.

Recently, the United States Football League was established. What was once an autumn-winter sport will now go into spring and summer. Pressures to recruit players before they graduate will get more intense, and the likelihood of abuse will increase. The truth is that a small but influential core of the nation's colleges and universities are caught in a corrupting web of activity that deceives students, distorts priorities on campus, and connects higher education to professional athletics, gambling, and vice.

The greatest tragedy, of course, is the terrible disservice to youth. Big-time sport is depicted as a way to fame and riches. The fact is, however, that only a tiny fraction of those who compete in big-time college sports will make it to the pros, and only a fraction of those who do will make the overpublicized salaries of top stars. Furthermore, they are academically diminished. In 1982, only about half the college seniors who competed in major college basketball conferences throughout the nation graduated in 4 years. In the Big Ten Conference alone, whose membership includes some of the most prestigious public institutions, less than a third of the basketball dribbling stars were able to score academically on time with a diploma. In the Southwest Conference, only 17% of those playing graduated in 4 years. Most of these young men will not find careers on professional teams. The vast majority who have poured all their energies into athletics will often find themselves consigned to a life of frustration, even failure, for playing instead of learning.

Frankly, there is something disgraceful about keeping athletes on campus for 4 years to use up their eligibility and then letting them go for failure to make academic progress; about a wire-service picture of the betting line inside a Las Vegas casino with the names of academic institutions in the background; about college coaches flying in university-owned jets to swoop down on young recruits and sign them up before the competition gets there; and about a university official screaming to his players from the sidelines and having his abusive language and childish tantrums reported in the local press. Yet, all of this goes on while the older generation wonders what has happened to the morals of our youth.

WHAT CAN BE DONE?

The 1929 Carnegie report on athletics (Savage, 1929) asked the central question, What should be done? The 1983 version of this agonizing question is, Can *anything* be done?

In the Carnegie Report, Henry Pritchett, the outspoken president of the Foundation, put the matter bluntly. He said,

> The paid coach, the gate receipts, the special training tables, the costly sweaters and extensive journeys on Pullman cars, the recruiting from high school, the demoralizing publicity showered on the players, the devotion of an undue proportion of time to training, the devices for putting a desirable athlete, but a weak scholar,

across the hurdles of examinations—these ought to stop and the inter-college and intramural sports be brought back to stage in which they can be enjoyed by large numbers of students and where they do not involve an expenditure of time and money wholly at variance with any ideal of honest study.

It is interesting to note, however, that in 1905, over 2 decades before the Pritchett statement, the President of Stanford, David Starr Jordan, had a solution of his own. Jordan said,

Let the football team become frankly professional. Cast off all the deception. Get the best professional coach. Pay him well and let him have the best men the town and alumni will pay for....Let the teams struggle in perfectly honest warfare, known for what it is and with no masquerade of amateurism or academic ideas....The evil in current football rests not in the hired men, but in academic lying and in the falsification of our own standards as associations of scholars and men of honor.

ATHLETICS TODAY

What about today? Can anything be done today? Quite frankly, I am enormously pessimistic. For almost 100 years, scandals in athletics have been noted, exposés have been written, reforms have been proposed, and still abuses grow. It may take an academic "Black Socks Scandal" or more to jolt the academic community into action. Meanwhile, we must continue to chip away. Recently, the National Collegiate Athletic Association approved tougher academic standards for players and stiffer rules for recruiting.

Also, there is new talk of barring all freshmen from intercollegiate basketball and football competition. Recently, Joe Paterno, one of the winningest coaches in the business was quoted in *The New York Times* (1983) as saying, "I've always been opposed to freshmen eligibility for varsity sports....I think a student needs his first year as a period of adjustment to college life." Such an arrangement would say to the new arrival on the campus: "You have come here as a student, first and foremost. You are just the same as all other students with no special training requirements or perks." Indeed, in entering the "culture" of the student rather that of the athlete, the potential team player may at least have time to sort out priorities on his own.

More than rule-changing and tinkering is needed, however. Reduction of sports' abuse will come only when a wave of moral indignation sweeps the campuses. Perhaps the time has come for faculty at universities engaged in big-time athletics to organize a day of protest, to set aside a time to examine how the purpose of the universities is being subverted and how integrity is lost.

Furthermore, I propose that when serious athletic violations are discovered, the accreditation status of the institution should be revoked—along with the eligibility status for NCAA. It's ironic that one periodically hears that a university has lost its athletic eligibility, but never does one hear that a college has been put on accreditation probation or has been academically suspended because of unethical behavior or for the abuse of students. And yet nothing strikes closer to the integrity of the institution. I also propose that presidents of universities and colleges begin to say publicly what they acknowledge privately: that big-time sports are out of control.

In a caustic criticism of presidential leadership, Henry Pritchett in the 1929 Carnegie Report on Athletes (Savage, 1929) said that

> Perhaps our fundamental error has consisted in an inability to distinguish between undue expansion and requisite growth....Be that as it may at a time when the college president might have curbed his alumni in their hue and cry for numbers, *he ran with the noisiest.*

and Pritchett added

> There can be no doubt as to where lies the responsibility to correct this situation. The defense of the intellectual integrity of the college and universities lies with the president and (athletic) faculty.

It is not quite that simple, as every president clearly understands. Indeed, several years ago the president of one of this nation's most sports active institutions said that every president in his conference would be fired if he said what he actually felt about athletics.

However, presidents can begin to take some very specific steps. Campus leaders can meet with each other and talk about cutting back expenditures for recruitment and training, and they can continue to get involved in NCAA deliberation. It is a sign of hope that 100 college leaders participated in the last NCAA deliberation.[1] By reaching agreements within the various conferences, we can begin scaling back on commitment to big-time athletics without individual schools jeopardizing their standing.

Furthermore, governing boards have an absolutely critical role to play in stopping the corruption of big-time sports. When a president wants to fire a coach and is told by the board that he will have to go before the coach does, as has happened, then we see how much erosion of academic integrity has been lost. I get the clear impression that some trustees would rather see a Heisman Trophy than a Nobel Prize on campus.

---

[1]Robert Atwell, Bruce Grimes, and Donna Lopiano write about SALT-type negotiations to get the process started in the *Money game: Financing collegiate athletics.* (1980). Washington, DC: American Council on Education. (A good idea, I believe.)

A RENEWED INTEREST IN WELLNESS

Many institutions have athletic programs that do not involve the destructive spirit I have just described. At these institutions competitive sports are kept in appropriate perspective, and at most of the nation's colleges, priority is given to the needs of all the students, not just a privileged few. Indeed, the silver lining in the dark cloud I have painted is the renewed interest in health on campuses today.

There is a growing respect for wellness among the students. Nutrition is better understood. Regular exercise is now a way of life for many. Intramural sports are popular. Life-destroying habits, such as smoking, are far less popular today. At Princeton University, for example, the health director reported that only about 5% of entering freshmen smoke. I propose that in the decade of the 1980s the nation's colleges and universities will shift priorities from destructive competition for the few to health-related programs for the many.

Specifically, I suggest that all students, as a part of high school or college general education, be introduced to the miracle of the human body. I suggest that all students be taught about nutritious food and about exercise, and begin to understand that caring for one's body is a sacred trust, and that wellness is a prerequisite to all else. Furthermore, I propose that all students participate in sports, and that the college not only help organize such programs, but provide facilities as well.

Recently, the director of health at a large East Coast university put the matter bluntly, stating, "Student health and big-time athletes have nothing to do with each other." Indeed, health directors at colleges and universities talk about how students, quite literally, "wear out" their bodies through grueling competition. Their bodies are battered, their bones broken. Turning to another sport, the director added,

> Think about the swimmer who spends six hours a day in the pool, whose shoulders have been worn out. What does looking at the bottom of a pool for six hours a day have to do with liberal education. It even ceases to be fun.

This leads to an important footnote: I am convinced the placement of the medical directors in the administrative hierarchy of the college is critically important. At large and highly competitive institutions, the sport medical doctor reports to the director of athletics—which is a conflict of interest and may jeopardize the medical doctor's integrity. The medical director should report to the general administration to retain independence and to assure his concern about the students—not the protection of the system.

BIG-TIME ATHLETICS' EFFECT ON STUDENTS

This brings me back to where I began. The tragedy of big-time athletics is not just corruption on the campus, but the damaging of students.

In writing of the recent Herschel Walker episode, columnist Richard Cohen (1983) said in the *Washington Post*,

> There is no escaping the conclusion that big-time football does nothing but corrode college life. It has nothing to do with education, which is what college is supposed to be about, except in the sense that it mocks it. You cannot be both a semi-pro player and a full-time student. No one has that kind of time. Even in college, the day has just twenty-four hours…You can't blame Walker for doing what he did. He was schooled by people who have little regard for education and tutored by institutions that have prostituted themselves to sports. (p. 61)

Cohen goes on to note that the Walker incident "reinforced the view that sports and not education is what pays off" (C.1). "This is actually the case for Walker," Cohen says, "but it is not the case for your average kid—not even for your exceptional kid….There is just not much room at the top. For most kids, sports is just another way to stay at the bottom" (C.1).

Recently, the Carnegie Foundation published a study entitled, *The Control of the Campus—A Report on the Governance of Higher Education* (1983). In glancing through that document, it seemed to shed some light on the problem of athletics in higher education. In discussing the integrity of higher education, we say that the academy must have full authority over the essential functions on the campus. While we warned against Washington interference and corporate interference, not a word was said about the loss of integrity through professional athletics or TV or even gambling interference. No mention is made of pressure from alumni, board members, coaches, in the misguided notion that a team must win at any cost. In the end, these pressures may be the most destructive threats of all. To the extent that colleges and universities allow standards to be compromised through athletics, the integrity of the campus is lost just as surely as if it had been taken by political interference. In our report on governance, we call for a renewal of presidential leadership that can help colleges define their own academic standards and social obligations rather than wait passively for such standards to be imposed by others.

More than a half-century ago, the Carnegie study on athletics stated,

> Commercialism…(has) been permitted to corrupt a form of activity that might have been of great value in training the powers of youth. Now that the current is flowing with its full force, the college president must consume years of persuasions to accomplish in athletics results that thirty or even ten years ago he might have achieved in months. *In this respect, he has been a leader who has not led.* (Savage, 1929).

The time has come for everyone who cares about the future of higher education, not just the president, to oppose the abuses of big-time athletics and, more importantly, to urge a larger vision on campus. That larger vision is the wellness of all students.

In the decade of the '80s, health and that old-fashioned word sport should become an essential part of campus life. The physical well-being of every student should be pursued not just as an indulgence or frill, but as an important and sacred obligation.

REFERENCES

COHEN, R. (1983, February 27). Suckers. *Washington Post*, p. c.1.

THE control of the campus—A report on the governance of higher education. (1983). The Carnegie Foundation for the Advancement of Teaching. Washington, DC.

EXPOSED—College football is a racket. (1938, November 22). *Look*, pp. 6-7.

PAUL, A. (1983, March 2). Gambling on college games said to be up dramatically. *Chronicle of Higher Education*, **1**, 16-18.

SAVAGE, H.J. (1929). *American college athletics*. New York: The Carnegie Foundation for the Advancement of Teaching.

Chapter 31

Take Athletics Out of College?

Barbara S. Uehling
University of Missouri at Columbia

When I started my academic career, I was a faculty member at a small institution in the South, where they are very enthusiastic about athletics. We had a basketball program, and we were quite good. But as a young faculty member, I asked some questions. Why do those basketball players get treated differently? They seem to have more financial aid. And why do we make such an effort to recruit them, when there are some other things we should be doing? It seems to me that maybe there is less control over this athletic program than any other program on the campus. In short, I made myself something of a nuisance.

So when a national TV network came to do a piece on college basketball, the coach called me and said, "Would you be willing to say all those things you're always telling me on national TV?" They came and interviewed me, and I voiced my concerns. Then they went to the game that night, where they wanted to film the most enthusiastic spectators, and I was filmed cheering more loudly than anyone else.

I think that story illustrates our problem. I doubt there are many people who don't like and perhaps love competitive athletics. We identify with our teams, we take pride in our youth, we watch a marvelous visual spectacle; and I must say, I think I've learned something about administration from watching coaches because they are able to produce a kind of teamwork which is often enviable.

TIME TO CLEAN UP OUR ACT

Yet, we have some serious questions about the place of intercollegiate athletics in our institutions today and, indeed, about the place of intercollegiate athletics in the U.S. I hear people express concern that if we don't clean up our act, intercollegiate athletics will not remain popular and, indeed, will not retain its present status in a few years.

Thus, we have reason to be concerned. A question I'd like to pose is, Can athletics remain a part of an academic institution, or should it be separated? That's always one alternative.

The second question is (regardless of the form that we use, whether the athletics program remains part of an institution or becomes a separate identity, associated in name), How should it be controlled? These are difficult questions which we have not tried to answer for some time partly because there are no clear-cut answers, and partly because the responsibility lies with the chief executive officers, but they will need the help, support, understanding, and criticism that trustees and regents can offer.

To get some perspective on the first question as to whether or not athletics can be a part of an institution, I would like to consider several related questions. Who are the participants in athletics, and who are the participants in higher education? Are these participants treated the same? Who pays for education, and who pays for athletics? Finally, who controls and evaluates those two sets of activities?

ONE AND THE SAME? OR NOT?

Consider the participants first. In the U.S. we have taken great pride in saying that the direct participants in higher education should be all who have the ability to participate in that activity. In athletics, there is a special purpose, and the direct participants are those who have a special ability beyond that which is appropriate for higher education. This lack of common criteria causes many of the problems because athletic ability becomes more important than academic ability.

But even among athletes we have separate classes. I'd like to mention two in particular. The now-famous *Sports Illustrated* article from 1980 might seem in places somewhat exaggerated, but it points out some very real problems in intercollegiate athletics. One was that of the minority athlete, in particular the black athlete. We do have a question as to whether we are graduating these black athletes at the same rate as other students (or for that matter, whether even white athletes are graduating at the rate of other students). Are we adequately preparing them for postgraduate employment? Many of the answers that we hear would suggest that we are not.

THE TROUBLE WITH WOMEN'S ATHLETICS

We now have more women in undergraduate institutions than men for the first time in the history of the United States, but our athletic programs do not reflect these proportions. We have made enormous progress since 1971. The number of colleges offering athletics for women increased from 280 to 825, and the number of teams has increased likewise. Yet we are still finding that women's athletics is to many of us, to many people who are in charge, something of a bother. The major reason is that it does not produce any revenue, and we have been concerned about revenue production.

We also have the feeling that the government is taking care of all that. The government passed Title IX, the government's going to come in and make us do certain things, and therefore that relieves us of some moral responsibility. Probably there are those who applaud a recent decision made by a District Court judge in Michigan who ruled in the case he was hearing that Title IX did not apply to athletics unless federal funds were being used for the specific sport. I am sure that decision will be reviewed and probably will reach the Supreme Court. It is a very important decision and it leaves us even more with the question, What is our responsibility to women's athletics? Should the federal government decide that it does not have a role?

We also have the question of indirect participants in sports. To what extent are students across the United States being served by our athletic programs? I read about a survey in which the undergraduates of a university were asked the primary reason for attending their university, and a large number said because of the football team. Maybe many of our students are being served by major athletics even though they are not directly participating. Certainly, we all recognize that athletics brings a kind of identity and spirit to the institution that may not be achievable in any other way. It is something we need to consider. But we also have to ask the question, Are there more students who want to be athletic participants, and how do we serve them?

ATHLETES AND STUDENTS: THE DIFFERENCES

On the question of whether participants in athletics and in higher education are treated the same way, the answer is clearly no. If we look at recruitment practices, we find very few who pursue the violinist in the same spirit as they do the star tight end. As we look at admission practices, we find that in some cases admission standards are different, or at least the committees reviewing admissions of athletics make more exceptions.

If we look at financial aid patterns, we again find differences, depending on the institution. The advising is vastly different for the athlete and the nonathlete in almost any institution. The academic support of athletes may be greater than for the average students, and we may have other students needing the same kind of support, but we don't have the funds—at least we say we don't have the funds—to offer it.

The length of time that an athlete stays in an institution often differs from that of the nonathlete. Their job experiences differ in the summer time. It is far easier to find the athlete a job that pays well and requires brawn than a job that will provide skills for later postgraduate employment.

I suspect one of the things that may be most interesting is that you might ask yourself how much of this information you possess about the institution for which you have some responsibility because often it is not known. We have not looked carefully at these questions until lately, but we need to look at them, because treatments are different, and we need to justify that, or at least rationalize it.

THE GOLDEN GLOVE TREATMENT

Who pays? The same revenue sources are available to both education and athletics: state and federal funds, student fees, private donations. In addition athletics has available gate receipts, income from TV appearances and bowl allocations as well as conference allocations. The extent to which the athletic department has independent sources of revenue is the extent to which there can be differences in the academic and the athletic programs. Those receipts and also those special private donations often given to athletics provide an independence for the athletics department which may be very difficult to control at times.

Gate receipts, interestingly enough, are a decreasing proportion of athletic departments' budgets. How have these programs attempted to make up for that deficit? It has been met differently by different divisions of the NCAA. In Division I, the effort has been to seek private donations; Division II has sought to use federal funds, scholarships, and institutional support; in Division III, student fees are used more, together with institutional funds. Thus, even among the NCAA divisions, we are building in differences which will be reflected in the athletic and academic programs. The trend in Division I is for greater separation between these programs, while in Divisions II and III, the trend is for greater integration of the academic and athletic programs.

TV FOR THE ATHLETES?

We are familiar with increasing demands for revenue in academic programs as well as in our athletic programs, but it seems to me that the pressure to keep up with the Joneses is much greater for athletics than for academics. Occasionally, a professor will come into my office and say, "I'd like to have such-and-such a piece of equipment because I saw it at Institution X,"; but far more frequently I hear that the other athletic programs in the conference are doing such-and-such, so we have got to do the same thing. If another team travels by plane, it would be unheard of that we would travel by bus. If another team provides a TV set for each athlete, it would be unheard of not to do the same thing because we have got to have the same kind of recruiting commitment. If another institution builds a separate dorm, a residence ball for women athletics, then we have got to do the same thing because after all we have got to get in this women's athletic business and we have got to compete. The pressure to keep up with the Joneses seems even sharper because we are interested in winning teams, teams that produce revenue.

Finally, who controls athletics and who controls academics? The control of academic programs can be complex, it can be varied but the duties are reasonably well assigned and there is an understanding about who is in charge. In athletics, in my opinion, the control is much more dispersed and much less clearly understood. There is often a real question: Who within the institution is in charge? Is it the chief executive officer? Often it is not because there is so much alumni interest and so much pressure from other places and because the CEO is so busy.

Our institutions are also voluntary members of conferences—voluntary, and yet we could not compete if we were not members, or at least we could not compete in the same way. The conferences are interested in students and their academic progress and they have rules about that. But they are more interested in evening up the competition to generate the most interest and consequently the most revenue. Those motivations come into conflict in their rules because men's and women's athletics are at different stages of development.

We also have alumni/alumnae involved in the control of athletics, probably more than we would like to recognize. To the extent that they are organized and giving private donations to a program, they naturally feel that they should participate in control.

We also have some spectator control, because after all, they can vote not to go to the game, not to buy a ticket.

How does one pull all these elements of control into a rational balance? It is a tough question, and again I would say that I think the CEO of an institution has that responsibility. If the CEO does not assume the responsibility directly, he or she should insure that it is being effectively assumed.

FIVE STEPS TOWARD A SOLUTION

I have suggested that participants in athletics and academics are not quite the same because athletes have a special responsibility and a special skill. I have suggested that we do not treat these two groups of people the same. I have suggested that the source of revenue is often different, and can be independent. And I have suggested that the controls may be different, and that in the case of athletics, control is more diffuse. Is the solution simply to say, let's split athletics off and set up a franchise operation, and we'll let them use our name? I can remember in my early years, when I was being critical of that basketball team, I said, "Why don't we just go hire the players and call it College team?" I no longer believe in that as a solution. I think athletics can contribute value to any institution, and I would not like to see it split off. I want rather to see a greater integration of athletic and academic programs, and I have a few suggestions which might help to accomplish that.

Who's in charge?

First, we need to insure that the institution is in fact in charge of academic standards, that we do not leave it to conferences to enforce, or we do not get caught between competing sets of rules, but that we say, these athletes are here because they are students, and we, the institution, are first and foremost going to set those standards.

Second, we need institutional representatives responsible for athletics to make a commitment to the integrity of practice within our own institution. That sounds easy, but making that commitment—that we will have a clean program—is an important step.

Third, we need to establish mechanisms to insure that in fact we are appropriately monitoring athletics. Now I have made this kind of speech before, and having made it, I began to take myself seriously, which is always a problem, and I went back home and said, "I'm telling all these people out there that they should monitor athletics. What are we doing on our campus?"

So I sat down with our athletic director, with our faculty representative, with the person who keeps the books, and with some other people who are interested, and I said, "What can we do to insure even better that we are appropriately monitoring this?"

We divided the question into institutional controls, recruiting progress, academic eligibility, and financial aid, and we devised a new set of steps. I am convinced that we were doing a good job before. We devised a new set of monitoring controls which will not be burdensome, but which will insure that each year I get a clear picture of what's going on that we can review, instead of waiting for a crisis to occur.

We shared that document with the NCAA, and I think they in turn are sharing it with some of their institutions, and so we are sort of pleased with ourselves right now. Watch out! Next week we will have a problem. One should never brag too soon.

Time to reduce pressure

Fourth, I think we chief executive officers need to lessen our pressure, and our alumni need to lessen their pressure to have revenue-producing sports. The poor athletic director is under fire all the time because I, for one, am always saying, "You've got to balance the books. We can't spend more than we're taking in, and you've got that responsibility," and he says, "But we have travel budgets and all those things." We have got to lessen some of that pressure.

Finally, we have got to set up cooperative agreements among institutions to reduce the need to spend. I can say, in our institution, "There's got to be a limit to this and we're not going to spend any more than a certain amount," but that can be very self-defeating, because if other institutions go on in this race to be better and to produce more revenue, we are going to be losers. It is only with cooperation among institutions, and particularly in conferences, that we will be able to stem this ever-burgeoning demand for more resources for athletics.

Disraeli said, "Action may not always bring happiness, but there is no happiness without action." I think that in athletics it is time for action.

Epilogue

The way out is through the door. Why is it that no one will use this exit?

—Confucius

Throughout the differences of opinion expressed in these papers, there remains a commonality of view concerning the place of athletics in our institutions of higher education. While reformers criticize and proponents defend intercollegiate sport, with few exceptions, there is a similarity of view holding "sport" as somehow a significant part of the social institution of higher learning in America. For some reason, this strange relationship between sport and the work of the college and university seems to be vital and worth preserving.

This is not to say, however, that the intercollegiate athletic situation cannot be vastly improved. Clearly, the bulk of the papers in this volume suggest possible changes in the fulfillment of legal and moral obligations to students, to workers, and to women; the alteration of governance structures and procedures within and between the schools; and attendance to the growing specter of economic instabilities. Some papers call directly for change and offer proposals, while others comment on the reforms already forwarded.

The problems besetting college sport are as complex and varied as the institutions that house athletics. Certainly, the problems are deeper than superficial. As some of these chapters suggest, difficulties with campus sport may be related to the very heart of the free market system of higher education in this country. So long as insecurities in resource flow continue to plague the American college and university, then success in athletic programs may tease athletic and academic leadership as a means of "winning" the battle for students, money, and prestige, which may mean institutional and individual survival.

The campus sport which so captures public imagination may also be blinding. The whirlwind of emotions and loyalties, which is so invigorating, also hides from view the reality of intercollegiate athletics. The most dangerous blindness which results may be the obfuscation of the necessity to change, to alter the form of campus sport to suit the new economic, social, and educational environment in which the contemporary American college and university operates. As imposing an edifice as it is, sport has in the past had to accommodate itself to critics ranging from Teddy Roosevelt to John Underwood. Though fans may be enveloped by the heights and depths of favorite team fortunes, one must not lose sight of the fact that sport is a human creation and muteable to human will.

Change is not only possible, but change in intercollegiate athletics is required. Change is required to suit new social realities. If indeed the place of women in American society is one next to rather than behind the male, then the reformation of women's athletic programs is absolutely necessary. Change is also required to suit economic realities of limited federal and state funds and of the influence of "booster" groups and the media. With limits as to increased revenue available from the traditional sources such as ticket and concession sales, there is mounting pressure from groups external to the college and university to accept their monies. In exchange for dollars, which might flow into the athletic coffers, campus leaders must determine whether or not the influence these outside groups hold over college matters is worth that money. Is it worth it to the university to gain bowl appearance money at the expense of disruption of the academic calendar? Is it worth it to the university to gain a star high school recruit at the expense of impugning the school's good name due to some booster's indiscretion? Is it worth it to gain money at the expense of losing control over one's programs and reputation?

Questions like these are not easily answered. With careers built upon long years of toil, with the hopes and wishes of family, friends, and colleagues resting on continued good work, it is exceedingly difficult to give up job and concrete future plans for the abstractions of "institutional philosophy." Before necessary change can take place, support is necessary, support for the necessity of change among those capable of effecting change and among those capable of backing up the champions of change in college sport. Clearly institutional leadership must be convinced of the need for alteration of existent norms which glorify winning athletics above academic performance. Not only must college presidents and their staff be so convinced, but so must their colleagues at other schools. The American college president is not omnipotent. He or she is not usually capable of autonomous decisions. Intraorganizational leadership must instead consider their decisions within the context of the board of trustees and others in the environment of the school who "make a difference"—whose opinions will effect the livelihood of the institution. In trying economic and politically tricky times, cautious college presidents must be convinced that serious inspection and studied change in campus sport is supported by the board, by governance agencies, and by educational foundations and public opinion leaders.

The diversity of intercollegiate athletics today parallels the pluralistic society which has spawned the wide breadth of American higher education. As the contributors to this volume have indicated, college sport comes in many levels of play, is governed by many forms of structure, and is funded through diverse means. In all its various forms, however, college sport is the most visible representative of the institutions that house them. Perhaps due to a human need to reduce complex realities into symbolic representations, Americans often identify a school's quality with the teams that represent them.

Of paramount importance, then, is the need to convince both the public and college presidents, influential trustees, accrediting agencies, foundation leadership, and alumni of the need for studied change—of the existence of problems requiring immediate attention. Prematurely forwarded solutions are of no consequence if those capable of action are not convinced of the existence of a problem. What is required at this stage of the problem is information.

Information is required to remove the hypocrisy about college sport—the hypocrisy which impugns the integrity of the social institution of higher education. Does sport really build character? Does sport make money? Who is governing college sport? Which role is primary—the student or the athlete? Answers to questions such as these require both the strength of scientific evidence and the impact of journalistic reporting. For action to be affected, it is as necessary to derive indisputable conclusions as it is necessary to make awareness of this information incumbent upon those involved in education who can use this information. Science without dissemination of findings is impotent. Journalism without facts is vacuous. Before we can leave by the door, we must be convinced of the need to exit.

Given the legitimation of intercollegiate athletic concerns and communication of options for dealing with the ills that beset campus sport, the course of action taken by officers of our colleges and universities will tell us much about the American society that supports or criticizes such change. While the American society respects rationality, it certainly also demands emotional elevation and involvement. While the individual is extolled, so are group and cooperative concerns valued. While humanistic self-realization is deemed important, so are financial concerns legitimated. The determination of appropriate reform measures for intercollegiate athletics will be dependent upon the particular prioritization of values constructed by educational leadership who are themselves dependent upon environmental support.

This book was compiled as one means of disseminating studied conclusions about campus sport. It is hoped in some way that this book will contribute to the recognition of the importance of consideration of intercollegiate athletics and to the resolution of the ills that threaten the integrity of both the higher learning and sport.